Born in Chatham, Kent, **Henry Stedman** has been writing guidebooks for more than a decade now and is the author or co-author of half a dozen titles, including Trailblazer's *Dolomites Trekking*, *Coast to Coast Path* and *Hadrian's Wall Path*, as well as *The Bradt Guide to Palestine* and the *Rough Guide* ...... *Southeast Asi*...... surpassed c ...... obsession th ...... up it, collec ...... and setting u ...... ing it, 🖳 **www.climbmountkilimanja** ......

When not travelling, Henry lives ...... guidebooks and putting on weight. Frie ...... anyone can climb Kilimanjaro.

D1041362

.....oof that almost

Kilimanjaro – The trekking guide to Africa's highest mountain
First edition: 2003; this edition September 2006

Publisher
Trailblazer Publications
The Old Manse, Tower Rd, Hindhead, Surrey, GU26 6SU, UK
Fax (+44) 01428-607571
Email: info@trailblazer-guides.com
www.trailblazer-guides.com

British Library Cataloguing in Publication Data
A catalogue record for this book is available from the British Library

ISBN 1-873756-91-7
EAN 978-1873756-911

Editor: Jim Manthorpe
Series editor: Patricia Major
Typesetting and layout: Henry Stedman
Proof-reading: Jane Thomas and Patricia Major
Cartography: Nick Hill
Index: Jane Thomas

Warning: mountain walking can be dangerous
Please read the notes on when to go (p20) and on mountain safety (pp200-8).
Every effort has been made by the author and publisher to ensure that the information
contained herein is as accurate and up to date as possible. However, they are unable
to accept responsibility for any inconvenience, loss or injury sustained by anyone as a
result of the advice and information given in this guide.

Printed on chlorine-free paper from farmed forests by
D2Print (☎ +65-6295 5598), Singapore

KILIMANJARO

The trekking guide to
Africa's highest mountain

HENRY STEDMAN

TRAILBLAZER PUBLICATIONS

Dedication

This book is dedicated to Mohammed 'Moody' Limotko, guide and companion on my first trek to the summit of Kilimanjaro, who died before the publication of this second edition.

A request

The author and publisher have tried to ensure that this guide is as accurate and up to date as possible. However, things change quickly in this part of the world. Agencies come and go, trails are re-routed, prices rise and ... well, rise some more, governments are toppled and glaciers shrink. If you notice any changes or omissions that should be included in the next edition of this guide, please email Henry Stedman (henry.stedman@trailblazer-guides.com) or write to Trailblazer (address on p2). You can also contact us via the Trailblazer website at ⌨www.trailblazer-guides.com. Those persons making a significant contribution will be rewarded with a free copy of the next edition, an acknowledgement in the front of that edition, and my undying gratitude.

Acknowledgements

For this second edition I should like to thank those trekkers, locals and expats who kindly offered advice and suggestions. In no particular order (and Tanzanian unless otherwise stated) thanks are due to: Fons Van der Leen (Netherlands); Frank Fischer (Netherlands) and Jef Vercammen (Belgium) for their help with the Arusha chapter; Matthew Dee (UK, UN) for looking even worse than me on the top of Meru; Derek Eames (UK) for leading our team up Meru with incredible fortitude and skill and showing extraordinary bravery in climbing to Uhuru peak one week later *in his shorts*! I also want to thank him for writing this acknowledgement, which saves me having to think of one; Lazarus Mirisho Mafie for his help in organizing my Mount Meru trip, and Joseph Samba, Said Said Kawawa and Isaack Elias for getting me to the top; Ali Whitehouse and Ollie Watson (UK); Inga Benestad (Norway) for her information on Marangu; Gappers Phillip Woodhall, Peter Gocke, Louise Acres, Sophia Greenhough, Kathleen Epstein and Karen Cross (UK & US); Keith Kegley (US); Karen Valenti (US), Program Director of the Kilimanjaro Porters Assistance Project, for information on the plight of porters; Joseph Nyabasi and Nzuamkende Mkoma of the KGPU; John Eastwood (UK); Stephen and Katie Phillips and Bryce Florian (US) for introducing me to the delights of Serengeti beer; Richard Evans (UK) for having that uniquely British instinct of knowing which bar is showing the football, and for all his diligent work on the Marangu Route; Renata Haas (US) for her work on the litter problem and help with the article on p199 – you did a great job Renata; Amy Symons (US); Tina Thakor-Rankin (UK); Andrew Eckert; Mark Burgmans (Netherlands); Nyamakumbati N Mafuru, boss of KINAPA, for his help (and his receptionist Margaret for the cup of tea); Joseph H and Aloyse D Lyimo and David for showing me just how gorgeous Marangu village was and explaining the intricacies of Chagga culture; David and Amy Nespoli (US), honeymooners at Arrow Glacier; Philip Tribble for a moving and enjoyable morning at the Amani Children's Home; George Mtaki, his wife Victoria and children Paolo and Flora for the lovely day I spent with them at Machame; Titus Amasi at Umbwe Gate for the T-shirt; Claire, Teddy and Velly, the receptionists at the Buffalo Hotel; Joseph, the gentleman of Moshi, now at Zebra Hotels; Cuthbert Swai; Fredrick Munna, Ernest, Matthew, Julius and Salim for getting me to the summit on the Lemosho Route; guide Dismas Mlay, and porters Edward Mariwa, Kenedy Mboro, Tumanieli Kileo and Immanuel Sisti for performing a similar task on the Umbwe Route; and Ally Ibrahim for arranging it all. And finally to Harriet Auty and Henry (UK), for all the fun in Serengeti and Arusha.

Out of Africa I would like to thank the many readers who wrote in with their corrections, compliments, advice and experiences, all of which I have thoroughly enjoyed reading, mainly because they took me from my cold and wintry garret in Hastings back to the sun, fun and beauty of Kilimanjaro. In no real order I wish to acknowledge the help of Janet Bonnema (US) for her lesson on air pressure and burning damp toilet roll(!); Duncan Butchart (SA) for his corrections to the *Avifauna* section, as mentioned in his flattering review of the book in *Wildwatch*; Rick Smith (UK); Maureen Twichen (US); Maisy Luk (UK); Stephen J Davies; Pam Pickett; Gard Karlsen (No); John Rees-Evans (UK) for his help in compiling the altitude graphs – and proving to me that there are others who are slightly too obsessed about the mountain; Steve Goldstein (US); Brent Gwaltney (US), Jeremy Gane (UK), Robert M Rowlett II (US), Jay Rusek (US); Thomas Kimaro; and the stalking stars of Montreal, namely Anneliese and Valdina Di Betta, Maria Mangiocavallo and Isabelle Gryn; Judith and Jim Rowe. I hope you all find that, thanks largely to your input, this second edition is even better than the first.

At Trailblazer I'd like to thank Nick Hill for transforming my childlike scribbles into maps of beauty; Patricia Major for turning my incoherent ramblings into English in the first edition, and Jim Manthorpe for performing similar miracles in the second; Jane Thomas for the index; and Bryn, as ever, for making the whole thing possible.

CONTENTS

INTRODUCTION

Kilimanjaro is a snow covered mountain 19,710 feet high, and is said to be the highest mountain in Africa. Its western summit is called the Masai 'Ngàʹje Ngàiʹ, the House of God. Close to the western summit there is the dried and frozen carcass of a leopard. No one has explained what the leopard was seeking at that altitude.
Ernest Hemingway in the preamble to *The Snows of Kilimanjaro*

On 22 November, 2001, Bruno Brunod of Italy stood at Marangu Gate on the southern slopes of God's greatest mountain, Kilimanjaro. We can imagine the scene at the gate that day, for it's a scene that's repeated there every day of the year. There would be the noisy, excitable hubbub as porters, guides and rangers packed, weighed, re-packed and re-weighed all the equipment; the quiet murmur of anticipation from Bruno's fellow trekkers as they stood on the threshold of the greatest walk of their lives; maybe there was even a troop of blue monkeys crashing through the canopy, or the scarlet flash of a turaco's underwing as it glided from tree to tree, surveying the commotion below.

Signore Brunod's main goal that day was no different from the ambitions of his fellow trekkers: he wanted to reach the summit. Unlike them, however, Bruno planned to forego many of the features that make a walk up Kili so special. Not for him the joys of strolling lazily through the mountain's four main eco-zones, pausing occasionally to admire the views or examine the unique mountain flora. Nor did Bruno want to experience the blissful evenings spent scoffing popcorn, sharing stories and gazing at the stars with his fellow trekkers. Nor, for that matter, was Bruno looking forward to savouring the wonderful *esprit de corps* that builds between a trekker and his or her crew as they progress, day by day, up the mountain slopes; a sense of camaraderie that grows with every step until, exhausted, they stand together at the highest point in Africa.

It is these experiences that make climbing Kilimanjaro so unique and so special. Yet Bruno had chosen to eschew all of them; because, for reasons best known to himself, he had decided to *run* up the mountain. Which is exactly what he did, completing the ascent in a matter of 5 hours 36 minutes and 38 seconds – on a trail that takes the average trekker anywhere from four to six days to complete!

A mountain for eccentrics

Barking mad though Bruno may be, in his defence it must be said that he isn't exactly alone in taking an unorthodox approach to tackling Africa's greatest mountain. Take the Crane cousins from England, for example, who cycled up to the summit, surviving on *Mars* bars that they'd strapped to their handlebars. Or the anonymous Spaniard who, in the 1970s, drove up to the summit by motorbike. And what about Douglas Adams, author of the *Hitchhikers' Guide to the Galaxy*, who in 1994 reached the summit for charity while wearing an eight-foot rubber rhinoceros costume. Then there's the (possibly apocryphal) story of the man who walked *backwards* the entire way in order to get into the *Guinness Book of Records* – only to find out, on his return to the bottom, that he had been beaten by somebody who had done exactly the same thing just a few days previously.

And that's just the ascent; for coming back down again the mountain has witnessed skiing, a method first practised by Walter Furtwangler way back in 1912; snowboarding, an activity pioneered on Kili by Stephen Koch in 1997; and even hang-gliding, for which there was something of a fad a few years ago.

Don't be fooled

Cyclists to skiers, heroes to half-wits, bikers to boarders to backwards walkers: it's no wonder, given the sheer number of people who have climbed Kili over the past century, and the ways in which they've done so, that so many people believe that climbing Kili is a doddle. And you'd be forgiven for thinking the same.

You'd be forgiven – but you'd also be wrong. Whilst these stories of successful expeditions tend to receive a lot of coverage, they also serve to obscure the tales of suffering and tragedy that often go with them. To give you just one example: for all the coverage of the Millennium celebrations, when over 7000 people stood on the slopes of Kilimanjaro during New Year's week – with 1000 on New Year's Eve alone – little mention was made of the fact that well over a third of all the people who took part in those festivities failed to reach the summit, or indeed get anywhere near it. Or that another 33 had to be rescued. Or that, in the space of those seven days, three people died.

The reason why most of these attempts were unsuccessful is, of course, altitude sickness, brought about by a trekker climbing too fast and not allowing his or her body time to acclimatize to the rarified air. Because Bruno Brunod didn't just set a record in climbing Kilimanjaro in under six hours; he also unwittingly set a bad example. For once, statistics give a reasonably accurate impression of just how difficult climbing Kili can be. According to the park authorities, almost one in four people who climb up Kilimanjaro fail to reach even the crater. They also admit to there being a couple of deaths per annum on Kilimanjaro, though independent observers put that figure as high as ten. Sadly, as I write this in early 2006, three American climbers have just died in a rockslide near the summit.

There's no doubt the joys of climbing Kili are manifold; unfortunately, so are the ways in which it can kill you. Because the simple truth is that Kilimanjaro is a very big mountain and, like all big mountains, it's very adept at killing off the unprepared, the unwary or just the plain unlucky. The fact that the Masai call the mountain the 'House of God' seems entirely appropriate, given the number of people who meet their Maker every year on Kili's slopes.

At one stage we were taking a minute to complete thirty-five small paces. Altitude sickness had already hit the boys and two were weeping, pleading to pack up. All the instructors with the exception of Lubego and myself were in a bad way. They were becoming violently ill. It was becoming touch and go. The descent at one stage was like a battlefield. Men, including the porters, lying prone or bent up in agony. Tom and Swato though very ill themselves rallied the troops and helped manhandle the three unconscious boys to a lower altitude.
From the logbook of **Geoffrey Salisbury**, who led a group of blind African climbers up Kilimanjaro, as recorded in *The Road to Kilimanjaro* (1997).

The high failure and mortality rates speak for themselves: despite appearances to the contrary, climbing Kilimanjaro is no simple matter.

'Mountain of greatness'

But whilst it isn't easy, it *is* achievable. After all, no technical skill is required to reach the summit of Africa's highest mountain beyond the ability to put one foot in front of the other; because, unless you go out of your way to find a particularly awkward route, there is no actual *climbing* involved at all – just lots and lots of walking. Thus, anyone above the age of 10 (the minimum legal age for climbing Kilimanjaro) *can*, with the right attitude, a sensible approach to acclimatization, a half-decent pair of calf muscles and lots of warm clothing, make it to the top. Even vertigo sufferers are not excluded, there being only one or two vertical drops on any of the regular trekking routes that will have you scrabbling in your rucksacks for the Imodium.

Simply put, Kilimanjaro is for everyone. Again, statistics can back this up, for with the youngest successful summiteer aged just nine and the oldest, the venerable Frenchman Valtée Daniel, aged 87, it's clear that Kili conquerors come in all shapes and sizes. Amongst their number there are a few who have managed to overcome enormous personal disabilities on their way to the summit. Virtually every year there is at least one group of blind trekkers who, incredibly, make it to the top by using the senses of touch and hearing alone. And in January 2004 four climbers, who had been disabled on previous expeditions on other mountains, all managed to make it to the summit. The party consisted of Australian Peter Steane, who has permanent nerve damage and walks and climbs with the help of two leg braces; his compatriot Paul Pritchard, who has limited control over his right side; Singaporean David Lim, partially disabled in his right leg and left hand after contracting the rare nerve disorder Guillain-Barre Syndrome; and Scotland's Jamie Andrew, an amazing man who had to have his hands and feet amputated after suffering severe frostbite during a climbing expedition near Chamonix, France, in January 1999, and yet who made it to the top of Kilimanjaro with artificial limbs and prosthetic arms.

It is this 'inclusivity' that undoubtedly goes some way to explaining Kilimanjaro's popularity, a popularity that saw 34,530 trekkers visit in 2004, thereby confirming Kili's status as the most popular of the so-called 'Big Seven', the highest peaks on each of the seven continents. The sheer size of it must be another factor behind its appeal. This is the Roof of Africa, a massive massif 60km long by 80km wide with an altitude that reaches to a fraction under 6km above sea level. Writing in 1924, the renowned anthropologist, Charles Dundas, claimed that he once saw Kilimanjaro from a point over 120 miles away. This enormous monolith is big enough to have its own weather systems (note the plural) and, furthermore, to influence the climates of the countries that surround it.

The aspect presented by this prodigious mountain is one of unparalleled grandeur, sublimity, majesty, and glory. It is doubtful if there be another such sight in this wide world.
Charles New, the first European to reach the snow-line on Kilimanjaro, from his book *Life, Wanderings, and Labours in Eastern Africa* (1873).

See pp312-4 for more sights and sounds of Kili

But size, as they say, isn't everything, and by themselves these bald figures fail to fully explain the allure of Kilimanjaro. So instead we must look to attributes that cannot be measured by theodolites or yardsticks if we are to understand the appeal of Kilimanjaro.

In particular, there's its beauty. When viewed from the plains of Tanzania, Kilimanjaro conforms to our childhood notions of what a mountain should look like: high, wide and handsome, a vast triangle rising out of the flat earth, its sides sloping exponentially upwards to the satisfyingly symmetrical summit of Kibo; a summit that rises imperiously above a thick beard of clouds and is adorned with a glistening bonnet of snow. Kilimanjaro is not located in the crumpled mountain terrain of the Himalayas or the Andes. Where the mightiest mountain of them all, Everest, just edges above its neighbours – and look less impressive because of it – Kilimanjaro stands proudly alone on the plains of Africa. The only thing in the neighbourhood that can even come close to looking it in the eye is Mount Meru, over 60km away to the south-west and a good 1420m smaller too. The fact that it's located smack bang in the heart of the sweltering East African plains, just a few degrees (330km) south of the equator, with lions, giraffes, and all the other celebrities of the safari world running around its base, only adds to its charisma.

Then there's the scenery on the mountain itself. So massive is Kilimanjaro that to climb it is to pass through four seasons in four days, from the sultry rainforests of the lower reaches through to the windswept heather and moorland of the upper slopes, the alpine desert of the Saddle or Shira Plateau and on to the arctic wastes of the summit. There may be a fair few higher mountains on the globe; but there can't be many that are more beautiful, or more tantalizing.

In sitting down to recount my experiences with the conquest of the "Ethiopian Mount Olympus" still fresh in my memory, I feel how inadequate are my powers of description to do justice to the grand and imposing aspects of Nature with which I shall have to deal. **Hans Meyer**, the first man to climb Kilimanjaro, in his book *Across East African Glaciers – an Account of the First Ascent of Kilimanjaro* (1891)

Nor is it just tourists that are entranced by Kilimanjaro; the mountain looms large in the Tanzanian psyche too. Look at their supermarket shelves. The nation's second favourite lager is called Kilimanjaro. There's Kilimanjaro coffee (grown on the mountain's fertile southern slopes), Kilimanjaro tea (ditto), Kilimanjaro mineral water (bottled on its western side) and Kilimanjaro honey (again, sourced from the mountain). While on billboards lining the country's highways, Tanzanian models smoke their cigarettes in its shadow and cheerful roly-poly housewives compare the whiteness of their laundry with the mountain's glistening snows. And to pay for all of these things you may use Tanzanian Ts500 or Ts2000 notes – both of which just happen to have, on the back of them, a member of Tanzania's vaunted animal kingdom (namely a buffalo and a lion respectively) posing in front of the distinctive silhouette of Africa's highest mountain.

It is perhaps no surprise, therefore, that when Tanganyika won its independence from Britain in 1961, one of the first things they did was plant a torch on its summit; a torch that the first president, Julius Nyerere, stated would

'...shine beyond our borders, giving hope where there was despair, love where there was hate, and dignity where before there was only humiliation.'

To the Tanzanians, Kilimanjaro is clearly much more than just a very large mountain separating them from neighbouring Kenya. It's a symbol of their freedom, and a potent emblem of their country. And given the tribulations and hardships willingly suffered by thousands of trekkers on Kili each year – not to mention the money they spend for the privilege of doing so – the mountain obviously arouses some pretty strong emotions in non-Tanzanians as well.

Whatever the emotions provoked in you by this wonderful mountain, and however you plan to climb it, we wish you well. Because even if you choose to walk rather than run, leave the bicycle at home and forego the pleasures of wearing a latex rhino outfit, climbing up Kilimanjaro will still be one of the hardest things you ever do.

But it will also, without a doubt, be one of the most rewarding.

We were in an amiable frame of mind ourselves and, notwithstanding all the toil and trouble my self-appointed task had cost me, I don't think I would that night have changed places with anybody in the world.   **Hans Meyer** on the evening after reaching the summit, as recorded in *Across East African Glaciers (*1891)

IN THIS EDITION

For this second edition we have added comprehensive descriptions of the Lemosho and Umbwe routes, thereby completing our review of all the major trails to the summit (with Shira Plateau Route now little more than a road, we no longer consider it to be a regular trekking route, though we do still describe it for those few people who wish to take it). After the first edition was published, several readers wrote in and bullied us into compiling a whole new chapter covering the trek up Mount Meru; and having now experienced the joys of trekking in Arusha National Park up to Meru's summit, we're jolly glad you did. You'll find our description of that climb beginning on p209.

With the arrival of KPAP (Kilimanjaro Porters Assistance Project) in Moshi and an increased awareness in general of the mistreatment of porters – thanks to the work of organizations such as Tourism Concern, International Porters Protection Group and International Mountain Explorers Connection – for this second edition we have devoted more space in this book to their plight and how trekkers can help alleviate their suffering. Huge thanks must therefore go to Karen Valenti for her help with this matter. If you're in Moshi do pop into the KPAP office (for the address, see p40) to say hello – she's lovely – and to find out how you can do your bit.

One of the saddest parts of trekking on Kilimanjaro this time has been seeing the vast increase in litter on the mountain. I am therefore grateful both to fate for putting her in the same hotel as me at the same time and to the lady herself, Renata Haas, for her contribution to this edition on that very subject. Kilimanjaro is a beautiful, wonderful mountain – let's not bury that beauty under a pile of rubbish.

🖥 www.climbmountkilimanjaro.com

One of the most frustrating aspects of writing a guidebook is the inability to keep that book as up to date as we'd like it to be. To try to solve this problem and keep readers informed of the latest developments on and around the mountain we've set up 🖥 **www.climbmountkilimanjaro.com**.

As well as providing updates, the site has additional information to complement this guidebook and allows trekkers past, present and future to exchange their views and tips. Enter 'Kilimanjaro' into a search engine on the web and the screen fills with the sites of dozens of trekking agencies. As such, it is very difficult to find *unbiased* information from a site that isn't also trying to sell you a tour. With this guidebook we pride ourselves on our independence: we try to be anonymous when researching so that we can give you a fair and frank opinion of hotels, restaurants, trekking agencies etc. Our impartiality is, we believe, one of the reasons why the first edition of this book became the established text on the mountain; and this is also the aim for the website. It includes:

● **Kili news** Route alterations, park-fee increases and all the tragedies and triumphs that occur on the mountain
● **Readers' Forum** Tell us your opinions, recommendations, criticisms and experiences – and anything else you want to get off your chest
● **Your questions answered** Use the forum to post any questions you may have about the mountain
● **Weblogs** Compiling a weblog for your climb? Link it to the site so others can follow your progress
● **Charity climbs** If you're involved in a charity climb or trying to organize one, you'll find space here for you to tell the world about your climb
● **Links to Kili-based websites** Links to sites that we think you should look at
● **The Kilimanjaro Hall of Fame** Celebrate your achievements with the world by posting your photos of yourself and your friends on the summit!

We hope you'll find the site a useful and entertaining addition to this guidebook. Get online now!

PART 1: PLANNING YOUR TRIP

With a group or on your own?

INDEPENDENT TREKKING NOT AN OPTION

In 1991, the park authorities made it compulsory for all trekkers to arrange their walk through a licensed agency. Furthermore, they insist that all trekkers must be accompanied throughout their walk by a guide supplied by the agency. When these laws were first introduced, it was for a while still feasible to sneak in without paying, and many were the stories that arose about trekkers who managed to climb Kilimanjaro independently, tales that were often embellished with episodes of encounters with wild animals and even wilder park rangers.

Fortunately, the authorities have tightened up security and clamped down on non-payees, so these tedious tales are now few in number. Don't try to climb Kilimanjaro without a guide or without paying the proper fees. It's very unlikely you'll succeed and all you're doing is freeloading – indeed, stealing isn't too strong a word – from one of the poorest countries in the world. Yes, climbing Kilimanjaro is expensive. But the costs of maintaining a mountain that big are high. Besides, whatever price you pay, trust us, it's worth it.

WITH FRIENDS . . .

It's Kili time! Time to kick back, relax and take it easy with your friends.
Printed on the labels of Kilimanjaro Beer

So you have decided to climb Kilimanjaro, and have thus taken the first step on the path that leads from the comfort and safety of your favourite armchair to the untamed glory of the Roof of Africa. The second step on this path is to consider with whom to go.

This may not be as straightforward as it sounds, because Kilimanjaro breaks friendships as easily as it breaks records. The tribulations suffered by those who dare to pit themselves against the mountain wear down the most even of temperaments, and relationships are often the first to suffer. Idiosyncrasies in your friend's behaviour that you previously thought charming now simply become irritating, while the most trivial of differences between you and your chum could lead to the termination of a friendship that, before you'd both ventured onto its slopes, you thought was as steadfast and enduring as the mountain itself. Different levels of stamina, different levels of desire to reach the top, different attitudes towards the porters and guides, even differences in the film speeds you're using or the colour of your socks: on Kilimanjaro these things, for some reason, suddenly matter.

Then there's the farting. It is a well-known fact that the regular breaking of wind is a sure sign that you are acclimatizing satisfactorily (for more about acclimatization, see pp200-206); while the onset of a crushing headache, combined with a loss of sleep and a consequent loss of humour, are all classic symptoms suffered by those struggling to adapt to the rarified atmosphere. Problems occur, of course, when two friends acclimatize at different rates: ie, the vociferous and joyful flatulence of Friend A is simply not appreciated by Friend B, who has a bad headache, insomnia and ill-temper. Put the two parties together in a remote, confined space, such as that provided by a two-man tent on the slopes of a cold and lonely mountain, and you have an explosive cocktail that can blow apart even the strongest of friendships.

It rained terrible all night, and we put most of the Wachaga porters in our tent. It was rather distressing to the olfactory nerves ... At 4am a leopard visited us but did not fancy our scent.
Peter MacQueen, *In Wildest Africa* (an account of an expedition of 1907, published in 1910)

Of course, the above is just one possible scenario. It may be that both of you adapt equally well/badly to the new conditions and can draw pleasure/comfort from each other accordingly. People from Northern Europe seem particularly good at making the best of the windy conditions: while researching the first edition of this book we encountered a party of four Germans holding a farting competition, and one particularly talented Dutch pair who even managed a quick game of Name that Tune. (It may or may not surprise you to know that all but one of the participants in these competitions was male.)

And there are plenty of advantages in going with a friend too. There's the companionship for a start. It's cheaper, too, because away from the mountain you'll probably be sharing rooms, which always cuts the cost, and if you are planning on booking your climb through an agency in Tanzania your bargaining position is so much stronger if there are two of you. Having a companion also cuts the workload, enabling, for example, one to run off and find a room while the other looks after the luggage. It also saves your being paired with someone you don't know when you book with an agency; someone who may snore and blow off more violently than your friend ever would. And if you *do* both make it to the top, it's good to know that there will be somebody to testify to your achievements upon your return.

Climbing Kili with a companion has its problems, but there's no doubting the extra pleasure that can be gained as well. As the graffiti on the walls of Room 3 in the Kibo Huts tells us: '*What does not break us makes us stronger*'. If you are planning on travelling with a friend this, perhaps, should be your motto for the trek.

. . .OR ON YOUR OWN?

Those without friends, or at least without friends willing to climb a mountain with them, should not worry. For one thing, you'll never truly be on your own, simply because the park authorities forbid your climbing without a guide (see previous page) and you'll need at least one other crew member to act as porter. Furthermore, planning to go on your own means you can arrange **the trek that**

you want; you choose the trail to follow, the time to go and for how long; the pace of the walk, the number of rest-stops, when to go to bed – these are all your decisions, and yours alone. You are the boss; you have nobody else's feelings to consider but your own.

If you want to join up with others, for companionship or simply to make the trek a little cheaper, that's not a problem: you can book your trek in your home country with a tour operator (they always insist on a minimum number of participants before the trek goes ahead); or you can book in Tanzania, and ask to be put with other trekkers (which will often happen anyway, unless you specifically say otherwise). And even if you are walking alone, you can always meet other trekkers at the campsite in the evening if you so desire.

Trekking by yourself is fun and not the lonely experience many imagine; unless, of course, you enjoy the bliss of solitude and *want* to be alone. That's the beauty of walking solo: everything is up to you.

Budgeting

The most significant cost of your holiday, unless you opt for a few days at Serengeti's Kirawira Camp at the end of your stay (top suites US$950 per night in season – and this is not even the most expensive place!), is the walk itself. Set aside US$900-plus for a budget trek, more if you plan on ascending by an unusual route or insist on walking without other trekkers. Once on the mountain, however, you won't need to pay for anything else throughout the trek, except for the occasional chocolate bar or beer which you can buy at the rangers' huts on the way.

Away from the mountain and the other national parks, by far the most expensive place in Tanzania is Zanzibar. Elsewhere, you'll find transport, food and accommodation, the big three day-to-day expenses of the traveller's life, are pretty cheap in Tanzania and particularly in Moshi and Arusha.

The Tanzanian shilling (Ts) is the national currency. For exchange rates and more on money see p73.

ACCOMMODATION

Basic tourist accommodation starts at around £2-3/US$3.50-5. You can get cheaper, non-tourist accommodation, though this is often both sleazy and unhygienic and should only be considered as a last resort. We have not reviewed these cheap hotels individually in the book, but we do give some indication of where they can be found in the introduction to the accommodation sections in the city chapters.

At the other end of the spectrum, there are hotel rooms and luxury safari camps going for anything up to US$2000 per night in the high season.

FOOD

Food can be dirt cheap if you stick to the street sellers who ply their wares at all hours of the day – though dirt is often what you get on the food itself too, with hygiene standards not always of the highest. Still, even in a clean and decent budget restaurant the bill should still be only £2-3/US$3.50-5.

TRANSPORT

Public transport is cheap in Tanzania, though it could be said you get what you pay for: dilapidated buses, potholed roads, inadequate seating and narcoleptic drivers do not a pleasant journey make, but this is the reality of public transport, Tanzanian-style. Then again, at around £0.40/US$0.70 per hour for local buses and *dalla-dallas* (the local minibuses; see p74), it seems churlish to complain. Extra safety and comfort are available on the luxury buses, and at only a slightly higher price.

When to go

The two main trekking seasons for Kilimanjaro correspond with the mountain's two dry seasons (an imprecise term, the weather being occasionally inclement during these periods too) namely January to mid-March and June to October. Of course you can walk in the rainy season but not only is there a much higher chance of walking in the rain, the summits of Kibo and Mawenzi are likely to be wreathed in thick cloud too. Indeed, several agencies even suspend their operations in November and December, deciding that any trek is foolhardy at this time and the rewards for the trekkers considerably less. Curiously, however, Christmas and New Year, when the weather is far from perfect, are actually the most popular times to go.

As to the relative merits of the two trekking seasons, the differences are small though significant. The **January to March season** tends to be colder and there is a much greater chance of snow on the path at this time. The days, however, are often clearer, with only the occasional brief shower. It is usually an

DAR ES SALAAM

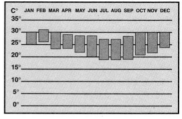

Average Rainfall (mm)

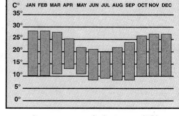

Average max/min temp (°C)

ARUSHA

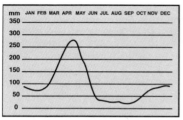

Average Rainfall (mm)

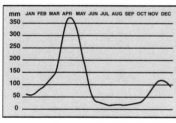

Average max/min temp (°C)

PLANNING YOUR TRIP

exceptionally beautiful time to climb and is often a little quieter than the other peak season of **June to October**, which coincides with the main academic holidays in Europe and the West. In this latter season the clouds tend to hang around the tree-line following the heavy rains of March to May. Once above this altitude, however, the skies are blue and brilliant and the chance of precipitation minimal (though still present).

Although the June to October season tends to be busier, this is not necessarily a disadvantage. For example, if you are travelling independently to Tanzania but wish, for the sake of companionship or simply to cut down on costs, to join up with other travellers for the trek, then the high visitor numbers in the June-October peak season will give you the best chance of doing this. And even if you do crave solitude when you walk, it can still be found on the mountain during this peak season. The trails are long, so you can always find vast gaps between trekkers to allow you to walk in peace; some of the routes – Rongai, for example, or the two trails across the Shira Plateau – almost never have more than one or two trekking groups on them at any one time, and are often completely deserted. And besides, Kilimanjaro is just so huge that its presence will dwarf your fellow trekkers to the point where they become, if you wish them to be, quite unnoticeable.

❏ **Star gazing**

Having decided which period you wish to travel in, you may wish to refine your dates still further by timing your walk so that on the final push to the summit, which is usually conducted at night, you will be walking under the brightness of a **full moon**. Stargazers may also wish to coincide their trip with a major astronomical happening; the views of the night sky from Kili are, after all, quite exceptional.

It's good to know that it isn't just the costs of climbing Kilimanjaro that are astronomical; the rewards can be too.

Booking your trek

With the decision over whether or not to climb independently taken out of your hands, and you've chosen who is going to join you on this trip of a lifetime, the next thing to decide is which agency is going to get your business.

The next few pages deal with exactly this matter. This may seem like overkill but booking with the right agency is perhaps **the single most important factor in determining the success or otherwise of your trek**: they are the ones who arrange everything, supply the equipment, and designate somebody to be your guide. So take your time choosing one. Because unless you are a guide, porter, guidebook writer or just plain daft, climbing Kilimanjaro will be a once-in-a-lifetime experience – and an expensive one too – so make sure that you get it right.

BOOKING WITH AN AGENCY AT HOME

Between 85 and 90% of trekkers on Kilimanjaro book their climb before they arrive in Tanzania through an agency in their home country. Despite this overwhelming majority, there is a fair case to be made for waiting until you arrive in the country before booking; see p32.

Booking your trek with an agency in your home country gets rid of the hassle. It depends what kind of package you have booked, of course, but few tour companies will sell you a climb up Kilimanjaro and nothing more. Nearly all will include in their Kili package such things as airport pick-up, accommodation, sightseeing trips, transport to and from the mountain, and maybe even the odd safari or Zanzibar excursion. Pay them some more and they'll throw in the flights and insurance and sort out your visas too. With no need to arrange these things yourself, booking from home will save you a considerable amount of time. It also ensures that you know exactly when you'll be walking, rather than having to wait around for a few days, as you may have to if you wait until you've arrived in Tanzania before booking.

Booking from an agency in your country also means you can plan your trek more precisely months in advance, and ask your agent any questions you may have well before you even arrive in Tanzania. Your agency at home will also either have their own guide to lead you up the mountain or, more probably, will be acting on behalf of one of the larger and better trekking operators in Moshi, providing you with peace of mind. (Where possible we have tried to find out exactly which Tanzanian trekking agency each company uses, so you can look them up and read a review of them in this book, too.) And if the trek still turns out to be a disaster, then the big advantage of booking from home is that you have a lot more comeback and thus more chance of receiving some sort of compensation.

A run-down of the larger overseas tour operators who arrange treks up Kilimanjaro follows. Before booking with anybody, have a look at the next section, *Booking with an agency in Tanzania*, and in particular the advice given in the sections headed *Choosing an agency in Tanzania* and *Signing the contract*. Both contain useful hints that are also relevant when dealing with agents and operators in your own country.

All prices quoted in the list below include park fees unless stated otherwise but exclude flights – again, unless stated. For details of the various routes up Kilimanjaro mentioned in the following list, please see p50.

Trekking agencies in the UK

● **7 Summits Expeditions** (☎ 01633-259844; 🖥 www.7summits-expeds.co.uk) Summit House, 5 Gold Tops, Newport, South Wales NP20 4PG. Company specializing in climbs up each of the continents' highest peaks, including Aconcagua and Everest. Their Kili climb follows the Umbwe/Western Breach Route, the most difficult trekking route on the mountain, and uses Zara International (see p187). Land-only prices start at £1225 including a Meru climb.

● **Abercrombie & Kent** (☎ 0845-0700 610; 🖥 www.abercrombiekent.co.uk) St George's House, Ambrose Street, Cheltenham, Gloucestershire GL50 3LG. Upmarket holiday company with treks on the Marangu Route from £2000 upwards including flights. Accommodation is at Moshi's Ameg Lodge (p176).

● **Acacia Africa** (☎ 020-7706 4700; 🖥 www.acacia-africa.com), Lower Ground Floor, 23A Craven Terrace, London W2 3QH. Africa specialist with a budget seven-day trip including Marangu trek (with five days/four nights on the mountain), using Springlands as a base (so it looks like Moshi's Zara International, see p187, are the local trekking agency concerned here), for £325 excluding park fees (for which they say you should add on another US$540). For six days on Machame it's £475 plus US$580.

● **The Adventure Company** (☎ 0870-794 1009) 15 Turk Street, Alton, Hampshire GU34 1AG. Offer Marangu, Machame and Rongai routes starting from £999 plus US$580 local payment including flights.

● **Africa Travel Resource** (☎ 01306-880770; 🖥 www.africatravelresource.com) Milton Heath House, Westcott Road, Dorking, Surrey RH34 3NB. Often recommended, very reliable and extremely knowledgeable company that uses the excellent African Walking Company (see p162) for their Kili climbs. Though they offer all the routes up the mountain, they concentrate on the relatively untramelled Rongai and Shira/Lemosho routes; and to further guarantee that your time on the mountain is a peaceful one, they try where possible to use their own campsites. Their website is a no-nonsense comprehensive place to find lots of information, too, for as well as promoting their own climbs they also have general stuff on booking a trek with other companies and a review of some of the local hotels. Their very helpful telephone staff quoted us US$1995 for the Shira Route, US$1495 for Rongai (why they quote in dollars we've no idea) – both of these joining a group on a set departure date – or they can arrange a private Lemosho trek for US$2403/4026/5553 for 1/2/3 people. Recommended.

● **Charity Challenge** (☎ 020-8557 0000; 🖳 www.charitychallenge.co.uk) Seventh Floor, Northway House, 1379 High Road, London N20 9LP. This company arranges expeditions to various parts of the world in order to raise money for charity. In order to participate, therefore, you need to raise a substantial amount of sponsorship – in Kili's case, almost £3000. Fail, and you could be kicked off the trip! Apart from all the fundraising, the cost for climbing Kili is £1875 – not cheap, though you pay for their expertise.

● **Exodus Travels** (☎ 0870-240 5550; 🖳 www.exodustravels.co.uk) Grange Mills, Weir Rd, London SW12 ONE. Offers a 17-day Kilimanjaro, Serengeti and Zanzibar trip using the Rongai Route (6 days and 5 nights) for upwards of £1732 (excluding park fees, so add on about US$640). Also offers Kilimanjaro-only treks using the Shira/Rongai routes for £760/650 respectively, or Marangu for £535 – all plus around US$640 in park fees – and a 'Roof of Africa' tour that combines a trek up Meru with the Shira Route (from £1465 plus US$640). They even offer a climb on the Rongai Route with a trip to see the mountain gorillas of Rwanda (£1679 plus park fees). Said to use African Walking Company (p162).

● **Explore Worldwide** (☎ 01252-391 140; 🖳 www.exploreworldwide.co.uk) Nelson House, 55 Victoria Road, Farnborough, Hants GU14 7PA. Long-established company offering treks on the Machame and Marangu routes, either on their own or combined with a safari or trip to Zanzibar. Machame Route starts at £1125, Marangu £1095, including flights but excluding park fees (US$585; we think this is remarkably cheap considering, by our estimate, the total park fees amount to US$635! Might be worth asking them why their estimate is so low.) Also operates an interesting 'Tanzanian Volcano' trek taking in Kili, Meru and a safari in Ngorongoro (from £1775). For the Kili section at least they use Shah Tours of Moshi (see p186), so accommodation is at the Mountain Inn.

● **Footprint Adventures** (☎ 01522-804 929; 🖳 www.footventure.co.uk) 5 Malham Drive, Lincoln LN6 0XD. The tour company arm of the well-known guidebook publishers. Offers guided treks on Kilimanjaro (beginning at £620) on all the established trails as well as a nip up Mount Meru (£450). Uses Zara International (p187) as their local trekking agent and thus accommodation off the mountain is at the Springlands (see p177). They also run an equipment-hire service, eg four-season sleeping bags £25.

● **Gane & Marshall International** (☎ 020-8445 6000; 🖳 www.ganeandmarsh all.co.uk), 7th Floor, Northway House, 1379 High Road, London N20 9LP. A small company that, using the Lemosho Route, claims to have a 95% success rate of trekkers reaching the summit. Also offers a Mount Meru climb followed by a trek up Kili on the Umbwe/Western Breach Route – the latter recognized as the toughest trekking route on the mountain. Uses GMTanzania (a Tanzania-based trekking agency). Prices start at £1136 for Lemosho though this depends on the number of trekkers in the group; add on another £524 at least for a trek up Mount Meru. Flights aren't included in this price, though two nights at Moivaro Lodge (see p154) are.

● **Guerba Expeditions** (☎ 01373-826 611; 🖳 www.guerba.co.uk), Wessex House, 40 Station Rd, Westbury, Wilts BA13 3JN. Offers the Rongai, Machame, Lemosho (which, like so many companies, they call the Shira Route) and Marangu routes. This is not unusual, but what *is* out of the ordinary is the ethical nature of their company. Not only do they have their own policy guidelines regarding porters and use the Marangu Hotel (p192), a KPAP partner, to ensure their fair treatment, but they also support the Amani Children's Home in Moshi (see p178). Prices begin at just less than £1000 plus a 'local payment' of US$600. Well worth checking out.

● **Hoopoe** (☎ 020-8428 8221; 🖳 www.hoopoe.com, email: hoopoeUK@aol.com) Suite F1, Hartsbourne House, Carpenders Park, Watford, Herts, WD1 5EF. Hoopoe Safaris has long been known as a trustworthy organization with high ideals – very eco-friendly, involved in many community projects and a KPAP partner (see pp40-41). Run treks on all the popular routes (though Marangu Route only reluctantly), and offer two sorts of trip, one where you join a group on a set departure, or a private trek (or FIT trek as they know it) for between two and eight people. Costs for the two alternatives: US$2695 for seven days on Machame on a set departure, or between US$2686 (for 11 or more of you) and US$3484 (if travelling solo) for a private trek on the same route. The set departure price includes two nights' accommodation at the Rivertrees Country Inn (p155) and transfer from Kili Airport; the FIT trek quote is for the climb only.

● **Imaginative Traveller** (☎ 0800-3616 2717; 🖳 www.imaginative-traveller. com) 1 Betts Avenue, Martlesham Heath, Suffolk IP5 7RH. Runs small-group tours including treks up Kili on the Umbwe (£665) and Marangu (£540) trails.

● **IntoAfrica Eco Travels Tanzania** (☎ 0114-255 5610; 🖳 www.intoafrica. co.uk) 4 Huntingdon Crescent, Sheffield, S11 8AX. Company that professes fair-trade ideals and supports several worthy causes in Tanzania, including support for schools and self-help projects. Recommended more than once by readers, they operate treks on the Machame Route (from US$1545) as well as a 3- or 4-day climb up Meru (from US$585). Also has offices in Arusha and Nairobi.

● **Jagged Globe** (☎ 0845-345 8848; 🖳 www.jagged-globe.co.uk) The Foundry Studios, 45 Mowbray Street, Sheffield, S3 8EN. Serious mountaineering company that leads four 12-person trips up 'trekkable' Kili per year on the Rongai and the more difficult Lemosho/Western Breach Route, with an *hors d'oeuvres* trek up Meru. Prices start at £1780 land only. Uses the Key's Hotel (see p183).

● **KE Adventure Travel** (☎ 01768-773 966; 🖳 www.keadventure.com) 32 Lake Rd, Keswick, Cumbria CA12 5DQ. Worldwide trekking specialists running a popular seven-day Rongai Route trek (including rest day at Mawenzi Tarn Hut) for £695 as well as a 13-day combined Mount Meru and Kilimanjaro holiday, climbing the latter via the Lemosho trail (though they misleadingly call it the Shira trail, presumably to advertise to customers that it crosses the Shira Plateau) and Western Breach. Prices for the Kili climb start at £1195 plus park fees and around £590-plus for the flights. Also claims to offer a combined Mount Kenya/Kilimanjaro tour for around £1500 plus park fees.

● **Kumuka** (☎ 020-7937 8855; 💻 www.kumuka.com) 40 Earls Court Rd, London, W8 6EJ. Offer a lightning seven-day trip starting and finishing in Nairobi and including a trek up Kili on the Marangu Route for £450 plus local payment US$605. Experienced and reliable, Kumuka is also one of the few established companies to demonstrate a social conscience, using the Kilimanjaro Guides and Porters Union (see p165) for their climbs.

● **Mountain Travel & Sobek** (☎ 01494-448 901; 💻 www.mtsobek.com) 67 Verney Ave, High Wycombe, Bucks, HP12 3ND. See *Trekking Agencies in the USA*, p29.

● **Sherpa Expeditions** (☎ 020-8577 2717; 💻 www.sherpa-walking-holidays.co.uk) 131a Heston Rd, Hounslow, Middx TW5 0RF. Offers a ten-day package including Machame trek for a very reasonable £799 *including* park fees, or a Mount Meru-Machame combination for £1093.

● **Team Kilimanjaro** (☎ 020-7193 5895 – note the clever number, with the last four digits corresponding to the height in metres of Kili; 💻 www.teamkilimanjaro.com) 5 Church Walk, Bideford, Devon EX39 2BP. This company comes at Kilimanjaro from a whole different angle. Established by a group of English mountaineers who now live permanently in Arusha and who lead their clients up the mountain themselves, they are reliable, reasonably priced and delightfully obsessed about the mountain, taking GPS systems up the mountain and holding a library filled with thousands of Kili photos. They also specialize in arranging record attempts for climbing the mountain. As far as their treks go, they concentrate on the southern three routes only (ie Machame, Marangu and Umbwe), charging £640 per person for six days, £730 for seven; meals and accommodation off the mountain are not included, though they can book a room for you. There's a single person's supplement of £75. Climb for one of their charities, however, and the trek can be heavily discounted; see their website for details. Overall a great little company and well worth checking out.

● **Terra Firma** (☎ 01691-870 321; 💻 www.terrafirmatravel.com) 'eunant', Lake Vyrnwy, Wales, SY10 0NF. Runs three or four seven-day Rongai treks per year for £795 (land only) plus park fees. Uses Zara International (see p187), so accommodation is at Moshi's Springlands Hotel (p177).

● **Tribes Travel** (☎ 01728-685 971; 💻 www.tribes.co.uk) 12 The Business Centre, Earl Soham, Woodbridge, Suffolk IP13 7SA. Award winning, eco-friendly, fair-trade company offering all the routes including the chance to spend the night on Kibo and visit the Reusch Crater and Ash Pit (£1900 excluding flights). Depending on which route you use, their base in Tanzania is either at the Key's Hotel or at the Moivaro Coffee Plantation Lodge. Pricey but impressive and well worth investigating.

● **World Expeditions** (☎ 0800-0744 135, 020-8870 2600; 🖳 www.worldexpeditions.co.uk), 3 Northfields Prospect, Putney Bridge Rd, London SW18 1PE. See p31, *Trekking Agencies in Australia*.

Trekking agencies in Continental Europe

● **Austria** **Hauser Exkursionen**, Favoritenstraße 70, A-1040 Wien (☎ 1-5 05 03 46; 🖳 www.hauser-exkursionen.at); branch of German agency (see below); **Supertramp** (☎ 01-533 51 37; 🖳 www.supertramp.co.at), Helferstorferstraße 4, A-1010 Wien.

● **Belgium** **Joker Tourisme** (☎ 02-502 19 37; 🖳 www.joker.be) Handelskaai 27, Brussels, and ten offices throughout the country; **Divantoura** (☎ 09-223 00 69; 🖳 www.divantoura.com), Bagattenstraat 176, B-9000, Ghent; **Road-runner** (☎ 052-21 15 11; 🖳 www.road-runner.be), Grote Markt 22, 9200 Dendermonde.

● **Denmark** **Inter-Travel** (☎ 33-15 00 77; 🖳 www.intertravel.dk), Frederiksholms Kanal 2, DK-1220 Kobenhavn K; **Marco Polo Tours** (☎ 33-76 67 00; 🖳 www.marcopolo-tours.dk), Borgergade 16, 1300 Kobenhavn K; **Topas** (☎ 86-89 36 22; 🖳 www.topas.dk), Bakkelyvej 2, 8680 Ry; offers a trek via the Rongai Route using Zara International (see p187).

● **France** **Allibert** (☎ 0476 45 2226; 🖳 www.allibert-trekking.com) Route de Grenoble, 38530, Chapareillan. **Club Aventure** (☎ 08-26 88 20 80; 🖳 www.clubaventure.fr), 18 rue Séguier, 75006 Paris; offers treks on the Machame and Marangu routes.

● **Germany** **Afrika Maximal Erleben** (aka **Afromaxx**; ☎ 036-02 97 45 88; 🖳 www.afromaxx.com), Ratsstrasse 02, D-99996 Urbach. **Hauser Exkursionen** (☎ 089-2 35 00 60; 🖳 www.hauser-exkursionen.de/main.asp) Spiegelstraße 9, D-81241 München; also has offices in Berlin at Klaus Peter Grätz, Brunnernstraße 167, D10119 (☎ 030-88 67 81 030) and Frankfurt at Reiseberatung Carmen Klopfstock, Postfach 1372, D65703, Hofheim (☎ 0619-2 90 17 82); one of Germany's larger trekking operators, currently running Kili climbs on the Lemosho and Machame routes. **DAV Summit Club** (☎ 089-64 24 20; 🖳 www.dav-summit-club.de), Am Perlacher Forst 186, 81545 München; **Explorer Fernreisen** (☎ 0211-99 49 01; 🖳 www.explorerfernreisen.com) Hüttenstrasse 17, 40215 Dusseldorf; **Olifants Tours and Safaris** (☎ 04293-78 98 89; 🖳 www.olifants.de) Wilhelmshauser Straße 3, D-28870 Fischerhude; **Skantur** (☎ 047-61 21 53 55; 🖳 www.skantur.de), Skandinavisches Reisezentrum DA, Ulvoldsveien, N-2670 Otta.

● **Netherlands** **SNP Reiswinkel** (☎ 024-327 7000; 🖳 www.snp.nl), Bijleveldsingel 26, Nijmegen; run treks up the Marangu Route with prices starting from just under €700. **Snow Leopard Adventure Reizen** (☎ 070-388 28 67; 🖳 www.snowleopard.nl), The Globe, Outdoor & Travel Center,

Waldorpstraat 15M; **Himalaya Trekking** (☎ 0521-55 13 01; 🖳 www.htwande lreizen.nl), Ten Have 13, 7983 KD Wapse; **Nederlandse Klim en Bergsport Vereniging** (☎ 0348-40 95 21; 🖳 www.nkbv.nl) Houttuinlaan 16A, 3447 GM Woerden; **Flach Travel Company** (☎ 0343-59 26 59; 🖳 www.flachtravel.nl); agents for Exodus UK (see p24).

● **Norway** EcoExpeditions (☎ 47-90 04 13 30; 🖳 www.ecoexpeditions.no/), PO Box 2028 Hillevåg, 4095 Stavanger; **Hvitserk** (☎ 47-23 21 30 70; 🖳 www. hvitserk.no), Prof Dahlsgt 3, 0355 Oslo; **Worldwide Adventures** (☎ 22-40 48 90; 🖳 www.worldwide.no), AS Nedre Slottsgate 12, Oslo 0157. Agents of UK's Explore Worldwide (see p24) and African Horizons (US; see below).

● **Spain** Giroguies (☎ 972-30 38 86; 🖳 www.giroguies.com).

● **Sweden** Aventyrsresor (☎ 08-55 60 69 00; 🖳 www.aventyrsresor.se) Hornsgartan 110, 117 26 Stockholm. Offers the Machame and Marangu routes.

● **Switzerland** Acapa Tours (☎ 056-443 32 21; 🖳 www.acapa.ch), Underdorfnstrasse 35, CH5107, Schinznach Dorf; agents for Exodus UK (see p24); **b&b travel** (☎ 01-380 4343; 🖳 www.b&btravel.ch) Bellerivestrasse 217, CH-8008 Zurich.

Trekking agencies in the USA
North American trekking agencies tend to quote land cost only.

● **Adventure Center** (☎ 510-654 1879, 800-228 8747; 🖳 www.adventurecen ter.com) 1311 63rd St, Suite 200, Emeryville, CA 94608. Agents for Guerba Expeditions (see p25), offering Marangu, Machame, Shira and Rongai routes, with prices starting from around US$1000.

● **African Horizons** (☎ toll free 877-256 1074; 🖳 www.africanhorizons.com) 2730 Lincoln Lane, Wilmette, IL 60091. Organizes treks up the Marangu and Machame routes, usually using Shah Tours (see p186). Reasonably inexpensive.

● **F&S Kiliwarrior** (☎ 703-827 5785; 🖳 www.go-kili.com), PO Box 275, Troutville, VA 24175. US contact of highly regarded Arusha-based company (see p164) and KPAP partner (see pp40-41).

● **Geographic Expeditions** (☎ 415-922 0448, 800-777 8183; 🖳 www.geoex. com) 1008 General Kennedy Ave, San Francisco, CA 94129-0902. Offer an 18-day 'Real Kilimanjaro' trek up the Lemosho/Western Breach Route with trips to Ngorongoro Crater and Serengeti afterwards as a reward for your exertions. Prices start at US$5695.

● **Good Earth** (☎ 813-615 9570, 877-265 9003; 🖳 www.goodearthtours.com), 18912 Wood Sage Drive, Tampa, Florida 33647. American office of Arusha-based company (see p164).

● **Journeys International** (☎ 734-665 4407, 800-255 8735; 🖳 www.journeys-intl.com) 107 Aprill Drive, Suite 3, Ann Arbor, MI 48103-1903. Does Rongai, Marangu and Lemosho routes (from US$2365/2045/2695 respectively) as well as a 'Full Moon' trek up Rongai with Kenyan safari add-on (US$4195).

● **Journey to Africa** (☎ 877-558 6288; 🖳 www.journeytoafrica.com), 1302 Waugh Drive, Houston, TX 77019. Currently organizes Marangu Route treks

followed by a safari trip to Tarangire, Ngorongoro and Serengeti national parks.
● **Mountain Madness** (☎ 206-937 8389, 800-328-5925; 🖳 www.mountainma
dness.com), 4218 SW Alaska Suite 206, Seattle, WA 98116. Founded by the late
Scott Fischer, after whom Kili's Fischer Campsite is named, the highly regarded
Mountain Madness and their sister company African Environments (see p162)
have a long association with the mountain, pioneered Kili's Lemosho Route
across the Shira Plateau and boast a 98% success rate in reaching the top. These
days in addition to Lemosho they also offer the Umbwe Route, combining the
trip with an optional jaunt to the Serengeti. Climb-only prices start at
US$3625/2575 for Lemosho/Umbwe. One of the best.
● **Mountain Travel & Sobek Expeditions** (☎ 510-594 6000, ☎ 888-687 6235;
🖳 www.mtsobek.com) 1266 66th Street, Emeryville, CA 94608. Upmarket
trekking company offering 10-day hikes on the Machame/Western Breach trail
(with 8 days actually on the mountain) including a night on the crater. The
climb-only option is US$3390 plus park fees.
● **Thomson Safaris** (☎ 617-923 0426, toll free 800-235 0289; 🖳 www.thomso
ntreks.com) 14 Mount Auburn Street, Watertown, MA 02472. American office
of popular and reputable Tanzanian agency based in Arusha, and recommended
by David Breasher, the director of the IMAX film *Kilimanjaro: To the Roof of
Africa*. They are also a KPAP partner (see pp40-41). They offer just the 6-day
Umbwe (from US$4990, including airfare) and 9-day Lemosho/Western Breach
(from US$6190) routes, as well as a 3- or 4-day jaunt up to the summit of Meru.
● **Tusker Trail** (☎ toll free 800-231-1919; 🖳 www.tusker.com) 924 Incline
Way, Suite H, Incline Village NV 89451-9423. Highly recommended, highly
regarded and very experienced company that's being operating for almost 30
years. Cited by Kilimanjaro Porters Assistance Project for their exemplary treatment of porters (see pp40-41), and a proportion of every client's trip costs goes
to Amani Children's Home (see p178). Offer the Machame and Lemosho
routes, the latter with an option to climb via the Arrow Glacier with a night at
the Crater Campsite. Trips start at just under US$2000.
● **Wilderness Travel** (☎ 510-558 2488, toll free 800-368 2794; 🖳 www.wilder
nesstravel.com) 1102 9th St, Berkeley, CA 94710. Offers 11-day upmarket trek
on the 'Shira Plateau' Route (essentially the Lemosho Route with variations)
combined with an optional Serengeti safari add-on. Climb-only prices US$3495
plus park fees. Uses KPAP partner Afrcan Environments (see p162).
● **World Expeditions** (🖳 www.weadventures.com) 580 Market St, 6th floor, San
Francisco, CA 94104. Australian company with office in California. See World
Expeditions under *Trekking Agencies in Australia* (p31) for details of their treks.

Trekking agencies in Canada
● **Canadian Himalayan Expeditions** (☎ 416-360 4300, toll free 1-800-563
8735; 🖳 www.himalayanexpeditions.com) 2 Toronto St, Suite 302, Toronto,
Ontario M5C 2B6. This is one of the few Canadian outfits that run their own
treks, rather than acting as agents for foreign companies. Run a couple of standard treks on the Machame and Marangu routes. Land costs are around
CA$1550 and CA$1790 respectively.

● **G.A.P. Adventures** (☎ 416-977 0433, 1-866-732-5885; 🖳 www.gapadve ntures.com) 355 Eglinton Ave East, Toronto, Ontario M4P 1M5. Agents for Exodus UK (see p24). Run standard Marangu and Rongai routes in seven days to and from Nairobi.

● **Trek Escapes** (☎ 403-283 6115; 🖳 www.trekescapes.com) 336-14 Street NW, Calgary, Alberta, T2N 1Z7. Agent for companies such as Dragoman, Guerba, Imaginative Traveller (see *Trekking Agencies in the UK*, p23) and Australia's Peregrine Adventures (see opposite).

● **Trek Holidays** (☎ toll free 1-888-456-3522; 🖳 www.trekholidays.com). Agents for Explore (see p24), have office in **Edmonton** (☎ 403-439 9118), 8412 109th St, Edmonton, Alberta T6G 1E2 and elsewhere.

● **Worldwide Adventures Inc** (☎ 1-800 567 2216; 🖳 www.worldexpediti ons.ca); offices in **Ottawa** (☎ 613 241 2700) 78 George St, Ottawa, Ontario K1N 5W1; **Montreal** (☎ 514 844 6364) 1795 St Denis St, Montreal, Quebec

---

It's not just about the climbing – other things to do on Kili

I suppose it's inevitable that, as more and more people climb and conquer Kili and the tourist industry surrounding the mountain grows, so certain individuals and companies will look for and organize other activities on or near the mountain. One of the more established is the **Kilimanjaro Marathon**, which usually takes place in February (🖳 www.kilimanjaromarathon.com). The race is run over the standard 26 miles/42.2km though there is a half marathon option too. The race starts in Moshi, heads out along the road to Dar, then returns to climb towards Mweka, before turning round to head back to Moshi and the finishing line. As such, it doesn't actually enter into the national park at all – though given the levels of exhaustion suffered by your average marathon participant, it's probably just as well that they don't have to climb a mountain too. There are prizes, with US$2500 each to winners of the men's and women's race, plus flights and free entry to the Rome Marathon in 2007.

However, for those for whom a marathon is not testing enough, there is always the **Kiliman Challenge** (🖳 www.kilimanjaroman.com). The itinerary for this particular brand of torture begins with a saunter up the Machame Route to Uhuru Peak for seven days, followed by a couple of days in the saddle of a mountain bike cycling around Kili to Rongai and back again, before rounding it all off with participation in the marathon as described above. The organizers are at pains to point out that only the last two events are races; with the climb, of course, it's too dangerous to race up. If it all sounds too much, you can opt to take part in just one or two of the activities.

For details of how to participate in either the marathon or the Kiliman challenge, contact the South African operator Wild Frontiers (see opposite) who organize the latter event and are the official tour agency for the marathon.

While all of these events will doubtless test your stamina and teach you much about yourself, if you'd rather learn more about the country instead then may we recommend that you try a simple **bike tour**. Afrigalaxy (see p182) of Moshi currently organize a four-day circuit of the mountain for US$400, including the hire of the 4WD and a security guide who accompanies the rider. Considering the tour will take you through the remote north-west side of the mountain, sandwiched between Kili and Kenya's Amboseli National Park, we think this is a great idea. Accommodation is either at guesthouses or camping.

H2X 3K4; **Toronto** (☎ 416 633 5666) 1170 Sheppard Ave, Suite 45, West Toronto, Ontario, M3K 2A3. Agents of World Expeditions (see below).

Trekking agencies in Australia

● **Peregrine Adventures** has several branches including one in **Melbourne** (☎ 03-9663 8611; 🖳 www.peregrineadventures.com) 258 Lonsdale St, Melbourne, Vic 3000. One of the larger agencies in Australia and the agents for Exodus UK (see p24). Offers Rongai and Machame routes with optional Zanzibar/safari add-ons from US$2200 to US$4330 land only.

● **World Expeditions** (☎ 1300-720-000; 🖳 www.worldexpeditions.com.au) Level 5, 71 York St, **Sydney** NSW 2000. Branches also in **Melbourne** (☎ 03-9670 8400) 1st Floor, 393 Little Bourke St, Melbourne Victoria 3000 and **Brisbane** (☎ 07-3216 0823), Shop 2, 36 Agnes St, Fortitude Valley, Queensland 4006. The main competition for Peregrine Adventures and a KPAP partner (see pp40-41), offering a challenging 16-day Twin Peaks trekking trip encompassing both Mount Kenya and Kilimanjaro (Rongai Route; from A$3990), or simple Rongai/Shira treks (A$1950/2150). They also organize a 'Volcanoes of Tanzania' (A$3990) tour, a neat combination of safari and trekking which climbs of Oldinyo Lengai, Meru and Kili; and, weirdly, a special Kilimanjaro Medical Trek (A$3690), a climb up the Rongai Route led by author and doctor Jim Duff and exclusively for medical professionals and their partners. Uses African Walking company (see p162) for their treks.

Trekking agencies in New Zealand

● **Adventure World** (☎ 09-524 5118) 101 Great South Rd, Remuera, PO Box 74008, Auckland. Agents for Explore (see p24).

● **Aspiring Guides** (☎ 03-443 9422; 🖳 www.aspiringguides.com) 99 Ardmore Street, PO Box 345, Lake Wanaka 9192. Partners of Jagged Globe (see p25).

● **World Expeditions** (☎ 09-368 4161, toll free 0800 350 354) Level 2, 35 High Street, Auckland CBD. Branch of World Expeditions of Australia (see above).

Trekking agencies in South Africa

● **Destination Africa Tours** (☎ 12-333 7110; 🖳 www.climbingkiliman jaro.com) 671 31st Avenue, Villeria, Pretoria 0186. Agency that covers all routes and claims to have a 96% success rate for leading trekkers to the top. Accommodation is at the Springlands Hotel in Moshi, so presumably there's a Zara International connection there (see p187). Also offers gear rental, and their comprehensive website includes full-moon dates, Swahili terms, a fitness programme and a menu.

● **Wild Frontiers** (☎ 11-702 2035; 🖳 www.wildfrontiers.com) PO Box 844, Halfway House, 1685. Established company, noteworthy for their involvement in the Kili Marathon and Kiliman events (see opposite). They also – and may they, their children and their children's children be forever blessed for doing this – arrange an annual 'Clean up Kili' trip to tackle one of the major problems with the mountain, offering trekkers a discount if they agree to pick up litter en route. They also organize regular trips up Kili, and are a partner of KPAP (see pp40-41) We like these people, and think they're well worth investigating.

For a review of **trekking agencies in Tanzania and Kenya**, see p126 (Dar es Salaam), p138 (Nairobi), p162 (Arusha), p182 (Moshi) and p192 (Marangu); and read the following section.

BOOKING WITH AN AGENCY IN TANZANIA

The main advantage of booking in Tanzania is one of economy: simply put, you're cutting out the middleman. Many foreign tour operators don't actually use their own staff to take the treks. Instead, they use the services of a Tanzanian tour operator. By booking in Tanzania, therefore, you are dealing directly with the people who are going to take you up the mountain and not the Western agent.

So it can be quite a bit cheaper booking your trek in Tanzania after you've arrived, particularly if you are willing to shop around and especially if you are willing to bargain. There are other advantages too. If you ask, there should be no reason why you cannot meet the guides and porters before you agree to sign up – and even your fellow trekkers, all of whom have a huge role to play in making the trek an enjoyable one. You can also personally check the tents and camping equipment before booking. Furthermore, the fact that you can book a trek up to 24 hours beforehand (but note proviso on p221) gives you greater flexibility, allowing you to alter your plans so that you can pick a day that suits you – when booking with an agency at home you often have to book months in advance, the tour is usually organized to a pretty tight schedule and altering this schedule at a later date is often impossible. Another point: while the money you spend on a trek may not be going to the most destitute and deserving of Tanzania's population, at least you know that *all* of it is going to Tanzanians, with none going into the

---

 Extending your time on the mountain

Although it's never made clear, it is in fact possible to extend your permit while you're on the mountain. So, for example, if you are booked on a six-day trek, you can in fact extend it to seven days or more. All you have to do is pay for the extra day(s) spent in the national park when you leave, either at Mweka or Marangu Gate. This means, of course, that should you fail to reach the summit, you can wait a day and try again. (The exception to this rule is those people on the Marangu Route who have to book their hut spaces in advance. As such, they have to specify the number of days they will be on the mountain before they start their trek and stick to it.)

At least, that's the theory. In practice, of course, it's not that easy. For a start, you have to make sure you have enough food for everyone to cover the extra time spent on the mountain. Secondly, you have to get permission from everybody else on your trek, including the guides, porters, the trekking company and, of course, other trekkers, that it's OK to delay your return back to civilization – and work out who's going to pay for the extra fees involved. This shouldn't be too difficult if you're the only trekker in the group, or the other trekkers you're with failed to reach the summit too and want another try at it. But both of these situations are unlikely – and it's perhaps unsurprising that we've never yet met anyone who has actually extended their time on the mountain. Still, it's worth knowing that the option exists.

pockets of a Western tour company. And finally, with the rise of the Internet, you don't even need to wait until you arrive in Tanzania before booking: most agencies in Arusha and Moshi (see p162 and p182) now have Internet booking services and, while it may seem a little scary sending a deposit to people in East Africa you've never met, the bigger companies at least are used to receiving bookings this way and can be relied upon.

What's more, if you go with an agency that's been recommended in this book or by friends, then there's no reason why it should be any more risky than if you were booking at home; indeed, there's a slim chance that you might even end up joining a group who *did* book their tour abroad, and paid more as a consequence.

Choosing an agency in Tanzania

The best place to look for an agency is either **Arusha**, which has the greatest number of tour and trekking operators, or **Moshi**. A third option, Marangu, is smaller and has fewer agencies, though it is also covered in this book on p192. Agencies in Dar es Salaam and other Tanzanian towns are usually nothing more than middlemen for the operators in Moshi and Arusha: book a tour with an agency in Dar, for example, and the chances are you'll still end up on a trek organized by an agency in Moshi or Arusha, only you would have paid more for it. Furthermore, if you book outside of Arusha or Moshi, you have less chance of inspecting the equipment or testing your guide before you set off.

Regarding the difference between Arusha and Moshi: in general the former is the home of the more established and larger safari companies/trekking agencies. However, perhaps due to its location, the Arusha-based companies tend to concentrate just as much on safaris in the Serengeti, Ngorongoro and Arusha National Park (including climbs up Meru) as they do on treks up Kilimanjaro. Indeed, some just act as middlemen for one of the agencies in Moshi, and don't actually arrange Kili treks themselves. Moshi, on the other hand, is a smaller place and one where the agencies tend to concentrate more on climbing Kili than on safaris. It would also be fair to say that the Moshi-based companies tend to be a little cheaper than those in Arusha, and most budget operators have their offices in Moshi.

Reading the above, therefore, it would seem that we are suggesting that you should base yourself in Moshi rather than Arusha, particularly if you are in the market for a budget trek. But it's not that simple. In particular, if you are thinking of taking a safari before or after your Kili climb, the Arusha-based companies may be able to offer you a better package for both than those in Moshi.

Our advice, therefore, is as follows. If you want a budget trek, the operators in Moshi tend to be cheaper. But before booking with any of them, do check out KPAP's website, download their questionnaire, and use this to grill any agency about their treatment of porters (many of them are cheaper because they pay porters poorly). And if you're unsatisfied with any of the answers given by an agency, let your conscience be your guide and go somewhere else. And don't dismiss the Arusha companies, particularly if a safari also features in your plans.

Wherever you decide to shop for your trek, do check out our reviews of the agencies on p162 (Arusha) and p182 (Moshi), which will guide you to the better companies. The golden rule when shopping around in either town is: **stick to those agencies that have a licence**, and check that licence thoroughly to ensure it covers trekking. If they don't have a licence, or the one that they show you looks a bit suspect, is out of date, or looks fake, take your business elsewhere. (That said, one or two of the agencies we've reviewed may not have a licence; we've pointed out which ones they are, but have included them just to show what kind of service they offer.)

Other advice includes:

● Decide what sort of trek you want, what route you wish to take, how long you wish to go for, and with how many people.

● Ask other travellers for their recommendations of a good agency.

● Shop around: don't sign up with the first agent you talk to; consult other agencies first to compare.

● Read the section opposite on signing contracts and learn it off by heart (or take this book with you!), so you know what to ask the agency.

● Ask about the number of other people on your trek and the number of porters you'll be taking.

● Ask if you can see their **'comments book'**. This is a book where previous clients have written their thoughts on the agency. Nearly every agency will have one, and if they are any good they will show it to you with little or no prompting. Indeed, if they don't have one, or are reluctant to show you, be very suspicious.

● If you have any dietary requirements or other special needs, ask them if these will be a problem, if it will cost any more, and how exactly they propose to comply with your requirements. For example, if you are a vegetarian, ask the agent what kind of meals you can expect to receive on the trek.

● Ask to see a print-out of the day-to-day itinerary (though some, admittedly, will not have this, all agencies should be able to describe the trekking routes and their itineraries without any problem); if you're negotiating with an agency at the upper end of the market, you may even be able to get a preview of the daily menus.

● If you think you've found a good company, ask to see the equipment you will be using and make sure the tent is complete, untorn and that all the zips work.

● Check the sleeping arrangements, particularly if you're not trekking with friends but have joined a group: are you going to have a tent to yourself, or are you going to be sharing with somebody you've never met before.

● If you are alone and on a budget, ask if it is possible to be put with a group, which should make things cheaper. (This is normally done automatically anyway; indeed, if you are travelling alone and were quoted a very low price, you can expect to be put with another group.)

Following on from the last point, many of the operators at the budget end often band together to lump all their customers into one large trekking group, thereby making it cheaper for them (because there are fewer guides required). So don't be surprised if, having signed up with one company, you end up being joined by trekkers who booked with another company. Once again, make sure you know in advance about any arrangements like this *before* you sign anything or hand over any money. And if you want to be on your own, tell them.

The sleeping arrangements are just one of the potential hazards of booking with a budget company. Or rather, it's one of the advantages of paying a bit more and going with a company that won't spring any nasty surprises on you. Sign up with a more expensive company and you should find that they have better safety procedures and emergency equipment such as gamow bags and oxygen bottles, more knowledgeable guides and, with companies at the top end, their own mobile toilets which means that you can use campsites (such as Fischer's Camp on the Shira Plateau) away from the masses. So unless money is really tight don't look for the cheapest company but the best value one; and hopefully our reviews will help you to decide which agencies offer the best deals.

For a list of trekking agencies in Tanzania, see the relevant sections in the Arusha, Moshi and Marangu chapters on p162, p182 and p192 respectively.

SIGNING THE CONTRACT

You've found a suitable agency offering the trek you want for the required duration at an acceptable price. Before you sign on the dotted line, however, there are a number of questions to be asked, matters to consider and points to discuss with the agency. (And if there is no dotted line to sign on – ie no contract – then don't even think about handing over any money or going with them.) What is vitally important is that you **sort out *exactly* what is and isn't included in the price of the trek**. Don't just ask what is included in the price: ask what isn't included – ie what you yourself will need to pay for.

The following is a brief checklist of **items that should be included**:
● All park fees, rescue fees, hut/camping fees for both yourself and the porters and guides.
● Hire of porters, assistant guides and guides, their wages and food.
● Food and water for the entire trek. Get a breakdown of exactly how many meals per day you will be getting: normally trekkers are served three meals per day plus a snack – typically a hot drink with popcorn and biscuits – upon arrival at camp at the end of the day; see p223 for more details on food on the trek.
● Transport to and from the park at the beginning and end of the trek.
● Hire of camping and cooking gear. If you have brought your own gear, you should be able to persuade the agency to reduce the cost of your trek, though it will be only by a small amount.
● Hire of any equipment – torches, ski poles, spare water-bottles etc – that you have forgotten to bring with you.
● Any special dietary requirements or other needs, all of which should be stipulated in the contract.
● Any free night's accommodation at the beginning or end of your trek that the trekking company has agreed to pay for.

Please note that items that are rarely, if ever, included in the package include cigarettes, soft drinks and the tips you dish out to your crew at the end.

PLANNING YOUR TRIP

Having sorted that out, you then need to make sure that *everything* that the agency has said they will provide, including everything listed above, is **specified in the contract**. This is important because, as you probably already know, a verbal contract is simply not worth the paper it isn't written on. The trekking companies all have standard contracts already drawn up which should include most of the above but will not include specific things such as the hire of any equipment that you need or any free nights' accommodation that you have managed to negotiate into the package. However, these will need to be written in as well. It is also useful to have a breakdown of the **day-by-day itinerary** written somewhere into the contract. Though it's rare now, in previous years some trekkers failed to reach the summit simply because they started out too late on the final, night-time push to the top.

THE COST: WHY IS IT ALL SO EXPENSIVE?

With little change from US$800 for even the cheapest trek, it cannot be denied that climbing Kili is a relatively expensive walk, particularly when compared to other famous treks (the Annapurna Circuit in Nepal, for example, has an

---

❑ AN EXAMPLE: THE MACHAME TREK

A six-day Machame trek, taking one guide, one assistant guide and two porters, would cost as follows:

Park fees

Rescue fee	US$20
Park entry fee (US$60 x 6 days)	US$360
Camping fee (US$50 x 5 nights)	US$250
Porter/guide entrance fees	US$4

Wages

Two porters (assuming they're paid the recommended wage of US$8 per day, though in reality it's usually less)	US$96
Assistant guide (assuming US$9 per day)	US$54
Guide (assuming US$15 per day)	US$90

Food

Five people at Ts10,000, which using current exchange rates, is... US$43

Transport

Estimate per person	US$20
TOTAL	**US$937**

Obviously if there are more of you then some costs, such as the food, wages and the transport costs, can be divided between the group, thus making it cheaper. Nevertheless, the above example gives you an idea of just how quickly the costs add up. Any excess over these costs goes straight to the agency but they have significant costs of their own, including an annual licence fee of US$2000 (US$5000 for foreigners), not to mention tax that amounts to nearly 30%. Remember, too, when working out your budget, to add on **tips** for your crew; see p38 for details.

entrance fee of US$30, while the Inca Trail is around US$60 for the permit); with no refund available to those who fail either, at first sight this trek can seem very bad value too – though to those who successfully reach the summit, of course, the sense of achievement and the enjoyment of the trek makes any amount seem worth it.

Since January 2006 and the doubling of the park entry fees, the cost of the trek has become even more extortionate. To give you some idea of where your US$800-plus is going, the following is a breakdown of fees, wages and other costs incurred on the trek, while the box opposite is an example of the breakdown of costs for an average trek. Don't forget that, in addition to the official costs outlined below, there is also the matter of tips: see p38 for further details.

Park fees

Rescue fee	US$20 per trip
Park entry fee	US$60 per day
Hut fee (Marangu Route only)	US$50 per night
Porter/guide entrance fees	US$1 per person per trip
Camping fee	US$50 per night.

Take a quick look at these figures and already you can see just why the cost of climbing Kilimanjaro is so high. Even if you took the quickest (and thus not recommended) five-day yomp up the Marangu Route, your fees alone still come to $520 plus porter/guide entrance fees. See opposite for how much a typical trek could cost.

Other costs

Wages (per trip) Wages vary from company to company, of course, though no agency pays their porters or staff that well – which is why they rely so heavily on the tips you give out. The subject of porters' wages is given further attention in the box on pp40-41.

Porters	Ts6000 (Marangu Route) to Ts8000 (other routes) per day (recommended by KINAPA, though more likely to be Ts4000-5000 per day).
Assistant guides	Ts8000-10,000 per day (US$7.50-9)
Guide	Ts12,000-20,000 per day (US$11-18)

Transport The only significant cost (other than wages) that can be divided between trekkers, a gallon of premium petrol is Ts1129 per litre (almost a dollar), with diesel a little more. The total cost for your trek will depend, of course, on which route you are taking and how long the journeys to and from the trek are, with Rongai and Lemosho/Shira routes the priciest, being the furthest away.

Food Difficult to calculate precisely, the best guess we can come up with for the food bill is around Ts10,000 per person (just over US$8); remember, though, that your total bill has to cover not only *your* food but the food of the porters and guides too.

TIPPING

Like a herd of elephants on the African plains, the subject of tipping is a bit of a grey area. What is certain is that, in addition to the cost of booking your trek, you will also need to shell out tips to your crew at the end of it all. The gratuity system on Kilimanjaro follows the American-style: that is to say, a tip is not so much a bonus to reward particularly attentive service or honest toil, as a mandatory payment to subsidize the poor wages the porter and guides receive. In other words, tipping is obligatory.

To anybody born outside the Americas this compulsory payment of gratuities seems to go against the very spirit of tipping. Nevertheless, it is very hard to begrudge the guides and porters a decent return for their labours – and depriving your entourage of their much-needed gratuities is not the way to voice your protest against this system.

As to the **size of the remuneration**, there are no set figures or formulas, though we do urge you to let your conscience instruct you on this matter as much as your wallet. One method that's currently very popular is for everybody to contribute 10% of the total cost of their trek towards tips. So if you paid US$850 for your trek, you should pay US$85 into the tip kitty. (If there are only one or two of you, it would be better to pay slightly more than 10%.) Another approach we've heard about is where each member of the trekking staff receives a set amount, from US$20 to each of the porters to US$40-50 to the assistant guides, and US$60-70 to the guides; or a *per diem* amount such as US$5 per porter per day, US$7 for the assistant guide, US$10 for the guide. These are mere guidelines, and you may wish to alter them if you feel, for example, a certain porter is deserving of more than his normal share, or if your trek was particularly difficult.

Having collected all the money, the usual form is to hand out the individual shares to each porter and guide in turn. Whatever you do, **do not hand all your tips to the guide**; sadly, often he'll end up trousering most of it. For more details of this, see the KPAP box on pp40-41.

The crew

PORTERS

My guide was as polite as Lord Chesterfield and kindly as the finest gentleman of the world could be. So I owe much to the bare-footed natives of this country, who patiently for eight cents a day bear the white man's burden. **Peter MacQueen** *In Wildest Africa* (1910)

The wages may have gone up – a porter today will earn on average Ts24,000-36,000 (around US$20-30) for a six-day trip, though do see the box on pp40-41 for details of just how low it can be – and all now have footwear of some description, but the opinion expressed way back at the beginning of the twentieth century by the intrepid MacQueen is much the same as that voiced by thousands of trekkers at the beginning of the twenty-first.

These men (and the ones hired by trekkers are nearly always male) never fail to draw both gratitude and, with the amount they carry and the minimum of fuss they make it about it, admiration from the trekkers who hire them. Ranging in age from about 18 (the minimum legal age, though some look a good deal younger) to 40 (though occasionally way beyond this), porters are amongst the hardest workers on Kilimanjaro. To see them traipsing up the mountain, water in one hand, cooker in another, rucksack on the back and picnic table on the head, is staggering to behold. And though they are supposed to carry no more than 15kg, many, desperate for work in what is an over-supplied market, carry much, much more.

And if that isn't enough, while at the end of the day the average trekker spends his or her time at camp moaning about the hardships they are suffering – in between cramming down mouthfuls of popcorn while clasping a steaming hot cup of tea – these hardy individuals are putting up the tents, helping with the preparation of the food, fetching more water and generally making sure every trekker's whim is, within reason, catered for.

Yet in spite of appearances, porters are not indestructible. Though they rarely climb to the summit themselves, a few still expire each year on the slopes of Kilimanjaro. The most common cause of death, perhaps unsurprisingly given the ragged clothes many wear, is exposure. For this reason, if you see a porter dozing on the wayside and it's getting a bit late, put aside your concerns about depriving him of some much needed shut-eye and wake him up: many are the tales of porters who have perished on Kilimanjaro because they took forty winks and then couldn't find their way back to camp in the dark. It's this kind of horror story that has caused so much concern over recent years and led to the formation of organizations such as the Kilimanjaro Porters Assistance Project (see pp40-1).

How many . . .

The first question regarding porters is: how many do you actually need? This issue won't actually concern many people, for agencies typically work this out for you. Those looking to save every last shilling, however, often ask the agency to cut down on the number of porters. But this is neither easy nor – given that the cost of a porter's wages is usually less than the food bill – a particularly brilliant idea. Remember that even if you do carry your own rucksack, there is still all the food, cooking equipment, camping gear and so forth to lug up the mountainside. Then there is the guide's rucksack too, for which he will expect you to hire a porter. What's more, you're also tempting the agency to overload each porter in order to reduce their total number – leading to the kind of illegal practices described in the box on pp40-1. So, in general, accept the agency's recommendations as to the number of porters and make sure that they're not overloaded.

As a general rule, the larger the number of trekkers, the less porters per person required and, if you take the Marangu Route (where no tent is required), you can probably get away with about two per trekker, and often less if the group is large. On other routes, where tents are necessary, two to three porters per person is the norm. (Just for the record, and just in case taking porters up a mountain makes you feel a little less virile, you may like to know that the great Count Teleki – see p101 – took no less than 65 of them up the mountain with him!)

A PORTER'S LOT IS NOT A HAPPY ONE

Nobody should underestimate the achievement of climbing Kilimanjaro. For five days you've dragged yourself up 4500m-plus of slopes, through four different seasons, on terrain that may be as alien to you as the moon. Imagine then, trying to do the same trek while eating only one square meal a day, with nothing but a pair of secondhand plimsolls on your feet and tatty cast-offs for clothes; that your days on the mountain are spent carrying up to 40kg on your back or head, while your nights are spent sharing a drafty four-man tent with up to nine other people, often with no ground mats and inadequate sleeping bags. And that, should anything go wrong – which, given the conditions you're expected to work in, they very well might – there'll be no insurance to cover you.

Imagine, furthermore, climbing not out of desire to be on Africa's highest mountain, but out of necessity, for if you don't submit yourself to these deprivations then you won't be able to fund yourself through college (which costs about US$300 per year) or feed your children. Imagine, too, that your reward for putting up with such conditions is somewhere between Ts3000-4000 per day; and that, out of that, you have to pay for your transport to and from the mountain (Ts3000 each way from Arusha to Marangu Gate), your food whilst on the mountain (which is why you only eat once a day) and even have to bribe the trekking guide (at least Ts5000) in order to be allowed on the mountain in the first place. No wonder you often end up relying on tips from tourists in order to take home any money from your labours. Tips that, if you're unlucky, may end up in the pocket of that same guide you bribed in order to get a job in the first place.

Such is the lot of the porters on Kilimanjaro: a precarious existence that, at best, involves hardship and indignity; and at worst can lead to death, as happens every year on the mountain. It is these kind of conditions that various organizations are now trying to improve.

The Kilimanjaro Porters Assistance Project (KPAP)
🖳 *www.kiliporters.org*

Registered at the beginning of 2003, KPAP is an initiative of the American-based International Mountain Explorers Connection (🖳 www.mountainexplorers.org), which fights for porters' rights worldwide including those working in other tourist hotspots such as Nepal's Annapurna Sanctuary and Peru's Inca Trail. With offices on the ground floor of the Hotel Da'Costa in Moshi, KPAP currently has a staff of three, including local man Zamo and American Karen Valenti. According to their manifesto, the organization's focus is on improving the working conditions of the porters on Kilimanjaro. They do this in three main ways:

● Lending trekking equipment and clothing at no charge. KPAP have a couple of wardrobes full of good quality trekking gear, much of it donated by American skiing companies and couriered over by American trekkers. For a returnable deposit (which can be anything from a school certificate to a mobile-phone) the porter can borrow items of clothing or fleeces.

● Providing classes on English, first-aid, HIV awareness and money management for the benefit of porters.

● Educating the climbers and general public on proper porter treatment.

In addition, we think it's fair to say that they are also trying to educate the trekking agencies and, hopefully, with a mixture of pressure and incentives, encourage them to treat their porters better – and pay them better too. (*Continued opposite*)

Among those incentives, KPAP are currently organizing an '**African Partnership for Responsible Travel**' scheme. In order to join the scheme, companies have to conform to certain guidelines issued by KPAP. They include directives on porters' wages, the amount the porters are required to carry, the food and water they receive on the mountain, what the sleeping conditions are like and how they're treated in the event of an accident or sickness. In order to be considered as a partner, the trekking agency must not only adhere to these guidelines but must allow KPAP to monitor them, too, to make sure they continue to stick to them.

Manage to fulfil all these criteria and the benefits, in terms of increased marketing opportunities and the extra demand that comes from being known as a Partner for Responsible Travel, are considerable. Perhaps unsurprisingly, however, there are only a dozen or so companies that are being considered by KPAP for this partnership scheme (see below). It's a depressing but accurate reflection of the current state of play.

In addition to the partnership scheme, KPAP also promotes the rights of porters in other ways. For one thing, at the end of your trek you may well bump into a KPAP staff member at Marangu or Mweka gates conducting a survey. If you should see one, do try to go out of your way to help them by filling in one of their questionnaires (if you haven't already picked one up from their website or office). It is hoped that, eventually, these questionnaires will help to build up a comprehensive and accurate picture of exactly which companies treat their porters well...and which don't. KPAP also sell maps and T-shirts from their office, the proceeds of which go towards their campaign. They have also recently instigated the 'Spend a day with a porter' scheme, about which you can read more on p45.

So how can you help?

There are many things trekkers can do to help the campaign. Sign up for a trek with one of the companies recommended by KPAP (see below for details) is one obvious way, of course. Though less accurate, in Britain at least you can check that your agency follows an ethical policy by going online to the Tourism Concern website: they have international guidelines for employing porters and encourage companies to sign up to them. (We say 'less accurate' because some of the companies that have signed up are still using Tanzanian companies that KPAP have found to be less than fair in their treatment of porters.)

To give you a helping hand in this matter, the following Tanzanian-based companies have joined KPAP's African partners scheme. As you can see, most of them are foreign (and indeed America-based), perhaps reflecting the fact that the fight to end the mistreatment of porters' has a higher profile abroad than it does in Tanzania. The companies are: **African Environments** (p162) and **Africa Walking Company** (p162) from Arusha, Moshi's **Summit Expeditions and Nomadic Experience** (p186) and the **Marangu Hotel** (p193) in Marangu Village. UK's **Hoopoe** (see p25) and Australia's **World Expeditions** (p31) In addition, there are other companies who are already part of IMEC's Responsible Travel Program, namely Arusha's **Thomson Safaris** (who are actually American-based – see p29 – though they use Arusha's **Nature Discovery** – p165 – for their treks), **F&S Kiliwarrior** (p164; another company with a large American input) and the American **Tusker Trail** (p29) who use Key's Hotel but organize their own climbs. To find out the latest situation and see if any other companies have become partners, access the 'Partner' section on the KPAP website. *(Continued on p42)*

❑ A PORTER'S LOT IS NOT A HAPPY ONE   (Continued from p41)

Other ways to help

Another way to help is to donate your camping equipment and clothing at the end of your trek to KPAP. You can also give it directly to a porter on your trek, though please note this should not be seen as a substitute for a tip but a supplement to it, no matter how good the equipment/clothing you're donating. Furthermore, you have to accept that the porter will probably sell those clothes when money is tight.

In addition, KPAP recommend the following on their website:

1 Make sure your porters are outfitted with appropriate clothing Porters need adequate footwear, socks, waterproof jackets and pants, gloves, hats, sunglasses, etc. Clothing can be borrowed at the KPAP office in Moshi – make sure they know this.

2 Fair wages should be paid to the porters The Kilimanjaro National Park recommends Ts6000 per day on the Marangu Route and Ts8000 per day on all of the other routes (where you camp, so equipment is heavier and there's more work to do). Ask your porters how much they are paid and if it includes food. Showing that you care about such things will encourage all operators and guides to treat their porters fairly.

3 Make sure porters have proper food and water If they are required to purchase their own food, wages should be increased accordingly.

4 Check the weights of porters' loads The Kilimanjaro National Park has a maximum carrying weight per porter of 25kg. which includes the porter's personal gear which is assumed to be 5kg. Thus the load they carry for the company should not exceed 20kg. If you can, be there at the weighing of the luggage at the start of the trek to make sure no funny business is going on. By checking that the bags are the recommended weight you ensure that the guide is using the correct amount of crew. If additional porters need to be hired, do make sure that the tour company is paying each porter their full wage when you return.

5 Count the number of porters every day Know the number of people in your crew. After all, you are paying for them. Do make sure, too, that porters are not sent down early, as often happens; if they are, they won't receive their tips; what's more, the other porters will then be overloaded.

6 Make sure your porters are provided with proper shelter Where no shelter is available (ie on all routes other than Marangu), porters need proper accommodation: that means their own tents and sleeping bags. Make sure they have enough tents and that they don't have to sleep in the mess tent: sleeping in the mess tent means that they have to wait, sometimes in inclement weather, for climbers to finish their meals.

. . . and how much?

The porters' wages are paid by the agency you sign up with. All you need to worry about is how much to give them as a **tip** at the end of the trek. Given the privations they suffer over the course of an average trek and their often desultory wages, their efforts to extract as much money as possible from the over-privileged *mzungu* (Swahili for 'white person') is entirely forgivable. One elaborate yet surprisingly common method is for the porters to pretend that there are more of them than there actually are; which, given the vast numbers of porters running around each campsite and the fact you don't actually walk with them on the trail,

Other ways to help (cont'd)

7 Ensure that your porters are given the tips you intend for them If you give the tips to the guide you run the risk that they may not pass on the full amount to the crew. Tipping directly to each individual member of your crew ensures that they receive their fair share. Alternatively, you can make sure your tour company has a transparent method of distributing tips.

8 Take care of any sick or injured porters Porters deserve the same standard of treatment and care as their clients. Sick or injured porters need to be sent back with someone who speaks their language and understands the problem. If available, porters should also be provided with insurance.

9 Get to know your porters and thank them Some porters speak English and will appreciate your making an effort to speak with them. Basic Swahili language cards are available for free at KPAP's office in Moshi. The word *pole* (pronounced 'polay') – which translates loosely as 'I'm sorry for you' – shows respect for porters after a hard day of carrying your bags. *Ahsante* ('asantay') means 'Thank you'.

10 Report any instances of abuse or neglect To both the trekking agency concerned and, more importantly, to KPAP on 🖳 info@kiliporters.org

11 Complete the post-climb survey This is perhaps the most important and one of the easiest things you can do. Before heading off up the mountain, pick up a questionnaire from the KPAP office or the website 🖳 www.kiliporters.org, as this will remind you of what you should be looking out for on the mountain. By providing KPAP with your feedback regarding the tour company's treatment of its staff, they will then be able to share with the company any problem areas that need to be corrected. KPAP eventually hopes to collect enough data to post a list of conscientious companies who treat their porters well.

In addition to the above, if you're travelling from America and have some spare luggage allowance, you may wish to contact IMEC before heading to Africa to see if you can help courier some of their donated clothing to Moshi.

Further details
Kilimanjaro Porters Assistance Project (KPAP) 🖳 www.kiliporters.org
International Mountain Explorers Connection (IMEC)
    🖳 www.mountainexplorers.org
    Umbrella organization of which KPAP is a part.
International Porter Protection Group (IPPG) 🖳 www.ippg.net
Tourism Concern 🖳 www.tourismconcern.org.uk

is a lot easier to achieve than you may think. It's a technique hinted at by John Reader in his excellent 1982 book *Kilimanjaro*:

I hired four porters for part of my excursion on Kilimanjaro. The fourth man's name was Stephen, or so the other three told me. I never met Stephen himself. Our gear seemed to arrive at each campsite without his assistance and I am not aware that he ever spent a night with us. I was assured that he was engaged elsewhere on tasks essential to the success of my journey, but I occasionally wondered whether Stephen actually existed. I was particularly aggrieved when he failed to collect his pay in person at the end of the trip. The other guides collected it for him. They also collected his tip.

This sort of thing shouldn't happen if you're with a reputable company but it's a good idea anyway to make sure you meet your team at the start of the trail before you set off. This will help to prevent this sort of scam, and it's good manners too. While at the end, to ensure each porter gets his fair share, dish the tips out yourself – *do not* give them to your guide to hand them out on your behalf; see the box on pp40-41 for why this is so.

Spend a day with a porter

Have you ever stared out of a bus window as it drives around the prettier, more rural parts of Tanzania and wished you could just jump out and explore the countryside at your own pace? Or have you ever climbed Kili and wished you could get to know your crew a little better, and found yourself wondering what their lives away from the mountain were like: Where did they live? Did they have any family? And what did they do when they weren't lugging picnic tables and other inessentials up the side of a bloody great mountain?

If you have, then a new initiative by those lovely people at KPAP could be just what you are looking for. Provisionally titled 'Spend a day with a porter', this new scheme does exactly what it says on the tin, offering you the chance to hang out with one of Kili's finest and see what a day in the life of your average porter entails. It also provides you with the opportunity to witness the reality behind all the current brouhaha concerning the rights and plights of porters – and all while strolling through some of the prettiest scenery East Africa has to offer.

Actually, though I said 'average porter' in the last paragraph, George Mtaki, the porter with the onerous duty of entertaining me for the day, was anything but average. For a start, when he met me as I alighted from the dalla dalla at Machame's village square, George immediately and unwittingly managed to allay one of my worst fears; namely that he wouldn't speak any English and thus, thanks to my almost complete lack of both Swahili and Chagga, we'd spend a rather awkward and uncomfortable day in near silence, communicating only via the medium of primitive grunts, facial expressions and charades. Because, apart from being charming and intelligent, George's command of English was such that he momentarily made me contemplate handing him my laptop so he could write this second edition – while I spent the next three months in Moshi's East Africa Pub, drinking Serengeti and watching Chelsea.

Despite his undoubted talents and virtues, however, life is just as tough for George as it is for his fellow porters, as he explained to me during a morning stroll to Machame Gate. A typical day during the trekking season would see him rising just after dawn to help see his two young children off to school, before setting off on the one-hour walk to Machame Gate, a breathtakingly beautiful march that in our opinion could be improved only by making the gradient about 30 degrees less steep, and by bringing the gate about 45 minutes closer to the village. For the dozens of porters of Machame, however, this was no aimless, once-in-a-lifetime amble but a daily commute undertaken in the relentless (and often fruitless) hunt for employment. Once there, it was a case of waiting for the trekking parties to turn up and hoping that one of them would need an extra porter or two – and that you'd be the lucky one, out of all the porters hanging around the gate, to be chosen. Small wonder that the walk uphill, particularly outside the high season, would often be in vain, leaving the porters jobless, penniless and very, very bored.

Please note that however much money and equipment you lavish on them at the end, the porters' reaction will always be the same. Simply put, porters are not above play-acting, in the same way that the sea is not above the clouds. On being given their gratuity all porters will grimace, sigh, tut, shake their head, roll their eyes in disgust and stare at the money in their hand with all the enthusiasm and gratitude of one who has just been handed a warm jar of the contents of the

For the afternoon, George had planned a two-hour hike to some 'nearby' waterfalls. However, with our intestines clogged with ugali and onions courtesy of George's wife Victoria, who cooked us a meal at their smart but spartan home, it soon became clear that this was over-ambitious, and instead we waddled down to the nearby river to look for monkeys and sleep off lunch. It was a beautiful afternoon and – though the monkeys were conspicuous only by their absence – an interesting one too as we discussed the lot of the porter. I also quizzed him on which companies treated their porters well (with George unsurprisingly listing the usual shining examples: Tusker Safaris, African Environments, African Walking Tours, Thomson Safaris etc) and which companies had particularly poor reputations (which, alas, the threat of legal action forbids me from naming in this book). It leaves the porters with a dilemma: refuse to work with some of the worst companies and you risk not working at all; agree to work for them, on the other hand, and you may not get paid as much as you hope – and you're only encouraging these companies to continue treating porters unfairly.

In many ways, George is one of the luckier ones. He's smart, for one thing, and his fine command of English should provide him with the opportunity to move up in the trekking/tourism industry. (Indeed, if it wasn't for a lack of money George would already have trained as a guide – which pretty well sums up the Catch 22 position in which many porters find themselves.) He also has a reasonably successful sideline producing furniture which enables him to support himself and his family during the rainy season. (As George explained, the KGPU – see p165 – of which he is a member, is currently looking at ways to help the porters earn money in the off season, and to this end is hoping to set up training courses in carpentry and other trades.) But for others, portering is their main and only reliable source of income; and for this reason, if no other, it's important that companies take more of an interest in the porters' welfare, particularly out of season.

A final stroll took us to the main road, calling in at the local hospital on the way, and with addresses swapped and promises to keep in touch exchanged, I bade him farewell at the end of an enlightening and extremely enjoyable day.

Though it's still in its earliest days, the 'Spend a day with a porter' scheme is a great way to discover what the day-to-day existence of a porter is like. But it is much more too. It is also a wonderful way to see one of the prettier villages on Kilimanjaro; to get an insider's view of what makes the village tick; and to see how important the tourist industry is to these villages on the mountain's slopes. And most importantly of all, it's a wonderful way to make a friend. Just go easy on the ugali.

For more information on the 'Spend a day with a porter' scheme, contact KPAP's offices below the Da'Costa Hotel in Moshi. Currently it costs just Ts5000, including lunch, though plans are to double this to a still-very-reasonable Ts10,000 soon.

Barranco Camp toilets. A few of the more talented ones may even manage a few tears. Nevertheless, providing you have paid a reasonable tip (and for guidance over what exactly is the correct amount, see p38), don't fall for the melodramatics but simply thank them warmly for all their endeavours over the course of the trek. Once they realize your conscience remains unpricked it will all be handshakes and smiles and, having trousered the money, they'll soon trot off happily enough.

GUIDES

Mzee Yohana Lauwo, the porter guide who accompanied the first Europeans up the Kilimanjaro Mountain a century ago, was the centre of attention in a commemorative ceremony in Moshi on Friday.

Mzee Lauwo, now over 118 years, was presented with a prize in cash. The Deputy Minister for Lands, Natural Resources and Tourism, Ndugu Chabanga Hassan Dyamwalle, suggested that Mwee Lauwo also be given a house to be built in his own village.

The ambassador to the Federal Republic of Germany (FRG) to Tanzania, Christel Steffler, presented Mzee Lauwo with a letter which expressed gratitude for his service in cementing German-Tanzanian relations. She said it was high time porters and guides were given the recognition they deserved for their work.

At the same ceremony, the deputy minister presented cash prizes and certificates to the winners of the Bonite tree planting competition.

Press cutting from the *In Brief* section of a local newspaper, found stuck on the wall of the *Kibo Hotel*, Marangu.

If portering is the first step on the career ladder of Kilimanjaro, then it is the guides who stand proudly on the top rung. Ornithologist, zoologist, botanist, geologist, tracker, astronomer, chef, butler, manager, doctor, linguist and teacher, a good guide will be all of these professions rolled into one. With luck, over the course of the trek he'll also become your friend.

The metamorphosis from porter to guide is a lengthy one. Having served one's apprenticeship by lugging luggage as a porter, a few lucky and ambitious ones are eventually promoted to the position of **assistant guide**. These gentlemen are probably the hardest working people on the mountain. While they still essentially remain a porter, in that they have to carry their fair share of equipment, they are also expected to perform many of the duties of a fully fledged guide – including, most painfully of all, the escorting of trekkers on that final, excruciating push to the summit.

Their reward for all this effort is a slightly higher wage than a porter (Ts54,000-60,000 per six-day trip), a commensurately greater proportion of the tips – and, perhaps most importantly, the knowledge that they have taken that first crucial step towards becoming a guide, when they can leave all this hard graft behind and wallow in the privileges that seniority brings.

Standing between them and a guiding licence is a period of intensive training conducted by the park authorities. This mainly involves a two- to three-week tour of the mountain, during which time they cover every designated route up and down Kilimanjaro. On this course they are also taught the essentials of being a guide, including a bit about the fauna and flora of Kili, how to take care of the mountain environment, how to spot the symptoms of altitude sickness in trekkers and, just as importantly, what to do about it.

Training complete, they receive their licences and are free to tout themselves around the agencies looking for work. While a few of the better guides are snapped up by the top agencies and work exclusively for them, the majority are freelance and have to actively seek work in what is already an over-supplied market; at the moment there are about 700 guides working on the mountain. For this reason, guides' wages are not that stratospheric considering the work they do and the time and effort they've put in to qualifying, being about Ts72,000-115,000 for a six-day trip.

Choosing a guide

At the moment, all guides carry the same licence regardless of their ability. As a result, tourists have no idea whether they are hiring a knowledgeable guide who can instruct them in the geology, flora, fauna and so on of the mountain, or whether they are getting a guide whose knowledge extends little beyond knowing where the path is and how to cook popcorn. For this reason, KINAPA are planning to introduce a system whereby the guides will be categorized according to their ability: so, for example, the top guides (who for the moment have been given the title of Chief Interpreters by KINAPA) will be issued with one licence, while those of lesser ability (dubbed, temporarily at least, Route Guides by KINAPA) hold another. Naturally, those who hold the Chief Interpreter licences will command a higher wage and will tend to be employed by the more expensive agencies. But the Route Guides should still be able to find employment among the cheaper agencies catering to those trekkers who want to climb the mountain, but aren't overly interested in its features; in other words, those who are hiring a guide simply because the rules say they have to.

This initiative, if it works, can only be good news for trekkers: your guide is one of the most important factors in determining whether your trek is an enjoyable one, and a good guide can truly enhance any walk on Kilimanjaro. It's particularly important because the examinations taken by would-be guides in order to gain their guiding licence do not appear to be particularly stringent: the last time these exams were held, for example, of the 244 who enrolled on the course, 226 passed – in other words almost 93% became licenced guides, suggesting that the exams do little to distinguish between the very good and the very, very bad.

Unfortunately, we first heard about this scheme four years ago – and despite promises, it doesn't appear to be any nearer fruition. So unless and until that initiative is introduced, it is very important that you meet your guide before you go, in order to test his abilities and, even more importantly, to make sure that you can trust him: remember, you are putting your life into his hands for the next five or six days, and his decisions could determine whether you come down with a gold certificate – or on a stretcher. It's not just his talent on the mountain that needs to be tested either. You need to make sure you can get along with him, so his ability with the English language could be crucial too. You may even, if you're feeling particularly vindictive, test him on his knowledge of Kilimanjaro by asking him about a few facts that you've gleaned from this book (though bear in mind, knowledge of the mountain is only one area in which he should be proficient). Remember, it's you who is paying for this trek, and it's a lot too. For that reason alone you should be entitled to check that you are getting your *shilingis'* worth.

PLANNING YOUR TRIP

Getting to Kilimanjaro

One of the gladdest moments in life, methinks is the departure upon a distant journey into unknown lands. Shaking off with one mighty effort the fetters of habit, the leaden weight of routine, the cloak of many cares and the slavery of home, man feels once more happy... The blood flows with the fast circulation of childhood ... afresh dawns the morn of life.

Diary entry of **Richard Burton** (the explorer, not the actor), 2 December 1856.

BY AIR

Tanzania has three major international airports: Dar es Salaam, Zanzibar and Kilimanjaro. The latter as you may expect is the most convenient for Kilimanjaro, standing only 48km away from the mountain town of Moshi and a similar distance from Arusha. An approximate timetable of international flights to and from KIA (the acronym for Kilimanjaro International Airport, though the three-letter international airport code more commonly used is JRO) can be found in *Appendix B*, p305. Unfortunately, the lack of airlines flying into Kilimanjaro – KLM, Ethiopian, Air Tanzania and Air Kenya being the major ones – results in airfares from Europe and elsewhere being rather inflated; this, combined with the fact that many trekkers will want a few days on a beach at the start or end of their holiday, means that most visitors to Tanzania fly to one of the other two airports. Of the two, Zanzibar is often, surprisingly, the cheaper destination. It is, however, rather inconveniently located for Kilimanjaro, being around 40km off the Tanzanian coast, and as such those flying out for the specific purpose of climbing the mountain should really discard this option and look instead at flights to Dar es Salaam.

In addition to the Tanzanian destinations, you may also wish to consider Mombasa and Nairobi in Kenya, both of which are conveniently situated for Kilimanjaro and which are usually a little cheaper to fly to. This also gives you the chance of taking in one of Kenya's world-renowned game reserves (which are cheaper when compared to Tanzanian park fees). Note, however, that by choosing this option you may need a multiple-entry visa (if you are flying out of Kenya, too, for example, and spend longer than a fortnight in Tanzania) for Kenya, which for Brits and others can be as much as £70/US$122 – thereby reducing or eliminating any saving you may have made in airfares. (For details of whether you will require a multiple-entry visa, or can get away with a single-entry visa for Kenya, see p72.) Furthermore, there is all the extra travelling to and from Kilimanjaro to consider.

You will find brief guides in this book to Dar es Salaam (p124) as well as Nairobi (p134) and Kilimanjaro International Airport (p144); while a timetable for flights to Kilimanjaro International can be found in *Appendix B*, p305.

From the UK
A cheap flight to Kilimanjaro from London with KLM via Amsterdam will set you back a minimum of £500, while for Dar the determined may be able to find one for around £420. You have to add on to these places departure taxes from both the UK and Tanzania (from the latter it's around US$30 and not usually included as part of the ticket price).

In addition to the travel agencies listed below, net-heads may also like to check out 🖳 www.cheapflights.co.uk, which gives a summary of the flight offers to your destination from a number of different agents. A couple of other online agencies to recommend are Airline Network (🖳 www.airline-n etwork.co.uk) and Expedia (🖳 www.expedia.co.uk).

The larger travel agents include STA Travel (☎ 08701 630026; 🖳 www.stat ravel.com), Flight Centre (☎ 0800 58 700 58; 🖳 www.flightcentre.co.uk) and Trailfinders (☎ 0845 058 9858; 🖳 www.trailfinders.com). All have branches around the country.

From North America
In the US, check out Air Brokers International of San Francisco (🖳 www.airb rokers.com; ☎ 1-800-883 3273), Travel Cuts (🖳 www.travelcuts.com; ☎ 1-800-592-2887, in Canada ☎ 1-686-246-9762) and STA Travel (🖳 www.statravel. com; ☎ 1-800-781 4040).

From Australia and New Zealand
In Australia and New Zealand try Flight Centre (🖳 www.flightcentre.com/au; Australia ☎ 133 133, New Zealand ☎ 0800 2435 44), Trailfinders (🖳 www.tra ilfinders.com; ☎ 1300-780-212) and STA Travel (🖳 www.statravel.com; ☎ 1300-733-035).

OVERLAND

A big country lying at the heart of East Africa, Tanzania has borders with many countries including Burundi, Kenya, Malawi, Mozambique, Rwanda, Uganda and Zambia. The **Burundi** border has been shut since 1995 due to the ongoing civil war in that country. Positive murmurs have been coming out of the country of late after voters backed a power-sharing constitution in a referendum in March 2005, and elections in August brought the Hutu Pierre Nkurunziza to power. Unfortunately, the last rebel group still operating, FNL, has rejected peace talks and unrest continues. The border remains shut for the moment.

The borders with **Rwanda**, **Uganda** (most commonly crossed at Mutukula, north-west of Bukoba), **Zambia** (main crossing Tunduma), **Mozambique** (Kilambo), **Malawi** (Songwe River Bridge) and **Kenya** (see the Nairobi chapter for details) are all relatively straightforward and served by public buses. Tanzania and Zambia are also linked by express train, running twice weekly between Dar es Salaam and Mbeya.

PLANNING YOUR TRIP

Route options

GETTING TO THE MOUNTAIN

This book aims to take you from your armchair to the summit of Africa's highest mountain. If you have booked a package from home, of course your transport to and from the mountain will already have been sorted out and you needn't worry. If you haven't then this book will tell you about the city you are flying to and the towns of Arusha, Moshi and Marangu that lie nearest to the mountain. It also goes into some detail about which trekking company to book with and where you can find them; having booked your trek with a company in Tanzania, you will invariably find that it includes transport to and from the Kilimanjaro National Park gates. From there, it's all about the walking...

GETTING UP THE MOUNTAIN   [SEE COLOUR MAP, p322]

Kilimanjaro has two main summits. The higher one is Kibo, the glacier-clad circular summit that stars on all the pictures of Kilimanjaro. While spiky Mawenzi, to its east, is impossible to conquer without knowledge of advanced climbing techniques and no small amount of courage, it is possible to *walk* up to the top of Kibo at a height of 5892-5896m (for a discussion of the exact height of the mountain, see p84).

   Look down at Kilimanjaro from above and you should be able to count seven paths trailing like ribbons up the sides of the mountain. Five of these are ascent-only paths (ie you can only walk *up* the mountain on them and you are not allowed to come down on these trails); one, Mweka, is a descent-only path, and one, the Marangu Route, is both an ascent and descent trail. At around 4000m these trails meet up with a path that loops right around the Kibo summit. This path is known as the Kibo Circuit, though it's often divided into two halves known as the Northern and Southern circuits. By the time you reach the foot of Kibo, only three paths lead up the slopes to the summit itself. For a *brief* description of the trails and a look at their relative merits, read on; for a map, see p322, while for further details check out the **full trail descriptions**, beginning on p220. Note that some trekking agencies vary the routes slightly, particularly on the Shira Plateau, but any agency worth its salt will provide you with a detailed itinerary so you can check exactly which path you'll be taking each day.

Ascending Kilimanjaro: the options

There are six ascent trails leading up to the foot of Kibo peak. These are (running anti-clockwise, beginning with the westernmost trail): the little-used Shira Plateau Route, the Lemosho Route, Machame Route, Umbwe Route, Marangu Route and, running from the north-east, the Loitokitok (Rongai) Route. Each of these six routes eventually meet with a path circling the foot of the Kibo cone, a path

known as either the **Northern Circuit** or the **Southern Circuit** depending on which side of the mountain you are. (It is possible and very worthwhile to walk right around Kibo on this path, though this needs to be arranged beforehand with your agency, takes a long time, and permission from KINAPA may need to be sought before embarking on such an expedition.) The trails mix and merge, so that by the time you reach Kibo just three trails lead up to the crater rim: the **Western Breach Route** (aka the **Arrow Glacier Route**), **Barafu Route**, and the nameless third path which runs up from Kibo Huts to Gillman's Point, and which we shall call the **Kibo Huts Route**. Which of these you will take to the summit depends upon which of the six paths you took to get this far: the Shira, Lemosho, Machame and Umbwe routes can use either the difficult Western Breach Route or the easier (but longer) Barafu Route, while the Marangu and Rongai trails use the Kibo Huts Route. You can deviate from this rule and design your own combination of trails to take you to the summit and back, but it will require special permission from KINAPA and the agencies charge a lot more to organize such a trek.

A brief description of each of the six main trails follows:

The Marangu Route (5-6 days) is the oldest and, officially at least, still the most popular trail on the mountain (though most guides now consider Machame, below, to be more popular). It is also the one that comes closest (though not very) to the trail Hans Meyer took in making the first successful assault on the summit. It is also the only ascent trail where camping is not necessary, indeed not allowed, with trekkers sleeping in dormitory huts along the way. From the Kibo Huts, trekkers climb up to the summit via Gillman's Point. The trail should take a minimum of five days and four nights to complete, though an extra night is usually taken after the second day to allow trekkers to acclimatize.

The Machame Route (6-7 days) is possibly now the most popular trail on the mountain. Whether this is true or not, it's certainly the one the majority of guides consider the most enjoyable. Though widely regarded as more difficult than the Marangu Route, the success rate on this trail is higher, possibly because it is a day longer at six days and five nights (assuming you take the Barafu Route to the summit) which gives trekkers more time to acclimatize; an extra acclimatization day can also be taken in the Karanga Valley. You can also take the more difficult Arrow Glacier Route though this shortens the trek by a day or two.

The Shira Plateau and Lemosho routes (5-8 days each) Both of these routes run from west to east across the centre of the Shira Plateau. The **Shira Plateau Route** is the original plateau trail, though it is seldom used these days, for much of it is a 4WD track and walkers embarking on this trail often begin their trek above the forest in the moorland zone. After traversing the plateau the trekker has a choice of climbing Kibo via the Western Breach/Arrow Glacier Route, or the longer and easier Barafu Route. If opting for the former, expect the trek to last a total of five nights and six days. By the latter trail the walk could last as many as eight days if extra overnight stops on the plateau and in the Karanga Valley are taken – if not, six days is more likely.

The **Lemosho Route** improves on the Shira Plateau Route by starting below the Shira Ridge, thus providing trekkers with a walk in the forest at the start of

---

 The topography of Kilimanjaro

And surely never monarch wore his royal robes more royally than this monarch of African mountains, Kilimanjaro. His foot rests on a carpet of velvety turf, and through the dark green forest the steps of his throne reach downward to the earth, where man stands awestruck before the glory of his majesty. Art may have colours rich enough to fix one moment of this dazzling splendour, but neither brush nor pen can portray the unceasing play of colour – the wondrous purples of the summit deepening as in the Alpine afterglow; the dull greens of the forest and the sepia shadows in the ravines and hollows, growing ever darker as evening steals on apace; and last, the gradual fading away of all, as the sun sets, and over everything spreads the grey cloud-curtain of the night. It is not a picture but a pageant – a king goes to his rest.

Hans Meyer *Across East African Glaciers* (1891)

Kilimanjaro is not only the highest mountain in Africa, it's also one of the biggest volcanoes on the entire planet, covering an area of approximately 388,500 hectares. In this area are three main peaks that betray its origins as the offspring of three huge volcanic eruptions.

The oldest and smallest peak is known as **Shira**, and lies on the western edge of the mountain. This is the least impressive of the three summits, being nothing more than a heavily eroded ridge, 3962m tall at its highest point, **Johnsell Point**. This ridge is, in fact, merely the south-western rims of the original Shira crater, the northern and eastern sides being covered by later material from Kibo (see below).

The Shira Ridge separates the western slopes from the **Shira Plateau**. This large, rocky plateau, 6200ha in size, is one of Kilimanjaro's most intriguing features. It is believed to be the caldera of the first volcano (a caldera is a collapsed crater) that has been filled in by lava from later eruptions which then solidified and turned to rock. The plateau rises gently from west to east until it reaches the youngest and main summit on Kilimanjaro, **Kibo**. This is the best preserved crater on Kilimanjaro; its southern lip is slightly higher than the rest of the rim, and the highest point on this southern lip is **Uhuru Peak** – at 5895m the highest point in Africa and the goal of just about every Kilimanjaro trekker.

Kibo is also the only one of the three summits which is permanently covered in snow, thanks to the large **glaciers** that cover much of its surface. Kibo is also the one peak that really does look like a volcanic crater; indeed, there are not one but three concentric craters on Kibo. Within the inner **Reusch Crater** (1.3km in diameter) one can still see signs of volcanic activity, including fumaroles, the smell of sulphur and a third crater, the **Ash Pit**, 130m deep by 140m wide.

the trek, giving them more time to acclimatize. As with the Shira Plateau Route, you can ascend Kibo either by the Arrow Glacier Route or by the Barafu Route; allow five nights for the former, up to seven nights for the latter if stops at Shira 1, Shira Huts and in the Karanga Valley are taken. It's becoming very common for trekking agencies to refer to the Lemosho Route as the Shira Route, which is of course confusing. If you have already booked your 'Shira' trek and want to know what route it is you will be taking, one way to check is to see where your first night's campsite will be; if it's the Big Tree Campsite – or Mti Mkubwa in the local language – then it's actually the Lemosho Route that you'll be using.

The outer, **Kibo Crater** (1.9 by 2.7km), is not a perfect, unbroken ring. There are gaps in the summit where the walls have been breached by lava flows; the most dramatic of these is the **Western Breach**, through which many climbers gain access to the summit each year. The crater has also subsided a little over time, leading to a landslide 100,000 years ago that created the **Barranco** on Kibo's southern side. On the whole, though, Kibo's slopes are gentle, allowing trekkers as well as mountaineers to reach the summit. For more details on the Kibo summit, see p300.

Separating Kibo from Kilimanjaro's second peak, Mawenzi, is the **Saddle**, at 3600ha the largest area of high-altitude tundra in tropical Africa. This really is a beautiful, eerie place — a dusty desert almost 5000m high, featureless except for the occasional parasitic cone dotted here and there, including the **Triplets**, **Middle Red** and **West Lava Hill**, all running south-east from the south-eastern side of Kibo. (A parasitic cone is a mini cone on the side of a volcano caused by a later, minor eruption; amazingly, there are said to be some of the 250 parasitic cones on Kilimanjaro!)

Nothing could be more marked than the contrast between the external appearance of these two volcanoes – Kibo, with the unbroken, gradual slopes of the typical volcanic cone – Mawenzi with its bewildering display of many-coloured lavas and its fantastically carved outlines, the result of long ages of exposure, combined with the tendency of its component rocks to split vertically rather than horizontally. The hand of time has left its impress upon Kibo too, but the havoc it has wrought is not to be detected at a distance. **Hans Meyer** *Across East African Glaciers* (1891)

Seen from afar, **Mawenzi** looks less like a crater than a single lump of jagged, craggy rock emerging from the Saddle. This is merely because its western side also happens to be its highest and hides everything behind it. Walk around Mawenzi, however, and you'll realize that this peak is actually a horseshoe shape, with only the northern side of the crater having been eroded away. Its sides too steep to hold glaciers, there is no *permanent* snow on Mawenzi, and the gradients are enough to dissuade all but the bravest and most technically accomplished climbers. Mawenzi's highest point is Hans Meyer Peak at 5149m but so shattered is this summit, and so riven with gullies and fractures, that there are a number of other distinctive peaks including Purtscheller Peak (5120m) and South Peak (4958m). There are also two deep gorges, the Great Barranco and the Lesser Barranco, scarring its north-eastern face.

Few people know this, but Kilimanjaro does actually have a crater lake. **Lake Chala** (aka Jala) lies some 30km to the south-east, and is said to be up to 2.5 miles deep.

For details on how exactly Kilimanjaro came to be this shape, see the geology section on p81; for flora and fauna that can be found growing on the mountain, see p110.

The Rongai Route (5-6 days) is the only trail to approach Kibo from the north. Indeed, the original trail began right against the Kenyan border, though recently the trail shifted eastwards and now starts at the Tanzanian town of Loitokitok, after which the new trail has been named (though everybody still refers to it as the Rongai Route). For the final push to the summit, trekkers on this trail take the Kibo Huts Route, joining it either at the huts themselves or at the 5000m mark just below Hans Meyer Cave. Again the trek can be completed in five days and four nights, though trekkers usually take a detour to camp beneath Mawenzi peak, adding an extra day.

The Umbwe Route (5-6 days) is the hardest trail, a tough vertical slog through the jungle, in places using the tree roots as makeshift rungs on a ladder. Having reached the Southern Circuit, trekkers then traditionally continue north-west to tackle Kibo from the west and the more difficult Arrow Glacier/Western Breach Route, though you can also head east round to Barafu and approach the summit from there. The entire walk up and down takes a minimum of five days if going via the Barafu Campsite (though this is much too rapid; take six minimum, with a day at Karanga Valley); or four/five minimum (six is again better) if going via the Western Breach, with additional days if sleeping in the crater.

Descending Kilimanjaro – the designated descents

In an attempt to control the number of people walking on each trail, and thus limit the amount of soil erosion on some of the more popular routes, KINAPA

 Day trips

If for some reason you cannot climb all the way to the top but nevertheless wish to experience the pleasure of walking on Africa's most beautiful mountain, it is possible to enter the Kilimanjaro National Park for one day only. There are some advantages to doing this. It's safer for one thing, for few will get beyond 3000m at most in one day, so altitude sickness shouldn't be an issue. With no camping or rescue fees, porters' wages or food to pay, it will work out much cheaper too: just US$30 per day entry fee plus a wage for the compulsory guide. And as well as being wonderfully pleasant, if you're fit and start out early enough there's no reason why you can't climb above the tree-line to the heathland, thereby covering two vegetation zones and giving yourself a good chance of a reasonably close-up view of Kibo and Mawenzi. There are even designated picnic spots on the way.

Marangu Gate has a **three-hour nature loop** through the cloud forest which is lovely, and from which you can descend either via the trekkers' trail or the less scenic but faster porters' route. There are also a number of seldom visited waterfalls in the area. The ambitious can attempt to reach the Mandara Huts (p228) and descend again in one day. Furthermore, just 15 minutes beyond the Mandara Huts, through a small patch of forest alive with monkeys, is the Maundi Crater (p228), with excellent views of Kibo and Mawenzi to the north-west, and the flat African plains stretching away to the east.

The other place where day trips are allowed is on the Shira Plateau, where your chances of spotting big game are much greater (though still very small). However, the time taken in entering the park from the west deters most day-trippers.

introduced regulations regarding the descent routes and which ones you are allowed to take. In general, the main rule is as follows: those ascending Kilimanjaro from the west, south-west or south (ie by taking the Machame, Umbwe, Lemosho or Shira routes) must take as their descent route the **Mweka** trail; whereas if you have climbed the mountain from the south-east or north (ie on the Marangu or Rongai/Loitokitok trails) you must descend by the **Marangu Route**. See p292 for descriptions of these trails.

Those trekkers who wish to **deviate from these rules** should first seek permission from KINAPA.

What to take

CLOTHES

The best head-gear for all weathers is an English sun-helmet, such as are supplied by Messrs. Silver & Co., London; while a soft fez or smoking cap should be kept for wearing in the shade – one with flaps for drawing down over the ears on a cold night to be preferred.
Hans Meyer *Across East African Glaciers* (1891)

According to his book *Life, Wanderings, and Labours in Eastern Africa*, when Charles New attempted to climb Kili in 1861 he took with him a party of thirteen porters, all of whom were completely naked. New and his crew became the first to reach the mountain's snow-line, which is a rather creditable effort considering their lack of suitable apparel. Assuming your goal is to reach more than just snow, however, you will need to make sure you (and indeed your porters) are appropriately attired for the extreme conditions.

The fact that you will be paying porters to carry your rucksack does, to some degree, make packing simpler – allowing you to concentrate on warmth rather than weight. However, packing for warmth does not mean packing lots of big jumpers. The secret to staying warm is to **wear lots of layers**. Not only does this actually make you warmer than if you just had one single, thick layer – the air trapped between the layers heats up and acts as insulation – but it also means you can peel off the layers one by one when you get too warm, and put them on again one by one when the temperatures drop.

A suitable mountain wardrobe would include:

● **Walking boots** Mountaineering boots are unnecessary unless you're taking an unusual route that demands them. If you're not, a decent pair of trekking boots will be fine. The important thing about boots is comfort, with enough toe room, remembering that on the ascent up Kibo you might be wearing an extra pair or two of socks, and that on the descent the toes will be shoved into the front of the boots with every step. Remember these points when trying on trekking boots in the shop. Make sure they are also sturdy, waterproof, durable and high enough to provide support for your ankles. Finally, ensure you break them in *before* you

PLANNING YOUR TRIP

Cameras and camera equipment

Regarding **regular film**, there is plenty of light on Kilimanjaro, so 100 or 200ASA film should be fine. Film is readily available in the larger towns of Tanzania, though the choice is limited and the films are sometimes either past their sell-by date or have been stored in the baking hot sun and have perished. Therefore, you are strongly advised to **bring all your film from home**. The same applies if you have a **digital camera**: bring plenty of memory cards, for though the situation is improving, you'll be lucky to find the exact one you want out here, and they'll be more expensive too.

A **polarizing filter** is also a good investment to bring out the rich colours of the sky, rocks and glaciers. A **tripod** is useful for those serious about their photography, in order to keep the camera steady and allow for maximum depth of field – though remember, you're the one who's going to have to carry it if you want to use it during the day. You should also bring a couple of sets of **spare batteries** with you; the cold on Kibo can play havoc with batteries, and you may be extremely glad of them, particularly as both digital cameras and automatic SLRs seize up altogether without power. One other useful investment is a **camera-cleaning kit**. Your camera goes through a lot of hardship on Kili, not least because of the different vegetation zones you pass through, from the humidity of the forest to the dusty desert of the Saddle. Either buy a ready-made kit from a camera shop, or make one yourself by investing in a soft cloth, cotton buds, a blow brush and tweezers.

Finally, many people with expensive SLR cameras also bring along a cheap point-and-shoot **compact**; this is not a bad idea, as it doubles your chances of getting some photographic record of your journey. As an alternative, why not invest in a disposable panoramic camera – you can pick them up for about a tenner in the UK – which both acts as a back-up to your main camera *and* offers an alternative picture of the mountain.

---

come to Tanzania, so that if they do give you blisters, you can recover before you set foot on the mountain.

● **Socks** Ahhh, the joy of socks ... a couple of thick thermal pairs and some regular ones should be fine; you may stink but you'll be comfortable too, which is far more important. Some people walk in one thick and one thin pair of socks, changing the thin pair regularly, rinsing them out in the evening and tying them to their pack to dry during the day.

● **Down jacket** Not necessary if you have enough fleeces, but nevertheless wonderfully warm, light, compact – and expensive. Make sure it is large enough to go over all your clothes.

● **Fleece** Fleeces are light, pack down small, dry quickly and can be very, very warm. Take at least two: one thick 'polar' one and one of medium thickness and warmth. Make sure that you can wear the thinner one over all of the T-shirts and shirts you'll be taking, and that you can wear your thick one over all of these – you'll need to on the night-walk up Kibo.

● **Thermals** The value of thermal underwear lies in the way it draws moisture (ie sweat) away from your body. A thermal vest and long johns are sufficient.

● **Trousers** Don't take jeans, which are heavy and difficult to dry. Instead, take a couple of pairs of trekking trousers, such as those made by Rohan, preferably one light and one heavy.

● **Sun-hat** Essential: it can be hot and dazzling on the mountain ...

● **Woolly/fleecy hat** ... but it can also be very cold. Brightly-coloured bobble hats can be bought very cheaply in Moshi; or, better still, invest in one of those knitted **balaclavas** which you can usually find on sale in Moshi, which look a bit like a pizza oven but which will protect your face from the biting summit wind.

● **Gloves** Preferably fleecy; many people wear a thin thermal under-glove too.

● **Rainwear** While you are more likely to be rained on during the walk in the forest, where it's still warm, once you've got your clothes wet there will be lit- tle opportunity to dry them on the trek – and you will not want to attempt to climb freezing Kibo in wet clothes. A **waterproof jacket** – preferably made from Gore-tex or similar breathable material, hopefully with a warm or fleecy lining too, and big enough to go over all your clothes so you can wear it for the night-walk on Kibo – is ideal; waterproof trousers are perhaps a luxury rather than a necessity, but if you have a pair bring them with you. Alternatively, one reader suggests a cheap waterproof **poncho** 'from a dollar store', preferably one that goes over the backpack as well as yourself.

● **Summer clothes** T-shirts and shorts are the most comfortable things to wear under the humid forest canopy. You are strongly recommended to take a shirt with a collar too, to stop the sun from burning the back of your neck.

OTHER EQUIPMENT

Any trekking agency worth its licence will provide a **tent**, as well as **cooking equipment, cutlery and crockery**. You will still need to pack a few other items, however, if you don't want to return from your trek as a sun-burnt, snow- blinded, dehydrated wretch with hepatitis and hypothermia. Some of these items can be bought or rented in Moshi or Arusha. Your agency can arrange equipment rental, which is the most convenient way, though you may well find it cheaper to avoid going through them as they will, of course, take their cut. Note that the following lists concern the trek only. It does not include items nec- essary for other activities you may have planned on your holiday, such as binoc- ulars for your safari or a bucket and spade for Zanzibar.

Essentials

● **Sleeping bag** The warmest you've got. A three-season bag is probably the most practical, offering a compromise between warmth and cost. A two-season plus **thermal fleecy liner**, the latter available in camping shops back at home for about £20-30/US$35-50, is another solution.

● **Sleeping mat** Essential in camping but unnecessary if you're following the standard Marangu Route when you'll be sleeping in huts. Trekking agencies usually supply these.

● **Water bottles/Platypus Hoser system** You'll need to carry two litres of water up Kibo *at the very least*. Indeed, many people take enough bottles to carry four litres, with one reader saying it's essential for summit day. It's certainly good to take a lot of water, though do remember that you've got to carry it with you, and four litres is a lot of water to carry; We recommend two or three litres.

Make sure your bottles are thermally protected or they will freeze on the summit. Regular army-style water bottles are fine, though these days many trekkers prefer the new Platypus Hoser-style systems, a kind of soft, plastic bladder with a long tube from which you can drink as you walk along. They have a number of advantages over regular bottles in that they save you fiddling about with bottle tops and you can keep your hands in your pockets while you drink – great on the freezing night-time walk to the summit. But while they encourage you to drink regularly, which is good for dealing with the altitude, they also discourage you from taking a break, which is bad. What's more, these systems can also freeze up, especially the hose and mouthpiece. So if you are going to bring one of these with you, make sure it's fully insulated – and don't forget to take frequent breaks!

Medical kit

According to Meyer, the Chagga treated their cuts and scars with the liberal application of cow dung. We advise, however, that you don't; instead take a medical kit with you onto the mountain as few agencies, at least at the budget end, will have one. In theory, many of the mountain huts have first-aid kits but take one anyway just to be on the safe side, for you never know what they'll have, how old it will be or how far you'll be from the nearest station when you need help.

A medical kit should include the following:

- **Antiseptic cream** For small cuts and grazes.
- **Plasters** Ditto.
- **Bandages** Useful for twists and sprains as well as for larger flesh wounds.
- **Compeed** For blisters.
- **Elastic knee supports** For steeper gradients, particularly if you have knee problems.
- **Anti-malarials** Though you're highly unlikely to catch malaria on the mountain, if you're on a course of anti-malarials you should continue taking them.
- **Ibuprofen/Aspirin/Paracetamol** Or other painkillers, though do read the discussion on AMS (p200) and the medical indications in the packet before scoffing these.
- **Bismuth subsalicylate** The active ingredient in Pepto-bismol, which could be useful for settling upset stomachs.
- **Imodium** Stops you going when you don't want to go, which could come in handy.
- **Insect repellent** Useful on the first and last day, though above the tree-line the climate is too cold for most insects to survive.
- **Rehydrating powders** Such as Diarolyte. Usually prescribed to people suffering from diarrhoea but useful after a hot day's trekking as well.
- **Lip salve or chapstick/vaseline** See under *Highly desirables* opposite.
- **Throat pastilles** Useful, as the dry, dusty air causes many a sore throat.
- **Any current medication you are on** Bring with you all your needles, pills, lotions, potions and pungent unguents.
- **Diamox** Diamox is the brand name for Acetazolamide, the drug that fights AMS and which many people use prophylactically on Kilimanjaro. See the box on p204 to help you decide whether you want to bring a course of these with you.
- **Sterile needles** If you are having an injection in Tanzania, insist that the doctor uses your new needles.

Carry everything in a **waterproof bag or case**, and keep at least the emergency stuff in your daypack – where hopefully it will lie undisturbed for the trek's duration.

● **Water purifiers/filter** Also essential, unless you intend to hire an extra porter or two to transport your drinking water up from the start. While you can get your cooking crew to boil you some water at the end of every mealtime, you'll still find purifiers and/or a filter essential if you're going to drink the recommended four to five litres every day, for which you'll have to collect water from the mountain streams. Of the two, purifying tablets such as iodine are more effective, as they kill everything in the water, though they taste awful. A cordial will help to mask this taste; you can buy packets of powdered flavouring in the local supermarkets. Filters are less effective and more expensive, though the water they produce tastes much better.

● **Torch** A head-torch, if you have one and don't find it uncomfortable, is far more practical than a hand-held one, allowing you to keep both hands free; on the last night this advantage is pretty much essential, enabling you to keep your hands in your pockets for warmth.

● **Sunscreen** High factor essential.

● **Ice axe/ski stick** Only useful if you plan to take the Arrow Glacier Route to the summit and the conditions are very bad. Otherwise leave it, your snow boots, rope, karabiners and all that other mountaineering gear at home.

● **Towel** The controversy here is over which sort of towel to bring. Many just bring one enormous beach towel, because they plan to visit Zanzibar after the trek and don't see the point of packing two towels. At the other extreme there are the tiny so-called 'travel towels', a sort of chamois-cloth affair sold in camping shops and airport lounges the world over. Some people swear by these things, but others usually end up swearing at them, finding that they have all the absorbency of your average block of obsidian stone. Nevertheless, we grudgingly admit that they do have their uses on Kilimanjaro, where opportunities to wash anything other than face and hands are minimal. You can dry your towel by attaching it to the outside of your rucksack with clothes-pegs (see p60).

● **Sunglasses** Very, very necessary for the morning after you've reached the summit, when the early morning light on Kibo can be really painful and damaging. If you're climbing via the Arrow Glacier Route or are going to spend some time on the summit, they could be essential for preventing snow-blindness.

● **Money for tipping** For a rough guide as to how much you should take, see p38 – then add a few dollars, just in case.

● **Toothbrush and toothpaste** Ensure your dental checks are up-to-date; if there is one thing more painful than climbing to the summit of Kili, it's climbing to the summit of Kili with toothache.

● **Toilet paper**

● **Tampons/sanitary towels**

● **Contraceptives**

Highly desirables

● **Ski poles** If you've done some trekking before you'll know if you need ski-poles or not; if you haven't, assume you will. While people often use them the whole way, poles really come into their own on the descent, to minimize the strain on your knees as you trudge downhill. Telescopic poles can be brought from trekking/camping outfitters in the West, or you can invest in a more primitive version, a stick freshly chopped from the nearby forest, at Machame or Marangu gates – and anywhere else where enterprising local children gather.

● **Boiled sweets/chocolate** For winning friends and influencing people. Good for energy levels too. And morale.

● **Chapstick/ lip salve or vaseline** The wind on the summit will rip your sunburnt lips to shreds. Save yourself the agony by investing in a chapstick, available in strawberry and mint flavour from pharmacists in Moshi and Arusha.

● **Money** For sundry items on sale at huts en route.

● **Camera and equipment** See box on p56.

Usefuls

● **Earplugs** Some porters have stereos and mobile phones, and they love advertising this fact by playing the former and speaking into the latter extremely loudly at campsites. A set of earplugs will reduce this disturbance.

● **Gaiters** Useful on the dusty Saddle. Indeed, more than one trekker has written in to say that gaiters are essential. However, we've also met more than one trekker who can't see the point. It's a matter of preference, really.

● **Face mask** Again, we never would have thought of it but two people have written in to say they were bothered by the dust on the Saddle and would have worn some sort of surgical mask if they'd had one. Don't worry if you don't have one, however: we've never seen anybody actually wearing one on the mountain.

● **Soap** Though you won't get through much of it on the mountain and your trekking agency should provide some for you.

● **Plastic bags** Useful for segregating your wet clothes from the rest of your kit in your rucksack.

● **Aluminium sheet blanket** Provides extra comfort if your sleeping bag isn't as warm as you thought.

● **Sandals/flip-flops** Useful in the evenings at camp, but make sure they are big enough to fit round a thick pair of socks.

● **Candles** But don't use them in the tent, and keep them away from everybody else's tent too.

● **Bootlaces/string**

● **Clothes pegs** Very useful for attaching wet clothes to the back of your rucksack to allow them to dry in the sun while you walk; a reader wrote in to recommend **binder clips** (also known as bulldog or office clips) as a smaller, stronger alternative.

● **Penknife** Always useful, if only for opening beer bottles at the post-trek party.

● **Matches** As with the penknife, always useful, as any boy scout will tell you.

● **Sewing kit** For repairs on the trail.

● **Insulating tape** Also for repairs – of shoes, rucksacks, tents etc, and as a last resort for mending holes in clothes if you have forgotten your sewing kit, or are incapable of using it.

● **Watch** Preferably cheap and luminous for night-time walking.

● **Compass** Not essential, but useful when combined with ...

● **Map** See p309 for a list of our preferred maps; again not essential but will, in combination with a compass, help you to determine where you are on the mountain, and where you're going.

● **Trowel** If you envisage needing to defecate along the trail at places other than the designated toilet huts, this will help to bury the evidence and keep the mountain looking pristine; see p198.

● **Whistle** It's difficult to get lost on Kilimanjaro but if you're taking an unusual route – on the northern side of the mountain, for example, or around Mawenzi – a whistle may be useful to help people locate which ravine you've fallen into.

Luxuries

● **Mobile phone** You should be able to get reception on much of the southern side of the mountain – including, so it is said, on the summit. What better place could there be from which to phone friends stuck behind their desks at work on a rainy day in Europe?

● **Walkmans/CD/MP3 players** and **iPods** Probably unnecessary, as you won't want to listen to music during the day and you'll probably be too tired to listen in the evening. Nevertheless, while most find the idea abhorrent, people do still bring their music on the trek with them, including many porters. There is nothing wrong with a little mountainside music, of course, but do remember that while you may think you've found the perfect soundtrack for climbing up Kili, others on the mountain may disagree: bring headphones, so as not to disturb.

● **Diary/reading material** Though you'll probably be too tired to read or write much. A list of appropriate reading matter can be found in *Appendix E* on p309.

● **Champagne** For celebrating, of course, though don't try to take it up and open it at the summit – the combination of champagne and altitude sickness could lead to tragedy and, besides, the glass could well crack with the cold.

WHAT TO PACK IT IN

You'll need two bags: a **rucksack** and a smaller, lighter **daypack**. While sensible trekkers spend a long time finding the rucksack that's most comfortable for them, few bother to spend as long when choosing a daypack; however, on Kili it is the porters who traditionally carry your rucksack for you (usually on their heads), while you will carry your daypack yourself. So make sure you **choose your daypack with care** and that it is both comfortable and durable. It also needs to be big enough to hold everything you may need with you when walking, as it is unlikely that you will see your main rucksack from the moment you break camp in the morning to the time you arrive at camp in the evening. See p223 for a possible list of these things.

One more thing: don't leave anything valuable in your rucksack; though porters are very trustworthy, it's only fair that you do not put temptation in their path.

Finally, put everything in **plastic bags** (or **bin bags**) inside your backpack and daypack to keep the contents dry.

Health precautions, inoculations and insurance

FITNESS

I ascribe the almost perfect health I have always enjoyed in Africa to the fact that I have made every step of my journey on foot, the constant exercise keeping my bodily organs in good order. **Hans Meyer** *Across East African Glaciers*

There's no need to go overboard with fitness preparations for climbing Kili. The main reason why people fail to reach the summit is due to altitude sickness rather than lack of necessary strength or stamina. That said, the trek will obviously be more enjoyable for you the fitter you are, so anything you can do in the way of training can only help. A weekend of walking would be a good thing to do; it won't improve your fitness to a great degree but it will at least confirm that you can walk for more than a few hours at a time, and for more than one day. Wear the clothes you plan to bring to Kilimanjaro with you – particularly your boots and socks – and carry the daypack that you hope to be carrying all the way to the top of Kibo too.

One more thing: if you're planning on relying on it on the mountain, try Diamox (see p204) before you go to make sure it has no severe adverse reaction on you.

INOCULATIONS

According to the latest bulletin, it is no longer compulsory to have the **yellow fever** vaccination to enter Tanzania. Nevertheless, this rule seems to change every few months so it's probably wise to have an inoculation against it, which in the UK can cost anywhere from £25-45 (US$45-80). Remember to collect a health card or some other written evidence from your doctor to prove you've had the jab.

Sort out your vaccinations a few months before you're due to fly. Recommended inoculations include:

● **Typhoid** This disease is caught from contaminated food and water. A single injection lasts for three years.

● **Polio** The polio vaccine used to be administered by sugar-lump, making it one of the more pleasant inoculations, though these days it's more commonly injected. Lasts for ten years.

● **Hepatitis A** This debilitating disease of the liver is spread by contaminated water, or even by using cutlery that has been washed in it. The latest inoculation involves two injections; the first will protect you for three years, the second, taken six to twelve months later, will cover you for ten years.

● **Tetanus** Tetanus vaccinations last for ten years and are absolutely vital for visitors to Tanzania. The vaccination is usually given in combination with one for **diphtheria**. Once you've had five injections, you're covered for life.

● **Meningococcal meningitis** This disease of the brain is often fatal; the vaccination, while not free, is safe, effective and lasts for three to five years.

● **Rabies** If you're spending some time with animals or in the wilderness, it's also worth considering having a course of **rabies** injections, though it isn't pleasant, consisting of three injections spread over one month.

Malaria
Malaria is a problem in Tanzania, which is considered one of the highest risk countries in the world. While you are highly unlikely to contract malaria on Kilimanjaro, which is too high and cold for the anopheles mosquito (the species that carries malaria), it is rife in coastal areas and on Zanzibar. There's even some cases just south of Moshi. When beginning a course of **anti-malarials**, it is very important to begin taking them before you go; that way the drug is established in your system by the time you set foot on Tanzanian soil and it will give you a chance to see if the drug is going to cause a reaction or allergy. Once started, complete the full course, which usually runs for several weeks after you return home.

Which anti-malarial you will need depends on which parts of Africa you are visiting and your previous medical history. Your doctor will be able to advise you on what drug is best for you. With Tanzania in the highest risk category, the chances are you will be recommended either Lariam (the brand name for mefloquine), Doxycycline or the new drug Malarone, which is supposedly free of side effects but very expensive. Stories of Lariam causing hallucinations, nightmares, blindness and even death have been doing the rounds in travellers' circles for years now but if you feel no adverse reaction – and millions don't – carry on taking them and don't worry.

Of course the best way to combat malaria is not to get bitten at all. A **repellent** with 30% Diethyltoluamide (DEET) used in the evenings when the malarial anopheles mosquito is active should be effective in preventing bites. Some use it during the day too, when the mosquitoes that carry yellow and dengue fevers are active. Alternatively, you could just keep covered up with long sleeve shirts and long trousers, sleep under a **mosquito net** and burn **mosquito coils**; these are available within Tanzania.

Travellers' medical clinics
For all your jabs, malaria advice and anything else you need to know regarding health abroad, visit your doctor or one of the following clinics:

● **Trailfinders Travel Clinic** (☎ 020-7938 3999; 💻 www.trailfinders.com) 194 Kensington High Street, London.

● **Nomad Travellers Store and Medical Centre** (☎ 020-7833 4114; 💻 www.nomadtravel.co.uk) 40 Bernard Street, Russell Square, London, as well as London's Turnpike Lane (☎ 020-8889 7014), Bristol (☎ 0117-922 6567) and Southampton (☎ 02380-234920).

High altitude travel
The most likely illness you are going to suffer from is altitude sickness; indeed, it's a rare trekker on Kilimanjaro who doesn't to some degree. Altitude sickness is caused by the body's inability to adapt quickly enough to the thinner mountain air present at high altitudes. It can be fatal if ignored or left untreated but is also entirely preventable. For an extensive run-down on the causes, symptoms and treatments of altitude sickness, read carefully the section on pp200-6.

Before you go, if you suffer from heart or lung problems, high blood pressure or are pregnant, you must visit your doctor to get advice on the wisdom of climbing up Africa's highest mountain; many of the deaths on the mountain are due to heart failure.

● **British Airways** (☎ 0845-600 2236; 🖳 www.britishairways.com/) 213 Piccadilly, London.

Also worth looking at is the informative website of the **US Center for Disease Control** (🖳 www.cdc.gov), packed full of advice and the latest news.

INSURANCE

When buying insurance you must make clear to the insurer that you will be trekking on a very big mountain. If you are going to be climbing and using ropes then you need to tell them that too. This will probably increase your premium (it usually doubles it), and may even exclude you from being covered altogether. But if you don't make this clear from the start and pay the lower premium you may find, should you have to make a claim, that you weren't actually covered at all.

Remember to read the small print of any insurance policy before buying, and shop around, too, for each insurance policy varies slightly from company to company. Details to consider include:

● How much is the deductible if you have to make a claim?
● Can the insurers pay for your hospital bills etc immediately, while you are still in Tanzania, or do you have to wait until you get home?
● How long do you have before making a claim and what evidence do you require (hospital bills, police reports etc)?
● Does the policy include mountain rescue services, helicopter call-out and so forth? (If it doesn't, don't buy it!)

Remember the premium for the entire trip will double when you mention that you are climbing Kilimanjaro, even though you will actually be on the mountain for only a few days. However, you will need to be covered for your entire trip: there are just as many nasty things that can happen to you – indeed more – when off the mountain than on it, and theft becomes a much bigger issue too.

PART 2: TANZANIA

'Strange country isn't it?'
'Yes. It seems so cruel one moment, then suddenly kind and very beautiful. Maybe there are parts God forgot about – he meant it all to be like this.'
Robert Taylor and **Anne Aubrey** discuss the land we now call Tanzania in the 1959 swashbuckling classic *Killers of Kilimanjaro.*

Although this book concentrates specifically on Kilimanjaro, some background knowledge of the country in which it stands, Tanzania, is necessary. For the chances are that climbing Kilimanjaro forms only one part of your trip to Tanzania, and as such you are going to need to know what this beautiful country is like and how you are going to negotiate travelling around it. With this in mind the following chapter is split into two halves. The first provides a background of the country by looking at the history, economy, culture etc. This should both increase your enjoyment of visiting Tanzania and serve to put Kilimanjaro in its national context. The second half of this chapter deals with the more practical side of things, offering advice and tips to help the visitor.

Facts about the country

GEOGRAPHY

Tanzania occupies an area of 945,087 sq km – a little over twice the size of California – made up of 886,037 sq km of land (including the offshore islands of Pemba, Mafia and Zanzibar) and 59,050 sq km of water. This makes it the largest country in the geo-political region of East Africa. It is bounded to the north by Uganda and Kenya, to the west by the Democratic Republic of Congo (DRC), Burundi and Rwanda, to the south by Mozambique, Malawi and Zambia, and to the east by the Indian Ocean. The terrain in that 886,037 sq km of land includes a wide, lush coastal plain and a large and dusty central plateau flanked by the eastern and western branches of the **Great Rift Valley** (see p82). There are highlands in both the north and south of the country, and in the centre of the plateau are some volcanic peaks, which again owe their existence to the Rift Valley. Interestingly, over a quarter of the country is given over to national parks or nature reserves.

Tanzania is also a land of extremes, housing Africa's largest game reserve, the **Selous** (covering approximately 55,000 sq km, and with an approximately equal number of elephants), and the Serengeti, the park with the greatest concentration of migratory game in the world. Its borders also encompass a share in the continent's largest lake, **Lake Victoria**, and a share in **Lake Tanganyika**, the longest and, after Lake Baikal in Siberia, deepest freshwater lake in the world. The third largest lake in Africa, **Lake Malawi**, also forms one of Tanzania's borders. These lakes were formed when the Great Rift Valley, which runs through the heart of the country, opened up about 30 million years ago. As a direct result of the formation of this valley, Tanzania contains Africa's lowest point, the floor of Lake Tanganyika, some 350m below sea level. It is also, of course, the proud owner of Africa's highest.

Beautiful as this country undoubtedly is, it is also beset by enormous environmental problems, from deforestation to desertification, soil degradation, erosion and reef bombing. Significant damage has already occurred, and is still occurring, with added pressures on the land caused by the meteoric rise in tourism over the past couple of decades. For details of how you can minimize your impact on the environment of Kilimanjaro, see p197.

CLIMATE

Tanzania's climate varies greatly, and you'll be encountering just about all of the variations in the four or five days it takes you to walk to the top of Kilimanjaro. For more about this, see the Kilimanjaro climate section on p85. Away from the mountain, the narrow coastal strip tends to be the most hot, humid and tropical part of the country with the inland plateau being of sufficient elevation to offer some cooler temperatures and respite from the heat. On the coast the average temperature during the day is a sticky 27°C; luckily the sea breezes temper this heat and make it bearable. On the inland plateau you're looking at an average temperature of around 20-26.5°C during the cooler months of June to August, up to a roasting 30°C between December and March. The **rainy seasons** extend from November to early January (the short rains), and from March to May (the long rains). On the coast the average annual rainfall is around 1400mm; inland it is a much drier 250mm, though in mountainous areas it can be a magnificent 2000mm; unsurprisingly, flooding can be a problem at this time.

HISTORY

We, the people of Tanganyika, would like to light a candle and put it on the top of Mount Kilimanjaro, which would shine beyond our borders, giving hope where there was despair, love where there was hate, and dignity where before there was only humiliation.
Julius Nyerere in a speech to the Tanganyika Legislative Assembly, 1959. Following independence in 1961, his wish was granted and a torch was placed on Kili's summit.

The discovery of the 1,750,000-year-old remains of an early hominid, **Australopithecus Zinjanthropus Boisei**, at Olduvai Gorge in the Ngorongoro Crater, (near footprints that could be as much as three and a half million years old), suggest that Tanzania has one of the longest histories in the world. We are now going to cram these three and a half million years into the next three and a half pages – a task made considerably simpler by the fact that this history has been, until the last 200 years or so, unrecorded. (For a detailed history of Kilimanjaro, see pp86-109.)

We know that **Khoisan speakers** (from southern Africa) moved into the area of modern Tanzania around 10,000 years ago, to be joined between 3000BC and 1000BC by Cushitic speakers from the Horn of Africa (Ethiopia and Eritrea), who brought with them more advanced agricultural techniques. Over the next few hundred years **Bantu speakers** from West Africa's Niger Delta and Nilotic peoples from the north and Sudan also migrated to the area we now know as Tanzania.

By 400BC merchants from Classical Greece knew about and traded with the coast of East Africa, which they called **Azania**. Some of them eventually settled here to take advantage of the trading opportunities, to be joined later by **traders from Persia** and, by the end of the first millennium AD as trade routes stretched into China, merchants from **India**. The majority of immigrants, however, proved to be the seafaring **traders from Arabia**, and soon the Swahili language and culture, an amalgamation of the cultures of Arabia and the Bantu speakers who had also settled on the coast, began to emerge there.

Life on the coastal strip of modern-day Tanzania continued, as far as we know, pleasantly enough for a number of centuries, a fairly idyllic existence that was rudely shattered by the arrival of the **Portuguese** following Vasco da Gama's legendary expedition at the end of the fifteenth century. As greedy as they were intrepid, they built the coastal village of Kilwa Kisiwani into a major trading port which, in typical Portuguese style, they later sacked. Understandably unpopular, the Portuguese nevertheless held on grimly and gamely to their East African possessions for almost 200 years until the end of the seventeenth century; that they managed to survive for so long is largely due to a lack of a united opposition, which didn't arrive until 1698 in the form of **Omani Arabs**, summoned to help by the long-suffering traders of Kilwa Kisiwani.

Portuguese, Arabs, Germans and British

Unlike the Portuguese, the Omani Arabs were keen to forge trading links with the interior. They pushed new routes across the plains to Lake Tanganyika, thereby facilitating the extraction of gold, **slaves** and ivory from the interior. The Arabs grew inordinately wealthy from the fat of Africa's land, to the extent that the Omani sultan eventually decided to pull up his tent pegs from the desert sands of Arabia and relocate, establishing his new capital at Stonetown on Zanzibar.

While this was going on, the Europeans returned to Africa. Initially it was just a trickle of **missionaries** and **explorers**, hell-bent (if that's the right term) on making converts and mapping continents respectively. Indeed, one man who famously combined both vocations, Dr David Livingstone, spent a while in Tanzania as part of his efforts to find the source of the Nile, and it was at the village of Ujiji, on the Tanzanian side of Lake Tanganyika, that HM Stanley is believed to have finally caught up with him and uttered those immortal words 'Dr Livingstone, I presume'.

With intrepid, independent Europeans now roaming all over the continent, it could only be a matter of time before one European country or another would come up with the idea of full-scale colonization. By the late **1880's** Britain had already secured a dominant role on Zanzibar. But over on the mainland it was Germany who was making the most progress.

Or rather, one German, for it was one **Carl Peters** who, acting independently of his government, established German influence on the mainland at this time, negotiating treaties with local chiefs in order to secure a charter for his **Deutsch-Ostafrikanische Gesellschaft** (DOAG, the German East Africa Company). A few years later, and with his homeland's government now supporting his work, Peters' DOAG was formally given the task of administering the mainland. This left the British on Zanzibar fuming – and not a little scared – at the German's impertinence, and war was averted between the two superpowers only with the signing of an accord in 1890, in which Britain was allowed to establish formally a protectorate over her Zanzibar territories. One year and further negotiations later and the land we now know as Tanzania (Zanzibar excluded) officially came under direct German control as **German East Africa**.

The Germans brought a Western education, a rail network, and a higher level of healthcare with them to Africa. They also brought harsh taxes, suppression, humiliation and no small amount of unrest. They were eventually replaced as colonial overlords after World War One by the **British** following a League of Nations mandate. The territory was renamed Tanganyika at this time. After World War Two a near bankrupt Britain clung on to administrative control, though officially Tanganyika was now a 'trust territory' of the fledgling United Nations.

Independence

Life under the British was marginally better than under the Germans, with greater political freedom and an improved economy thanks to the cultivation of export crops; but it *was* only marginal and soon political groups were springing up all over the country with each campaigning for the same thing: independence. The most important of these was the Dar es Salaam-based Tanganyika Africa Association, which in 1953 elected teacher **Julius Nyerere** as its president. Pressure from Nyerere and his party (now known as TANU, or the Tanganyika African National Union) forced Britain to agree to the formation of an internal self-government. Indeed, so impressed was Britain with Nyerere that the only condition they placed on the establishment of this new regime of self-government was that he should be its first chief minister.

Now a mere formality, **independence** for Tanganyika was eventually declared on the 9 December 1961; exactly one year later it was formally established as a **republic**, with Nyerere, as Britain had hoped, as the first president.

On **Zanzibar**, meanwhile, things were going less smoothly. Whilst the Zanzibaris won their independence not long afterwards (December 1963), the two parties that formed the first government did not enjoy popular support, but instead had been thrust into power by the departing British because of their pro-British leanings. With a tenure that was decidedly shaky, it came as no surprise when they were toppled in a revolution just a month later. In their place came the popular, radical Afro Shirazi Party (ASP). Less than a year after independence, on 26 April 1964 the ASP leader, Abeid Karume, was signing an act of union with his mainland neighbours and the **United Republic of Tanganyika** was formed.

In October of the same year the name was changed to the **United Republic of Tanzania**, the name being a neat combination of the two former territories. The two maintained separate governments, however, even after 1977 when ASP and TANU were combined by Nyerere to form **Chama Cha Mapinduzi**, or **CCM**, the party which maintains political control of Tanzania to this day.

Modern history

From 1967 to the late 1980s Nyerere and his party followed a socialist course; the economy was nationalized, the tax regime was deliberately aimed at redistributing wealth, and new villages were established in order to modernize the agricultural sector and give the rural poor greater access to social services. Unfortunately, the twenty-year experiment was eventually deemed a flop, with the economy in seemingly perpetual decline. By 1992 things had got so desperate that the CCM took the unprecedented step of legalizing opposition parties, after pressure from Western donors for more democracy in the country.

Curiously, this move seems to have done little to achieve this. Three years after the legalization of political opponents to CCM, the first democratic elections were held, with the CCM, now under the leadership of **Benjamin Mkapa** following Nyerere's resignation in 1985, emerging once again as the major force in Tanzanian politics. The elections of late 2000 confirmed their dominance, with over 95% of parliamentary seats won by CCM candidates. While they remain the most creditable political party in Tanzania, the scale of the victory suggests that proper political debate will be stifled for years to come.

On semi-autonomous **Zanzibar** things, as usual, have been a little more explosive. In 1995 the incumbent CCM president, Salmin Amour, was returned to office after an election that many believe was rigged. Fresh elections in 2000 resulted in yet more controversy, with widespread reports of ballot rigging and intimidation of opposition leaders. Zanzibar is still in political disarray and anger is fomenting between the two sides. In January 2001, 27 protesters were shot dead in Pemba as they marched through the streets protesting against these voting irregularities. And though the situation has quietened a little since then, following the latest bout of elections in late 2005 the Zanzibaris once more rioted. The new president of Tanzania, **Jakoya Kikwete**, has admitted that the unrest on Zanzibar will be his biggest problem in his first term.

The future

Tanzania is often portrayed as a model African nation, garnering international acclaim for its fight against corruption and its efforts to reform itself peacefully – as exemplified by the move towards democracy in the 1990s. The new government of President Jakoya Kikwete, who was brought to power with over 80% of the vote, has provided further evidence that Tanzania is one of the more enlightened nations with his promotion of female ministers to key finance and foreign posts.

It is, however, still a nation beset by problems. The usual African ailments – poverty, AIDS and a lack of clean water, basic healthcare and decent education – are as prevalent in Tanzania as they are over much of the continent. In addition, Tanzania has other local problems to contend with, from a lack of credible opposition to the main autocratic CCM party to the secessionist grumblings of many on Zanzibar who were never happy with the union with the mainland – a dissatisfaction that three subsequent decades of turmoil have done little to dispel. It remains to be seen whether the moderate line that Tanzania has taken throughout its independence will continue into the future; and whether this thoughtful, conservative (with a small 'c') attitude will be enough to help it to overcome these difficulties.

ECONOMY

Tanzania is one of the poorest countries in the world. Its per capita GDP stands at a modest US$700 and just over 36% live below the poverty line – though these are significant improvements on the figures recorded in the first edition of this book, when GDP per capita was US$264 and over 50% lived below the poverty line. Sadly, other statistics suggest that Tanzanians are worse off, not better, than they were in 2001 when this book was first published.

Infant mortality stands at a level of 98 per 1000 births (up from 85 per 1000 in 2001), and life expectancy is just 45.2 years, down from 49, presumably because of AIDS, with a remarkable 8.8% of the population now estimated to be infected. One of the biggest contributors to the economy is foreign aid: in 1997 it received US$973 million in donations; by 2001 it stood at US$1.2 billion.

Tanzania is still largely an **agricultural** country. The style of agriculture is mainly traditional, the large collective farms introduced under Nyerere's socialist experiment having been rejected on the whole in favour of the age-old system whereby each farmer cultivates a small plot of land called a *shamba*. The most popular home-grown crops are cotton, rice, sorghum, sugar and coconuts; sisal, coffee and tea are produced principally for the export market, while cloves and other spices are still grown on Zanzibar and the coast. Agriculture accounts for half of Tanzania's GDP, contributes an enormous 85% of its exports, and employs 80% of the workforce.

As well as agriculture, Tanzania has a solid **mining** base with oil, tin, iron, salt, coal, gypsum, phosphate, natural gas, nickel, diamonds and, of course, tanzanite, all extracted in the country. Tourism is now a major contributor to the GDP of the country and is a vital source of much-needed foreign currency, particularly in the north.

THE PEOPLE

With 36,766,356 people (CIA world factbook estimate) split into more than a hundred different ethnic groups, numerous local languages and dialects and three main religions, Tanzania is something of an ethnic and cultural hotchpotch, and it is a credit to the country that they exist largely in harmony, without succumbing to the sort of ethnic hatred that has riven many other countries around these parts. Native Africans make up 99% of the population; of these, the vast majority (estimate 95%) are of Bantu origin, though even here there are over 130 tribes. The other 1% are of European, Arabian or Indian origin. Around Kilimanjaro it is the Chagga people, one of the more wealthy and powerful groups in Tanzania, who dominate; for details about the Chagga, see p116.

The **religious** division is a lot more equal. The slight majority (35%) are now Muslim (in the last edition it was Christian), with 30% now professing the Christian faith and traditional indigenous beliefs accounting for the other 35%. These figures exclude Zanzibar, which is 99% Muslim. Presumably adherents of the Hindu and Sikh faiths are too small in number to register in the statistics, though they are undoubtedly a highly visible presence in Tanzania with some large, ostentatious Hindu temples in Dar, Arusha and Moshi. The Chagga people around Kilimanjaro are largely Christian; again, you can read more about them, their culture and beliefs on p116.

Language

The first and most common language in Tanzania is **Swahili**, the language originally used by traders on the coast and thus based on Arabic and various Bantu dialects. Zanzibar is still known as the home of Swahili, where the purest form of the language is spoken. A few words of Swahili will go a long way in Tanzania and, although the prefixes and suffixes used in the language can be a little tricky to grasp, any efforts to speak a few words will endear you to the local people. *Appendix A* on p303 provides an introduction to Swahili.

Around Kilimanjaro, however, it is not Swahili but the language of the Chagga people, a tongue sometimes known as Wachagga, that predominates, though there are several different dialects. See the box on p117 for a very brief introduction.

Practical information for the visitor

DOCUMENTS AND VISAS

Visas for Tanzania are required by most visitors **except** citizens of the following countries:

Antigua & Barbuda, Barbados, Belize, Bermuda, Botswana, Brunei, Cyprus, Dominica, Grenada, Guyana, Jamaica, Kenya, Kiribati, Lesotho, Malaysia, Malawi, Malta, Maldives, Mauritius, Namibia, Nauru, Sao Tome & Principe Island, Saint Lucia, Saint Vincent, Saint Christopher and Nevis, Seychelles, Singapore, Solomon Island, Swaziland, Tuvalu, Tonga, Uganda, Vanuatu, Zambia, Zimbabwe.

Note that while some Commonwealth countries are included in that list, citizens of Canada, India, Nigeria and the UK **do require visas**.

A single-entry visa costs £38 for UK citizens, US$50 for US citizens, and €50 for most European nations. A visa is typically valid for three months from the **date of issue**. Unless coming from a country without Tanzanian representation, you should buy your visa at the consulate/embassy beforehand (though it doesn't seem to be a problem to buy one both at Kilimanjaro International Airport and at the Namanga border crossing with Kenya). A list of the addresses of some of the more popular Tanzanian embassies and consulates is given in *Appendix C* on p306.

With all applications you will need to present a passport that's valid for at least six months and two passport photos. If applying in person, some consulates/high commissions (including the ones in London and Washington) insist that you pay in cash.

If you don't have a Tanzanian representative in your country you can pick up a visa only at one of the **four border controls**: Dar-es-Salaam International Airport, Kilimanjaro International Airport, Zanzibar International Airport, and the Namanga border crossing between Tanzania and Kenya.

Remember that, if flying in and out of Kenya you will need a **Kenyan visa** too (typically £30 for UK citizens, though a transit visa is only £10). If you plan to fly to Kenya and cross into Tanzania from there, you can return to Kenya using the same single-entry visa you arrived with *providing* your visit to Tanzania lasted for less than two weeks, and that your Kenyan visa has not expired. Apparently, you can do this only once (ie it's a double-entry visa, not a multiple-entry one), or so we were told at the Kenyan border the last time we did this. Otherwise, you will need to buy a multiple-entry visa, which typically costs double the single-entry (ie UK£60). See *Appendix C* (p307) for a list of addresses of Kenyan embassies abroad.

Yellow-fever vaccination certificate

Though it seems that the authorities have now dropped this requirement, a **yellow-fever vaccination certificate** used to be mandatory to prove that you have been immunized against the disease. This can be picked up from your doctor after you have received the jab, and is usually free – though the jab itself is not. This rule seems to change every few months.

AIRPORT TAX

Airport tax when departing from a Tanzanian airport is currently US$30 for international flights. Internal flights are subject to airport taxes too, though these vary from airport to airport (usually US$6-11).

MONEY

Currency

The Tanzanian shilling (Ts) is the national currency. It's fairly stable. Local currency cannot be imported except by residents of Tanzania, Kenya and Uganda, and cannot be exported.

Foreign currency

Foreign currency can be imported and exported without limit. **Dollars** and, to a lesser extent, **sterling** and **euros** are the best currencies to bring.

The question therefore is: in what form should you carry your money to Tanzania, ie: should you bring travellers' cheques, cash, or rely solely on your credit card and use that to get money out of cashpoints in Tanzania?

Unfortunately, the answer is not a simple one, as each have their advantages. **Travellers' cheques** are regarded as the safest way to bring money because they are replaceable. What's more, they also offer a certain level of convenience in that you can pay your national park fees directly in US$ travellers' cheques at the Machame, Marangu and Londorossi gates (the latter for the Lemosho and Shira routes). That said, Tanzanian banks usually offer a better rate for **cash** (US dollars are the only widely accepted currency) than for travellers' cheques and cash is very useful for those occasions when the Tanzanian shilling is not accepted, such as when paying for upmarket hotel rooms and air tickets, both of which, officially at least, must be paid for in hard currency (US$). Then there's the third option, **credit cards**, which are the easiest to carry around. However, all have their disadvantages too. Cash is the riskiest way to carry money. Travellers' cheques, on the other hand, are bulky and the rates you get are generally inferior to those you get for cash. While if you bring credit/debit cards, you run the risk that the cash machines will reject them or, worse, swallow them, leaving you stuck in Africa with no means of support.

Thus, we advocate **bringing all three forms**. That is to say, bring most of your money in travellers' cheques, a few hundred dollars in cash and a credit/debit card for back up. True, many experienced Africa hands advocate eschewing travellers' cheques and bringing cash and credit cards/debit cards only, particularly as cashpoints are becoming more and more common. But having tried unsuccessfully to get money out of any Standard Chartered bank in Tanzania on our last trip, we were glad that we'd brought with us a whole heap of travellers' cheques – and you may be too.

Banks and moneychangers

Banking hours are typically 8.30am-4pm Monday to Friday, and 8.30am-1pm on Saturday. As a general rule, only banks and the larger exchange bureaux can change travellers' cheques but since currency controls were relaxed a few years ago and the black market for foreign currency has largely disappeared, this is not the major drawback it once was. As for cash you get a significantly better rate for large denomination bills (US$50 and $100 bills) than small ones. Keep your **exchange receipts** so that when you leave the country you can change your spare shillings back into hard currency. They rarely check, but you never know.

> ❏ **Exchange rates**
> To get the latest rates visit www.expedia.com. At the time of writing they were:
> UK£1 = Ts2386
> €1 = Ts1615
> US$1 = Ts1258
> Can$1 = Ts1126
> A$1 = Ts947
> NZ$1 = Ts794
> SwissFr1 = Ts1013
> Ks1 = Ts17.14
> Japan Y1 = Ts10.77

TANZANIA

There are **ATMs** (**cashpoints**) in Tanzania and Kenya, including Standard Chartered ATMs in Arusha, Moshi, Dar and Nairobi, and Barclays have machines in Dar es Salaam, Arusha and Nairobi. Tanzania's own National Bank of Commerce (NBC) also has its own ATMs, though currently they are unreliable, particularly with foreign cards, and best avoided if possible.

Credit cards

Credit cards are useful in major tourist hotels, restaurants, gift shops and airline offices and their usefulness is growing every day. Visa is probably the more useful card in that you can withdraw money from more ATMs than with MasterCard.

TOURIST OFFICES

Dar es Salaam and Arusha have tourist offices (see p125 and p147) though they're the only ones that do. Outside Tanzania, there's a tourist office in New York (☎ 212 -972 9160), 8th Floor, 205 East 42nd Street, New York 10017. Consulates and embassies around the world also have the odd brochure, or you can look at the online information services on the net (see p308).

GETTING AROUND

Public transport in Tanzania is unreliable, uncomfortable, slow, and not recommended for those with either long legs or haemorrhoids. It is also dangerous. A little-known but highly pertinent fact about Tanzania's transport system is that 8% of deaths in Tanzanian hospitals are road-accident victims. According to one source, Tanzania suffers an average of 9780 road accidents annually, resulting in the loss of 1189 lives; and these are just the ones the authorities know about.

That said, Tanzanian transport is also cheap, convenient and, it must be said, cheerful: conversation usually flows pretty easily on a train, bus or dalla-dalla (providing you can make yourself heard above the noise of the stereo). And while the average road is little more than a necklace of potholes strung together with tyre tracks, the main roads between towns are splendid, well-maintained tarmac strips – with speed ramps to deter the bus drivers from going too fast.

The most luxurious form of ground transport is provided by the **express bus** companies; a few of them, such as Scandinavia and Dar Express, deserve their reputation for safety and comfort; you may want to ask your hotel or a local which bus company is currently the most reliable. These express buses run to a fixed timetable and will leave without you if you're late. Buy your tickets in advance. The cheaper alternative is the **ordinary buses**, which leave when full. These are cheap but you definitely pay for what you get. As with all forms of local transport, ask your fellow passengers what the correct fare is before handing any money over to the 'conductor'; rip-offs are the rule rather than the exception on many journeys.

In addition to the buses there are the indigenous **dalla-dallas**: minibuses plying routes around and between neighbouring towns. They're usually a tight squeeze as the drivers pile in the customers to maximize their takings. If you're being pushed into one that looks full-to-bursting, simply refuse to enter; there'll be another along in a minute. In Kenya these minibuses are known as **matatus**.

It is possible to **hire a car** in Tanzania; we give details of some of the more reliable companies in Dar es Salaam; you can also hire cars from many of the bigger tour and trekking agencies in Moshi and Arusha. Make sure you choose a vehicle that is suitable for your requirements. Don't, for example, be tempted to conduct your own off-road safari in a two-wheel drive.

You can, of course, **hitch** around the country, though payment will often be expected from a Western tourist; it is, of course, wiser not to hitch alone.

Tanzania does still have a skeleton **train** service; services to Arusha and Moshi have long since stopped, though the stations and tracks are still there in both towns and are interesting places to look around if you're very bored.

Flying is a great way to cover the vast distances of Tanzania, and there are a number of small chartered and scheduled airlines serving visitors, including Coastal Air, Precision Air, Air Excel and the national airline Air Tanzania. For details of airlines flying to Kilimanjaro see p305.

ACCOMMODATION

Tanzania's guesthouses and hotels can be split into three sorts: those that welcome tourists, those that accept them, and those that refuse them altogether. The latter are usually the cheapest, double as brothels, have minimum security, minimal advertising and can safely be ignored. Room rates for the other two start at about Ts5000 per night; dorms are a rarity. Always take your time when choosing a hotel, particularly in the towns featured here where there are lots of options. Standards vary widely, but you'll probably be surprised at how pleasant some of them can be, with mosquito nets and attached bathrooms and maybe even a telly. Bear in mind that most hotels, as with the shuttle buses and other services, have two tariffs, one for locals and people living in Tanzania (commonly known as the 'residents rate') and a more expensive one for foreigners. If business is slow, it doesn't take much effort to persuade some of the smaller hotels to charge you the residents rate, regardless of whether you live in Tanzania or not.

In Nairobi, safety is a concern in some of the hotels, though the ones we have chosen to recommend in this book were fine. Accommodation on Zanzibar, incidentally, is generally much more expensive. Note, too, that in Swahili *hotel* or *hoteli* means restaurant rather than accommodation.

For details of **accommodation on the mountain**, see p222.

❏ **Abbreviations**

Throughout this book we have used the following abbreviations when writing about accommodation: **s/c** is short for self-contained, a local term meaning that the room comes with a bathroom (ie the room is en suite or attached); **sgl/dbl/tpl** means single/double/triple rooms. So, for example, where we have written 's/c sgl/dbl/tpl US$35/40/45', we mean that a self-contained single room costs US$35 per night, a self-contained double costs US$40, and a self-contained triple costs US$45.

ELECTRICITY

Tanzania is powered by a 250V, 50 cycles, AC network. Those bringing electrical items from home may wish to invest in a power breaker: Tanzania's electricity supply can be erratic on occasions, and power surges could seriously impair the efficacy of your electrical instruments, if not melt them altogether. Plugs and sockets vary in style, though by far the most common are the British three-square-pin or European two-round-pin style.

TIME

Tanzania is **three hours ahead of GMT**, and thus two hours ahead of Western Europe, eight ahead of New York, eleven ahead of San Francisco, one ahead of Johannesburg, seven hours behind Sydney and nine behind Wellington.

A point of endless confusion for travellers, and with the potential to cause major problems for the uninitiated, is the concept known as **Swahili time**, used mainly on the coast and other regions where Swahili is the *lingua franca*. Swahili time begins at dawn, or more precisely at 6am. In other words, 6am is their hour zero (and thus equivalent to our midnight), 7am in our time is actually one o'clock in Swahili and so on.

To add further confusion, this system for telling the time is not prevalent throughout the whole of Tanzania, with most offices, timetables etc using the standard style for telling the time. Whenever you're quoted a time it should be obvious which clock they are using, but always double check.

POST AND TELECOMMUNICATIONS

Telephone

The yellow TTCL **cardphones** have been installed in the larger Tanzanian towns but they are seldom used and frequently vandalized. Furthermore, often the only place where you can buy the cards themselves is from a Telecom building anyway. The TTCL Telcards come in denominations of 10, 20, 40, 100, 150 and 500 units. Even if you do manage to secure the correct phonecard and find a phone that will accept it and hasn't been vandalized beyond use, there is still no guarantee that you'll be able to make a call. If

This 65c stamp from 1954 featured Kilimanjaro. British Empire stamps are starting to increase in value and this one is now worth about £3.00

you are having trouble ringing home, try tacking an extra '0' on to the front of the international dialling code: for example, if you wish to ring the UK but the phone continues to bar your call, dial ☎ 00044 (or ☎ 000144) rather than just ☎ 0044 (or ☎ 00144).

Given this hassle, you may consider it worthwhile spending a little more and using the phone service at the **Telecom building**, of which there is one in every major town (including Moshi and Arusha). Most Telecom offices open from 8am until 10pm on weekdays. The procedure is simple: pick up a scrap of

□ The telephone country access code for Tanzania is ☎ 255.

paper from the counter; if the office is posh you will have a form to fill out, but if it's not then you'll just have to write the name and number of the person you wish to call and how long you wish the call to last. Hand it over and the operator will dial the number and direct you to a booth where you can take the call. If you did not speak for your alloted time, the operators are usually scrupulously fair in giving back the correct change; if you do speak for the full number of minutes, the operator will come online to tell you when your time is up.

One of the reasons why placing a call with a landline in Tanzania is still rather inefficient is because of the inordinate rise in popularity of **mobiles** – to the extent that anyone who can afford one, has one. If you're in Tanzania a while and need to make a lot of phone calls it may be worth investing in a SIM card (Ts2000) and a pay-as-you-go voucher from one of the many mobile phone kiosks that have sprouted up over the past few years. If your existing phone is unlocked you can put the SIM card straight in there; if not, you can pick a phone up cheaply in Tanzania.

Email
In contrast to the phones, Tanzania's Internet cafés are havens of efficiency and value, at about Ts500 for thirty minutes (a rate that is continually tumbling as competition grows). Most cafés are open from about 9am until late (typically 9pm). Some of the equipment is a little dated, as you'd probably expect, and the speed of the connection, particularly in the afternoon, can be a little slow. Nevertheless, if you've already tried to make a phone call or post a letter here, you'll come to regard the Internet cafés with something approaching affection: they're your best chance of keeping in regular touch with home while you're in East Africa. In the city guides we have picked out some of the better cafés.

Post
Thanks to the presence of the English missionaries, matters have already advanced so far in Jagga that the Europeans stationed there get their letters and newspapers not more than a month old. **Hans Meyer** *Across East African Glaciers* (1891)

The postal system in Tanzania has improved since Meyer's day but not massively. Reasonably reliable and reliably sluggish, things do occasionally get 'lost in the post' but most gets through … eventually. You should allow about two weeks for letters to reach their destinations from Dar, a day or two longer from regional post offices. There is a **poste restante** system operating in Tanzania too; letters sent to post offices in Tanzania for collecting are generally held indefinitely, usually in a shoebox in a dusty corner somewhere.

Media
You'll find that **BBC World** and **CNN** are both popular in Tanzania and often fill air-time on the national channels during the day (ITV, for example, switches to BBC at 8am every morning). **Channel O** is Africa's MTV equivalent and a

HOLIDAYS AND FESTIVALS
The following are public holidays in Tanzania; note that some, (eg Zanzibar's Revolutionary Day) are not held nationwide but are celebrated locally only.

1 Jan	New Year	**7 July**	Industrial Day
12 Jan	Zanzibar Revolutionary Day	**8 Aug**	Farmers' Day
April	Good Friday/Easter	**9 Dec**	Independence/Republic Days
26 April	Union Day (National Day)	**25 Dec**	Christmas Day
1 May	International Labour Day	**26 Dec**	Boxing Day

Islamic holy days
The dates of the following holidays are determined according to the Islamic lunar calendar and as such do not fall on the same date each year. Their **approximate** dates for the next few years are given. The extent to which these days are celebrated and whether these celebrations will impact on your holiday depends to a great extent on where you are in Tanzania; remember that around Kilimanjaro the people are largely Christian and so the impact tends to be minimal, though there will be some shops and businesses closed.

Idul Fitri (End of Ramadan – a two-day celebration)
approx dates: 24 October 2006, 13 October 2007, 1 October 2008.
Eid El-Hajj (also known as Eid El-Adha or Eid Al-Kebir)
approx dates: 31 December 2006, 20 December 2007, 8 December 2008.

favourite with waitresses who often have it blaring out in the restaurant while you're trying to eat. **Radio Tanzania** is the most popular radio station, with some broadcasts in English. The *Guardian* is the pick of the English-language newspapers for world events, while the *Daily News* is more Tanzania-centric.

Office hours
These are typically 8am-noon and 2-4.30pm Monday to Friday, and 8am-12.30pm for some private businesses on Saturdays.

FOOD
The native foods do not offer much variety, though they do differ widely in different districts; but if the traveller is not too dainty and is prepared to make the best of what is to be had, it is wonderful what can be done.   **Hans Meyer** *Across East African Glaciers* (1891)

Tanzanian food is, on the whole, unsubtle but tasty and filling. If there's one dish that could be described as quintessentially East African, it would be **nyama choma** – plain and simple grilled meat. If the restaurant is any good they'll add some sauces – often curry and usually fiery – to accompany your meat and the whole lot will usually come with rice, chips, plantains or the ubiquitous **ugali**. This is a stodgy cornmeal or cassava mush. Usually served in a single cricket-ball sized lump that you can pick up with your fork in one go, ugali has the consistency of plasticine and gives the impression of being not so much cooked as congealed. A bit bland, it nevertheless performs a vital role as a plate-filler, and acts as a soothing balm when eating some of the country's more thermogenic curries. With the indigenous cuisine catering for carnivores, the country's significant Indian minority has cornered the market for vegetarian fare. Indian restaurants abound in Dar, Moshi, Arusha and Nairobi, catering mainly for the budget end of the market though the cuisine at a top-notch Indian restaurant in Tanzania is amongst the best served outside Britain or India.

For details about food on the trail, see p223.

DRINKS

The usual world-brand **soft drinks** are on sale in Tanzania. Juices are widely available and pretty cheap, though be warned: a lot of upset stomachs are caused by insanitary juice stalls. Far safer, coconuts are ubiquitous on the coast and Zanzibar. **Alcoholic** drinks include a range of beers including the tasty Serengeti (our favourite), Safari and Kilimanjaro from Tanzania, Tusker from Kenya, and the potent Chagga home-brew *mbege*, or banana beer.

THINGS TO BUY

kíRìmíyà – A Chagga term meaning a treat brought home by mother to kids upon completion of a successful day at market From **University of Oregon**'s *Word of the Week* website

Tanzania has the usual supply of weavings and woodcarvings, T-shirts, textiles and trinkets. Amongst the T-shirts, at least in Moshi, are a number of variations on the 'I climbed Kili'motif. Witchcraft items, battle shields, Masai beads and necklaces and bows and arrows are all up for grabs in the high streets of Moshi and Arusha. Kilimanjaro coffee makes for a good and inexpensive present for the person who's been feeding your cat while you've been away; buy it in a wooden box or velvet bag in a souvenir store, or pick a simple bag of it up for a third of the price in a supermarket. Though not grown on the slopes of Kilimanjaro, the organic Africafe has been described by one enthusiastic reader as the best instant coffee in the world and an affordable souvenir. Another popular souvenir is the *kanga*, the typical Tanzanian woman's dress that usually has a message or motto running through the print, or the similar but smarter and message-less *kitenge*.

In the afternoon I bought some small capes made of hyrax skins, of a style formerly much in vogue, and two long spears of the most modern narrow-bladed pattern, which were quite works of art. **Hans Meyer** *Across East African Glaciers* (1891)

It depends on your taste, of course, but Zanzibar is widely reckoned to have a better selection and higher quality of souvenirs. Some of them, particularly the carved door jambs and furniture, are lovely, though difficult to get home; furthermore, these people are extremely tough negotiators, know the true price of everything and bargains are few.

SECURITY

Tanzania is a pretty safe country, at least by the standards of its neighbours. That said, the standards of its neighbours are very, very low indeed – as anybody who has already been to Kenya's capital, known to many travellers as 'Nairobberi', will testify – so do take care. Violent crime is relatively rare, but not unknown, especially in Dar es Salaam, while pickpockets are common throughout the country and reach epidemic proportions in busy areas such as markets and transport terminals. The best (if somewhat contradictory) advice is to:

● Keep a close eye on your things. ● Don't flaunt your wealth.

● Wear a moneybelt. ● Be on your guard against scams and con merchants ... but at the same time don't let a sense of paranoia ruin your holiday and remember that the vast majority of travellers in East Africa spend their time here suffering no great loss beyond the occasional and inevitable overcharging. If you are unfortunate enough to become the victim of a mugging, remember that it's your *money* that they're after, so hand it over – you should be insured against such eventualities anyway. Report the crime as soon as possible to the police, who are generally quite helpful, particularly when the victim is a tourist. This will help to back up your claim from the insurers and may help to prevent further crimes against tourists in the future.

HEALTH

Diarrhoea is often symptomatic of nothing more than a change of diet rather than any malignant bacteria, so if you get a vicious dose of the runs and your sphincter feels like a cat flap in the Aswan Dam, don't panic and assume you've got food poisoning. That said, there are problems with hygiene in Tanzania, so it's wise to take certain precautions. Take heed of that old adage about patronizing only places that are popular – so food doesn't have a chance to sit around for long – as well as that other one about eating only food that has been cooked, boiled or peeled. Stick to **bottled**, **purified** or **filtered water** and avoid ice unless you're certain it has been made from treated water. Washing fruit, vegetables and your hands and ensuring food is thoroughly cooked can all help to prevent food poisoning. Shellfish, ice cream from street vendors and under-cooked meat should all be avoided like the plague, or you could end up feeling like you've got it. Slathering yourself in an **insect repellent** to prevent you from being eaten alive by the smaller members of Tanzania's animal kingdom is a good idea too.

We could go into a detailed examination here of all the possible diseases you could catch in Tanzania. But the truth is that for most of the worst ones you should have already had an inoculation or be taking some sort of prophylactic. Besides, it's unlikely that you'll suffer anything more in Tanzania than a dose of **the runs**, some **altitude sickness** or, if you're careless, a touch of **sunstroke**. If you've got the former, just rest up and take plenty of fluids until you recover; to protect against the latter wear a high-factor sun lotion and a hat, and drink a lot of fluids – maintaining a reasonable salt intake will also help to prevent dehydration. As for altitude sickness, which the majority of trekkers on Kili suffer from to some extent, as well as other ailments that you may contract on the trail, read the detailed discussion on pp200-07.

(Opposite) Passing the Rebmann Glacier on that final push to Uhuru from Stella Point.

Geology

Our geological work was especially delightful... Every rock seemed to differ from another, not only in form but in substance. In half-an-hour it was no uncommon thing for us to pick up specimens of as many as two-and-twenty different kinds.
Hans Meyer *Across East African Glaciers*

Rising 4800m above the East African plains, 270km from the shores of the Indian Ocean and measuring up to 40km across, Kilimanjaro is a bizarre geological oddity, the tallest freestanding mountain in the world and one formed, shaped, eroded and scarred by the twin forces of fire and ice. It is actually a volcano, or rather three volcanoes, with the two main peaks, **Kibo** and **Mawenzi**, the summits of two of those volcanoes. The story of its creation goes like this:

About three-quarters of a million years ago (making Kilimanjaro a veritable youngster in geological terms) molten lava burst through the fractured surface of the **Great Rift Valley**, a giant fault in the Earth's crust that runs through East Africa (see p82; actually, Kilimanjaro lies 50 miles from the East African Rift Valley along a splinter running off it, but that need not concern us here). The huge pressures behind this eruption pushed part of the Earth's crust skywards, creating the **Shira volcano**, the oldest of the volcanoes forming the Kilimanjaro massif. Shira eventually ceased erupting around 500,000 years ago, collapsing as it did so to form a huge caldera (the deep cauldron-like cavity on the summit of a volcano) many times the size of its original crater.

Soon after Shira's extinction, **Mawenzi** started to form following a further eruption within the Shira caldera. Though much eroded, Mawenzi has at least kept some of its volcanic shape to this day. Then, 460,000 years ago, an enormous eruption just west of Mawenzi caused the formation of **Kibo**. Continual subterranean pressure forced Kibo to erupt several times more, forcing the summit ever higher until reaching a maximum height of about 5900m. A further huge eruption from Kibo 100,000 years later led to the formation of Kilimanjaro's characteristic shiny black stone – which in reality is just solidified black lava, or **obsidian**. This spilled over from Kibo's crater into the Shira caldera and around to the base of the Mawenzi peak, forming the so-called Saddle. Later eruptions created a series of distinctive mini-cones, or **parasitic craters**, that run in a chain south-east and north-west across the mountain, as well as the smaller **Reusch Crater** inside the main Kibo summit. The last volcanic activity of note, just over 200 years ago, left a symmetrical inverted cone

---

(Opposite) Top: The chilly Barafu Campsite with the route to the summit beyond.
Bottom: Getting ready for the next leg of the trek at Horombo Huts – see p230.

of ash in the Reusch Crater, known as the **Ash Pit**, that can still be seen today.

Today, **Uhuru Peak**, the highest part of Kibo's crater rim and the goal of most trekkers, stands at around 5895m. The fact that the summit is around five metres shorter today than it was 450,000 years ago can be ascribed in part to some improved technology, which has enabled scientists to measure the mountain more accurately; and in part to the simple progress of time and the insidious glacial erosion down the millennia. These glaciers, advancing and retreating across the summit, created a series of concentric rings like **terraces** near the top of this volcanic massif on the western side. The Kibo peak has also subsided slightly over time, and about one hundred thousand years ago a landslide took away part of the external crater, creating **Kibo Barranco** or the **Barranco Valley** (see p246). The glaciers were also behind the formation of the valleys and canyons, eroding and smoothing the earth into gentle undulations all around the mountain, though less so on the northern side where the glaciers on the whole failed to reach, leaving the valleys sharper and more defined.

While eruptions are unheard of in recent times, Kibo is classified as being dormant rather than extinct, as anybody who visits the inner **Reusch Crater** can testify. A strong sulphur smell still rises from the crater, the earth is hot to touch, preventing ice from forming, while occasionally fumaroles escape from the Ash Pit that lies at its heart.

THE GLACIERS

It is now time to consider the discovery on which Mr Rebmann particularly prides himself, namely, that of perpetual snow.   **W D Cooley** *Inner Africa Laid Open* (see box p93)

At first sight, Kilimanjaro's glaciers look like nothing more than big smooth piles of slightly monotonous ice. On second sight they pretty much look like this too. Yet there's much more to Kili's glaciers than meets the eye, for these cathe-

---

The Great Rift Valley

According to the theory of plate tectonics, the Earth's exterior is made up of six enormous plates that 'float' across the surface. Occasionally they collide, causing much buckling and crumpling and the creation of huge mountain ranges such as the Himalayas. At other times, these plates deteriorate and break up because of the massive forces bubbling away in the Earth's interior. When this happens, valleys are formed where the Earth fractures.

The Great Rift Valley, whose origins are in Mozambique but which extends right across East Africa to Jordan, is a classic example of a fracture in the Earth's surface caused by the movement of these plates. The same monstrous internal forces that two million years ago caused the disintegration of the tectonic plate and the formation of the Rift Valley are also responsible for the appearance of volcanoes along the valley, as these forces explode through the surface, pushing the Earth's crust skywards and forming – in the case of Kilimanjaro – one huge, 5895m-high geological pimple.

Of Africa's sixteen active volcanoes, all but three belong to the Rift Valley. Kili was just one of a number of volcanic eruptions to hit the valley; others included Ol Molog (to the north-west of Kilimanjaro) and Kilema (to the south-east).

drals of gleaming blue-white ice are dynamic repositories of climatic history – and they could also be providing us with a portent for impending natural disaster.

You would think that with the intensely strong equatorial sun, glaciers wouldn't exist at all on Kilimanjaro. In fact, it is the brilliant white colour of the ice that allows it to survive as it reflects most of the heat. The dull black lava rock on which the glacier rests, on the other hand, does absorb the heat; so while the glacier's surface is unaffected by the sun's rays, the heat generated by the sun-baked rocks underneath leads to glacial melting.

As a result, the glaciers on Kilimanjaro are inherently unstable: the ice at the bottom of the glacier touching the rocks melts, the glaciers lose their 'grip' on the mountain and 'overhangs' occur where the ice at the base has melted away, leaving just the ice at the top to survive. As the process continues the ice fractures and breaks away, exposing more of the rock to the sun... and so the process begins again. The sun's effect on the glaciers is also responsible for the spectacular structures – the ice columns and pillars, towers and cathedrals – that are the most fascinating part of the upper slopes of Kibo.

One would have thought that, after 11,700 years of this melting process, (according to recent research, the current glaciers began to form in 9700BC) very little ice would remain on Kilimanjaro. The fact that there are still glaciers is due to the prolonged 'cold snaps', or ice ages, that have occurred down the centuries, allowing the glaciers to regroup and reappear on the mountain. According to estimates, there have been at least eight of these ice ages, the last a rather minor one in the fifteenth and sixteenth centuries, a time when the Thames frequently froze over and winters were severe. At these times the ice on Kilimanjaro would in places have reached right down to the tree line and both Mawenzi and Kibo would have been covered. At the other extreme, before 9700BC there have been periods when Kilimanjaro was completely free of ice, perhaps for up to twenty thousand years.

The slush of Kilimanjaro – where have all the glaciers gone?

Of the 19 square kilometres of glacial ice to be found on Africa, only 2.2 square kilometres can be found on Kilimanjaro. Unfortunately, both figures used to be much higher: Kili's famous white mantle has shrunk by a whopping 82% since the first survey of the summit in 1912. Even since 1989, when there were 3.3 square kilometres, there has been a decline of 33%. At that rate, say the experts, Kili will be completely ice-free within the next decade or two.

'We found that the summit of the ice fields has lowered by at least 17 metres since 1962,' said Professor Lonnie Thompson of Ohio State University. 'That's an average loss of about a half-metre (a foot and a half) in height each year.' You don't need to be a scientist to see that the glaciers on Kili are shrinking. Take a look at old photos of Kibo, even those taken as late as the 1960s, and compare them with the ice on the summit today and the difference is obvious.

The big question, therefore, is not whether they are shrinking, but why – and should we be concerned? Certainly glacial retreats are nothing new: Hans Meyer, the first man to conquer Kilimanjaro, returned in 1898, nine years after his ascent, and was horrified by the extent to which the glaciers had shrunk. The ice on Kibo's slopes had retreated by 100m on all sides, while one of the notches he had used to gain access to the crater in 1889 – and now called the Hans Meyer Notch – was twice as wide, with the ice only half as thick. Nor are warnings of the complete disappearance of the glaciers anything new: in 1899 Meyer himself predicted that they would be gone within three decades, and the top of Kili would be decorated with nothing but bare rock.

So how high is it then?

Ever since Hans Meyer ambled down from the summit of Kibo and told anybody who'd listen that he'd reached 19,833ft above sea level (6010m), an argument has been raging over just how high Africa's highest mountain really is. For though Meyer's estimate is now unanimously agreed to be a wild over-estimate (an inaccuracy that can be ascribed to a combination of the imprecise nineteenth-century instruments that he had at his disposal, and perhaps a touch of hubris) finding a figure for the height of Kili that meets with a similar consensus of opinion has proved altogether more difficult.

For years the accepted height of Kilimanjaro was 5892m, that being the figure set by the colonial German authorities some five years after Meyer's ascent. You'll see this figure crop up time and again in many a twentieth-century travelogue as well as on pre-World War Two maps of the Kilimanjaro region. Not many people at the time bothered to question this estimate; the few dissenting voices almost invariably belonged to climbers whose own estimates (which were, perhaps unsurprisingly, nearly always over-estimates, ranging from 5930m to 5965m) are today regarded as even more inaccurate than the German's figure.

Under British rule the figure was revised to 5895m following the work of the cartographers of the Ordnance Survey, who mapped Kilimanjaro in 1952; and it is this figure that those trekkers who reach the summit will find written on the sign at the top, as well as on the certificates they receive from KINAPA and on the souvenir T-shirts on sale back in Moshi.

The trouble was, of course, that whereas the Ordnance Survey's techniques and equipment may have been state of the art in the 1950s, so were vinyl records and the Ford Edsel. Technology has moved on a couple of light years since then. The Ordnance Survey's readings for Kilimanjaro had been taken from a distance of over 55km away from the mountain; as such, the probability that the OS's figure was not entirely accurate was rather high.

So in 1999 a team of specialists at the University College of Land and Architectural Studies in Arusha together with experts from Karlsruhe University in Germany set out to measure the precise altitude using a technique involving GPS (Global Positioning Satellites) that had previously been used on Everest, and which resulted in that mountain shrinking by a couple of metres to 8846.10m.

The result of their findings in Africa? Kilimanjaro was now a full 2.45 metres shorter than the traditionally accepted figure, at **5892.55m**.

So is Kilimanjaro shrinking? Or was the old estimate of 5895m just plain inaccurate. Unfortunately, the scientists have yet to tell us that. And while they have every confidence in the accuracy of their latest readings, the old figure of 5895m is still the official figure and the one you'll hear bandied about by tour operators, guides, porters and anybody else you care to speak to; and until we are told otherwise, 5895m is the one we're going to use in this book too.

What concerns today's scientists, however, is that this current reduction of Kili's ice-cap does seem to be more rapid and more extensive than previous shrinkages. But is it really something to worry about, or merely the latest in a series of glacial retreats experienced by Kili over the last few hundred years?

Professor Thompson and his team are attempting to find answers to all these questions. In January and February 2000 they drilled six ice cores through three of Kibo's glaciers in order to research the history of the mountain's climate over the centuries. A weather station was also placed on the Northern Icefield to see how the current climate affects the build-up or destruction of glaciers.

Although results are still coming in from Professor Thompson's work, early indications are not good. In a speech made at the annual meeting of the American Association for the Advancement of Science in February 2001, the professor declared that, while he cannot be sure why the ice is melting away so quickly, what is certain is that if the glaciers continue to shrink at current rates, the summit could be completely ice-free by 2015.

This doesn't surprise locals who live in the shadow of Kilimanjaro, some of whom believe they know why the ice is disappearing. According to an AllAfrica.com news report, a 50-year-old native of Old Moshi, Mama Judith Iyatuu, reckons that it's the evil eyes of the white tourists which are melting the ice, while 65-year old Mzee Ruaici Thomas from Meela village believes that the ice is disappearing because God is unhappy with mankind.

Whatever the reasons, if Kilimanjaro is to lose its snowy top, the repercussions would be extremely serious: Kilimanjaro's glaciers are essential to the survival of the local villages, supplying their drinking water, the water to irrigate their crops and, through hydroelectric production, their power; never mind the blow the loss of the snow-cap would deal to tourism.

And these are just the local consequences. If the scientists are to be believed, what is happening on Kilimanjaro is a microcosm of what the entire world could face in future. Even more worryingly, more and more scientists are now starting to think that this future is probably already upon us.

Climate

Kilimanjaro is big enough to have its own weather pattern. The theory behind this pattern is essentially very simple. Strong winds travel across the oceans, drawing moisture up as they go. Eventually they collide with a large object – such as a mountain like Kilimanjaro. The winds are pushed upwards as they hit the mountain slopes, and the fall in temperature and atmospheric pressure leads to precipitation or, as it's more commonly called, snow and rain.

In one year there are two rain-bearing seasonal winds buffeting Kilimanjaro. The south-east trade wind bringing rain from the Indian Ocean arrives between March and May. Because the mountain is the first main obstacle to the wind's progress, and by far the largest, a lot of rain falls on Kili at this time, and for this reason the March-to-May season is known as the **long rains**. This is the main wet season on Kilimanjaro. As the south-east trade winds run into the southern side of Kili, so the southern slopes tend to be damper and as a consequence more fertile, with the forest zone much broader than on the northern slopes.

Then there are the dry **'anti-trade' winds** from the north-east which carry no rain and hit the mountain between May and October. These anti-trade winds, which blow, usually very strongly, across the Saddle (the broad valley between Kilimanjaro's two peaks), also serve to keep the south-east trade winds off the upper reaches of Kilimanjaro, ensuring that the rain from the long monsoon season stays largely on the southern side below 3000m, with little falling above this. This is why, at this time of year, the first day's walk for trekkers following the Marangu, Umbwe or Machame routes is usually conducted under a canopy of cloud, while from the second day onwards they traditionally enjoy unadulterated sunshine.

A second seasonal rain-bearing wind, the north-east monsoon, having already lost much of its moisture after travelling overland for a longer period, brings a **short rainy season** between November and February. While the northern side receives most of the rain to fall in this season, it is far less than the rain brought by the south-east trade winds, and as a result the northern side of the mountain is far drier and more barren in appearance. Once again, the rain falls mainly below 3000m.

This theory seems fine in principle but it does pose a tricky question: if the precipitation falls below 3000m, how did the snows on the summit of Kibo get there in the first place? The answer, my friend, is blowing in the (anti-trade) wind: though these winds normally blow very strongly, as those who walk north across the Saddle will testify, they occasionally drop in force, allowing the south-east trade winds that run beneath them to climb up the southern slopes to the Saddle and on to the summit. Huge banks of clouds then develop and snow falls.

This, at least, is the theory of Kilimanjaro's climate. In practice, of course, the mountain is rarely so predictable. What is certain is that, with rain more abundant the further one travels down the mountain, life, too, is more abundant further down the slopes – as the *Flora and Fauna* section on p110 illustrates.

The history of Kilimanjaro

EARLY HISTORY

Thanks to several primitive **stone bowls** found on the lower slopes of Kilimanjaro, we know that man has lived on or around the mountain since at least 1000BC. We also know that, over the last 500 years, the mountain has at various times acted as a navigational aid for traders travelling between the interior and the coast, a magnet for Victorian explorers, a political pawn to be traded between European superpowers who carved up East Africa, a battlefield for these same superpowers, and a potent symbol of independence for those who wished to rid themselves of these colonial interlopers. Unfortunately, little is known about the history of the mountain during the intervening two thousand five hundred years.

It's a fair bet that Kilimanjaro's first inhabitants, when they weren't fashioning stone bowls out of the local terrain, would have spent much of their time hunting and gathering the local flora and fauna, Kilimanjaro being a fecund source of both. Add to this its reputation as a reliable location both for fresh drinking water and materials – wood, stones, mud, vines etc – for building, and it seems reasonable to suppose that Kilimanjaro would have been a highly desirable location for primitive man, and would have played a central role in the lives of those who chose to take up residence on its slopes.

Unfortunately, those looking to piece together a comprehensive history of the first inhabitants of Kilimanjaro rather have their work cut out. There are no documents recording the life and times of the people who have once lived on the mountain; not much in the way of any oral history that has been passed down through the generations; and, stone bowls apart, little in the way of archaeological evidence from which to draw any inferences. So while we can *assume* many things about the lives of Kilimanjaro's first inhabitants, we can be certain about nothing and if Kilimanjaro did have a part to play in the pre-colonial history of the region, that history and the mountain's significance within it has, alas, now been lost to us.

And so it is to the notes of foreign travellers that we must turn in order to find the earliest accounts of Kilimanjaro. These descriptions are usually rather brief, often inaccurate and more often than not based on little more than hearsay and rumour rather than actual firsthand evidence.

One of the first ever descriptions of East Africa is provided by the *Periplus of the Erythraean Sea*, written anonymously in AD45. The *Periplus* – a contender for the title of the world's first ever travel guide – is a handbook for seafarers to the ports of Africa, Arabia and India and includes details of the sea routes to China. In it the author tells of a land called Azania, in which one could find a prosperous market town, Rhapta, where 'hatchets and daggers and awls … a great quantity of ivory and rhinoceros horn and tortoise shell' were all traded. Yet interestingly, there is no mention of any snow-capped mountain lying nearby; indeed, reading the *Periplus* one gets the impression that the author considered Rhapta to be just about the end of the world:

Beyond Opone [modern day Ras Harun on the Somalian coast] *there are the small and great bluffs of Azania … twenty-three days sail beyond there lies the very last market town of the continent of Azania, Rhapta …*

Less than a hundred years later, however, **Ptolemy of Alexandria**, astronomer and the founder of scientific cartography, wrote of lands lying to the south of Rhapta where barbaric cannibals lived near a wide shallow bay and where, inland, one could find a '**great snow mountain**'. Mountains that wear a mantle of snow are pretty thin on the ground in Africa; indeed, there is only one candidate that is permanently adorned in snow, and that, of course, is Kilimanjaro.

Kilimanjaro – the name

The meaning of the name Kilíma Njáro, if it have any meaning, is unknown to the Swáhili... To be analysed, it must first be corrupted. This has been done by Mr Rebmann, who converts Kilíma Njáro into Kilíma dja-aro, which he tells us signifies, "Mountain of Greatness." This etymology... is wholly inadmissible for the following reasons: 1st. It is mere nonsense...

So said W D Cooley (see p90), leading British geographer during the mid-nineteenth century, in his book *Inner Africa Laid Open*. Nonsense Rebmann's suggestion may have been, but in the absence of better alternatives the translation is as valid as any other. For the fact of the matter is that despite extensive studies into the etymology of the name Kilimanjaro, nobody is sure where it comes from or what exactly it means.

When looking for the name's origin, it seems only sensible to begin such a search in one of the local Tanzanian dialects and, more specifically, in the language spoken by those who live in its shadow, namely the Chagga people. True, the name Kilimanjaro bears no resemblance to any word in the Chagga vocabulary; but if we divide it into two parts then a few possibilities present themselves. One is that Kilima is derived from the Chagga term *kilelema*, meaning 'difficult or impossible', while *jaro* could come from the Chagga terms *njaare* ('bird') or *jyaro* ('caravan'). In other words, the name Kilimanjaro means something like 'That which is impossible for the bird', or 'That which defeats the caravan' – names which, if this interpretation is correct, are clear references to the sheer enormity of the mountain.

Whilst this is perhaps the most likely translation, it is not, in itself, particularly convincing, especially when one considers that while the Chagga language would seem the most logical source for the name, the Chagga people themselves do not actually have one single name for the mountain! Instead, they don't see Kilimanjaro as a single entity but as two distinct, separate peaks, namely Mawenzi and Kibo. (These two names, incidentally, are definitely Chagga in origin, coming from the Chagga terms *kimawenzi* – 'having a broken top or summit' – and *kipoo* – 'snow' – respectively.)

How exactly Ptolemy came by his information is unknown, for he almost certainly never saw Kilimanjaro for himself. Nevertheless, based on hearsay though it may have been, this is the earliest surviving written mention of Africa's greatest mountain. It therefore seems logical to conclude that the outside world first became aware of the continent's tallest mountain in the years between the publication of the Periplus in AD45, and that of Ptolemy's work, sometime during the latter half of the second century AD.

THE OUTSIDERS ARRIVE

Arabs, An Anonymous Chinaman and some Portuguese

Following Ptolemy's description, almost nothing more is written about Kilimanjaro for over a thousand years. The Arabs, arriving on the East African coast in the sixth century, must have heard something about it from the local people with whom they traded. Indeed, the mountain would have proved essential to the natives as they travelled from the interior to the markets on the East African shore: as one of the few unmissable landmarks in a largely featureless

Assuming Kilimanjaro isn't Chagga in origin, therefore, the most likely source for the name Kilimanjaro would seem to be Swahili, the majority language of the Tanzanians. Rebmann's good friend and fellow missionary, Johann Ludwig Krapf, wrote that Kilimanjaro could either be a Swahili word meaning 'Mountain of Greatness' – though he is noticeably silent when it comes to explaining how he arrived at such a translation – or a composite Swahili/Chagga name meaning 'Mountain of Caravans'; *jaro*, as we have previously explained, being the Chagga term for 'caravans'. Thus the name could be a reference to the many trading caravans that would stop at the mountain for water. The major flaw with both these theories, however, is that the Swahili term for mountain is not *kilima* but *mlima* – *kilima* is actually the Swahili word for 'hill'!

The third and least likely dialect from which Kilimanjaro could have been derived is Masai, the major tribe across the border in Kenya. But while the Masai word for spring or water is *njore*, which could conceivably have been corrupted down the centuries to *njaro*, there is no relevant Masai word similar to *kilima*. Furthermore, the Masai call the mountain *Oldoinyo Oibor*, which means 'White Mountain', with Kibo known as the 'House of God', as Hemingway has already told us at the beginning of his – and this – book. Few experts, therefore, believe the name is Masai in origin.

Other theories include the possibility that *njaro* means 'whiteness', referring to the snow cap that Kilimanjaro permanently wears, or that Njaro is the name of the evil spirit who lives on the mountain, causing discomfort and even death to all those who climb it. Certainly the folklore of the Chagga people is rich in tales of evil spirits who dwell on the higher reaches of the mountain, and Rebmann himself refers to 'Njaro, the guardian spirit of the mountain'; however, it must also be noted that the Chagga's legends make no mention of any spirit going by that name.

And so we are none the wiser. But in one sense at least, it's not important: what the mountain means to the 35,000 who walk up it every year is far more meaningful than any name we ascribe to it.

expanse of savannah and scrub, and with its abundant streams and springs, the mountain would have been both an invaluable navigational tool and a reliable source of drinking water for the trading caravans. But whether the merchants from the Middle East actually ventured beyond their trading posts on the coast to see the mountain for themselves seems doubtful, and from their records of this time only one possible reference to Kilimanjaro has been uncovered, written by a thirteenth-century geographer, **Abu'l Fida**, who speaks of a mountain in the interior that was 'white in colour'.

The Chinese, who traded on the East African coast during the same period, also seemed either ignorant or uninterested in the land that lay beyond the coastline and in all their records from this time once again just one scant reference to Kili has been found, this time by an anonymous chronicler who states that the country to the west of Zanzibar 'reaches to a great mountain'.

After 1500, and the exploration and subsequent conquest of the African east coast by Vasco da Gama and those who followed in his wake, the Arabs were replaced as the major trading power in the region by the Portuguese. They proved to be slightly more curious about what lay beyond the coast than their predecessors, perhaps because their primary motives for being there were more colonial than commercial. A vague but once again unmistakable reference to Kilimanjaro can be found in a book, *Suma de Geographia*, published in 1519, an account of a journey to Mombasa by the Spanish cartographer, astronomer and ship's pilot **Fernandes de Encisco**:

West of Mombasa is the Ethiopian Mount Olympus, which is very high, and further off are the Mountains of the Moon in which are the sources of the Nile.

Amazingly, in the fourteen hundred years since Ptolemy this is only the third reference to Kilimanjaro that has been found; with the return of the Arabs in 1699, it was also to be the last for another hundred years or so. Then, just as the eighteenth century was drawing to a close, the Europeans once more cast an avaricious eye on East Africa.

THE 1800s: PIONEERS . . .

With British merchants firmly established on Zanzibar by the 1840s, frequent rumours of a vast mountain situated on the mainland just a few hundred miles from the coast now began to reach European ears. British geographers were especially intrigued by these reports, particularly as it provided a possible solution to one of the oldest riddles of Africa: namely, the precise whereabouts of the source of the Nile. Encisco's sixteenth-century reference to *the Mountains of the Moon in which are the sources of the Nile* (see above) is in fact a mere echo of the work of Ptolemy, writing fourteen hundred years before Encisco, who also cites the Mountains of the Moon as the true origin of the Nile.

But while these Mountains of the Moon were, for more than a millennium, widely accepted in European academia as the place where the Nile rises, nobody had actually bothered to go and find out if this was so – nor, indeed, if these mountains actually existed at all.

Interest in the 'dark continent' was further aroused by the arrival in London in 1834 of one Khamis bin Uthman. Slave dealer, caravan leader and envoy of the then-ruler of East Africa, Seyyid Said, Uthman met many of Britain's leading dignitaries, including the prime minister, Lord Palmerston. He also met and talked at length with the leading African scholar, **William Desborough Cooley**. A decade after this meeting, Cooley wrote his lengthy essay *The Geography of N'yassi, or the Great Lake of Southern Africa Investigated*, in which he not only provides us with another reference to Kilimanjaro – only the fifth in 1700 years – but also becomes the first author to put a name to the mountain:

The most famous mountain of Eastern Africa is Kirimanjara, which we suppose, from a number of circumstances to be the highest ridge crossed on the road to Monomoezi.

Suddenly Africa, long viewed by the West almost exclusively in terms of the lucrative slave trade, became the centre of a flurry of academic interest and the quest to find the true origins of the Nile became something of a *cause célèbre* amongst scholars. Long-forgotten manuscripts and journals from Arab traders and Portuguese adventurers were dusted off and scrutinized for clues to the whereabouts of this most enigmatic river source. Most scholars preferred to conduct their research from the comfort of their leather armchairs; there were others, however, who took a more active approach, and pioneering explorers such as Richard Burton and John Hanning Speke set off to find for themselves the source of the Nile, crossing the entire country we now know as Tanzania in 1857. This was also the age of Livingstone and Stanley, the former venturing deep into the heart of Africa in search of both knowledge and potential converts to Christianity, and the latter in search of the former.

. . . AND PREACHERS

Yet for all their brave endeavours, it was not these Victorian action men but one of the humble Christian missionaries who arrived in Africa at about the same time who became the first European to set eyes on Kilimanjaro. **Johannes Rebmann** was a young Swiss-German missionary who arrived in Mombasa in 1846 with an umbrella, a suitcase and a heart full of Christian zeal. His brief was to help **Dr Johann Ludwig Krapf**, a doctor of divinity from Tubingen, in his efforts to spread the Christian faith among East Africa's heathen. Krapf was something of a veteran in the missionary field, having previously worked for the London-based Church Missionary Society in Abyssinia. Following the closure of that mission, Krapf sailed down the East African coast to Zanzibar and from there to Mombasa, where he hoped to found a new mission and continue his evangelical work.

Instead, his life fell apart. His wife succumbed to malaria and died on the 9 July 1884. His daughter, born just three days previously, died five days after the death of her mother from the same disease, while Krapf too fell gravely ill with the same; and though he alone recovered, throughout the rest of his life he suffered from sporadic attacks that would lay him low for weeks at a time.

But though his body grew weak with malaria, his spirit remained strong, and over the next six months following the death of his wife, Krapf both translated the New Testament into Swahili and devised a plan for spreading the gospel throughout the interior of Africa. Estimating that the continent could be crossed on foot from east to west in a matter of 900 hours, Krapf believed that establishing a chain of missions at intervals of one hundred hours right across the continent, each staffed by six 'messengers of peace', would be the best way to promulgate the Christian religion on the dark continent.

Unfortunately for Krapf, Islam had got there first, which made his job rather tougher; indeed, in the six months following his arrival in Mombasa, the total number of successful conversions made by Krapf

David Livingstone preaching near Lake Tanganyika. (HG Adams, 1873)

KILIMANJARO

stood at zero. Clearly, if the faith was to make any inroads in Africa, fresh impetus was required. That impetus was provided by the arrival of Rebmann in 1846. Having recovered from the obligatory bout of malaria that all but wiped him out for his first month in Africa, Rebmann set about helping Krapf to establish a new mission at Rabai-mpia (New Rabai), just outside Mombasa. The station lay in the heart of Wanika territory, a tribe who from the first had proved resistant to conversion. Even the founding of a mission in their midst did little to persuade the Wanika to listen to Krapf's preaching: by 1859, 14 years after Krapf first arrived, just seven converts had been made.

It was clear early on that they would have little success in persuading the Wanika to convert. So from almost the start the proselyting pair began to look to pastures new to find potential members for their flock. In 1847 they founded a second mission station at Mt Kasigau, three days' walk from Rabai-mpia – the first in their proposed chain of such stations across the African continent – and later that same year they began to plan the establishment of the next link, at a place called **Jagga** (now spelt Chagga). Rebmann and Krapf had already heard a lot about Jagga from the caravan leaders who earned their money transferring goods between the interior and the markets on the eastern shore, and who often called into Rabai-mpia on the way. A source of and market for slaves, Jagga was renowned locally for suffering from extremely cold temperatures at times, a reputation that led Krapf to deduce that Jagga was probably at a much higher altitude than the lands that surrounded it. This hypothesis was confirmed by renowned caravan leader Bwana Kheri, who spoke to Krapf of a great mountain called 'Kilimanshaho' (this, incidentally, being the sixth definite reference to Kilimanjaro). From other sources, Krapf and Rebmann also learnt that the mountain was protected by evil spirits (known in the Islamic faith as *djinns*) who had been responsible for many deaths, and that it was crowned with a strange white substance that resembled silver, but which the locals simply called 'cold'.

Following protracted negotiations, Bwana Kheri was eventually persuaded to take Rebmann to Chagga in 1848 (Krapf, being too ill to travel, remained in Rabai-mpia). The parting caused great distress to both parties, as detailed in Krapf's diary:

Here we are in the midst of African heathenism, among wilful liars and trickish men, who desire only our property... The only earthly friend whom I have, and whom he has, does at once disappear, each of us setting our face towards our respective destinations while our friends at home do not know where we are, whither we go and what we are doing.

Rebmann's journey and the discovery of snow

And so, armed with only his trusty umbrella – along a route where caravans typically travelled under armed escort – Rebmann, accompanied by Bwana Kheri and eight porters, set out for Chagga on 27 April 1848. A fortnight later, on the morning of 11 May, he came across the most marvellous sight:

At about ten o'clock, (I had no watch with me) I observed something remarkably white on the top of a high mountain, and first supposed that it was a very white cloud, in which supposition my guide also confirmed me, but having gone a few paces more I could no more rest satisfied with that explanation; and while I was asking my guide a second time whether *that white thing was indeed a cloud and scarcely listening to his answer that **yonder** was a cloud but what that white was he did not know, but supposed it was **coldness** – the most delightful recognition took place in my mind, of an old well-known European guest called **snow**. All the strange stories we had so often heard about the gold and silver mountain Kilimandjaro in Jagga, supposed to be inaccessible on account of evil spirits, which had killed a great many of those who had attempted to ascend it, were now at once rendered intelligible to me, as of course the extreme cold, to which poor Natives are perfect strangers, would soon chill and kill the half-naked visitors. I endeavoured to explain to my people the nature of that 'white thing' for which no name exists even in the language of Jagga itself...* **Johannes Rebmann** from his account of his journey, published in Volume I of the *Church Missionary Intelligencer*, May 1849

An extract from the next edition of the same journal continues the theme:

The cold temperature of the higher regions constituted a limit beyond which they dared not venture. This natural disinclination, existing most strongly in the case of the great mountain, on account of its intenser cold, and the popular traditions respecting the fate of the

WD Faulty? – The great snow debate

The most relentless critic was a redoubtable person, for long years a terror to real explorers, Mr. Desborough Cooley, a kind of geographical ogre, who used to sit in his study in England, shaping and planning out the map of Africa (basing his arrangements of rivers, lakes and mountains on ridiculous and fantastic linguistic coincidences and resemblances of his own imagination), and who rushed out and tore in pieces all unheeding explorers in the field who brought to light actual facts which upset his elaborate schemes. **HH Johnston** *The Kilima-njaro Expedition – A Record of Scientific Exploration in Eastern Equatorial Africa* (1886)

Though Rebmann's accounts of Kilimanjaro caused a minor sensation amongst the wider reading public when first published in the *Church Missionary Intelligencer* of May 1849, the response it elicited from academic circles back in Europe was initially as cool as the top of Kibo itself. Leading the sceptics was one **William Desborough (WD) Cooley**. Cooley was widely regarded in his day as one of Britain's leading geographers and something of an expert on Africa (though he never actually ventured near the continent throughout his entire life). Indeed, Cooley had already added to the stock of knowledge about the mountain way back in 1845, a full four years before Rebmann's essay was published, by providing the world with a description of Kilimanjaro that he had managed to construct from details furnished to him by the slave dealer-cum-ambassador Khamis bin Uthman (see p90). But if he is remembered at all today it is as the man who refused to believe that Kilimanjaro could be topped with snow, as this response to Rebmann's first account (see opposite) makes clear:

I deny altogether the existence of snow on Mount Kilimanjaro. It rests entirely on the testimony of Mr Rebmann... and he ascertained it, not with his eyes, but by inference and in the visions of his imagination. **Athenaeum,** May 1849

Absurd as it seems now, Cooley's reputation in intellectual circles at that time was as high as Kili itself, and such was the reverence with which his every pronouncement was received in the mid-nineteenth century that it was his version of reality that was the more widely accepted: as far as people in Europe were concerned, if Cooley said Kilimanjaro did not have snow on it, then it did not have snow on it. *(Cont'd on p94)*

KILIMANJARO

only expedition which had ever attempted to ascend its heights, had of course prevented them from exploring it, and left them in utter ignorance of such a thing as 'snow', although not in ignorance of that which they so greatly dreaded, 'coldness'.

Still bent on spreading Christianity, and undeterred (or perhaps ignorant) of the scepticism with which his reports in the *Intelligencer* would soon be received in Europe (about which, see the box on p93), Rebmann returned to Rabai-mpia but continued to visit and write about Kilimanjaro and the Chagga region for a few more years. His second trip, made in November of the same year, was blessed by favourable weather conditions, providing Rebmann with his clearest view of Kilimanjaro, and the outside world with the most accurate and comprehensive description of the mountain that had yet been written:

There are two main peaks which arise from a common base measuring some twenty-five miles long by as many broad. They are separated by a saddle-shaped depression, running

---

❑ WD Faulty? – The great snow debate

(Continued from p93) A second report by Rebmann, following his trip to the Chagga lands in November 1848, did little to stem the scepticism, even though he – perhaps now aware of the controversy his first account had caused back home – went to great lengths to back up his earlier report:

.. during the night, I felt the cold as severely as in Europe in November; and had I been obliged to remain in the open-air, I could not have fallen to sleep for a single moment: neither was this to be wondered at, for so near was I now to the snow-mountain Kilimandjaro (Kilima dja-aro, mountain of greatness), that even at night, by only the dim light of the moon, I could perfectly well distinguish it.

If Rebmann hoped to persuade his critics, however, he was sadly mistaken: if he was capable of making a mistake once, they countered, then surely he could be wrong a second and third time too. And so for much of the next two years Rebmann's account of his time on Kili was treated with equal parts suspicion and derision. Indeed, it wasn't until 1850 and the publication of an account by Rebmann's friend and mentor, Dr Krapf, that doubts began to be cast on Cooley's ideas. In an edition of the *Church Missionary Intelligencer* in which he recounts his own experiences working in the Ukamba region immediately to the north of Kilimanjaro, Krapf baldly states that:

All the arguments which Mr Cooley has adduced against the existence of such a snow mountain, and against the accuracy of Rebmann's report, dwindle into nothing when one has the evidence of one's own eyes before one; so that they are scarcely worth refuting.

Suddenly it became that much harder to deny the existence of snow on Kili: after all, there were now two Europeans who had seen the mountain for themselves – and both of them had insisted that they'd seen snow there.

Yet Cooley remained adamant in his convictions and, thanks to the support of some pretty influential friends to back up his arguments, enjoyed popular public support. No less a figure than the President of the Royal Geographical Society, **Sir Roderick Murchison**, said that the idea of a snow-capped mountain under the equator was to *'a great degree incredulous'*, (even though there are other snow-capped mountains in the Andes and Papua New Guinea that fall 'under the equator', and which were already known about by the mid-nineteenth century). Even those who *had* *east and west for a distance of about eight or ten miles. The eastern peak is the lower of the two, and is conical in shape. The western and higher presents the appearance of a magnificent dome, and is covered with snow throughout the year, unlike its eastern neighbour, which loses its snowy mantle during the hot season.*

On this second trip Rebmann was also able to correct an error made in his first account of Kilimanjaro: that the local 'Jagga' tribe were indeed familiar with snow and did have a name for it – that name being 'Kibo'!

A third and much more organized expedition in April 1849 – at the same time as the account of his first visits of Kilimanjaro was rolling off the presses in Europe – enabled Rebmann, accompanied by a caravan of 30 porters (and, of course, his trusty umbrella), to ascend to such a height that he was later to boast that he had come 'so close to the snow-line that, supposing no impassable abyss to intervene, I could have reached it in three or four hours'. After Rebmann's pioneering work

been to Africa for themselves had serious reservations about the missionaries' claims. The esteemed Irish explorer **Richard Burton**, for example, having listened to Krapf give a talk on Kilimanjaro in Cairo, declared that *'These stories reminded one of a de Lunatico'*; while **David Livingstone**, recently returned from his latest adventures in Africa, lent further weight to Cooley's arguments during an address to the Royal Geographical Society. In it, Livingstone related a story about some mountains in the Zambezi Valley, which were described to him by locals as being of a *'glistening whiteness'*. Livingstone initially believed that these mountains must be covered by snow, until, having seen the mountains for himself, he realized that they were in fact composed of *'masses of white rock, somewhat like quartz'*. As if to drum home the point of the tale, Sir Roderick Murchison later declared at the same meeting that Livingstone's account

... may prove that the missionaries, who believed that they saw snowy mountains under the equator, have been deceived by the glittering aspect of rocks under a tropical sun.

The next broadside fired by either side occurred in 1852 and the publication of Cooley's grandly (but inaccurately) titled *Inner Africa Laid Open*. This, Cooley clearly hoped, was to be his masterpiece: the culmination of a lifetime's armchair studying, this was the opus that would secure his reputation during his lifetime and ensure his name lived on in perpetuity as one of the great intellectual heavyweights of the nineteenth century. As it transpired, the book did indeed serve to preserve Cooley's name for posterity – though, presumably, not quite in the way that he had hoped.

To read the book now, it is clear that Cooley hoped it would once and for all dismiss all this nonsense about snow on Kilimanjaro. Within the first few pages almost every part of Rebmann's account is called into question, with the claim of snow on Kilimanjaro being treated with particularly vehement derision:

... it is obvious that the discovery of snow rests much more on 'a delightful mental recognition' than on the evidence of the senses... But in his mind the wish was father to the thought, the 'delightful recognition' developed with amazing rapidity, and in a few minutes the cloudy object, or 'something white,' became a 'beautiful snow mountain', so near to the equator. (Continued on p96)

KILIMANJARO

it was the turn of his friend Krapf, now risen from his sickbed, to see the snowy mountain his friend had described in such detail. In November 1849 he visited the Ukamba district to the north of Kilimanjaro, and during a protracted stay in the area Krapf became the first white man to see Mount Kenya. Perhaps more importantly, he was also afforded wonderful views of Kilimanjaro, and was able to back up Rebmann's assertion that the mountain really was adorned with snow.

❏ WD Faulty? – The great snow debate

(Continued from p95) Later on in the book Cooley forgets the conduct becoming to a 19th-century English gentleman, and the attacks on Rebmann border on the personal, beginning with an attack on Rebmann's eyesight:

Various and inconsistent reasons have been assigned for this failure [by Rebmann to see Kilimanjaro from a nearby hill], *but the only true explanation of it is contained in Mr Rebmann's confession that he is very short-sighted. He was unable to perceive, with the aid of a small telescope, Lake Ibe, three days distant to the south, which his followers could discern with the naked eye; nor could he even see the rhinoceroses in his path.*

And he goes on to finish his onslaught with this rather uncompromising, hysterical summary of Rebmann's accounts:

... betraying weak powers of observation, strong fancy, an eager craving for wonders, and childish reasoning, could not fail to awaken mistrust by their intrinsic demerits, even if there were no testimony opposed to them.

To further back up his argument, Cooley was able to point out a number of inconsistencies between Rebmann's and Krapf's accounts, such as the postulation by Krapf that the mountain is 12,500 feet (3800m) high – this after Rebmann had estimated the height to be closer to 20,000 feet (6000m, a remarkable guess by the myopic Rebmann).

Cooley's desire to prove Rebmann wrong was fuelled by more than just a desire to crush a young upstart in a field in which he considered himself the ultimate authority. He was also frightened that the existence of snow on Kilimanjaro would provide support for his rivals' theories at the expense of his own. In the big debate that raged in academic circles in the mid-1800s on the exact location of the source of the Nile, Cooley was firmly of the opinion that the river started from a large lake in Central Africa called Lake N'yassi. (Indeed, in the 1830s he even organized an expedition to prove his theory, though unfortunately it failed abysmally for reasons that remain rather obscure.) Aligned against him, Cooley's opponents, such as the geographer **Charles Beke**, preferred the idea that the Nile had its source in a range of mountains in the interior – possibly, as Encisco had stated in the sixteenth century, the legendary Mountains of the Moon – and looked upon the discovery of snow on an East African mountain as evidence to back up their theories. Indeed, when Rebmann and Krapf's accounts first reached Britain, Beke was only too keen to accept their every word as the gospel truth, and even went so far as to suggest that Kilimanjaro was now the most likely source of the Nile.

And that, for the next decade or so, was that: Rebmann and Krapf continued to visit Kilimanjaro, and continued to see snow there, while Cooley and the gang back in England continued to refute their every utterance and enjoy the majority of public opinion. Then in 1862, **Baron Carl von der Decken** visited Kilimanjaro (see top p97). Travelling with Richard Thornton, the baron was the first European to have another

FIRST ATTEMPTS AT THE SUMMIT

Baron von der Decken and Charles New

After the missionaries came the mountaineers. In August 1861 Baron Carl Claus von der Decken, a Hanoverian naturalist and traveller who had been residing in Zanzibar, accompanied by young English geologist Richard

European with him to back up his account. In trying to climb the mountain, the baron also came as close to the snow as any European ever had. His account of the expedition exploded Cooley's theories once and for all. As the brave baron wrote in his report:

During the night it snowed heavily and next morning the ground lay white all around us. Surely the obstinate Cooley will be satisfied now.

There was now a third eyewitness claiming to have seen snow on Kilimanjaro, and a baron at that; Cooley's position as a result began to look increasingly untenable, and his support began to ebb quietly away. If the baron really believed his testimony alone would persuade Cooley, however, he was much mistaken:

So the Baron says it snowed during the night...In December with the sun standing vertically overhead! The Baron is to be congratulated on the opportuneness of the storm. But it is easier to believe in the misrepresentations of man than in such an unheard-of eccentricity on the part of nature. This description of a snowstorm at the equator during the hottest season of the year, and at an elevation of only 13,000 feet, is too obviously a 'traveller's tale', invented to support Krapf's marvellous story of a mountain 12,500 feet high covered with perpetual snow.

But the redoubtable Cooley was fighting a lonely battle now. The Royal Geographical Society withdrew their backing, with Sir Roderick Murchison – presumably between mouthfuls of humble pie – finally admitting that Rebmann and Krapf were probably right after all. As if to add insult to Cooley's injured pride, the Society even awarded their Gold Medal in 1863 to von der Decken for his contributions to the sum of geographical knowledge of Africa. Fourteen years after Rebmann had first announced that there was snow on the equator, the world was finally listening to him. Cooley meanwhile, resolutely refused to believe in the existence of snow on Kilimanjaro, carrying his scepticism with him to the grave and leaving behind a reputation for stubbornness and ignorance that has survived to this day.

In Cooley's defence, one has to remember just how little was known about the continent then: few people from Europe had ever visited Africa; fewer still had penetrated beyond the coast; and of those who had, even fewer had survived to tell the tale. So the armchair scholars of Europe were forced to rely upon the sketchy mentions of Kili in historical records for their information; and of those descriptions, none since Ptolemy mentions anything about snow. As some compensation, perhaps, Cooley at least had the satisfaction of knowing that, while defeated in this particular battle, he gained at least a partial victory in the wider war: in 1858 a large body of water in the heart of central Africa was discovered, and was named **Lake Victoria** after Britain's sovereign. This lake would later be proved to be one of the sources of the Nile. Cooley may have got the name and location of this body of water wrong, but his supposition that the Nile had a lake as its source, and not a mountain, had been proved correct after all.

KILIMANJARO

Thornton, himself an explorer of some renown who had accompanied (and been sacked by) Livingstone during the latter's exploration of the Zambezi, made the first serious attempt on Kilimanjaro's summit. Initially, despite an entourage of over fifty porters, a manservant for von der Decken and a personal slave for Thornton, their efforts proved to be rather dismal and they had to turn back after just three days due to bad weather, having reached the rather puny height of just 8200ft (2460m). Proceeding to the west side of the mountain, however, the pioneering baron did at least enjoy an unobstructed view of Kibo peak on the way:

Bathed in a flood of rosy light, the cap that crowns the mountain's noble brow gleamed in the dazzling glory of the setting sun... Beyond appeared the jagged outlines of the eastern peak, which rises abruptly from a gently inclined plain, forming, as it were, a rough, almost horizontal platform. Three thousand feet lower, like the trough between two mighty waves, is the saddle which separates the sister peaks one from the other.

Von der Decken also provided the most accurate estimate yet for the height of both Kibo – which he guessed was between 19,812 and 20,655 feet (5943.6m to 6196.5m) – and Mawenzi (17,257-17,453 feet, or 5177.1-5235.9m). Thornton, for his part, correctly surmised that the mountain was volcanic, with Kibo the youngest and Shira the oldest parts of the mountain.

The following year, without Thornton, von der Decken reached a much more respectable 14,200ft (4260m) and furthermore reported being caught up in a snow storm. On his return to Europe, the baron described Kibo as a 'mighty dome, rising to a height of about 20,000 feet, of which the last three thousand are covered in snow'.

Following this second attempt, von der Decken urged Charles New (1840-75), a London-born missionary with the United Free Methodist Church in Mombasa, to tackle the mountain, and in 1871 New made a laudable attempt to reach the summit. That attempt failed, as did a second attempt in August of the same year; nevertheless, by choosing on the latter occasion to climb on the south-eastern face of Kibo where the ice cap at that time stretched almost to the base of the cone, New inadvertently wrote himself into the history books as the first European to cross the snow-line at the African Equator:

The gulf was all that now lay between myself and it, but what an all! The snow was on a level with my eye, but my arm was too short to reach it. My heart sank, but before I had time fairly to scan the position my eyes rested upon snows at my very feet! There it lay upon the rocks below me in shining masses, looking like newly washed and sleeping sheep! Hurrah! I cannot describe the sensations that thrilled my heart at that moment. Hurrah!

On this second expedition New also discovered the crater lake of Jala, the mountain's only volcanic lake, at Kilimanjaro's foot to the south-east of Mawenzi.

New's experiences on Kilimanjaro fanned his passion for the mountain and two years later he was back preparing for another assault on the still-unconquered peak. Unfortunately, the volatile tribes living at the foot of the mountain had other ideas and before New had even reached Kilimanjaro he was forced to return to the coast, having been stripped of all his possessions by the followers of the Chief of 'Moji' (Moshi), a highly unpleasant man by the name of Mandara (see p228). Broken in both health and spirits, the unfortunate New died soon after the attack.

As rumours of New's demise trickled back to Europe, enthusiasm among explorers for the still unconquered Kilimanjaro understandably waned, and for the next dozen years the mountain saw few foreign faces. Those that did visit usually did so on their way to somewhere else; people such as **Dr Gustav A Fischer** in 1883, who stopped in Arusha and visited Mount Meru on his journey to Lake Naivasha, and declared Kilimanjaro to be fit for 'European settlement', a statement that would have greater resonance later on in the century; and the Scottish geologist, **Joseph Thompson**, who became one of the first to examine properly the northern side of the mountain during an attempt to cross the Masai territories. He also attempted a climb of Kili, though having allowed himself only one day in which to complete the task his attempt was always doomed to failure, and in the end he reached no higher than the tree-line at about 2700m. (Failure though he may have been in this instance, his name lives on as a species of gazelle.)

The first European to venture back to the region with the specific intention of visiting Kilimanjaro arrived in the same year, 1883. In an expedition organized by the Royal Geographical Society, **Harry Johnston** arrived in East Africa with the aim of discovering and documenting the flora and fauna of Kilimanjaro. Though his work did little to further our understanding of the mountain, Johnston's trip is of anecdotal interest in that he later claimed in his biography that he was actually working undercover for the British Secret Service. No documentary evidence has ever turned up to back this claim (though there is a letter written by him to the foreign office in which he asks for 40 men and £5000 for the purpose of colonizing Kilimanjaro). Much doubt has been cast, too, upon his boast that he reached almost 5000m during his time on the mountain; while his (quite correct) suggestion that it was 'a mountain that can be climbed even without the aid of a walking stick' was widely ridiculed when first broadcast later that year. But whatever the inaccuracies and falsehoods of Johnston's recollections, his journey did at least assure other would-be Kilimanjaro visitors from Europe that the region was once again safe to visit. His visit also served to bring the mountain to the attention of European powers...

COLONIZATION

... a country as large as Switzerland enjoying a singularly fertile soil and healthy climate, ... within a few years it must be either English, French or German ... I am on the spot, the first in the field, and able to make Kilima-njaro as completely English as Ceylon
HH Johnston *The Kilima-njaro Expedition – A Record of Scientific Exploration in Eastern Equatorial Africa* (1886)

In describing the mountain thus, HH Johnston brought Kilimanjaro to the attention of the world's leading powers. Soon the two great colonizers in East Africa, Germany and Britain, were jockeying for position in the region. British missionaries were accused of putting the temporal interests of their country over the spiritual affairs of their flock, while for their part certain German nationals made no secret of the fact they wished to colonize Kilimanjaro. In 1884, the **Gesellschaft fur Deutsche Kolonisation** (GDK), a political party founded by

The biggest present ever?
There is a widely held belief that the kink in the border between Kenya and Tanzania near Kilimanjaro was created to satisfy the whim of Britain's reigning monarch at the time the border was first defined, Queen Victoria. According to the story, she magnanimously decided to give Kilimanjaro to her grandson, the future Wilhelm II, as a birthday present, following a complaint from him that while Britain had two snowy mountains in her East African territories (mounts Kili and Kenya), Germany was left with none. In order to effect the transfer of such a generous gift, the border had to be redrawn so that Kili fell to the south of the boundary in German territory, which is why the border has a strange kink in it to the east of the mountain.

Alas, however poetic the story, it is simply not true. The kink is there not because of Victoria's largesse, but as part of the agreement struck between Germany and Britain, and it exists not because of Kili, but Mombasa. Britain's territories in East Africa needed a port: the Germans already had Dar, and if the border between the two was to continue on the same bearing as it had taken to the west of Kilimanjaro, the Germans were going to end up with Mombasa too. So a kink was placed in the border to allow Mombasa to fall in British territory.

the 28-year old **Dr Carl Peters** with the ultimate goal of colonizing East Africa, persuaded a dozen local chiefs to throw off the rule of the (British controlled) **Sultan of Zanzibar** and, furthermore, to cede large sections of their territory to the German cause; one of Dr Peters' envoys, Dr Juhlke, even managed to establish a protectorate over Kilimanjaro in 1885. The British fought fire with fire in response, forcing two dozen chiefs (including some of those who had sided with the Germans) to swear allegiance to the sultan – and therefore indirectly to them. The situation was becoming dangerously volatile, with war looking increasingly likely. After further bouts of political manoeuvring, in October 1886 the two sides met in London and Berlin to define once and for all the boundary between British- and German-controlled East Africa and head off the possibility of war: the border between the British-ruled Kenya and German East Africa was now in place.

The first period of German rule over Kilimanjaro proved to be exceptionally harsh, and many Germans soon felt uneasy about the excesses of Dr Peters and his followers. In 1906 an enquiry opened in the Reichstag into the conduct of the doctor and his men, in which an open letter was read out to the court. Its contents give an idea of the hatred that the doctor and his men aroused in the locals:

What have you achieved by perpetual fights, by acts of violence and oppression? You have achieved, Herr Doctor, I have it from your own mouth in the presence of witnesses – that you and the gentlemen of your staff cannot go five minutes' distance from the fort without military escort. My policy enables me to make extensive journeys and shooting trips in Kilimanjaro and the whole surrounding country with never more than four soldiers. You have cut the knot with the sword and achieved that this most beautiful country has become a scene of war. Before God and man you are responsible for the devastation of flourishing districts, you are responsible for the deaths of our comrades Bulow and Wolfram, of our brave soldiers and of hundreds of Wachagga. And now I bring a supreme charge against you: Necessity did not compel you to this. You required deeds only in order that your name might not be forgotten in Europe.

Soon German soldiers were being attacked and killed and, with opposition to their rule growing stronger and more organized, they suffered a massive defeat at Moshi at the hands of the Chagga, led by Meli, Mandara's son (see p228).

Though the Germans regained control, it was clear to them that a more benevolent style of government was required if they were to continue ruling over their East African territories. This new 'caring colonialism' paid off, and for the last decade or so of their rule the Germans lived largely at peace with their subjects and even forged a useful alliance with the Chaggas during the German's push against the rebellious Masai tribes. The Germans also started the practice of hut-building on Kilimanjaro, establishing one at 8500ft (2550m), known as **Bismarck Hut**, and one at 11,500ft (3450m) known as **Peters' Hut**, after Dr Karl.

KILIMANJARO CONQUERED

While all this was going on, attempts to be the first to conquer Kilimanjaro continued apace. In 1887, **Count Samuel Teleki** of the Austro-Hungarian Empire made the most serious assault on Kibo so far, before 'a certain straining of the membrane of the tympanum of the ear' forced him to turn back. Then the American naturalist, **Dr Abbott**, who had primarily come to investigate the fauna and flora of the mountain slopes, made a rather reckless attempt. Abbott was struck down by illness fairly early on in the climb but his companion, Otto Ehlers of the German East African Company, pushed on, reaching (according to him) 19,680ft (5904m). Not for the first time in the history of climbing Kilimanjaro, however, this figure has been sceptically received by others – particularly as it is at least 8m above the highest point on the mountain!

Both Teleki and Abbott, however, played a part in the success of the eventual conqueror of Kilimanjaro, **Dr Hans Meyer**: Teleki, by providing information about the ascent to Meyer in a chance encounter during Meyer's first trip to the region in 1887; Abbott, by providing accommodation in Moshi for Meyer and his party during their successful expedition of 1889. Hans Meyer was a geology professor and the son of a wealthy editor from Leipzig (he himself later joined the editorial board and became its director, retiring in 1888, one year before the conquest of Kili, to become professor of Colonial Geography at Leipzig University). In all he made four trips to Kilimanjaro. Following the partial success of his first attempt in 1887, when he managed to reach 18,000ft (5400m), Meyer returned the following year for a second assault with experienced African traveller and friend Dr Oscar Baumann. Unfortunately, his timing couldn't have been worse: the **Abushiri War**, an Arab-led revolt against German traders on the East African coast, had just broken out and Meyer and his friend Baumann were captured, clapped into chains and held hostage by Sheikh Abushiri himself, the leader of the insurgency. In the end both escaped with their lives, but only after a ransom of ten thousand rupees was paid.

However, on his third attempt, in 1889, Meyer finally covered himself in glory. Though no doubt a skilful and determined climber, Meyer's success can largely be attributed to his recognition that the biggest obstacle to a successful assault was the lack of food available at the top. Meyer solved this by establishing camps at various points along the route that he had chosen for his attempt, including one at 12,980ft (3894m; Abbott's camp); one, Kibo camp, 'by a conspicuous rock' at 14,210ft (4263m); and, finally, a small encampment by a lava cave and just below the glacier line at 15,260ft (4578m). Thanks to these intermediary camps, Meyer was able to conduct a number of attempts on the summit without having to return to the foot of Kili to replenish supplies after each; instead, food was brought to the camps by the porters every few days.

Meyer's route to the top and the modern trails: a comparison
While no modern path precisely retraces Hans Meyer's original route to the summit, some of today's paths do occasionally coincide with the trail he blazed. For instance, Meyer and his climbing partner, Purtscheller, began their assault on the summit, on 28 September, 1889, from **Marangu** village. From there they headed due north up through the trees, arriving two days later at the very upper limits of the forest, where they made camp. Trekkers on the Marangu trail follow a similar itinerary today, though their starting point is a good deal higher than Meyer's at Marangu Gate, rather than Marangu village – which explains why trekkers today need only one day to reach the edge of the forest, while Meyer took two. It is also worth noting that, according to the beautifully drawn maps by Dr Bruno Hassenstein in Meyer's book *Across East African Glaciers*, his camp on this second night lay to the south-west of Kifunika Hill at an altitude of 8710ft (2613m), whereas the Mandara Huts lie a couple of hours' walk to the east of Kifunika, at a loftier 2743m.

On the third day, Meyer struck a westerly course, crossing the Mdogo (lesser) and Mkuba (greater) streams before making camp at an altitude of 9480ft (2844m). This was the all-important **Halfway Camp**, the intermediate station that Meyer would use as his base for tackling Kibo. In the history of climbing Kibo, no single spot on the entire mountain, save Uhuru Peak itself, has played a more prominent role: Harry Johnston had built some huts nearby during his reconnaissance mission of 1883; Meyer himself had camped here during his first expedition on the mountain, with Baron von Eberstein in 1887, and Abbott and Ehlers had also camped nearby in 1889, just a few months before Meyer and Purtscheller arrived. There's even evidence to suggest Count Teleki had also stopped here in 1887; in his account of their attempt on Kili in *Discovery by Count Teleki of Lakes Rudolf and Stefanie*, Lieutenant Ludwig von Höhnel speaks of making camp at 9390ft by a brook, near some old huts built originally by HH Johnston.

So where is this spot? There are plenty of clues. It is no coincidence, for example, that all these different parties chose to make camp at this site. Then, as now, campsites would have been chosen largely for their proximity to water and other amenities, so we can guess that a mountain stream or brook must run nearby. We also know that Meyer headed almost due west from his camp of the night before, and that the spot lies at around 2844m, above the tree-line. No modern campsite exactly fits this description – the Horombo Huts, the second night's accommodation on the Marangu trail, are too high up at 3657m. Rau Campsite, however, on the sadly now defunct Alternative Mweka/Kidia Route, seems a more plausible candidate: though this campsite is too high at 3260m, just below it is a glorious stretch of grasslands bordering the forest and near a mountain stream that would appear to fit the description given by Meyer. If the nineteenth-century explorers really did camp around there, they are to be congratulated on choosing one of the most beautiful places on the mountain. *(Continued opposite)*

He also had a considerable back-up party with him, including his friend and climbing companion, Herr Ludwig Purtscheller – a gymnastics teacher and alpine expert from Salzburg – two local headmen, nine porters, three other locals who would act as supervisors, one cook and one guide supplied by the local chief, Mareale, whom he had befriended during his first trip to the region. These men would help to carry the equipment and man the camps, with each kept in order by Meyer's strict code of discipline, where minor miscreants received ten lashes, and serious wrongdoers twenty.

Leaving most of his porters behind at this site – it would be their duty from now on to ferry supplies up to the camp from Marangu – Meyer then struck due north up to the Saddle, past the **Spring in the Snow**, or Schneequell (12,910ft, 3873m) and on to **Abbott's Camp** at 12,980ft (3894m), so-called by Meyer because he found an empty Irish stew tin and a sheet of the Salvation Army newspaper *En Avant* at this spot, and guessed that this must have been where his missionary friend Dr Abbott had camped a few months previously. As to their location, according to the maps in Meyer's book the Schneequell lies almost exactly due south of the East Lava Hill, the easternmost of the parasitic cones on the Saddle, and would seem to tie in fairly neatly with the Last Water Point, the Mua River, that lies below the Zebra Rocks on the Marangu Route (see p292). Abbott's Camp, meanwhile, lies to the north-north-west of here, at a point between the two Marangu Route paths to the Saddle.

From here, Meyer's path and the Marangu Route diverge for good. Where Marangu trekkers head roughly north across the Saddle, keeping Kibo to their left, in 1889 Meyer and his two companions, the alpine expert Purtscheller and Mwini Amani, their guide, set off directly for the summit in a more westerly direction, stopping for the night by a prominent rock at 14,200ft (4260m). This is **Viermannstein**, the Rock of Four Men, a place popular with Kili explorers in the nineteenth century. Unfortunately, because it lies far from any trail today, the site rarely features on modern trekking maps; for an approximate location, draw a line running east from the Barafu Campsite, and a second due south from the easternmost Triplet: the rock stands near to where they coincide.

Meyer's aim in 1889 was the **Ratzel Glacier**, on the south-eastern rim of Kibo. The glacier, though much reduced in size, is still there today: those walking up to the summit from the Barafu Campsite will see it on their right as they approach Stella Point. In Meyer's day the glacier covered the entire south-eastern lip of Kibo, and it was into this glacier that Meyer and Purtscheller, on 3 October, carved a series of steps that led all the way up to the crater rim and a height of 19,260ft (5778m).

On this occasion, considerations of time and weather forced them to withdraw back down to camp, having seen – but not scaled – the highest point on Kibo. After a day's rest and contemplation, however, and having decided to bivouac at **Lava Cave** on the slopes of Kibo at 15,960ft (4788m), the duo were ready for another assault on the summit. From there, at 3am on a cold October morning, they set off. At dawn they were at the foot of the glacier where, to their delight, they found the glacial stairway that they'd built two days previously was still there. By 8am they had reached and crossed a large crevasse, the only serious obstacle on the way to the summit. Just 45 minutes later they were back standing on the crater rim, the limit of their achievements two days previously. On this occasion, however, both time and weather were on their side. Walking around the southern rim of Kibo, they climbed three small hillocks, the middle of which they found by aneroid to be the highest by some 40 feet or more. *(Continued overleaf)*

KILIMANJARO

❑ **Meyer's route to the top and the modern trails: a comparison**
(Cont'd from p103) Thus at 10.30am on 6 October 1889, Meyer and Purtscheller wrote themselves into the history books as the first to make it to the highest point in Africa.

So where exactly did they gain **access to the crater**? According to Dr Hassenstein's maps, the Lava Cave lies at the northern end of the large South-East Valley, due west of the middle of the three triplets. That puts it somewhere to the north-east of the Barafu Campsite, and more than 150m higher, on one of the rocky spurs that run south-east down from Kibo. Where it certainly is *not*, though many a guide will tell you otherwise, is the Hans Meyer Cave on the Marangu Route, which at 5151m is simply too high and too far north. The notch by which they gained access to the crater lay almost exactly north-west of this Lava Cave Camp. Though again this is pure guesswork, all the evidence does seem to point to the fact that Meyer and Purtscheller on this particular occasion passed into the crater rim from a spot very near to **Stella Point** (5745m); the difference in height (Meyer estimated the height at this point on the crater to be 5778m) can possibly be ascribed to the fact that Meyer's estimates tend to be over-estimates (his height for Uhuru Peak, for example, is over 6000m) – perhaps because in Meyer's day there was a lot more ice at the summit, which would have raised the altitudes.

Having christened the summit after their Kaiser and taken the topmost stone from the summit as a souvenir (a stone that Meyer later gave to the Kaiser, who used it as a paperweight), the pair then hurried back to Abbott's camp on the Saddle. The next few days were spent trying to conquer **Mawenzi**, but with no success, the mountain peak defeating them wholly on the first occasion on 13 October, and an attack of colic brought on by some over-ripe bananas stalling their second attempt two days later. Before returning to civilization, however, they spent five more days revisiting Kibo: on 17 October they headed to the crater's northern side, where they reached 5572m before confronting a sheer wall of ice that forced them to retreat; and then finally, on the 18th, they approached the crater from the east.

The path Meyer took up to the crater on this occasion is not too dissimilar to the trail up to Gillman's from the Kibo Huts. Meyer and Purtscheller on this final climb bivouacked at a location they called **Old Fireplace** because, to their considerable surprise, they found the remains of a recent campfire there, along with the bones of an eland and some pieces of banana matting. This camp, according to Meyer, sat at an altitude of 15,390ft (4617m). It's just possible, therefore, that the Old Fireplace is in fact the site that we now call **Jiwe Lainkoyo**, which many local mountain guides insist was once a popular hunters' campsite. From the Old Fireplace, Meyer and Purtscheller climbed up the snow-clad slopes of Kibo once more, gaining access into the crater via a cleft in the rim that is now known as **Hans Meyer Notch**, and which lies just a few hundred metres to the north of Gillman's Point. Though they failed in their attempts to reach the inner cone of the volcano, they were at least able to confirm that the floor of the crater was made up of a mixture of mud and ashes. They were also startled when, peering into the first cone, they came across the carcass of an antelope (which possibly explains what the leopard, whose frozen body was found up here many years later, was doing at this altitude).

After one more unsuccessful attempt on Mawenzi, Meyer and Purtscheller finally decided to call it a day, and on 22 October they said goodbye to the Saddle for the last time. The pair had spent 16 days between 15,000 and 20,000 feet. During this time they had made four ascents of Kibo, reaching the crater three times and the summit once, and three sorties on Mawenzi, reaching the 5049m summit of Purtscheller's Spitze but failing to reach the very top.

The size of his entourage, however, shouldn't detract from the magnitude of Meyer's achievement: as well as the usual hardships associated with climbing Kilimanjaro, Meyer also had to contend along the way with deserters from his party, a lack of any clear path, elephant traps (large pits dug by locals and concealed by ferns to trap the unwary pachyderm), as well as the unpleasant, rapacious chief of Moshi, Mandara (see p228). It is also worth noting here that Meyer did not begin his walk *on* the mountain, as today's visitors do, but in Mombasa, 14 days by foot, according to Meyer, from the Kilimanjaro town of Taveta!

Then there was the snow and ice, so much more prevalent in the late 1800s on Kili than it is today. Above 4500m Meyer had to trek upon snow for virtually the whole day, even though his route up Kibo from the Saddle is not too dissimilar to that taken by the vast majority of the thousands of trekkers every year – and today there is no snow on the route. The added difficulties caused by the snow are well described in Meyer's book *Across East African Glaciers*. Rising at 2.30am for their first assault on the summit, Meyer and Purtscheller spent most of the morning carving a stairway out of a sheer ice-cliff, every stair laboriously hewn with an average of twenty blows of the ice axe. (The cliff formed part of the Ratzel Glacier, named by Meyer after a geography professor in his native

The conquest of Kilimanjaro
Taking out a small German flag, which I had brought with me for the purpose in my knapsack, I planted it on the weather-beaten lava summit with three ringing cheers, and in virtue of my right as its discoverer christened this hitherto unknown and unnamed mountain peak – the loftiest spot in Africa and the German Empire – Kaiser Wilhelm's Peak [now known as Uhuru Peak]. Then we gave three cheers more for the Emperor, and shook hands in mutual congratulation. **Hans Meyer** *Across East African Glaciers*

Leipzig.) As a result, by the time they reached the eastern lip of the crater, the light was fading fast and the approach of inclement weather forced them to return before they could reach the highest point of that lip.

On their second attempt, however, three days later on 6 October 1889, and with the stairs still intact in the ice from the first ascent, they were able to gain the eastern side of the rim by mid-morning; from there it was but a straightforward march to the three small tumescences situated on the higher, southern lip of the crater, the middle one of which was also the highest point of the mountain.

AFTER MEYER

Mawenzi, Pastor Reusch and a frozen leopard
In the decades following Meyer's successful assault on Kili, few followed in his footsteps. Meyer himself climbed again in 1898, though this time he got only as

KILIMANJARO

far as the crater rim. In 1909 surveyor M Lange climbed all the way to Uhuru Peak, and in doing so became only the second to reach the summit of Kilimanjaro – a full twenty years after the first.

The conquest of the last peak on Kilimanjaro, that of the summit of Mawenzi (called, somewhat perversely, Hans Meyer Peak), was achieved by the climbers **Edward Oehler** and **Fritz Klute** on 29 July 1912. Thus, 64 years after the first European had clapped eyes on Kilimanjaro, both of its main peaks had been successfully climbed. As an encore, Oehler and Klute made the third successful attempt on Kibo and the first from the western side. In the same year, **Walter Furtwangler** and **Ziegfried Koenig** achieved the fourth successful climb, and became the first to use skis to descend. Two more successful assaults occurred before the outbreak of World War One, and **Frau von Ruckteschell** kept up the German's impressive record on Kilimanjaro by becoming the first woman to reach Gillman's Point.

Fresh attempts on Kilimanjaro were suspended for a while during World War One. The countryside around Kilimanjaro became the scene of some vicious fighting, including Moshi itself, which was attacked by British forces in March 1916. Paul von Lettow Vorbeck, the German commander, went down in military history at this time as the man who led the longest tactical retreat ever. With the German's defeat, however, Kilimanjaro, along with the rest of German East Africa, reverted to British rule.

After the war, attention turned away from Kibo to the lesser-known Mawenzi. In 1924 **George Londt** of South Africa became, by accident, the first to climb South Peak (he was aiming for Hans Meyer Peak but got lost); the peak (4958m), was named after him. Three years later three English mountaineers climbed Mawenzi, including **Sheila MacDonald**, the first woman to do so; the trio then climbed Kibo, with Ms MacDonald writing her name into the record books again as the first woman to complete the ascent to Uhuru Peak. In 1930 two famous British mountaineers, HW Tilman and Eric Shipton, names more usually associated with Everest, climbed Mawenzi's Nordecke Peak – again, like Londt, by accident.

While all this was happening on Mawenzi, over on Kibo another man was writing himself into the history of Kili: **Pastor Richard Reusch**. Missionary for the Lutheran Church, former officer in the Cossack army and long-time Marangu resident, Reusch climbed the mountain on no less than 40 different occasions. During his first assault on the summit in 1926 he discovered the frozen leopard on the crater rim that would later inspire Hemingway (Reusch cut off part of an ear as a souvenir), while on another sortie the following year he became the first to gaze down into the inner crater, a crater that he was later to give his name to. Later work by mountaineer **HW Tilman** and vulcanologist **JJ Richard** led to confirmation, in 1942, that Kilimanjaro was still active, and while this led to some local panic, in 1957 the Tanganyika Geological Survey and the University of Sheffield were able to allay fears by declaring the volcano to be dormant and almost extinct.

❏ **A war-time climb**

By great good fortune, I was recently introduced to someone who had climbed Kilimanjaro over 60 years ago while on leave during World War II. Petty Officer Jim Rowe, together with his friend, radio operator John Hemsley, were stationed for nearly three years at the Royal Naval Air Station at Tanga and in 1944 they decided to spend their leave climbing God's greatest mountain. Accompanying them on their expedition was Lieutenant Peter Paul, on leave from Nairobi, whom they met at the Kibo Hotel.

Climbing Kilimanjaro 60 years ago was a decidedly trickier affair than it is today. For one thing, the equipment and clothing would have been heavier and 'colder' than that used by today's Gore-tex lined, fleece-clad trekkers. Our understanding of the causes and symptoms of altitude sickness has also improved a great deal in the last 60 years. This is perhaps one reason why the party allowed only five days for the entire expedition – which in turn goes some way to explaining why only Jim made it to the crater!

These differences are, of course, only to be expected. What did surprise me, however, were the *similarities* between their expedition and today's treks. For example, not only is the Kibo Hotel, who organized their trek, still operating (see p192) but the composition of their crew – six porters, a cook and a guide, Yohanne – is not too dissimilar to those accompanying today's parties. Furthermore, they followed a path that bears a strong resemblance to today's Marangu Route, with nights spent at Bismarck, Peters and Kibo Huts (where today we stop at Mandara, Horombo and Kibo huts); and in his diary, Jim bemoans the lack of wildlife on the mountain, with nothing but a few lizards spotted during the five days – a complaint that will resonate with many a trekker today.

The striking similarities continue when one compares the emotions and opinions of Jim and his party and those of today's trekker. Take Jim's diary entry, for example, of the final, steep ascent to Gillman's Point:

'*Here, on the scree, I think that it is willpower that keeps one going more than anything else. The oxygen is scarce and I took ten steps and then stopped for a while to regain my breath. The top never seems to get any nearer and one feels inclined to say "Oh what's the use anyway" and turn round and come back.*'

Then there's Jim's assessment upon returning to Earth at the end of the trek:

'*I think, to sum up, I can say that it was a very good experience and I'm glad that I went. But I do not think that I should want to do it again.*'

As most trekkers, whether successful or not, would surely agree, it's a description that is just as true today as it was over sixty years ago.

KILIMANJARO TODAY

The twentieth century witnessed the inevitable but gradual shift away from exploration towards tourism. The most significant change occurred in 1932 with the building of Kibo Hut; name plates and signs were put up too, as the mountain was gradually made more tourist-friendly. With a ready base for summit assaults now established, tourists began to trickle into Tanzania to make their own attempt on Africa's greatest mountain.

In 1959 the mountain became the focus for nationalist feelings and a symbol of the Tanganyikans' independence aspirations following Julius Nyerere's speech to the Tanganyika Legislative Assembly (see p66 for quote). Nyerere eventually got his wish and, after independence was granted in 1961, a torch

For the record

● **Fastest ascent of Kilimanjaro** As mentioned in the introduction to this book, in 2001 Bruno Brunod of Italy managed to reach Uhuru Peak from Marangu Gate in just 5 hours 38 minutes and 40 seconds. This remains the fastest verified ascent of Kilimanjaro. There are a couple of unverified claims, however, with Sean Burch of Virginia claiming to have made it to the top on 7 June 2005 in 5 hours 28 minutes, and Christian Stangl of Austria claiming to have achieved the summit in 5 hours 36 minutes in October 2004.

Incidentally, Bruno then ran back down the same way, reaching Marangu Gate just 2 hours 56 minutes and 12 seconds after summiting. Adding these up, his total time on the mountain was just over 8 hours 30 minutes. Impressive, but it's not the record...

● **Fastest ascent and descent** This belongs to Simon Mtuy (Tanzania), who runs the Summit Expeditions and Nomadic Experience trekking agency in Moshi (see p186). On December 26, 2004, Simon achieved the incredible time of 8 hours 27 minutes. Apparently, it took Simon 6 hours exactly to reach the summit via the Umbwe Route, and after seven minutes to catch his breath, just two hours 20 minutes to complete the descent to Mweka Gate. In fact, it's likely that Simon will be the holder for a while. His ultrarunning background combined with the fact that he climbs the mountain regularly mean that even if his rivals do beat his time, their reign is likely to be shortlived.

Nor is that the end of Simon's record-breaking exploits, for on the 22 February 2006 Simon climbed from Umbwe Gate to the summit and back again in a time of 9 hours and 19 minutes and, in doing so, achieved the **fastest ever unaided ascent and descent** (by unaided, they mean that Simon carried his own food, water and clothing). This despite suffering from a nasty bout of diarrhoea, as well as a three-minute break at the top to video himself, plus two further breaks to vomit!

● **Fastest ascent (female)** Rebecca Rees-Evans (UK), part of the Team Kilimanjaro organization that organizes most of these record attempts, achieved the time of 13 hours 16 minutes and 37 seconds in reaching Uhuru Peak via the Marangu Route.

● **Youngest person to reach the summit** Though we've heard rumours of a 7-year-old boy who climbed Kili, we have been unable to find any details. However, according to a report in a South African newspaper, Joshua Schumacher, a South African now living in Swaziland, managed to reach the summit early in 2002 aged just 9! An impressive feat, not least because in breaking the record he must also have broken all sorts of rules, including the one that says you have to be at least ten to climb Kili! He beat the previous record holder, another South African kid by the name of Antoine van Heerden, who was a geriatric 10 years and 11 months – though at least Antoine can comfort himself with the fact that he remain the youngest *legal* conqueror of Kili.

● **Oldest person to reach the summit** Curiously, according to the *Guinness Book of World Records* American Carl Haupt holds the record for the oldest man to summit Kilimanjaro, being 79 when he reached the top in 2004. This must have come as something of a surprise to Frenchman Valtée Daniel, who has long been regarded as the oldest man ever to reach Africa's highest point – and considering he was 87 when he made it to the top, we can see no reason why he's not still the record holder. One can assume only that Monsieur Daniel's expedition could not be verified according to the regulations governing Guinness records – though it seems a bit rough on the old fella to have his record snatched away by such a whippersnapper. However, as you may have already noticed in the introduction to this book, Valtée's achievement hasn't been entirely forgotten and most people, including us, continue to consider Valtée the main man. So come back when you're older, Carl, and try again.

was indeed placed on the summit of Kilimanjaro. Independence also provided Tanganyika with the chance to rename many of the features of the mountain; in particular, the very summit, named Kaiser Wilhelm Peak by Hans Meyer, was renamed Uhuru Peak – Uhuru meaning, appropriately, 'Freedom' in Swahili.

Since this mountain's moment of patriotic glory, the story of Kilimanjaro has largely been about tourism. The early trickle of tourists of seventy years ago is nowadays more akin to a flood, with visitor numbers still increasing exponentially, from less than a thousand in the late 1950s to 11,000 in the mid-1990s, to the 35,000-plus we see today.

What has been an economic boon to the people of Kilimanjaro, however, has brought little benefit to the mountain itself. With the increase in the number of trekkers comes commensurately greater numbers of pressures and problems. Its soil is being eroded, its vegetation is being burnt or chopped, its wildlife is disappearing and its glaciers are melting. Along with these environmental pressures come challenges to its dignity, too, as climbers dream up ever more bizarre ways of climbing to the top, whether it's driving up by motorcycle or walking in fancy dress, as we discussed in the introduction to this book.

Then there's the problem of fire. In February 1999 a huge blaze swept across the upper slopes of Kilimanjaro. The fires were first discovered on 6 February and over the next five days 70 hectares were destroyed. Thanks to the combined efforts of 347 villagers, park rangers and 40 soldiers of the 39th Squadron of the Tanzanian People's Defence Force, the main blaze was eventually brought under control, though not before considerable damage had been done to the mountain. Evidence of fire can still be seen in places on Kili, particularly in the moorland zone on the Marangu and Machame routes where new plants now grow between the charred remains of branches and shrubs. Further fires, particularly on the Shira Plateau, have caused yet more lasting damage.

Depressingly but unsurprisingly, human activity is believed to have been behind the fires. Twenty-two men from the Kamwanga and Rongai districts were arrested for the 1999 fire, having been identified as the culprits by six hundred villagers in a secret ballot. The men were all squatters living illegally in the protected areas of the national park; according to one minister who visited the scene of the devastation, there were up to ten thousand such squatters living in Kilimanjaro's forests, most of whom made their living by collecting honey. It is believed that a cigarette butt discarded by one of them started the blaze, though others have pointed an accusing finger at local farmers who like to clear their farms by fire before the start of the annual rains the following month.

Yet no matter how many indignities are heaped upon it, Kilimanjaro continues to inspire both awe and respect in all who gaze upon it. And while man will continue to visit in droves and in his clumsy, careless way will carry on defacing and demeaning Africa's most charismatic place, setting it ablaze and covering it with litter, the mountain itself remains essentially the same powerful, ineffably beautiful sight it always was; perhaps because, while we throw all that we can at it, the Roof of Africa does what it always has done – and what it does best: it simply rises above it all.

Flora and fauna

FLORA

It is said that to climb up Kilimanjaro is to walk through **four seasons in four days**. It is true, of course, and nowhere is this phenomenon more apparent than in its flora. The variety of flora found on Kilimanjaro can be ascribed in part to the mountain's tremendous height and in part to its proximity to both the equator and the Indian Ocean. Add to this the variations in climate, solar radiation and temperature from the top of the mountain to the bottom (temperatures are estimated to drop by 1°C for every 200m gain in altitude), and you end up with the ideal conditions for highly differentiated and distinctive vegetation zones. In all, Kilimanjaro is said to have between four and six distinctive zones depending on who you read. A description of each follows, while a picture chart of the more common species of flower can be found opposite p112.

Cultivated zone and forest (800m-2800m)

The forest zone, along with the cultivated zone that lies below it, together receive the most rainfall – about 2300mm per year – of any part of the mountain. The forest zone also houses the greatest variety of both fauna (see p112) and flora.

Enormous **camphorwoods** flourish at this altitude, as do **fig**, **podocarpus** and, around Marangu Gate, the grey-barked **eucalyptus**, one of the few non-natives and a tree that the authorities are currently trying to eradicate. Giant ferns enjoy these damp conditions too, as, clearly, does *Usnea sp.*, or **old man's beard**, which lies draped over most of the branches, particularly at the upper limit of the forest zone. Also hanging from the trees is the *Begonia meyeri johannis*, with sweet smelling white and pink flowers that often litter the path like confetti. On the drier northern and western slopes **juniper** and **olive trees** proliferate, with one species, *Olea kilimandscharica*, indigenous to the mountain. Back on the southern side, towards the upper limit of the zone the smooth

Protecting Kilimanjaro

Kilimanjaro has enjoyed some form of protection since the early years of the twentieth century under German rule, when the mountain and surrounding area were designated as a game preserve. In 1921 this status was upgraded to become a forest and game preserve, thereby protecting the precious cloud forest that beards Kili's lower slopes. Another change in 1957 saw the Tanganyika National Parks Authority propose that the mountain become a national park, though this wasn't actually realized until 1973, when Kilimanjaro National Park (KINAPA) was formed; a park that, for simplicity's sake, the authorities decided would include all land above 2700m. KINAPA didn't actually officially open until 1977; twelve years later, in 1989, the park was declared a World Heritage Site by UNESCO.

grey *Ilex mitis*, with its characteristic red and yellow fruit, becomes the dominant tree, before finally giving way to the first of the giant heathers as the forest zone comes to an end. The star of the montane forest zone, however, is the beautiful flower ***Impatiens kilimanjari***, an endemic fleck of dazzling red and yellow in the shape of an inch-long tuba. You'll see them by the side of the path on the southern side of the mountain. Vying for the prime piece of real estate that exists between the roots of the trees are other, equally elegant flowers including the beautiful violet *Viola eminii* and *Impatiens pseudoviola*.

Perhaps the most unusual aspect of Kilimanjaro's forest zone, however, is not the plants and trees that it does have, as one that it doesn't. Kili is almost unique in East Africa in not having any bamboo at the upper limit of the forest zone, possibly because it is one of the driest mountains and cannot support bamboo stands the way other African mountains can. As a result, the forest zone ends suddenly, with little warning, throwing us immediately into the less shady trails of the ...

Heath and moorland (2800m-4000m)

These two zones overlap, and together occupy the area immediately above the forest from around 2800m to 4000m – known as the **low alpine zone**. Temperatures can drop below 0°C up here and most of the precipitation that does fall here comes from the mist that is an almost permanent fixture at this height.

Immediately above the forest zone is the **alpine heath**. Rainfall here is around 1300mm per year. The giant heather *Erica excelsa* and the similar but less bushy *Erica arborea* both grow in abundance. The latter also exists in the upper part of the forest zone, where it can grow to ten metres or more; the higher you go, however, the less impressive the specimens, with many refusing to grow beyond 2.5-3m. Grasses now dominate the mountain slopes, too, picked out here and there with some splendid wild flowers including the yellow-flowered *Protea kilimandscharica*, an indigenous rarity that can be seen on the Mweka and Marangu trails and, so we've been told, around Maundi Crater – the best place for botanists to spot wild flowers. Another favourite, and one most readers will recognize instantly, is the back-garden favourite *Kniphofia thomsonii*, better known to most as the **red-hot poker**. A whole raft of *Helichrysum* species – some yellow, daisy-like flowers, others looking grey and shiny like living potpourri – make their first appearance here too, though certainly not their last. Climbing higher, you'll begin to come across **sedges** such as *Mariscus kerstenii*.

The shrubs are shrinking now: *Philippia trimera* is the most common of them, along with the gorse-like *Adenocarpus* which it often grows beside; the prettiest shrub in the upper reaches of the heath zone is the pink-flowered *Blaeria filago*. Climbing ever further, you'll soon reach the imperceptible boundary of the moorland zone, which tends to have clearer skies but an even cooler climate. Average per annum precipitation is now down to 525mm. The most distinctive plant in this area – indeed, on the entire mountain – is the senecio, or **giant** or **tree groundsel**, of which there are two different species thriving on Kilimanjaro: the *Senecio kilimanjari* occurs between 2450 and 4000m, can grow up to 5m high, and on the rare occasion it flowers the petals themselves are yellow and grow from a one-metre-long spike; while the *Senecio* *johnstonii cottonii* is found only above 3600m, and has duller, mustard-coloured flowers. Groundsels tend to favour the damper, more sheltered parts of the mountain, which is why you'll see them in abundance near the Barranco Campsite as well as other, smaller valleys and ravines.

Sharing roughly the same kind of environment is the strange *Lobelia deckenii*, another endemic species and one that bears no resemblance to the lobelias that you'll find in your back garden. These strange, either phallic or cabbage-shaped plants take eight years to flower (the blue flowers are hidden inside the leaves to protect them from frost), and are a favourite with the *Nectarinia johnstoni*, the dazzling green malachite sunbird.

Alpine desert (4000m-5000m)

By the time you reach the Saddle, only three species of tussock grass and a few everlastings can withstand the extreme conditions. This is the **alpine desert**, where plants have to survive in drought conditions (precipitation here is less than 200mm per year), and put up with both inordinate cold and intense sun, usually in the same day. Up to about 4700m you'll also find the *Asteraceae*, a bright yellow daisy-like flower and the most cheerful-looking organism at this height.

Ice cap (5000m-5895m)

On Kibo, almost nothing lives. There is virtually no water. On the rare occasions that precipitation occurs, most of the moisture instantly disappears into the porous rock or is locked away in the glaciers.

That said, specimens of *Helichrysum newii* – an everlasting that truly deserves its name – have been found near a fumarole in the Reusch Crater, a good 5760m above sea level, and moss and lichen are said to exist right up to the summit. While these lichens may not be the most spectacular of plants, it may interest you to know that their growth rate on the upper reaches of Kilimanjaro is estimated to be just 0.5mm in diameter per year; for this reason, scientists have concluded that the larger lichens on Kilimanjaro could be amongst the oldest living things on Earth, being hundreds and possibly thousands of years old!

FAUNA

URGENT MESSAGE:
Location: *Amboseli Game Park, Kenya*
Human population: *150*
Baboon population: *90,000*
Meteorological conditions: *Severe drought*
Water supplies: *Nil*
Situation: *Mutilated bodies discovered. Baboons have turned into man-eating primates –*
POSITION DESPERATE!
Taken from the advertising blurb of the terrible 1980s' horror film *In the Shadow of Kilimanjaro*, supposedly based on a true story. You may like to consider that when you're walking past a troop of them on the first day of your Meru climb!

In order to see much in the way of fauna, you have to be either very lucky or, it would seem, an author of a book on Kilimanjaro. When Hans Meyer was coming down from the mountain in 1889 he spotted an elephant on the slopes. In

Lantana camara

Cannaceae Red-spotted canna

Cassia didymobotrya

Impatiens pseudoviola

Impatiens kilimanjari

Desmodium repandum

Begonia meyeri-johannis

Dracaena afromontana

Fragraria Wild strawberry

Parochaetus communis

Plectranthus sylvestris

Bearded lichen

Hypericum revolutum
St John's Wort

*Bidens
kilimandsharica*

*Gladiolus
watsonides*

*Trifolium
usambarensis*

Cycnium

Kniphofia thomsonii
Red hot poker

*Leonotis
nepetifolia*

Solanaceae brugmansia
Angel's trumpet flower

Thunbergia alata
Black-eyed Susan

*Dierama
pendulum*

*Stoebe
kilimandsharica*

Protea kilimandsharica
(above and right with
malachite sunbird)

*Carduus
keniensis*

*Hebenstretia
kilimandscharium*

Lobelia deckenii

Helichrysum brownei

Lobelia deckenii
(flowers)

Helichrysum newii

*Helichrysum meyeri-
johannis*

Senecio kilimanjari
Tree Groundsel

Colobus monkey

Tree hyrax

Arusha National Park: Giraffe

Baboon

Suny deer

Arusha National Park: Buffalo

Two-horned chameleon

White-necked raven

Mountain buzzard

Streaky seed-eater

1926 a leopard was found frozen in the ice at a place we now call Leopard Point – providing Hemingway with the inspiration for *The Snows of Kilimanjaro*. The mountaineer, HW Tilman, saw 27 eland on the Saddle when he passed this way in 1937, with each, according to him, especially adapted for the freezing conditions with thicker fur. In 1962, renowned travel writer Wilfred Thesiger and two companions were accompanied to the summit by five African hunting dogs. Though the dogs then turned round and disappeared after the three men made the summit, paw-prints in the ice proved that this wasn't the first time they had climbed to the top.

More recently, Rick Ridgeway claimed he saw a leopard on his ascent, as did Geoffrey Salisbury while leading his group of blind climbers to the summit; and in 1979 a local guide called David was savaged by a pack of African hunting dogs above the Mandara Huts and lost a finger.

We mention these stories to demonstrate that the more exotic fauna of East Africa does occasionally venture onto the mountain. It just doesn't happen very often, with most animals preferring to be somewhere where there aren't 35,000 people marching around every year. So in all probability you will see virtually nothing during your time on the mountain beyond the occasional monkey or mouse. Nevertheless, keep your mouth shut and your eyes open and you never know...

Forest and cultivated zones

Animals are more numerous down in the forest zone than anywhere else on the mountain; unfortunately, so is the cover provided by trees and bushes, so sightings remain rare. As with the four-striped grass mice of Horombo (see p230), it tends to be those few species for whom the arrival of man has been a boon rather than a curse that are the easiest to spot, including the **blue monkeys**, which appear daily near the Mandara Huts and which are not actually blue but grey or black with a white throat. These, however, are merely the plainer relatives of the beautiful **colobus monkey**, which has the most enviable tail in the animal kingdom; you can see a troop of these at the start of the forest zone on the Rongai Route, by Londorossi Gate in the west and, so we've been told, near the Mandara Huts. **Olive baboons**, **civets**, **leopards**, **mongooses** and **servals** are said to live in the mountain's forest as well, though sightings are extremely rare; here, too, lives the **bush pig** with its distinctive white stripe running along its back from head to tail.

Then there's the **honey badger**. Don't be fooled by the rather cute name. As well as being blessed with a face only its mother could love, these are the most powerful and fearless carnivores for their size in Africa. Even lions give them a wide berth. You should too: not only can they cause a lot of damage to your person, but the thought of having to tell your friends that, of all the bloodthirsty creatures that roam the African plains, you got savaged by a badger, is too shaming to contemplate. Of a similar size, the **aardvark** has enormous claws but unlike the honey badger this nocturnal, long-snouted anteater is entirely benign. So fear not: as the old adage goes, aardvark never killed anyone. Both aardvarks and honey badgers are rarely, if ever, seen on the mountain. Nor are **porcupines**, Africa's largest rodents. Though also present in this zone,

KILIMANJARO

they are both shy and nocturnal and your best chances of seeing one is as roadkill on the way to Dar es Salaam.

Further down, near or just above the cultivated zone, **bushbabies** are more easily heard than seen as they come out at night and jump on the roofs of the huts. Here, too, is the **small-spotted genet** with its distinctive black-and-white tail, and the noisy, chipmunk-like **tree hyrax**.

One creature you definitely won't see at any altitude is the rhinoceros. Although a **black rhinoceros** was seen a few years ago on the north side of the mountain, it is now believed that over-hunting has finally taken its toll of this most majestic of creatures; Count Teleki (see p101) is said to have shot 89 of them during his time in East Africa, including four in one day, and there are none on or anywhere near Kilimanjaro today.

Heath, moorland and above

Just as plant-life struggles to survive much above 2800m, so animals too find it difficult to live on the barren upper slopes. Yet though we may see little, there are a few creatures living on Kilimanjaro's higher reaches.

Baboons in the branches of a Dum palm
(from *Across East African Glaciers*, Hans Meyer, 1891)

Above the treeline you'll be lucky to see much. The one obvious exception to this rule is the **four-striped grass mouse**, which clearly doesn't find it a problem eking (or should that be eeking?) out an existence at high altitude; indeed, if you're staying in the Horombo Huts on the Marangu Route, one is probably running under your table while you read this, and if you stand outside for more than a few seconds at any campsite you should see them scurrying from rock to rock. Other rodents present at this level include the **harsh-furred** and **climbing mouse** and the **mole rat**, though all are far more difficult to spot.

For anything bigger than a mouse, your best chance above 2800m is either on the Shira Plateau, where **lions** are said to roam occasionally, or on the northern side of the mountain on the Rongai Route. Kenya's Amboseli National Park lies at the foot of the mountain on this side and many animals, particularly **elephants**, amble up the slopes from time to time. **Grey** and **red duikers**, **elands** and **bushbucks** are perhaps the most commonly seen animals at this altitude, though sightings are still extremely rare. None of these larger creatures live above the tree-line of Kilimanjaro permanently, however, and as with the **leopards**, **giraffes** and **buffaloes** that occasionally make their way up the slopes, they are, like us, no more than day-trippers.

On **Kibo** itself the entymologist George Salt found a species of **spider** that was living in the **alpine zone** at altitudes of up to 5500m. What exactly these high-altitude arachnids live on up there is unknown – though Salt himself reckoned it was probably the flies that blew in on the wind, of which he found a few, and which appeared to be unwilling or unable to fly. What is known is that the spiders live underground, better to escape the rigours of the weather.

Hornbill

Avifauna

Kilimanjaro is great for birdlife. The cultivated fields on the lower slopes provide plenty of food, the forest zone provides shelter and plenty of nesting sites, while the barren upper slopes are ideal hunting grounds for raptors.

In the **forest**, look out for the noisy dark green **Hartlaub's turaco** (there was one nesting near the first-day lunch stop on the Machame Route), easy to distinguish when it flies because of its bright red underwings. The **silvery-cheeked hornbills** and **speckled mousebirds** hang around the fruit trees in the forest, particularly the fig trees. There's also the **trogon** which, despite a red belly, is difficult to see because it remains motionless in the branches. Smaller birds include the **Ruppell's robin chat** (black and white head, grey top, orange lower half) and the **common bulbul**, with a black crest and yellow beneath the tail.

White-necked raven

Further up the slopes, the noisy, scavenging, garrulous **white-necked raven** is a constant presence on the heath and moorland zones, eternally hovering on the breeze around the huts and lunch-stops on the lookout for any scraps. Smaller but just as ubiquitous is the **alpine chat**, a small brown bird with white side feathers in its tail, and the **streaky seed-eater**, another brown bird (this time with streaks on its back) that often hangs around the huts. The **alpine swift** also enjoys these misty, cold conditions. The prize for the most beautiful bird on the mountain, however, goes to the dazzling **scarlet-tufted malachite sunbird**. Metallic green save for a small scarlet patch on either side of its chest, this delightful bird can often be seen hovering above the grass, hooking its long beak in to reach the nectar from the giant lobelias or feeding on the lobelias.

Augur buzzard

Climbing further and we come to raptor territory. You'll rarely see these birds up close as they spend most of the day gliding on the currents looking for prey. The **mountain** and **augur buzzards** are regularly spotted hovering above the Saddle (a specimen of the former also hangs about the School Huts when it's quiet); these are impressive birds in themselves – especially if you're lucky enough to see one up close – though neither is as large as the enormous **crowned eagle** and the rare **lammergeyer**, a giant vulture with long wings and a wedge tail.

The People of Kilimanjaro: The Chagga

With regard to the Chagga people, they are a fine, well-built race. Their full development of bone and muscle being probably due to the exercise they all have to take in moving about on steep hills: they seem intellectually superior to the general run of coast Natives, and despite their objectionable traits (almost always present in the uneducated Native), such as lying, dirty habits, thieving, &c., they are certainly a very nice and attractive race.
Rev A Downes Shaw in 1924 in his book *To Chagga and Back — An Account of a Journey to Moshi, the Capital of Chagga, Eastern Equatorial Africa.*

Mount Kilimanjaro is the homeland of the **Chagga** people, one of Tanzania's largest ethnic groups. It is fair to say that when you are in Moshi, Marangu or Machame, there is little indication that you are in a 'Chagga town'. Yet in the smaller villages, though waning year by year, traditional Chagga culture remains fairly strong and occasionally a reminder of the past is uncovered by today's tourist, particularly when passing through the smaller villages on the little-visited eastern and western sides of Kilimanjaro. Such finds make visits to these villages truly fascinating.

Do not, however, come to Kilimanjaro expecting to witness some of the more extreme practices described below. This point needs emphasizing: the Chaggas' traditional way of life has been eroded by the depredations of Western culture and, as far as we know, is now largely extinct. Indeed, much of the material on which the following account is based is provided by the reports of the nineteenth- and early twentieth-century Europeans who visited the area; in particular, Charles Dundas' comprehensive tome, *Kilimanjaro and its People*, which was first published way back in 1924.

This, of course, begs the question: why have we included in a modern guide to Kilimanjaro descriptions of obsolete Chagga practices and beliefs that were largely wiped out almost 100 years ago? Well, research revealed the relevance of this inclusion since there are still faint echoes of their traditional way of life that have survived into the present day. What's more, reading this admittedly detailed account of the Chagga and how they lived and thought could provide you with a better understanding — and thereby some insight — into the mind, beliefs and behaviour of the people who live in Kilimanjaro's shadow today. It was a fascinating subject to research and we hope that at least some readers will find it as interesting to read.

Chagga language — a quick introduction
The language of the Chagga, Kichagga, is classified as a Niger-Congo language and has various dialects including Vunjo, Rombo, Machame, Huru and Old Moshi. The following is a very brief introduction to the Vunjo dialect of Chagga, taken from the book by Bernard Leeman (see p311), to whom we are indebted. The Vunjo district covers Kirua, Kilema, Marangu, Mamba and Mwika. Attempt to speak a little Chagga and you'll have your porters eating out of the palm of your hand. Or laughing at you. Note that there are different dialects of Chagga and, as such, your Chagga friend may not understand this particular one ... nevertheless, it's worth a try.

Yes	Yee
No	Ote
Please	Tafadhali
Thank you	Aika
Good morning, how are you?	Shimbonyi sha ngamenwi?
Very well, thank you, and how are you?	Nashica kapisa, aika, ungiwie shapfo?

ORIGINS

The Chagga are believed to have arrived between 250 and 400 years ago from the north-east, following local upheaval in that area. Logically, therefore, the eastern side of the mountain would have been the first to have been settled. Upon their arrival these new immigrants would have found that the mountain was already inhabited. An aboriginal people known as the Wakonyingo, who were possibly pygmies, were already living here, as indeed were the Wangassa, a tribe similar to the Masai, and the Umbo of the Usambara mountains. All of these groups were either driven out or absorbed by the Chagga.

Initially, these new immigrants were a disparate bunch, with different beliefs, customs and even languages. With no feelings of kinship or loyalty to their neighbour, they instead settled into family groups known as **clans**. According to Dundas, in his day some 732 clans existed on Kilimanjaro; by 1924, however, when his book was published, some of these clans were already down to just a single member.

These family ties were gradually cut and lost over time as people moved away to settle on other parts of the mountain. Thus, in place of these blood ties, people developed new loyalties to the region in which they were living and the neighbours with whom they shared the land. Out of this emerged twenty or so states or chiefdoms, most of them on a permanent war footing with the other nineteen. Wars between the tribes, and indeed between villages in the same tribe, were commonplace, though they usually took the form of organized raids by one village on another rather than actual pitched battles. Slaves would be taken during these raids, cattle rustled and huts burned down, though there was often little bloodshed — the weaker party would merely withdraw at the first sign of approaching hostilities and might even try to negotiate a price for peace.

KILIMANJARO

**Traditional Chagga
beehive hut**
(from *The Kilima-njaro Expedition,*
HH Johnston, 1886)

Eventually the number of different groups was whittled down to just six tribes, or states, with each named after one of the mountain's rivers. So, for example, there are the Wamoshi Chaggas (after the Moshi River) and the Wamachame Chaggas who settled near the Machame River. With all this intermingling going on, a few words inevitably became used by all the people living on the mountain — and from this unlikely start grew a common language, of which each tribe had its own dialect. Similar customs developed between the tribes, though as with the language they differed in the detail. However, it was only when the Germans took control of the region during the latter part of the nineteenth century and the local people put aside their differences to present a united front in disputes with their colonial overlords that a single ethnic group was identified and named the Chagga. From this evolved a single, collective Chagga consciousness.

Today the Chaggas, despite their diverse origins, are renowned for having a strong sense of identity and pride. They are also amongst the richest and most powerful people in Tanzania, thanks in part to the fertile soils of Kilimanjaro, and in part to the Western education that they have been receiving for longer than almost any other tribe in Africa, Kilimanjaro being one of the first places to accept missionaries from Europe.

SOCIAL STRUCTURE AND VILLAGE LIFE

Hans Meyer notes in his book that the biggest Chagga settlement when he visited in 1889 was Machame, with 8000 people. 'Moji' (Moshi) had 3000, as did Marangu. Each family unit, according to him, lived in two or three extremely simple thatched huts in the shape of beehives, with a granary and small courtyard attached. There are several examples of these **'beehive' huts** still dotted around Kilimanjaro's slopes. Only the **chief**, the head of village society and its lawmaker, lived in anything more extensive. The chief of every village was often venerated by his subjects and to meet him required going through an elaborate ceremony first. According to his report in the *Church Missionary Intelligencer*, Johannes Rebmann, the first white man to see Kiliman-jaro, had to be sprinkled with goat's blood and the juice of a plant and was then left waiting for four days before being granted an audience with Masaki, the chief of Moshi. While modern society has reduced his role to a largely ceremonial one, the chief is still a widely respected person in village life today — though thankfully there is now less ceremony involved when paying him a visit.

There are other similarities between the Chagga society of yesterday and today. The economy was, then as now, largely agricultural, using the environmentally destructive slash-and-burn technique for clearing land. **Bananas** were once the most common crop, and though banana bushes were largely replaced by **coffee** plantations in the early twentieth century, both are still grown today.

When it came to trading these bananas and coffee in former times, instead of the Tanzanian shilling people used red and blue glass beads as currency, or lengths of cloth known as *doti*. One hundred beads were equal to one *doti*, with which you could buy, for example, twenty unripe bananas; twelve *doti* would get you a cow.

RELIGION AND CEREMONIES

Unsurprisingly for a people that has been subjected to some pretty relentless missionary work for over a century, the majority of the Chagga are today **Christian**. Traditional beliefs are still held by some in rural areas, though the intensity of the beliefs and the excesses of many of the rituals have largely disappeared. Superstition played a central role in traditional Chagga religion: witchcraft (*wusari* in Chagga) played a major part, **rainmakers** and rain-preventers were important members of society, and dreams were infallible oracles of the future; indeed, many Chagga were said to have dreamt of the coming of the white man to Kilimanjaro.

The traditional faith was based around belief in a god called **Ruwa**. Ruwa was a tolerant deity who, though neither the creator of the universe nor of man, nevertheless set the latter free from some sort of unspecified incarceration. Ruwa had little to do with mankind following this episode, however, so the Chagga instead **worshipped their ancestors**, whom they believed could influence events on Earth.

Chagga mythology had many parallels with stories from the Bible, including one concerning the fall of man (though in the Chagga version, a sweet potato was the forbidden fruit, and it was a stranger rather than a serpent that persuaded the first man to take a bite); there are also stories that bear a resemblance to the tales of Cain and Abel, and the great flood.

The Chagga faith also had its own **concept of sin** and its own version of the Catholic practice of confession. In the Chagga religion, however, it is not the sinner but the person who is sinned against who must be purified, in order that the negative force does not remain with him or her. This purification would be performed by the local medicine man, with the victim bringing along the necessary ingredients for performing the 'cleansing'. These included the skin, dung and stomach contents of a hyrax; the shell and blood of a snail; the rainwater from a hollow tree and, as with all Chagga ceremonies, a large quantity of banana beer for the medicine man. All of this would then be put into a hole in the ground lined with banana leaves and with a gate or archway built above, which the victim would then have to pass through. This done, the victim would be painted by the medicine man using the mixture in the hole. This entire ceremony would be performed twice daily over four days.

KILIMANJARO

Medicine men did more than care for one's spiritual health; they also looked after one's physical well-being. For the price of one goat and, of course, more banana beer, the medicine man would be able to cure any affliction using a whole host of methods – including spitting. If you were suffering from a fever, for instance, you could expect to be spat upon up to 80 times by the medicine man, who would finish off his performance by expectorating up your nostrils and then blowing hard up each to ensure the saliva reached its target. For this particular method, the traditional payment was one pot of honey – and probably some more banana beer.

Traditional Chagga society also practised preventative medicine, and not just in matters of health. If, for example, a prominent man in the village was for some reason worried about his own safety, the medicine man would order him to lie with his favourite wife in a pit dug in the ground. With the man and wife still inside, the hole would then be decked with poles and covered with banana leaves. They would remain there until evening, while the man's friends above would cook food.

Medicine men also performed the vital role of **removing curses**. Curses took many forms: a cheated wife, for example, might curse her husband by turning her back on him, bowing four times and praying for his death. The most feared curse, however, was that of the deathbed curse, issued by somebody shortly before they expired. These were widely held to be the most difficult to reverse, for to have any hope of removing it the medicine man would require the victim to get hold of a piece of the curser's corpse.

Funerals

If the medicine man's efforts at lifting the curse proved to be in vain, a funeral would be the most likely outcome. As with most Chagga ceremonies, this would vary slightly from place to place and from tribe to tribe, and also depended on the status of the deceased. Only married people with children, for example, would be buried: dead youths and girls would be wrapped in banana leaves and left in a banana grove, while babies were merely covered in cow dung and left out for jackals and hyaenas. (It is said that this practice was stopped after a jackal dropped the severed head of a small baby at the feet of a local chief.)

For married adults, the corpse would be stripped and bent double, with the head and legs tied together. **Animal sacrifices** would take place on the day of the burial, with the hide of a sacrificed bull used to cover the grave. Interestingly, the corpse would face Kibo in the grave – as if the Chagga believed that the summit of Kilimanjaro was in some way connected with the afterlife. A lot of beer-drinking was also involved. Sacrifices would continue for the next nine days until, it was believed, the soul had finally crossed the harsh desert separating the earthly world from the spirit world. The afterlife, incidentally, was said to be very like our temporal world, only not as good, with food less tasty and the scenery less majestic.

The Chagga view of Kilimanjaro

The summit of Kilimanjaro is and always has been as enchanting to the Chagga as it has been to visitors. According to Dundas, the Chagga view the Kibo summit as something beautiful, eternal and strengthening, its snows providing streams that support life, while the clouds that gather on its slopes provide precious rainfall. By comparison, the plains that lie in the opposite direction are seen as oppressively hot, where famine stalks, drought and malaria are rife and large creatures such as crocodiles and leopards prey on man. Indeed, so venerated is Kilimanjaro that the Chagga dead are traditionally buried facing towards Kibo, and the side of the village facing the summit is known to be the honourable side, where meetings and feasts are held and chiefs are buried. Furthermore, when meeting somebody, he who comes from higher up the slopes of Kilimanjaro should traditionally greet the other first, for it is he who is coming from the lucky side.

Intriguingly, some Chagga myths about Kilimanjaro are remarkably accurate. In particular, the Chagga traditionally believed that the mountain was formed by a volcano – even though the main eruption that formed Kibo occurred around half a million years ago, way before the arrival of man. What's more, there is a story in Chagga folklore concerning the twin peaks of Mawenzi and Kibo, in which Mawenzi's fire burns out first, and the Mawenzi peak is forced to go to Kibo whose fire was still burning. Parallels between this story and what scientists now believe really happened – with Kibo continuing to erupt long after Mawenzi expired – are remarkable.

But the question remains: did the Chagga ever actually climb all the way to the top of Kilimanjaro before the Europeans? The answer is, probably not. The quote on pp93-4 by Rebmann in which he talks about '*the popular traditions respecting the fate of the only expedition which had ever attempted to ascend its heights*' suggests that he had information that they had tried only once – and failed.

True, their belief that Kibo was covered in a magic silver which melted on the way down does suggest that they had at least reached the snow-line before. Furthermore, Rebmann's guide refers to the snow on the summit of Kilimanjaro as 'coldness' (see pp92-3), and Meyer found traces of a hunting expedition on the Saddle, both of which seem to confirm this idea. But the fact that Charles New's entourage of porters and guides were buck naked when they climbed up to the snow-line suggests that they were, on the whole, unused to the conditions on Kibo; that, and the fact that the name Kilimanjaro, if it is of Chagga origin (about which, see p88), roughly translates as 'That which is impossible for birds', suggests that they thought that it was therefore impossible for man to reach the top.

Charles Dundas is equally sceptical of the notion that the Chagga climbed Kilimanjaro before Meyer:

It is inconceivable that natives can ever have ascended to the crater rim, for apart from cold, altitude and superstitious fears, it is a sheer impossibility that they could have negotiated the ice. Nor is there any tradition among the natives that anyone went up as high... Rebmann tells us that Rengwa, great-grandfather of the present chief of Machame, sent an expedition to investigate the nature of the ice, which descends very low above Machame, but is impossible to scale. Only one of the party survived, his hands and feet frozen and crippled for life; all the rest were destroyed by the cold, or by evil spirits, as the survivor reported.

KILIMANJARO

The Ngasi

One of the occasions in which children frequently died was during the initiation ceremony known as **Ngasi**. This was a brutal rite-of-passage ceremony to mark the passing of boys into adulthood. The ceremony was presided over by the so-called King of Ngasi, a man who had the authority to viciously flog any boy taking part in the ceremony who displeased him.

Before the Ngasi proper started, the boys who were to take part were summoned from their houses by the singing of lugubrious songs at the gate of their homes. From there they were taken to the place of ceremony deep in the forest and the proceedings began. **Hunting** formed a large part of the Ngasi; boys were tested on their ability to track down and kill game, the animals caught being smeared with the novices' excrement. Another test they had to undergo was to climb a tree on the riverbank and cross the river by clambering along its branches to where they intertwined with the branches of the trees on the other side. After this, a chicken would be sacrificed and the boys ordered to lick the blood.

The final part of the initial stage was the most brutal, however: orders were secretly given to the boys to slay a crippled or deformed youth amongst their number. Traditionally, the victim was killed in the night. The parents were never actually told what had happened to their son and, as all present at the Ngasi ceremony were sworn to silence, they rarely found out the whole story. The boys then moved to a new camp. They were now called Mbora, and were free to collect their clothes (one set of boy's clothes, of course, was left unclaimed). They then repaired to the chief's house for a feast, from where they headed home.

After the tribulations of the ceremony, the boys were allowed a month's holiday, before they returned to the chief's house to participate in the sacrificing of a bull. They were then free to head back to their homes, raping any young women they chanced to meet on the way; the poor women themselves had no redress. The Ngasi was now at an end, and the boys who had successfully completed the ceremony were now men.

Matrimony

Ver hard on Wachaga to get wife, but when he get her she can make do plant corn, she make wash and cook and make do work for him. Ingreza [English] man very much money to spend. She wife no can wash, no plant corn, herd goats or cook. All money, much merkani (cloth), heap money, big dinner. She eat much posho. She no can cook dinner. She only make 'Safari' and look. Porr, porr Ingreza man. A local's view of matrimony as recorded in **Peter MacQueen**'s book *In Wildest Africa*, published in 1910

After the Ngasi, boys were free to marry. **Marriage** was arranged by the parents, though the boy and girl involved were allowed to voice their opinions – and unless the parents were particularly inflexible, these opinions would count for something. Furthermore, in order for the boy to stand a chance with his potential suitor, he had to woo her. The Chaggas' courtship process involved, as elsewhere in the world, a lot of gift-giving, though the gifts followed a strict set of rules: spontaneity played little part in this process. The first gift, for example, from the man to the woman, was always a necklace. The Chagga male would be well rewarded for his generosity, for traditionally in return the girl would dance naked all day with bells attached to her legs by her mother. Over the following days other gifts were exchanged until the time came when the girl, having visited all her relatives, would be shut away for three months. No work would be done by the girl during this time but instead she would be given fattening food and would be kept in a cage. At the end of this period a **dowry** would be paid, the marriage ceremony performed and the bride would be carried on the back of the Mkara (the traditional Chagga equivalent of the best man) to her new husband's house.

KILIMANJARO ECONOMY

Tourism is now the biggest earner in the region, though agriculture, as you will discover, is still very much part of the local economy. The volcanic soil of the mountain slopes, so rich with nutrients, is amongst the most fertile in East Africa. Thanks to the regular and reliable rainfall blown in from the Indian Ocean (see p85) and the proliferation of springs trickling forth from the bare rock, Kilimanjaro is also one of the damper parts of the region, and the south-eastern slopes particularly so, thus increasing still further the agricultural fecundity of the mountain.

Chagga warriors
(from *Across East African Glaciers,* Hans Meyer, 1891)

On the lower slopes of Kilimanjaro annual staple crops such as beans, maize and millet are grown, while cash-crops such as Arabica coffee are planted in the *kihamba* land further up the mountainside. Bananas are also grown at this altitude, their leaves and stems providing both a nutrient-rich mulch for the coffee trees and fodder for the livestock that are traditionally grazed at this height. In Chagga society it is customary for a farmer's land to be divided between his sons on his death; whilst this may seem a fair way of dividing land, it also means that farmer's landholdings diminish in size with every generation, and many farms are now less than a hectare in size.

The Chagga are also keen bee-keepers, the hives being hollow sections of a tree trunk closed at both ends by bungs and left to hang in the trees; you may well see these trunks (put there illegally) in the forest zone of Kilimanjaro. Once the swarm has taken possession and completed the combs the bees are smoked out, the bung removed and the honey collected.

KILIMANJARO

The following chapter is devoted to helping you take your first few steps in East Africa. It contains guides to the two cities that you are most likely to fly into — namely **Dar es Salaam** and **Nairobi** — as well as an introduction to Kilimanjaro Airport, for those landing there. The guides to the two cities are deliberately rather brief but they should be adequate for finding your way around and for choosing somewhere to sleep and eat, as well to experience something of metropolitan Africa. We also explain, at the end of each description, how to get to Kilimanjaro. **Kilimanjaro International Airport** is, of course, the most convenient airport for the mountain; details about it can be found on p144.

Dar es Salaam

Dar es Salaam is a city with an identity crisis: a large metropolis (population two million-plus) which behaves as if it were a small and sleepy seaside town; a city that was at the forefront of the country's struggle for independence in the 1950s and yet still contains the finest collection of dusty old colonial buildings in possibly the whole of East Africa; and a place that everybody thinks is the capital of Tanzania – but isn't. It *is* the commercial heart of the country, however, and has been almost since its inception in the 1860s by Sultan Sayyid Majid of Zanzibar. Intended as a mainland port for many of the goods and spices being traded on his island, the sultan, a man of poetic bent, named his new city Dar es Salaam ('Haven of Peace'). And peacefully was how it spent its first few years, too, as the sultan died soon after founding the city, allowing Bagamoyo, a dhow port to the north, to emerge as the pre-eminent harbour on this particular stretch of the east coast.

Missionaries from Europe added fresh impetus to Dar with their arrival in the 1880s but it was the coming of the Germans in 1891 that really gave this city a fillip, the colonials feeling that the harbour here was more suitable to their steam-powered craft than Bagamoyo. Having made Dar their seat of power, it remained the capital until 1973 when the Tanzanian government decided to move the legislature to Dodoma, smack in the geometric heart of the country – which probably seemed like a good idea at the time, until somebody pointed out the lack of available water and other basic amenities there.

So while the capital may be Dodoma, most of the politicking and indeed everything else of importance takes place here in Dar. For tourists, there's nothing particularly special to warrant a long stay in this city; but by the same token, don't fret too much if you do have to spend some time in Dar: it's pleasant, it's laidback and, compared to Nairobi, it's a whole lot saner too.

ARRIVAL

Though safer than arriving in Nairobi, it still pays to be on your guard when landing in Dar: like a recently hatched turtle taking to the ocean for the first time, you are at your most vulnerable when you land in a new country – and even in the Haven of Peace there are still plenty of sharks out there. There are two terminals at Dar airport, about 700m apart from each other. Arriving from overseas you will land at **Terminal Two**, the busier of the two, about 12km out from the town centre to the west. A **taxi** into town will set you back about Ts15,000 during the day, and about half as much again at night; ignore or haggle with those drivers who quote a price significantly higher than this. You could walk to the main road and take a **dalla-dalla** into town for Ts150, though this is not really practical if you have a lot of luggage. **Going to the airport**, look for the dalla-dalla signed U/Ndege (short for Uwanja wa Ndege, or airport) that departs from the front; leave in plenty of time – it can take well over an hour and drops you a ten-minute walk away. From town a taxi's a little cheaper at Ts8000-10,000.

Arriving by bus you'll be dropped in the city centre at Kisutu Bus Station.

ORIENTATION AND GETTING AROUND

Navigating your way around central Dar is no easy task. Things are fairly straightforward on the sea front, where Kivukoni Road/Ocean Road follows the shore from the train station to the Ocean Road Hospital and beyond. But step back from the shore and you find yourself in a labyrinth of small streets, many of which curve imperceptibly but dramatically enough to confuse and disorientate. Keep the map on p129 with you, using it first to help you find your way to the tourist office (see below) where they have a more detailed and extensive map of the city. They will also be able to help you out with the city's **public transport** system, which can also be rather confusing. Buses and dalla-dallas ply all the main routes, though finding where they start and stop can be difficult. Ask locals, your hotel, or take a cab. Fortunately, central Dar is compact enough to walk around.

SERVICES

Tourist office

There's a tourist office on Samora Avenue (Mon-Fri 8am-4pm; Sat 8.30am-12.30pm; ☎ 212 0373, 213 1555). It depends on who is working there when you call in but we found the staff to be really helpful, knowledgeable and patient. They may well have a copy of the free bi-monthly *Dar Guide* magazine, too, the most useful run-down of the city.

Banks

There are **cashpoints** at Standard Chartered on Garden Avenue (just up from the museum) and Sokoine Drive, and a Barclays ATM opposite the Mövenpick Hotel. Of the local banks, Bank Exim has Mastercard cashpoints (there's one on Sokoine opposite the Azania Front Lutheran Church), while the NBC also has ATMs (Visa) and is also the best place for cashing **travellers' cheques**. Their main office is on the corner opposite the Lutheran Church and the New Africa Hotel; for later opening hours, try the moneychangers down Samora Avenue. The AMEX rep is the Flying Rickshaw, in the Mövenpick Hotel.

Communications
The main **post office** is on Maktaba/Azikiwe Street (Mon-Fri 8am-4.30pm, Sat 9am-noon). The **telephone office** is on Bridge Street. You won't have any trouble finding an **Internet** café in Dar; they are everywhere. Most tourists head for the one in the Safari, probably just because of its convenient location, though it does offer an efficient service.

Car hire
Hertz (☎ 2112967; 🖳 www.hertz.com) are based in the Mövenpick Hotel. For a big four-wheel drive (4WD, the only vehicles allowed into the national parks) suitable for four people they charge US$145 per day plus 20% VAT; the first 100km per day are free; thereafter it's US$0.90 per km. For a smaller car suitable for two people, it's the same rules but the fee is US$79 per day plus 20%, and the excess over 100km is US$0.80 per km. Curiously, it is not much more expensive if you actually hire a driver with your rental vehicle.

As with all rental vehicles, check its condition carefully before setting out.

Trekking agencies
You *can* organize your Kili trek from here, though unless there are mitigating circumstances you'd be daft to do so, it being far easier and a lot cheaper to travel to Moshi and arrange it from there. The average price in Dar is about US$1200, though transport to the mountain from Dar is included in this. Recommended companies include:
● **Coastal Travels** Upanga Road, (PO Box 3052, ☎ 2117959; 🖳 safari @coastal.cc, aviation@coastal.cc). The most established agent in the city with offices in both Dar es Salaam and Zanzibar airports.
● **Easy** On the front to the east of the car park, on the first floor of Avalon House, Zanaki St, (PO Box 1428, ☎ 2123526; 🖳 easytravel@raha.com). Claims to do all the routes up Kili.
● **Rickshaw Travels** (☎ 2114094), Mövenpick Hotel. They are expensive but reliable.

WHERE TO STAY

The following are listed in **price order**, with the **cheapest first**. For details of the abbreviations, see overleaf.
● *YWCA* Ghana Ave (☎ 022 2122439, 0741 622707; 🖳 ywca.tanzania@ africaonline.co.tz); sgl/dbl US$9/$12. Perhaps the most popular budget hostel currently operating, the YWCA (men are allowed too) has pretty basic accommodation but it's clean, cheap and has a good location by the post office.

❏ Dar's area code is ☎ 022. If phoning from outside Tanzania dial ☎ +255-22.

● *Jambo Inn* (☎ 2110711 – though signs say that advance bookings are not allowed!) Libya St; s/c sgl/dbl with fan US$12/16, s/c sgl/dbl with air-con and TV US$25/30, or it's US$24 s/c air-con dbl with no TV. Just a few doors down from the Safari (see p128) on Libya Street, the Jambo is a scruffy but very welcoming hotel, slightly cheaper than its neighbour but way friendlier. The restaurant serves Indian, English, Chinese and Pakistani food, though with Chef's Pride so nearby it struggles for custom.

❏ **Diplomatic missions in Dar es Salaam**

Austria Samora Ave, PO Box 312; ☎ 2111722

Belgium NIC Investment House, Samora Machel Ave, PO Box 9210; ☎ 2114025/2112503/2112688

Burundi Lugalo Rd, Plot No.1007, Upanga East, PO Box 2752; ☎ 2126827/2113710

Canada 38 Mirambo Garden Ave, PO Box 1022; ☎ 2112831-5/2112865-6

Czech Republic Plot No.1067, Msasani Peninsula, PO Box 3054; ☎ 2666509/2666131

Democratic Republic of Congo 438 Malik Rd, Upanga, PO Box 975; ☎ 2150282

Denmark Ghana Ave, PO Box 9171; ☎ 2113887/90

Egypt 24 Garden Ave, PO Box 1668; ☎ 2113591/2117622

Finland NIC Investment House, 9th flr, Samora Machel Ave, PO Box 4255; ☎ 211 9170/2118788

France Ali Hassan Mwinyi Rd, PO Box 2349; ☎ 2666021/3

Germany NIC Building, l0th Floor, Samora Machel Ave, PO Box 9541; ☎ 211 7409/15

Ireland 1131 Msasani Rd, Oysterbay, PO Box 9612; ☎ 2602355

Italy Lugalo Rd (Upanga), PO Box 2106; ☎ 2115935/6

Japan Plot 10, 18 Upanga Rd, PO Box 2577; ☎ 2115935/2115828/2115831

Kenya NIC Investment House, PO Box 5231; ☎ 2112959

Malawi IPS Building, 9th Floor, PO Box 7616; ☎ 2113238/41

Norway Plot 160, Mirambo Street, PO Box 9012; ☎ 2113610

Poland 63 Ali Khan Rd, Upanga, PO Box 2188; ☎ 2115271

Russian Federation Plot 73 Kenyatta Drive, PO Box 1905; ☎ 2666005/6

Rwanda Plot 32 Upanga Rd, PO Box 2918; ☎ 2130119/2119098

South Africa Mwaya Rd, Oysterbay Peninsula, PO Box 10723; ☎ 2601800

South Korea Plot 1349, Haile Selassie Rd, Msasani, PO Box 1154; ☎ 2600200/2600496/2600499

Spain Plot 99B Kinondoni Rd, PO Box 842; ☎ 2666018/2666936

Sudan 64 Upanga Rd, PO Box 2266; ☎ 2117641

Sweden Mirambo Street, PO Box 9274; ☎ 2111265-68/2111235-40

Switzerland 17 Kenyatta Drive, PO Box 2454; ☎ 2666008-9

Uganda Extelcoms Building, Samora Machel Ave, PO Box 6237; ☎ 2116754/2117646-8

UK Hifadhi House, PO Box 9200; ☎ 2117659-64

United States 686 Old Bagamoyo Rd, PO Box 9123; ☎ 2668001

Zambia Plot 5, Junction of Ohio/Sokoine Drive, PO Box 2525; ☎ 2112977/2118481-2

Zimbabwe NIC Life Building, Sokoine Drive, PO Box 20762; ☎ 2116789

❏ **Abbreviations**
Throughout this book we have used the following abbreviations when writing about accommodation: s/c means self-contained, as in en suite (ie the room comes with a bathroom); **sgl/dbl/tpl** means single/double/triple rooms. For example, where we have written 'sgl/dbl/tpl US$35/40/45', we mean that a single room costs US$35 per night, a double US$40, and a triple US$45.

• *Safari Inn* (☎ 2138101; ✉ safari-inn@mailcity.com) Band St, off Libya Street; s/c sgl/dbl Ts10,000/16,500, or Ts12,000/18,500 with TV; with air-con Ts26,500 s/c dbl. Still a popular budget choice, despite the best efforts of the miserable staff to frighten travellers away. All the rooms are en suite, though some are a bit gloomy with many lacking windows. There's a popular Internet café here too. The room rates include something that resembles a breakfast, only smaller.

• *Econolodge* (☎ 2116048; ✉ econolodge@raha.com), Libya St; US$15/25 s/c sgl/dbl with fan, up to US$25/30 s/c sgl/dbl with air-con. Not quite as 'Econo' as it makes out, this is the smartest in this little huddle of hotels. Singles, doubles and triples are all spacious and all come with bathroom. Some tourists have complained about the hassle from touts, however.

• *Starlight Hotel* (☎ 2119387) Bibi Titi Mohamed St; US$42/48 s/c sgl/dbl. Another hotel, like the Peacock below, that seems to cater mainly for local businessmen and warrants a mention largely due to its position in the mid-range price bracket. Impersonal looking but friendly, central and – with all 150 rooms equipped with air-con, hot water, TV and fridge – fair value too.

• *Peacock Hotel* (☎ 2114071; ✉ www.peacock-hotel.co.tz) Bibi Titi Mohamed St; s/c sgl/dbl US$75/85; bigger s/c sgl/dbl rooms (with sofas!) US$100/125. Refreshingly free of any pretension, an ugly but friendly establishment that sees few tourists, reaping its custom instead from local businessmen. It's OK, with all the facilities you'd expect from a hotel of this class but to be honest is probably getting a mention here only because of the shortage of other mid-range hotels in Dar – and it's a tad overpriced too. However, as with the Starlight, it's so nice to see receptionists who seem genuinely glad you've dropped in.

Map key		
	⑤ Bank	⅄ Camping Site
	🏛 Museum	☆ Police
⇧ Place to stay	📖 Library / Bookstore	ⓒ Mosque
○ Place to eat	✝ Church	● Other
⊠ Post office	✝ Cathedral	Ⓐ Bus Station
ⓘ Tourist information	↗ Internet	⛴ Ferry Service

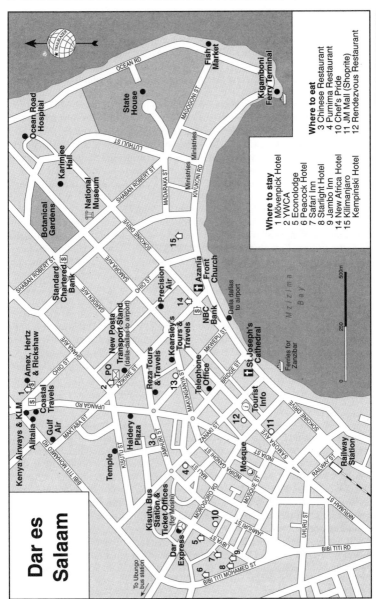

Dar es Salaam

Where to stay
1 Mövenpick Hotel
2 YWCA
5 Econolodge
6 Peacock Hotel
7 Safari Inn
8 Starlight Hotel
9 Jambo Inn
14 New Africa Hotel
15 Kilimanjaro Kempinski Hotel

Where to eat
3 Chinese Restaurant
4 Purnima Restaurant
10 Chef's Pride
11 JM Mall (Shoprite)
12 Rendezvous Restaurant

OCEAN RD
Fish Market
Kigamboni Ferry Terminal
MAGOGONI ST
State House
LUTHULI ST
Ocean Road Hospital
Ministries
Karimjee Hall
KIVUKONI RD
Ministries
National Museum
MADARAKA ST
SHABAN ROBERT ST
Botanical Gardens
SOKOINE DRIVE
SAMORA AVE
15
Azania Front Church
SHABAN ROBERT ST
Standard Chartered Bank
GARDEN AVE
GHANA AVE
Precision Air
OHIO ST
Dalla dallas to airport
Mzizima Bay
500m
250
0
Amex, Hertz & Rickshaw
1
New Posta Transport Stand (dalla-dallas to airport)
14
NBC Bank
Kearsley's Tours & Travels
MKWEPU ST
Ferries for Zanzibar
Kenya Airways & KLM
Alitalia
Gulf Air
Coastal Travels
PO
AZIKIWE ST
Reza Tours & Travels
13
St Joseph's Cathedral
UPANGA RD
2
MAKUNGANYA ST
Telephone Office
BRIDGE ST
SOKOINE DRIVE
MAKTABA ST
Haidery Plaza
3
JAMHURI ST
MALI ST
ZANAKI ST
12
Tourist Info
11
Railway Station
KISUTU ST
Temple
4
Mosque
MOSQUE ST
INDIA ST
SAMORA AVE
RAILWAY ST
BIBI TITI MOHAMED RD
NOROGORO RD
INDIRA GANDHI ST
UHURU ST
NKRUMAH ST
Kisutu Bus Station & Ticket Offices (for Moshi)
10
Mosque
BIBI TITI RD
To Ubungo bus station
Dar Express
5
LIBYA ST
JAMHURI ST
6
7
8
9
BIBI TITI MOHAMED ST

• *New Africa Hotel* (☎ 2117050; 🖥 www.newafricahotel.com) corner of Azikiwe/Sokoine Drive; s/c sgl/dbl US$150/170 up to US$200/220 in the executive suite. In a better location than the Mövenpick Hotel, though not with quite the same level of sophistication, the New Africa stands on the site of the Germans' original Kaiserhoff. Home to Dar's main casino as well as a host of bars and restaurants, the New Africa's rooms have everything you'd expect from a hotel of this calibre, including mini-bar, satellite TV, telephones with Internet hook-up and so on. If you're willing to pay over a hundred dollars for all this, you may as well pay the extra US$10 for one of the rooms with a sea view. A courtesy airport shuttle is available to passengers on certain flights.

• *Mövenpick Hotel* (☎ 2112416, 🖥 www.moevenpick-hotels.com) Ohio Street; s/c sgl/dbl US$210/230 up to US$1500 for the Presidential Suite. Formerly the Royal Palm and before that the Sheraton, this used to be the top place in the town centre. It has a swimming pool, gym and all mod-cons and is also the base for Dar's AMEX representatives, Hertz, British Airways, Rickshaw Travels and a bureau de change that is open from 8am to 8pm. Even if you're not staying here, do call in to have a peek at the photos of Kili's summit by John Cleare that adorn the shopping walkway, or simply to take advantage of their fierce air-con.

• *Kilimanjaro Kempinski Hotel* (☎ 2131111; 🖥 www.kempinski-dares salaam.com) Kivukoni St; rooms US$300 up to, wait for it, US$1800 for the Presidential Suite. Opened on 5 October 2005 after a massive refit, if you've got a rucksack full of money you won't find a more extravagantly glitzy or, given its name, *appropriate* place to stay. Actually, the hotel's association with the mountain is tenuous, other than the shared name and the fact that you need a bank balance the size of Kilimanjaro to be able to stay here. However, it *is* gorgeous, sophisticated and shiny and the rooms feature what are described as elegantly tropical interiors, wood floors, high-speed and wireless Internet access, international satellite LCD TV with movie channels, multilingual telephone voicemail and all the other bits 'n' bobs you'd expect of a hotel of this standard. The location overlooking the Indian Ocean is great, too.

WHERE TO EAT

Many eateries in Dar close on Sundays. One that doesn't and which is currently the most popular place in town amongst travellers – and indeed amongst many locals too – is *Chef's Pride* on Chagga Street. It is a popularity that is well deserved: tasty, huge portions of food, fair prices, a location close to the cheaper hotels and English football on the telly is a combination that for some is hard to resist, and many travellers, having tried the food once, venture nowhere else in the city. Another popular choice is *Rendezvous*, though it's definitely not as good.

If you can tear yourself away from there, for alternative cheap-eats the Indian quarter of central Dar, particularly around the junction of Indira Gandhi and Zanaki streets, is as good a place as any to start looking. *Purnima* on

Zanaki Street is a great little place, where a plate of bhajias with various sauces and curds will make you poorer by only Ts1000 or so. There are other similar places around here – follow your nose to find them. For the unadventurous there are fast-food snack stands at the JM Mall on the corner of Mission St and Samora Avenue, including *Nando's*, *Pizza Inn*, *Chick Inn* and the *Creamy Inn* ice-cream parlour. There's also an Italian-orientated *Hard Rock Café* on Makunganya Street.

For more refined cuisine in plusher surroundings, try the restaurants in the upmarket hotels, including the *Sawasdee Thai* or the Indian *Bandari Grill*, both at the New Africa, and the *Serengeti Buffet Restaurant* at the Mövenpick, where they have a Crab & Claws night every Wednesday. Your bank manager won't thank you for dining here, but your stomach certainly will.

A TOUR OF THE CITY

None of Dar's attractions is going to make your eyes pop out on springs from their sockets, but the following tour is fine for those with time to kill in the city and a cursory interest in the place. For those in a hurry, the National Museum at least is worth seeing (see box p132), being the most absorbing and, for Kili-bound trekkers, the most relevant attraction in Dar.

One word of warning: if any of the streets listed below seem unhealthily deserted – the lanes around State House and Ocean Road in particular can be a little *too* quiet at times – consider taking an alternative and safer route.

Your tour begins around the back of the **Azania Front Lutheran Church**, built on the seafront at the turn of the century by German missionaries. Heading east along the promenade past many old colonial buildings now used by the Tanzanian authorities to house various ministries, walk round the south-eastern tip of the peninsula and on to the **fish market**, Tanzania's most vibrant attraction. Having ensured all money and valuables are securely tucked away, feel free to take a wander around – it's at its best early in the morning – and see what the local fishermen have managed to catch overnight.

Retracing your steps for a few metres, take the first turning on the right (west) up Magogoni Street. Surrounded by spacious grounds, **State House**, built by the British in the years following World War One, stands to your right; you will get your best view of the house at the very end of the road at the junction with Luthuli St. Crossing this junction and continuing straight on along Shaban Robert St, to your right is the **National Museum** (see the box on p132); a right turn after that will land you on one of the prettier streets in central Dar, the eastern end of Samora Avenue, with the **botanical gardens** to your left and, on the opposite side towards the end of the street, steeple-topped **Karimjee Hall**, where Nyerere (see p68) was sworn in as Tanzania's first president. Facing the end of the street and hidden behind high walls is the now-defunct **Ocean Road Hospital**, another German building dating back to the last years of the nineteenth century. Stroll round to the sea-facing front of the hospital to

National Museum
Open 9.30am-6pm daily; US$3, US$2 for students, or you can pay in Tanzanian shillings at a rate currently of US$1=Ts900. Tanzania's National Museum fares badly when compared to Kenya's version but is still mildly diverting at times, and a cool escape from the heat of the day. And if you manage to avoid the marauding school parties you may well have the entire complex to yourself, with only the cleaner for occasional company.

Begin your tour by walking through the back door to a small courtyard, home to an even smaller **memorial garden** to the twelve victims who perished in the US Embassy bombing in Dar on 7 August 1998. Similar in style to the one in Nairobi (see p141), the **sculpture** here includes twisted metal and a window pane shattered by the blast, as well as a face emerging from concrete, presumably recalling those who were buried in the rubble.

The original museum building that stands beyond is of little relevant interest to those heading to Kilimanjaro with its displays of zoological and ethnographic items. If you hunt around in the latter you'll find a couple of old Chagga storage baskets and some interesting old photos of tribal customs, but nothing to keep you in the musty old building for too long.

The main building, however, is a different story. Here you'll find a number of absorbing displays including the **Hall of Man**, which describes our evolution with the help of some apposite objects from Leakey's discoveries at **Olduvai Gorge**, as well as a few items of particular interest to those climbing Kili in the **History Gallery** upstairs, which maps out in concise and thorough detail the story of Tanzania. Take your time wandering around – it's fascinating. Indeed, our only gripe is that the letter from Hans Meyer (the original conqueror of Kilimanjaro) to the German representative in Zanzibar, in which he begs for a ransom of 10,000 rupees to be paid to Chief Abushiri, by whom he had been taken hostage during his second expedition to Kilimanjaro (see p101), has been removed for some reason.

study the rather curious architecture, a hybrid of Arabic and European styles, and to view the curious spiked mace that sits atop the hospital roof.

From here you have two choices: one is to continue your walk along the coast road back to the fish market and on to the church; the other is to return to the junction behind the hospital, press on for another hundred metres or so southwards, then take a right and amble along attractive, tree-shaded Sokoine Drive back to the Lutheran church.

MOVING ON – TO KILIMANJARO

Buses

Most ticket offices are located in the Kisutu terminal right in the heart of downtown on Libya Street. Unfortunately, the buses do not depart from there but from Ubungo, a new terminal a fair distance out of town. A taxi from Kisutu to Ubungo will set you back about Ts5000-6000; you can try to catch a dalla dalla from outside the Peacock on Bibi Titi Mohammed Road, though it's not easy.

Choose your bus company carefully: despite the presence of speed ramps and traffic police along certain stretches, the Dar to Moshi highway is notorious for the number of accidents that occur along it and often it's the same few bus companies that are involved. Unfortunately, the number of touts operating at both of Dar's stations means that it can be difficult to buy the ticket you want. Be persistent and insistent and take anything the touts say with a pinch – no, make that a huge bucket – of salt.

Two companies to recommend are Scandinavia and Dar Express. Unfortunately, Scandinavia appear to be in considerable financial difficulty at the moment and much of their fleet was recently impounded by the authorities. If they are still operating by the time you read this, you may find the quality of their service has been lowered. The buses associated with the hotels in Moshi, namely Buffalo and Kindoroko, have the worst reputations.

Flights

Air Tanzania flies daily to **Kilimanjaro Airport**, at a different time everyday. The flight takes fifty minutes.

Air Excel have a daily flight to **Arusha Airport** at 4.20pm (1hr 50min; US$180), while Coastal Aviation on Upanga Road have daily flights from Dar via Zanzibar to Arusha at 9am, arriving at 11.30am at Arusha (US$190). Precision Air also have daily flights to Arusha via Zanzibar, as well as direct flights on Tuesdays, Fridays and Sundays (direct service US$165).

Crossing the plains to Kilimanjaro in the late nineteenth century, missionary Bishop Monseigneur Alexandre Le Roy recorded numerous encounters with wild animals in his book, *Au Kilima-Ndjaro (Afrique Orientale)* published in Paris in 1893.

Nairobi

As rough as a lion's tongue, East Africa's largest city has come quite a long way since its inception in May 1899 as a humble railway supply depot on the Mombasa to Kampala line. It is a city that has suffered much from plagues, fire and reconstruction – and that was just in its first ten years – yet it has continued obstinately to prosper and grow, rising from a population of exactly zero in 1898 to between 1.5 and 3 million today. Official recognition of the city's increasing importance arrived in 1907 when the British made it the capital of their East African territories, and you can still find the occasional colonial relic in the city today, from the Indian-influenced architecture of a few downtown buildings (shipped over from the subcontinent, the Indians supplied much of the labour force used in building the railway) to some distinctly elegant hotels and orderly public gardens (including one, just to the north of Kenyatta Avenue, which still bears a statue of Queen Victoria). But if you came with the specific purpose of seeing a faded colonial city you'll be disappointed: because as the capital of the Kenyan republic and the UN's fourth official 'World Centre', Nairobi is East Africa's most modern, prosperous and glamorous metropolis. It is also, first and foremost, black Africa at its loudest and proudest.

❑ **Nine useful things to know about Nairobi**
- Citizens of most countries need a **visa** for Kenya, including Britain and the US. Get your visa before leaving home. You can buy one at Nairobi's Jomo Kenyatta Airport, though this takes time and it is not unknown for officials to request bribes before issuing them. Welcome to Kenya.
- One thing to remember: as long as you remain in East Africa there is no need to buy a multiple-entry Kenya visa if you are flying into Kenya but wish to visit Tanzania or Uganda too, as long as you stay in those countries for less than two weeks and providing, of course, your Kenyan visa has not expired by the time you return to Kenya.
- The official **language** of Kenya is Swahili. For a quick guide to Swahili, see p303. In addition, many Kenyans speak both their own tribal language and English, which is widely spoken everywhere.
- As with Tanzania, Kenya is **three hours ahead of GMT**. Note that, in addition to standard time, many locals use **Swahili time**, which runs from dawn to dusk (or 6am to 6pm to be precise). See p76 for details on how to convert between East African time and Swahili time.
- The Kenyan **currency** is the shilling (Ks). At the time of writing, US$1=Ks72.81, UK1=Ks128.90. Don't change money on the street.
- Kenya's **electricity supply** uses the British-style three-pin plugs on 220-240V.
- The **international dialling code** for Kenya is ☎ 254; Nairobi's code is ☎ 02.
- The **emergency telephone number** is ☎ 999.
- The **opening hours** in Kenya are typically 8am to 5 or 6pm.

SECURITY

A few years back some genius dubbed Kenya's capital 'Nairobberi', and lesser geniuses have been retreading that joke ever since. Tired as the gag may be, however, it does still have relevance, for Nairobi's reputation as East Africa's Capital of Crime is well founded.

To be fair, the authorities are trying to improve matters, at least in the centre, blocking off many of the darker backstreets. There seem to be fewer beggars and touts populating the streets too. There is also a 'beautification' programme going on, which seems to involve a lot of tree-planting.

Nevertheless, the need to be wary when out on the streets of Nairobi remains paramount. The most notorious hotspot is the area immediately to the **east of Moi Avenue**, including **River Road** and the bus stations, a popular location with travellers because of the cheap hotels there. During the daytime violent robbery is rare though certainly not unheard of, simply because it's so packed with people; pickpocketing, on the other hand, is rife at this time, probably for the same reason. At night, both techniques are common. The **airport**, from the immigration counter and passport control to the arrivals' hall, is also a favourite with the local law-breakers, as is the **bus into town**.

To avoid being another victim, be vigilant, leave valuables with the hotel (having first checked their security procedures) and make sure that they give you a receipt for any goods deposited too. Furthermore, tuck moneybelts under your clothing and don't walk around at night but take a taxi, even if it's for just a few hundred metres. This last piece of advice applies particularly to the area around River Road: we've heard of people being attacked even as they made their way back to the (currently closed) Iqbal Hotel from the Taj restaurant, a walk of some twenty yards!

It can only be to your advantage if you are over-cautious for your first couple of days in the capital. After that, if you're still staying here, you can begin to appreciate Nairobi's charms – which do exist, and are not entirely inconsiderable – and can begin to moan, like the rest of the travellers here, about how unfair guidebook writers are about Kenya's capital.

ARRIVAL

If flying in, before landing at Nairobi's Jomo Kenyatta International Airport read the section about crime and security in the capital. Heed the advice about being vigilant and from the moment your foot hits the runway tarmac be on your guard against malefactors, and not only among your fellow passengers: signs above your head on the way to passport control warn against the giving and receiving of bribes, proving that some airport staff aren't above a little corruption. Arriving in Kenya without a **visa** does give crooked officials an opportunity to extort a little extra cash, so do try to arrange this before you arrive. If you haven't got a visa you should get one before passing through passport control, from the glass booth to the right of the hall (payment in US dollars or pounds sterling only). Through **immigration**, **luggage collection** is straight down the stairs. Once again be vigilant and, having retrieved your bags, check that nothing is missing: when climbing Kilimanjaro, there are few things more annoying than finding that your thermally insulated mountain hat that you thought was safely tucked away in the side-pocket of your rucksack, had in fact been taken by a light-fingered baggage handler and is now being used as a makeshift tea cosy in the staffroom of Jomo Kenyatta Airport.

On entering the arrivals' hall you'll find to your right a **moneychanger** offering, as moneychangers are wont to do at airports worldwide, dismal rates, and an **ATM** that accepts Visa cards – your best bet for a fair rate at the airport, though you could pay for your cab in dollars and wait to change money in town.

You have a number of choices in tackling the 15km from the airport to the centre of Nairobi. Taxis cost about Ks1000 with bargaining, or before 8pm you can take the number 34 bus that runs down River Road (Ks25). Remember to be careful of pickpockets on this route.

Arrive in Nairobi by shuttle bus and, if they don't drop you off at your hotel, you'll probably be dropped off by Jevanjee Gardens right in the heart of the action. **Arrive by bus**, on the other hand, and you could well be dropped off near infamous River Road – take care!

ORIENTATION AND GETTING AROUND

Despite decades of unplanned growth, a mass of sprawling suburbs and a wholesale aversion to street numbers, central Nairobi is actually very easy to navigate, with nearly everything of interest to the traveller within walking distance of Kenyatta Avenue. Two obvious landmarks are the enormous **KANU Tower**, to the south of City Hall, and the even more enormous **Nation Centre**, a red Meccano-type structure nestling between two giant cylindrical towers just off the eastern end of the avenue. Central Nairobi is fairly compact and the fit will be able to walk everywhere. Buses and matatus (Kenyan minibuses) run from early morning to late at night, though we strongly advise you to take taxis after dark. During the day things are much safer, though keep your wits about you. In the text we give the numbers of some of the buses you may need.

❏ **Diplomatic missions in Nairobi**
Australia Riverside Drive, 400m off Chiromo Rd (PO Box 39341; ☎ 445034)
Belgium Limuru Rd, Muthaiga (PO Box 30461; ☎ 522011)
Canada Comcraft House, Haile Selassie Avenue (PO Box 1013; ☎ 214804)
Denmark HFCK Building, 11th floor, Kenyatta Ave/Koinange St (PO Box 40412; ☎ 331088)
France Barclays Plaza, 9th floor, Loita St (PO Box 41784; ☎ 214848)
Japan 15F, ICEA Building, Kenyatta Ave (PO Box 60202; ☎ 332955)
Thailand Rose Ave, off Denis Pritt Rd (PO Box 58349; ☎ 715800)
Britain Upper Hill Rd (PO Box 30465; ☎ 714699)
United States United States Information Service, Barclays Plaza, Loita St (PO Box 30143; ☎ 240290).

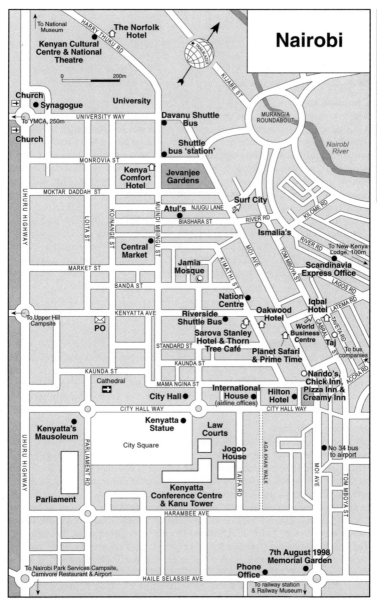

ARRIVING IN EAST AFRICA

SERVICES

Banks

Banks and foreign exchange bureaux tend to share roughly the same opening hours: Mon-Fri 9am-3pm, Sat 9-11am (noon for private exchange bureaux). Many of the banks have **ATMs** (cash machines) too, with most accepting Visa cards. Be on your guard when withdrawing money from an ATM.

Communications

Big, bright and gleaming, the new **post office** (Mon-Fri 7.30am-6pm) occupies a fairly large slice of valuable real estate at the western end of Kenyatta Avenue. Registered, recorded and normal deliveries can be made here, and there's a poste restante counter. The main **telephone** exchange stands 100m west down Haile Selassie Avenue from the American Embassy Remembrance Garden, though the cheapest way to phone home is to use the Internet. That said, we found the connection stuttering, though it's better at weekends when the Internet is less busy. A better or at least more reliable alternative is to pick up a Telcom Card (they come in denominations of Ks100, 200, 500, 1000 and 2000). With these all you have to do is dial 888, then the country code and then the number in the normal way. The rates to the UK are Ks15 per min. The phone office on Haile Selassie has details of this – and will be the best place to find if this service has been usurped by a superior one.

For **Internet**, head to the World Business Centre, a highfaluting name for what is essentially a shopping mall housed in the blue building opposite the end of Latema. The second floor is given over to Internet cafés all charging around Ks1 per minute (minimum Ks10). Or try Surf City, just off Jevanjee Gardens.

Camping equipment

Remember that you can rent everything you need from the trekking agencies in Arusha and Moshi or from the stall at Marangu Gate; see p226. But if you're not going there, **Atul's** (☎ 228064) on Biashara St, which is more a haberdashery than anything else, is the only place in the city that rents out camping gear. However, they're not cheap: Ks250 per day for a down sleeping bag for example.

Trekking agencies

It's a lot cheaper to book your trek in Tanzania, though booking in Nairobi may be worthwhile if you intend to climb via the Rongai Route, which starts at the border between the two countries. You may also consider visiting Amboseli National Park which lies just to the north-west of Kilimanjaro and has, in our opinion, the best views of the mountain. (Indeed, the photo on the front cover of this book was taken from Amboseli.) Safaris to Amboseli start at around US$70 per day. Those companies that also run hostels – namely **Prime Time**, **New Kenya Lodge** and **Planet Safari** (see opposite) are amongst the cheapest. They can also organize trips up Kili, though in reality are just acting as middlemen for Tanzanian operators. Another company worth checking out is **Kibo Slopes Safaris** (PO Box 58064; ☎ 2717373; 🖳 www.kiboslopessafaris.com), a smart and professionally run agent specializing in climbing Kilimanjaro from the northern side, ie up the Rongai Route, though they do offer other routes too. They are the partners of Snow Cap in Moshi (see p186), and include with their Kili trek optional excursions to Amboseli. Prices are steep, however, at US$2684 for eight days for one person, US$1868 each for two people.

WHERE TO STAY

The following list of hostels and hotels is arranged with the cheapest first. Those intending to **camp** should check out the **Nairobi Park Services Campsite** (☎ 889261; 💻 nps@swiftkenya.com) on Magadi Road, just past Langata Gate to the south of town, on the western perimeter of the Nairobi National Park. Clean, safe, cheap (US$3 per person per night camping charge), this campsite has some dormitory beds (US$6), tents for hire, a café and even satellite TV. Bus 126 or matatu 125 from the KBS bus station (3km east of town, take a cab to get there) will drop you off nearby. A little quieter, the **Upper Hill Campsite** (☎ 719662; 💻 campsite@alphanet.co.ke) lies in the grounds of a private house about 2km to the west of the city centre off Mara Road and has its own restaurant (in the house) and bar. Camping rates start at around Ks250.

● *Planet Safari* (☎ 229799; 💻 www.planetkenyasafaris.com), Sonalux House, 9th Floor, Moi Ave; dorm beds Ks300. Safari agency with tatty dorms attached. Use of the kitchen is also included as is the balcony café with a great view – well, an extensive one at least – over River Road and beyond. Agree to sign up for a safari (you'll almost feel obliged to if you stay here), and three nights' accommodation in the same tatty dorms are free, with reductions for stays beyond those three days. Other organizations such as Prime Time and New Kenya Lodge (see below) offer similar deals.

● *Prime Time* (☎ 215773; 💻 www.primetime.co.ke), on the top (9th) floor of Contrust House, Moi Ave. In the next building to Planet Safari and almost identical to it, with the same dorms, kitchen and balcony – and all at the same price of Ks300 for a dorm bed. They operate a similar deal regarding their safaris, too, though here they offer five nights free if you sign up to one of their trips, and then charge Ks200 after that.

● *New Kenya Lodge* (☎ 222202; 💻 www.nksafaris.com), River Road opposite the end of Latema Road; rates are Ks300 in a dorm, Ks500 sgl, Ks700 dbl. Another scruffy, old-style backpacker place that's friendly enough. Unlike those mentioned above it does have a few private rooms, but the chances are they'll be full and you'll be forced to share a dorm. Might be an idea to ring ahead. Like most such places, New Kenya also has a safari operation.

● *YMCA* (☎ 724116; 💻 www.kenya-ymca.org) University Way; non s/c dorm/sgl/dbl Ks540/690/1180; s/c dorm/sgl/dbl Ks640/940/1480; add Ks350-half-board, Ks700 full-board. Despite the name, women, atheists and the elderly are all welcome at this friendly, secure hostel, currently the number one destination for those on a budget who don't fancy their chances in the hurly-burly of the River Road area. The real clincher, however, is the pool (Ks50 residents, Ks80 non-residents).

• *Kenya Comfort Hotel* (☎ 2723414; 🖳 www.kenyacomfort.com) Jevanjee Gardens. Superbly situated just five minutes north of Kenyatta Avenue – and, more importantly, right next to where the shuttle buses pull in, which could be very handy if you've taken the afternoon shuttle and arrived after dark. Though it looks fairly small, features include a sauna and steam room, Internet and 91 bedrooms. With rates starting at US$30/40/50 for s/c sgl/dbl/tpl rising to US$40/50/60 if you want a TV and wardrobe thrown in, this is not a bad deal for central Nairobi and one of the better mid-range choices.

• *Oakwood Hotel* (☎ 220592/3; 🖳 www.madahotels.com/oakwood.html) Kimathi Street; s/c sgl/dbl/tpl US$60/75/85 including breakfast. Wooden floors, wooden walls, wooden ceiling and wooden doors – spending a night at the Oakwood can make you feel like Charles II hiding from Parliament. The Oakwood's strengths are its location opposite the Thorn Tree Café, its elegant antique lift, the TV and video in each room and the vague whiff of colonial charm. It's not spectacular, but it is convenient and fine.

• *The Sarova Stanley* (☎ 228830; 🖳 www.sarovahotels.com) Corner of Kenyatta Avenue and Kimathi Street; s/c sgl/dbl US$250/290 up to US$650 for Presidential Suite; breakfast US$17 extra. A luxury hotel with a bit of charac-ter, the Stanley first opened its doors to the very well-heeled in 1902 making it just a few years younger than the city itself. Edward, Prince of Wales, Ernest Hemingway and Hollywood's finest from Ava Gardner to Clark Gable have all rested their eminent heads on the Stanley's sumptuously stuffed pillows. Victorian elegance still abounds, though the demands of the modern client have led to the introduction of a shopping arcade, swimming pool and gymnasium. Also plays host to the Thorn Tree Café (see p141).

• *The Norfolk* (☎ 216940; 🖳 www.lonrhohotels.com) Harry Thuku Road; room-only prices: s/c sgl/dbl US$265/US$305; suites up to US$525; breakfast US$16. Nairobi's *other* historic hotel, and younger by two years, the Norfolk has been oozing class from its premises since it first opened its doors on Christmas Day 1904. Boasts the same facilities as The Stanley plus a fine col-lection of carriages and classic cars in the central courtyard and a more peace-ful, out-of-town feel.

WHERE TO EAT

Kenya's cuisine is virtually indistinguishable from Tanzania's, being hearty, meaty and with an emphasis firmly on quantity rather than quality. Embodying this description is the legendary tourist-attraction-cum-restaurant, *Carnivore* (Langata Road, near the Nairobi National Park; take a taxi from the town cen-tre), designed specifically for those people whose thoughts upon seeing the playful gambolling of a young impala for the first time is to wonder what it would taste like coated in a spicy barbecue sauce. Actually, the menu has had to be severely reduced in recent years though you can still find ostrich and ante-lope migrating across its pages most nights, and there are even a few vegetari-an options too. To be honest, some of it is revolting, but it's all good fun – and where else can you legitimately address the staff with that classic old chestnut 'Waiter, bring me some crocodile and make it snappy!'.

Vying with the celebrity of Carnivore is the *Thorn Tree Café*, something of a Mecca for travellers. Now on its third acacia, the original idea behind planting a tree in the middle of the courtyard was so that travellers could leave messages for other travellers on its thorns. Unfortunately, trees being trees, the roots of the previous two eventually started to undermine the building itself and had to be destroyed. As for the food here, it's a great place for a post-climb breakfast feed-up, while at other times of day it's an Italian restaurant.

For cheaper and more mundane fare, the *Taj*, on Taveta Road, one of a host of cheap eateries around River Road, is a reasonable African-style Indian curry house: don't expect hot towels, flock wallpaper and Cobra beer but do expect fast service, low prices and waiters who bring extra sauce if your rice or chapatis have outlasted your curry.

A TOUR OF THE CITY

This half- to full-day walking tour is best done on a Sunday morning, when the hassle from safari touts is at its lowest and the gospel choirs are out in force on the streets and in the parks. It begins at the the **Railway Museum** (daily 8.15am-4.45pm; Ks200/100 adults/students). To reach it, from the railway station head west for 5-10 minutes along the road running parallel to the tracks. The museum is a gem. If it's possible to feel nostalgia for a time that one never knew and a place that one has never visited before, then this is the museum that will prompt those feelings with its fading photos of British royalty riding in the cow-catcher seats and its old posters advertising the newly-opened Uganda railway. This is truly an endearing little museum, and the rusty locomotive graveyard out front is a fascinating place for a nose around too.

Returning to the station, head north along Moi Avenue. At the junction with Haile Selassie avenue is the **former site of the American Embassy**, blown to smithereens on 7 August, 1998 by Al-Qaeda. The site has now been landscaped into a very small **remembrance garden** (entry Ks20) where a concrete and stone memorial has been erected bearing the names of the Kenyan victims (who constituted all but twelve of the 263 who perished). At the back of the enclosure is a glass pyramid sculpture containing some of the debris from that day, namely some twisted metal, a lump or two of concrete and a door handle. It's a busy junction, and the Co-op building behind – also badly damaged in the blast – is from the eyesore school of architecture; yet still the park is suffused with an atmosphere of the deepest poignancy.

Continuing north along Moi, City Hall Way runs parallel to Haile Selassie, two blocks north. The **hall** itself lies about 400m along the road on the right (north). Opposite, to your left, is a **statue** of benign old first president Jomo Kenyatta, sitting regally overlooking the city square with his back to the **law courts**. To Kenyatta's left, rising imperiously from fountains, are the **Kenyatta International Conference Centre**, like a giant water-lily bud on the verge of opening, and the vertiginous **KANU Tower**, formerly the tallest building in the city and still one of the ugliest – though most locals would probably take issue with this opinion. (KANU, incidentally, are the most powerful party in Kenya and have dominated the political arena since independence.)

Continue along City Hall Way – past the **Holy Family Cathedral**, neatly juxtaposed with the casino directly opposite – and you'll see to the left of the road, lined with flags and guarded by two black lions and several bored-looking guards in neo-colonial ceremonial livery, the object of the Kenyatta statue's gaze: his own **mausoleum**. Next door and adorned with a rather quaint clock tower is the Kenyan **Parliament**, which can be visited; entry is gained through the entrance on Harambee Avenue.

Heading back north along the Uhuru Highway, 15 minutes later you'll come to a large roundabout and the centre of worship in the city, surrounded as it is by a **synagogue** (to the north-east) and no less than **four churches** (St Paul's Catholic Chapel to the north-west, with St Andrews behind it up the hill, the First Church of Christ Scientist further along the same road and the city's main Lutheran church on the roundabout's south-western edge). From the roundabout you can continue north for fifteen hot and dusty minutes along the highway to the National Museum (see below), or you can turn east along University Way, taking a right turn south through the business heart of Nairobi along Muindi Mbingu Street. On the way you might wish to take a short detour to visit the **Jamia Mosque** (Nairobi's most impressive mosque but closed to infidels), and the tawdry craft market, before rejoining Kenyatta Avenue. Take a left here, pausing on the way at one of the street vendors to pick up something to read at your table, and after a couple of hundred metres you'll come to the final port of call on this walk, the **Thorn Tree Café**, with its overpriced but wonderfully cold beer.

National Museum
(Off Museum Hill, near the Uhuru Highway; every day, 9.30am-6pm; Ks200). The National Museum, by far and away the number one sight in Nairobi, is unfortunately currently closed for renovation, though all being well by the time you read this it should have reopened with many of the museum's major attractions still on display. They include a model, faithfully cast in fibreglass, of the **nation's favourite pachyderm**, Ahmed, an elephant so huge its tusks alone weighed a whopping 65kg each; an exhibition celebrating Kenya's Asian immigrants, including a run-through of the building of the **Uganda Railway** from Mombasa to Kampala, a project that took over five years (August 1896 to December 1901) and claimed 582 lives; a wonderful collection of Joy Adamson's portraits of **Kenyan tribes** – look out for the depictions of people wearing ear stretchers and the priest enveloped in hippo teeth. But best of all, check out the startling prehistoric section, including the **1.6-million-year-old skeleton** of a boy and a couple of amusing and well-rendered 'caveman' dioramas.

MOVING ON – TO KILIMANJARO

With the sad demise of the **train** service between Voi and Moshi, on the Nairobi to Mombasa line, the only way overlanders can reach the towns and villages around Kilimanjaro now is by **bus**. It would be worth enquiring at the train station as to whether the train service has been resumed, for there can surely be no more splendid a way to travel through East Africa than in the faded colonial grandeur of a carriage belonging to Kenya Railways. The train to **Mombasa**, incidentally, leaves three times a week at 7pm from the terminus to the south of Haile Selassie Road, arriving, all being well – which it very often isn't – at 8.36am the next morning. Fares are Ks3160 in first class, Ks2275 in second, Ks400 third. If you've visited the Railway Museum, you'll want to catch it even if you've no intention of going to Mombasa!

As for the buses, for the best view of Kilimanjaro as you travel to Arusha, sit on the left-hand side of the vehicle. Scandinavia Express are one of the more reputable companies, though currently they are in a little financial trouble and it's touch and go whether they'll still be operating by the time you read this. Their offices are on River Road and they currently have a 7am bus daily to Arusha (Ks1500), or it's Ks1600 to Moshi.

Far more convenient and comfortable are the **shuttle buses**. Your hotel should be able to book these tickets for you and should be able to get you the cheaper residents' rate too. There are three main companies operating these minibuses to Arusha. **Riverside** (☎ 229618) on the third floor of Pan African House, Kenyatta Avenue, has two buses, at 8am (which continues on to Moshi) and 2pm (though note that this will not arrive in Arusha until after dark). Officially the fare is US$25 to Arusha, or US$30 to Moshi, but it doesn't take much bargaining to get the 'residents' price of Ks1000 to Arusha (Ks1500 to Moshi). The comparatively new **Impala** (☎ 2717373) in the Silver Springs Hotel by the Hurlingham Roundabout also operates buses to Arusha at 8am and 2pm for US$20/Ks1000 non-residents/residents. Cheap, but their offices are a little way from the centre. The third company is **Davanu** (☎ 222002), on the third floor of the Windsor Building, on the corner of Muindi Mbingu Street and University Way, which also operates two buses (8am to Moshi via Arusha and 2pm to Arusha only), though they're a little pricier (US$25, US$35 to Moshi), and trying to get the residents' price seems more difficult here. Though both of these companies promise to collect you from your hotel, in reality if you're staying anywhere in the centre of Nairobi they'll probably ask you to go to the Stanley or Norfolk hotels and pick you up there. All shuttles leave from Jevanjee Gardens.

Crossing the border

The drive between Nairobi and Arusha is fascinating, not least because you may find yourself sharing the road with Masai tribesmen on bikes, camels, zebras, impalas and giraffes, and all with Kili looking on from the east. Despite the chaos of souvenir hawkers and Masai warriors that surrounds the Kenya-Tanzania border crossing at Namanga, the border formalities themselves are straightforward enough. On the Kenyan side you'll doubtless have to queue to have your passport stamped, and on the Tanzanian side there's usually a little wait while the customs officials cast a cursory eye over your belongings and draw a little chalk cross on the side of your bag. It is possible to change money at the border though the crossing is renowned for its charlatans so you're probably better off waiting until Arusha.

Kilimanjaro International Airport

Is Kilimanjaro the first mountain to have its own international airport? It is situated equidistant between Moshi and Arusha, to the south of the disused rail-tracks. **Arriving** is straightforward: the terminal is small and you'll instantly be ushered into the arrivals hall. The baggage hall and immigration formalities are easily negotiated – Kilimanjaro is also one of only four places where you can pick up a visa if your own country of residence does not have a Tanzanian consulate or embassy. Indeed, in our experience even if there *is* a consulate in your country you should still be able to pick up a visa here – and the last time we checked they were charging only US$50 for it – which works out cheaper than the £38 (US$67) they charge at the consulate in London. Arriving in Tanzania without a visa is risky, however, for there's always the slight chance that the authorities will suddenly decide to enforce the rule that anyone coming from a country with Tanzanian representation must buy their visa beforehand, thereby putting you in very hot water with the authorities – which is no way to start your holiday. Our advice: get it beforehand if you can. Passing through customs (which is very rarely manned) you'll find a cash-only moneychanger here offering reasonable rates for the dollar, though as yet there's no ATM. To get to Arusha or Moshi, both about 45 minutes away, see pp145-6 and p169.

Departing from Tanzania, things are just as simple. The check-in desks face the door as you walk into the departure lounge. Don't be in too much of a hurry to get through customs, for there's even less to do on that side of the X-ray machine than there is on this side. Instead, go for a beer in the café to the right of the check-in desks, which isn't as big a rip-off as many airport establishments. The food isn't too nasty either.

Drink drunk and sandwich scoffed, you can then visit the small string of shops separating you from the departure lounge, which some tourists say offers the best-value souvenir shopping in the country. If you have any Tanzanian money you want to change, you can go and see if the cash-only bureau de change in the arrivals hall is open (the dollar and Kenya shilling rates are reasonable but the other rates are a bit stingy). All of these activities should take you less than seven minutes, leaving you plenty of time to visit the viewing platform upstairs, call in at the toilets in the basement, and have another beer.

(Opposite) The view east from the summit of Mount Meru with the Ash Cone in the foreground and Kilimanjaro in the background.

PART 5: ARUSHA, MOSHI AND MARANGU

Arusha

Arusha may only be Tanzania's sixth largest town but it is, nevertheless, one of considerable consequence. This importance has been rather thrust upon it, and has a lot to do with its location. As a Tanzanian city situated conveniently close to the border with Kenya and reasonably near to Uganda, Arusha was the obvious choice as headquarters of the East African Community when these three nations were part of an economic union in the seventies; it has latterly become the centre for recent attempts to revive this union by the Tripartate Commission for East African Collaboration. By coincidence, Arusha lies almost exactly halfway between Cape Town and Cairo and possibly as a result has become something of a venue for sorting out issues from all over Africa – including the Tanzanian-brokered peace talks on Burundi and, most famously, the Rwanda War Crimes Tribunal, still taking place in the Arusha International Conference Centre (AICC).

These momentous deliberations aside, Arusha is largely unremarkable and, it must be said, few visitors leave Arusha with fond memories, simply because of the inordinate amount of hassle that they are subjected to from the safari agents and their touts. This badgering begins the moment you set foot within 100m of the clock tower. (It should be stated here that the locals who aren't working as touts and who don't profess to be your best friend when you first meet them are, on the whole, very pleasant indeed.) Manage to survive the pestering and stick around for a few days in the town and you will find that it does have its charms, including some decent restaurants and other tourist amenities, some pretty suburbs filled with jacaranda trees and other blossoms, and a chaotic but occasionally fascinating central market. But with the call of the wild from Kilimanjaro, Ngorongoro and the Serengeti beckoning from east and west, it's a rare tourist who stays long enough to savour them.

ARRIVAL

Arusha Airport (or 'the little airport' as it's commonly called locally, to distinguish it from KIA) lies to the west of the city and serves internal flights only. There's not much to the place other than a tiny 'departure lounge', a great little bookshop crammed with English titles, a souvenir shop or two and several cafés. A taxi into town will set you back about Ts5000 (though they'll ask for double that), or you can walk to the main junction (about one hot, dusty kilometre) and wait for a dalla-dalla to pass by (Ts250).

(Opposite) **Marangu** (see pp190-6): Traditional Chagga house (top). The markets in Marangu (bottom) are amongst the most colourful sights in the region.

Not to be confused with Arusha Airport, **Kilimanjaro International Airport** lies to the other (eastern) side of town, some distance to the south of the road to Moshi. If you flew in with Air Tanzania, a shuttle bus should be waiting to ferry you into Arusha or Moshi (free with an Air Tanzania flight ticket, Ts5000 otherwise). KLM passengers have the chance to catch a shuttle to Arusha with Impala (US$10), their minibuses officially leaving at 9pm from the airport, though often if they've still got seats they'll wait until every last KLM passenger has passed through customs before setting off. Precision Air operate their own shuttle service (Ts2000) for their flights from Kenya, Dar, Zanzibar or Shinyanga. Fly in with any other airline, however, such as Ethiopian, and you'll have to take a cab, there being no public transport to and from the airport. These can be very expensive – the signs at the airport suggest a ridiculous US$50. From our own experience, a little haggling can reduce this figure to US$40, which is still a rip-off. However, as you're probably turning up in a strange country where you don't know the prices and where there's no other transport available, the odds are stacked against you; and after a long flight you may not feel inclined to argue anyway. For details on **going to the airports**, see below and the box on p168.

Arriving in Arusha by **public bus**, expect to be dumped (sometimes literally) at the terminus, reasonably close to the budget hostels at the southern end of Colonel Middleton Road, in the western half of town. If you've reached Arusha by **shuttle bus**, on the other hand, as you got in you should have told the driver where you wish to jump out; if not, the chances are you'll be dropped off at the New Mount Meru Hotel, in the north-eastern corner of town. From here, one of the drivers hanging around may offer to take you, free of charge, to the hotel of your choice. Whether they are working, as they often say they are, for the shuttle companies or whether they are working for one of the safari outfits in town and look upon this drive as a chance to hook another client, we have no idea. Suffice to say they will deliver you to your door without charge and, after a long journey, that is a good enough reason to accept their offer. If the offer of a free lift is not forthcoming, you'll have to catch a cab.

ORIENTATION AND GETTING AROUND

Arusha is bisected by the Naura River Valley, a narrow and shallow dip in the town's topography. The division is more than just geographical: to the west is downtown, the busier, noisier and more fun part of Arusha, where most of the cheap lodgings can be found. To the east of the valley lies the tourist centre, where most tourist hotels, safari companies and better restaurants are located.

Arusha is not a big place, most things are within walking distance of each other and **getting around** is not a major hassle, though to get from one half of town to the other it's a good idea to take a **dalla-dalla**. They charge Ts150 for short trips around town or Ts250 for destinations further afield. To the west of the post office on Sokoine is the stop for dalla-dallas heading west towards **Arusha Airport** (listen out for the touts shouting 'Kisongo'), dropping off passengers a kilometre from the terminal for Ts250; if you're carrying all your luggage, you've got to be seriously tightfisted to opt for this rather than take a taxi from town (about Ts5000, though they'll ask for more).

SERVICES

Tourist information

The **tourist information office** is on Boma Road (Mon-Fri 8am-4pm, Sat 8.30am-1pm). Full of brochures, it also stocks photocopied maps of the town but is only moderately helpful when dealing with any enquiries you may have about the city. Best of all, however, is the list of licensed tour agencies in both Moshi and Arusha that they keep. They also have a noticeboard where some people advertise for trekking companions.

Banks

Standard Chartered, at the southern end of Goliondoi Road, is probably the most central **cashpoint**, though if you've got a vehicle you may prefer to use the one at the Barclays building on the way down to The Outpost on the Serengeti Road, which we've always found to be more reliable. The best rates for **travellers' cheques** can be found at the NBC on Sokoine (Mon-Fri 8.30am-3pm, Sat 8.30am-noon), though you may have to queue for a long time to be served; if you haven't got the time or patience, the private exchange office over the road was offering the next best rates in town. The **AMEX** agent in Arusha is Rickshaw Travels in the Marshall Building on Sokoine (☎ 2506655).

Communications

The **post office** is by the clock tower (Mon-Fri 8am-4.30pm, Sat 9am-noon). The only reliable place to buy phonecards is from the **ATCO Telecom office** on Boma Road (Mon-Sat 7.30am-10pm, Sun 8am-8pm). Phoning is fairly expensive at Ts2300 per minute to the UK, Europe and the US (Ts2500 from the post office on Sokoine). Finding an **Internet** café in Arusha isn't difficult. All charge much the same with Ts500 for thirty minutes being the norm. The current favourite with most travellers is the Patisserie on Sokoine, though this is mainly because a) they have wi-fi facilities (for which they charge the same rate of Ts500 for thirty minutes); and b) all the overland tours stop there. I prefer the Klub Afriko, round the back of the New Safari Hotel, which charges the same but which offers a little more peace and privacy.

Airline offices

● **Ethiopian Air** Boma Road (PO Box 93; ☎ 2504231/2506167; 🖳 www.flyethiopian.com; Mon-Fri 8.30am-5pm, Sat 8.30am-1pm).
● **Air Excel** Bank Exim Building, first floor, (PO Box 12731; ☎ 2501597; 🖳 reservations@airexcelonline.com).
● **Coastal Aviation** Boma Road (☎ 2500087; 🖳 www.coastal.cc).
● **KLM and Northwest Airlines** Boma Road (☎ 2506063/2508062; 🖳 www.klm.com; Mon-Fri 8.30am-5pm, Sat 8.30am-12.30pm).
● **Precision Air** New Safari Hotel Building, Boma Road (PO Box 1636; ☎ 2506903; 🖳 www.precisionairtz.com; Mon-Fri 8am-5pm, Sat and Sun 8am-2pm).
● **Regional Air** (PO Box 14755; ☎ 2502541; 🖳 www.regional.co.tz).
● **Air Tanzania** Boma Road (☎ 2503201; 🖳 www.airtanzania.com; Mon-Fri 8am-1pm, 2-5pm, Sat 9am-1pm).

ARUSHA, MOSHI AND MARANGU

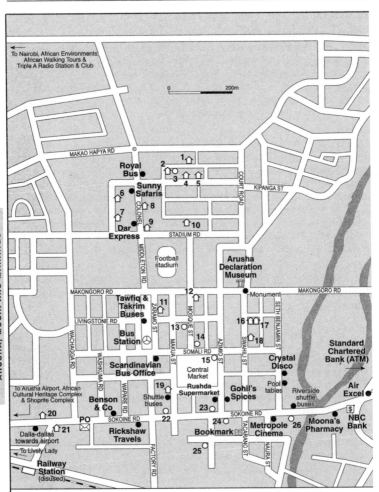

To Nairobi, African Environments, African Walking Tours & Triple A Radio Station & Club

0   200m

MAKAO HAPYA RD

Royal Bus

Sunny Safaris

Dar Express

KIPANGA ST

COURT ROAD

COLONEL MIDDLETON RD

STADIUM RD

Football stadium

Arusha Declaration Museum

MAKONGORO RD   Monument   MAKONGORO RD

Tawfiq & Takrim Buses

LIVINGSTONE RD

Bus Station

ZARAMO ST

MOSQUE ST

MAKUA ST

AZIMIO ST

SETH BENJAMIN ST

SWAHILI ST

Standard Chartered Bank (ATM)

SOMALI RD

Scandinavian Bus Office

WACHAGA RD

WASHKUMA RD

WAPARE RD

Central Market

Rushda Supermarket

Crystal Disco

Pool tables

Riverside shuttle buses

Air Excel

To Arusha Airport, African Cultural Heritage Complex & Shoprite Complex

Benson & Co

Shuttle buses

Gohil's Spices

NBC Bank

SOKOINE RD

PO

Rickshaw Travels

FACTORY RD

Bookmark

SOKOINE RD

Metropole Cinema

Moona's Pharmacy

NAURA ST

TACARANO ST

Dalla-dallas towards airport

To Lively Lady

Railway Station (disused)

Where to stay
1 Mashele Guest House
2 Casablance Mini Lodge
4 Monjes
5 Levolosi and Kitundu
6 Williams Inn
7 AM Hotel
8 Golden Rose
9 Annex Hotel
   Arusha By Night
10 Safari

11 Hotel 7-11
12 Arusha Crown
16 Arusha Centre
17 Hotel Fort des Moines
18 Sinka Court Hotel
19 Pallsons
20 Meru House Inn
21 Da'Costa Hotel
27 Arusha Naaz
29 Arusha Hotel
30 YMCA

32 New Safari Hotel &
   Easy Travel & Tours
34 Arusha Vision Campsite
35 Hotel Equatorl
37 New Mount Meru Hotel
40 Kibo Palace Hotel
   (unfinished)
42 The Outpost
43 Le Jacaranda
44 Spices and Herbs
45 Impala Hotel

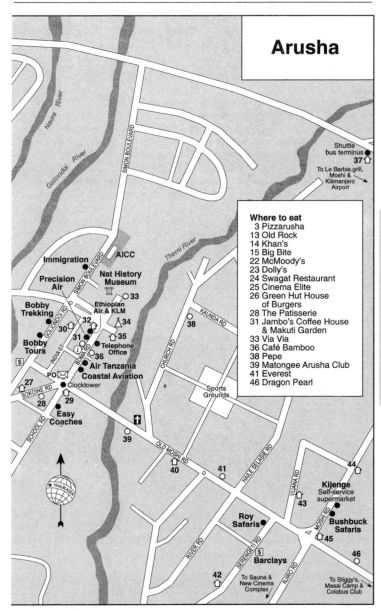

Arusha

Where to eat
3 Pizzarusha
13 Old Rock
14 Khan's
15 Big Bite
22 McMoody's
23 Dolly's
24 Swagat Restaurant
25 Cinema Elite
26 Green Hut House
   of Burgers
28 The Patisserie
31 Jambo's Coffee House
   & Makuti Garden
33 Via Via
36 Café Bamboo
38 Pepe
39 Matongee Arusha Club
41 Everest
46 Dragon Pearl

Immigration

The immigration office (Mon-Fri 7.30am-3.30pm) is on Simon Boulevard, south and across the road from the AICC.

Shopping

You can get most things in Arusha – it's just a question of knowing where to look. Some of the shops seem to have been deliberately set up with tourists and expats in mind, one such place being Bookmark, just south of Sokoine on Tacarano St. Part café, part **bookshop**, the place sells English-language books only, including an array of guide- and coffee-table books on Tanzania, shelf after shelf of fiction and non-fiction titles and even a secondhand section. Another tourist-orientated outlet is Explorer, opposite the Café Bamboo on the Boma Road. Though half of the floor space is given over to souvenirs, Explorer is also, as its name suggests, the place to come for **trekking equipment** such as torches, knives and even a few tents; though do remember that your trekking agency should provide you with any equipment you don't have.

Recommended by several travellers, Moona's **Pharmacy** lies near the eastern end of Sokoine, below the NBC Bank. The staff speak good English here, as they do at Benson & Company, about a kilometre further west on Sokoine, which should be your first port of call for **electrical goods**, repairs and camera film. This is also the first place to come if you need to have your phone unlocked (see p77). If you can't be bothered to schlep all the way to Shoprite (see below) for your **supermarket** needs, the Kijenge Self-Service Supermarket below the Spices and Herbs hotel/restaurant is good, though again a little out of the way for most people, while Rushda, just off Sokoine on Azimio Street, has a fair selection and just opposite is Gohil's, the place to come for dried **herbs and spices**.

● **The Shoprite Complex** The new **Shoprite**, at the western end of Sokoine, is Arusha's first full-blown supermarket: vast, cheap and with plenty of choice. Perhaps unsurprisingly, most of the customers at this latest branch of the pan-African chain appear to be expats. In the same vein and sharing the same complex are a number of quality outlets that, if not deliberately targeting the expat community, certainly derive much of their custom from it. They include *Stiggbucks* and *Chocolate Temptation* (see p159), *Msumbi Coffee* (a smart café-cum-coffee-retailers), the ice-cream purveyors *Ciao Gelati* (delicious ice cream in a range of flavours at Ts1200 per cup), a souvenir shop, a DVD-hire outlet, a couple of photographic stores, a few safari agencies and even the German Consulate (☎ 027-250 80 22). Beneath this last is a massage-parlour (☎ 0744 273557; Ts20,000 for one hour), perhaps the only place in town to advertise waxing and manicure/pedicures (US$16). This arcade may lack charm, being centred around a dusty parking lot next to a supermarket; nevertheless, if you're missing home, this place is unrivalled in Arusha.

❑ Arusha's area code is ☎ 027. If phoning from outside Tanzania dial ☎ +255-27.

WHERE TO STAY

As with much of the rest of Tanzania, the hotels in Arusha officially charge different rates for locals and foreigners. But, as usual, it doesn't take too much to persuade some hotels to let you have the cheaper residents' rate. For the prices listed below, however, we have usually opted to list the **non-residents' rate** only; the residents' rate is usually lower by 50% or more though not always; sometimes it's just the shilling equivalent of the non-resident price.

The following is written in **approximate price order**.

Camping

For those who wish to camp, the **Masai Camp** lies 3km from the centre on the Old Moshi Road and charges Ts3000 per person, including hot showers. It's a great place (see under *Where to Eat* and *Nightlife* on p158 and p159 respectively) but, with a disco on Friday and Saturday nights and a lively bar for the rest of the week, it's not the quietest place to camp. Unfortunately, the only other option is **Arusha Vision** on Boma Road opposite the Equator Hotel. It's the most central campsite, though it is rather noisy and said to be very unsafe.

Budget: under US$15

For years the backpackers' centre was a small cluster of roads to the north of the bus station and a few metres east of Col Middleton Road. Wandering around it today you find little has changed, with all the budget hotels still there – it's just the travellers who've disappeared. Still, if you're after the cheapest accommodation in town, this is the place to look. Places include the **Mashele Guest House** which, at just Ts4000 for a double with shared facilities or Ts7000 for those with bathroom, is fair value; the **Casablanca Mini Lodge** (☎ 2507062), on the corner of the same street; the spartan but acceptable **Kitundu** (☎ 2400466), **Levolosi** and **Monjes** on Kaloleni, the next street south; and the **Safari** (☎ 2507819), one or two blocks further south again. All charge roughly the same tariff as the Mashele and are similar in quality. One place round here that does still see the occasional backpacker, and deservedly so, is the curiously named **Annex Hotel Arusha By Night** (☎ 2501434), just north of the stadium. With rooms built either side of a long corridor, at first this place feels a bit like an institution but actually the rooms themselves – large, self-contained and comfortably furnished with fan and mosquito net – are quite pleasant. Rates are Ts7000/10,000 s/c sgl/dbl including continental breakfast.

However, the focus for budget travellers has moved a few hundred metres south to Sokoine Road. **Meru House Inn** (☎ 2507803; 🖳 meruhouseinn@hotm ail.com; non-s/c sgl/dbl/tpl Ts6000/7000/13,000, or Ts9000/11,000/16,000 with bathroom) has been around for a while and, unlike those previously mentioned, has managed to hold on to its popularity. It's another hotel often patronized by foreign tourists, which is surprising given that it makes little effort to attract them. Still, it's pleasant, relaxed, the manager and his staff are very friendly and there's a good Indian restaurant on the ground floor. But do avoid the rooms overlooking either the central courtyard or the road if you want a good night's sleep.

ARUSHA, MOSHI AND MARANGU

Virtually opposite, a new place has opened in town which, for the moment at least, offers the best value in the budget range. The *Da'Costa Hotel* (☎ 0744 377795; 💻 www.hoteldacosta.com) stands in an unpromising position in the forecourt of a petrol station by the Meru Post Office on Sokoine. Currently, the fumes of fresh paint and creosote pervade the entire building and some of the rooms (of which none are en suite) are unfinished (with fans yet to be put into some, for example). But at least this means they're smart and clean. The highlight, however, is the rooftop restaurant with perhaps the best view of Meru from the town. On a clear day, so it is said, you can even see Kilimanjaro. It's also a great place to stay if you have to catch an early flight in the morning: the noise of the traffic outside won't let you sleep beyond 6.30am. Rates, including breakfast, are just US$10/15/20 sgl/dbl/tpl though if it's quiet you may well be offered the 'tour operators rate' of US$5/10/15 – which represents great value. Just be sure to check a number of rooms before settling on any one, and check everything works in the room before agreeing to stay. Back north, *Williams Inn* (☎ 2503578) is run like a boarding school with notices everywhere reminding people of the rules of the house, including orders barring guests from bringing in both alcohol and 'women of immoral turpitude'. Given its location at the seamier side of town, however, such discipline is no bad thing and the rooms are comfortable, quiet and pleasant enough, and US$10/15 s/c sgl/dbl is fair value.

Finally in this bracket, the *YMCA* on India St (☎ 2544032; US$10/13/23 for non-self-contained sgl/dbl/tpl) is chaotic and a bit of a dump but the only budget place on this eastern side of town.

Mid-range: US$15-50

Adjacent to and overlooking the bus station, the *Hotel 7-11* (☎ 2501261, 0744 578459) on Zaramo St is still, as it was in the first edition, unfinished! But just as they were then, the tiled rooms are still clean, tidy and come with television and the only drawback is its location on one of the most threatening streets in Arusha – fine during the day but a bit menacing at night. If you can put up with that, however, the rates (US$15/20/25 s/c sgl/dbl/tpl) seem fair.

Just to the east, four new hotels have opened up in the last couple of years in the previously hotel-free area between the bus station and the Naura River. Of most interest to tourists are the two places standing side by side on Pangani Street. The *Hotel Fort des Moines* (☎ 2548523) is a 23-room affair and very comfy, with each room boasting TV, telephone and its own bathroom. Rates are a very reasonable US$20/25 s/c sgl/dbl including breakfast. It is probably a place that appeals more to the locals, at least when compared to the neigbouring *Arusha Centre Tourist Inn* (☎ 250 0421; 💻 icerestaurant@ yahoo.com) which has similar facilities, again with a TV (caged to prevent theft!) and mosquito net (though no fan) in every room, all of which are en suite. B&B rates are again very reasonable at US$18/20 s/c sgl/dbl. Round the corner on Swahili Street is the fourth option, the *Sinka Court Hotel* (☎ 2504961; 💻 sink acourthotel@hot-mail.com) with much the same facilities (en suite, TV) as the other two though perhaps slightly smarter, brighter and airier, a difference that's reflected in the price (US$30/40 s/c sgl/dbl). South of the market, *Hotel Pallsons* (☎ 2548123; 📧 pallsonshotel@yahoo.com; sgl/dbl/tpl US$25/30/40 including continental breakfast) on Makua St is surprisingly clean and comfy considering its location just off the central market. It appears their reception has of late become a venue for watching English football matches on the telly, but if you're not a fan you can sneak off to your room to watch something else, because as well as a bathroom all rooms have TV.

Across the other side of town, though we're not entirely happy with the upgrading of their restaurant, the renovations to the accommodation at the *Arusha Naaz* (☎ 2502087, 2508893; s/c sgl/dbl/tpl US$30/45/60) are great. Along with their eager-to-please staff the hotel now has squeaky-clean, sunny en-suite rooms, all with TV, and an equally brilliant roof terrace; mercifully, they've also managed to clean their drains. Try to get a room away from the road if possible.

The major landmark on Col Middleton Road is the *Golden Rose* (☎ 250 7959; s/c sgl/dbl/tpl US$36/48/60, all including English breakfast), a popular place that's now dwarfed by its neighbouring conference centre. The hotel's name is apt too, for this is a hotel with something of a gilt complex, many of its rooms now being decorated in shiny golden hues.

One block west of Col Middleton Road, the towering *AM Hotel* (☎ 0744 468225) is one of the older places in town, having been founded in 1988. Unfortunately, neither the papier-maché giraffe and elephant in reception nor the surly attitude of the staff does much to endear, and the rates (s/c sgl/dbl/tpl/suite US$40/60/80/100, though residents' rates are much cheaper at Ts12,000/18,000/24,000/36,000) suggest that they're not that interested in foreign custom.

Right over the other side of town, the Ethiopian *Spices and Herbs* restaurant (see p158; ☎ 2502279, 0744 313162; 📧 axum_spices@hotmail.com) has 18 en-suite rooms built around a central courtyard at the back of their premises. The rooms are clean and airy, but a tad overpriced at US$30/40 s/c sgl/dbl (all prices inclusive of breakfast). Also in this neck of the forest is *The Outpost* (☎ 2548405; 📧 www.outposttanzania.com) down Serengeti Road, a district so exclusive that Arusha's usual noise of traffic and touts is replaced by the soothing sound of birdsong and the gentle rhythm of people brushing the dust from the street. Popular with tour groups, the Outpost has its own Internet and laundry service and a lovely lounge area kitted out, as with the rooms, in a spartan but sophisticated style. The rooms do have TV, however, and all are en suite. B&B here costs US$38/US$49/US$63 s/c sgl/dbl/tpl: pretty good value.

However, our favourite in this price range is *Le Jacaranda Hotel* (☎ 254 4624, 0748 98 61116; 📧 www.chez.com/jacaranda), set to the east of town in a quiet street to the north of the Old Moshi Road. This is a great place, its exterior walls painted with cartoon animals, its communal seating areas comfy and relaxed, and its huge rooms furnished with four-poster beds and massive bathrooms (including bath!). There's even a mini-golf course in the garden. The tariff of US$45/50 s/c sgl/dbl with breakfast represents good value.

Upmarket: above US$50

Another newcomer to the city's hotel scene is the ***Arusha Crown Hotel*** (☎ 250 8523; 🖳 www.arushacrownhotel.com) on Makongoro Road by the south-eastern corner of the stadium. Very much a hotel for local businessmen, it's smart and comfy enough though a little bland and the walls cannot entirely block out the noise from the streets below. Rates start at US$60/70 s/c sgl/dbl, which in our opinion is a little cheeky. Moving back eastwards, the smart ***Hotel Equator*** (☎ 2508409; 🖳 nah@tz2000.com; the website 🖳 www.newarushaho-tels.com is due to begin operating soon) is hidden away behind the phone office. With every room fitted out with a shower, private balcony, satellite TV and phone – some with Internet connection – this is now one of the plushest places in the town centre, and the price is fair at s/c sgl/dbl US$60/70 including continental breakfast. Very nearby and occupying what it describes as a 'lavish location' on

❏ Accommodation – Arusha surroundings

There are a couple of lodges outside Arusha that are popular with tour groups, and thus if you booked your trek from abroad you may well end up in these. Stylish and salubrious, it's hard to criticize these places except that they tend to be in the middle of nowhere. A classic example is the ***Moivaro Coffee Plantation Lodge*** (🖳 www .moivaro.com), 16 cottages tucked away at the end of a bumpy dirt track, each located in their own little corner of a coffee plantation amidst some beautifully tended grounds. Each room has its own en-suite bathroom and veranda and the lodge also boasts a swimming pool and bar. A massage service is available, too, which will enable you to while away the hours when you're not on the mountain. The lodge lies about a twenty-minute drive from KIA on the way to Arusha.

Moivaro isn't the only coffee-themed lodge in the region, however; nor, for that matter, is it even the best coffee-themed lodge in the region. That award goes to the ***Arusha Coffee Lodge*** (🖳 www.arushacoffeelodge.com), twenty-three luxury chalets that are just gorgeous. Unlike the other hotels in this section, it actually lies to the west of Arusha on the way to the local airport but is still being used by a couple of trekking companies, particularly those who combine their treks with a safari after-wards. In addition there's a pool and massage service, and another thing in its favour is its renowned restaurant, Redds African Grill.

Continuing the theme of hotels located in the middle of coffee plantations, the ***Ngurdoto Mountain Lodge*** (PO Box 7302, Arusha; ☎ 2555217; 🖳 www.thengurdot omountainlodge.com) is a massive place squeezed between Mounts Meru and Kili, and exactly halfway between the airport and Arusha. The hotel consists of 79 rooms as well as 30 two-roomed chalets, all of which are en-suite and come with TV and mini-bar – and some even have their own jacuzzi. With two restaurants, coffee shop, 'BBQ ranch', tennis and badminton courts, swimming pool, health club and even its own golf course, this is just about as good as it gets facility-wise – though it must be said it's also a little soulless and a bit of a blot on the landscape that makes no attempt to blend into its surroundings. It's also geared more towards the business client than the tourist.

The ***Dik Dik*** (PO Box 1449, Arusha; ☎ 2553459; 🖳 www.dikdik.ch) is more homely and in a good location near Meru. Swiss-owned, it first opened its doors in 1990. Named after one of Africa's smallest antelopes, the Dik Dik is appropri-ately petite, particularly when compared to the nearby Ngurdoto. It boasts just

Boma Road is its sister establishment the *New Safari Hotel* (☎ 2503261/2; s/c sgl/dbl/tpl/suites US$70/95/120/150-60). In the last edition we described this place as a 'disappointment', where 'tired and threadbare corridors' lead to 'standardized rooms where charm, character and homeliness are all sadly absent', and we concluded our review by saying that it was reminiscent of 'a Stalinist housing estate in central Siberia'... My, how things have changed. Boasting of a makeover that would make Laurence Llewellyn-Bowen envious, the New Safari Hotel is now one of the smarter places in town, the gleaming, polished nature of the lobby mirrored by the spotlessly clean rooms, all with TV, Internet access and mini-bar.

Moving east down the Old Moshi Road, one can only guess at the number of woodland creatures that were made homeless in order to supply the *Impala Hotel* (☎ 2508448/49/50/51; 🖳 www.impalahotel.com) with its wood-heavy reception.

nine bungalows, each with fireplace, veranda, hammock and mini-bar, and there's a small pool here too. It's a pleasant, homely place and one that doesn't, unlike so many other hotels described here, hide itself away from the outside world – indeed, it even invites them in, hosting live music evenings at weekends.

Not far away, *Rivertrees Country Inn* (PO Box 235, Arusha; ☎ 2553894; 🖳 www. rivertrees.com) sits, as its name suggests, on the banks of the Usa River and plays host to only 24 guests in eight self-contained guestrooms. The inn also boasts its own pub. Perhaps the best feature, however, is the kitchen, which has a fine reputation and bakes its own bread; that and a lovely location with the river flowing through the grounds and some great old trees providing welcome shade. Peaceful and serene, it's a place that will appeal to the ornithologist in all of us.

Right by the airport, the *KIA Lodge* (PO Box 43, KIA; ☎ 2554194; 🖳 www. kialodge.com) has been recommended by more than one reader as a great place to spend your last night in Africa before flying out from the neighbouring Kilimanjaro International Airport. It's decorated in a smorgasbord of Tanzanian styles, too, from the Zanzibar-style reception, the Tinga-Tinga paintings in the restaurant and the Makonde woodcarvings in the rooms. Their hilltop location also allows you unequalled views of both Kili and Meru, as well as distant glimpses of the Blue Mountains and Maasai plains. Lovely.

The *Protea Hotel Aishi* (PO Box 534, Moshi; ☎ 2756948; 🖳 www.proteahotels. com/aishi), situated on the way to Machame, is a charming place with landscaped gardens and 30 rooms, all en-suite and with TV, and is the only hotel in the area with a heated swimming pool. It also boasts a fitness centre with sauna and steam room.

L'Oasis (PO Box 14280, Arusha; ☎ 2507089, 0741 510531) is a bit of a strange place, twenty-two 'African huts' with in-room facilities that are quite tired. The food is said to be great, however, and the birdlife fabulous, though we've read of more than one person who has failed to get any sleep due to the barking of the neighbourhood dogs.

Finally, some people are now staying at the *Ilboru Lodge* (PO Box 8012, Arusha; ☎ 0744 270357; 🖳 www.ilborusafarilodge.com), just a couple of kilometres north of the AICC in Arusha. With 4 acres of land and its own pool, it's not a bad place for those on a budget who want a night of relative luxury without breaking the bank.

ARUSHA, MOSHI AND MARANGU

Along with the New Mount Meru Hotel and the refurbished New Safari it's the main business centre in Arusha, with all the trimmings one would expect – a plethora of bars and restaurants (Indian, Chinese, Italian), a pool and conference facilities and colour televisions in every room. Rooms with breakfast are actually quite reasonably priced at s/c US$72/83/132/210 sgl/dbl/tpl/suite. As for the *New Mount Meru Hotel* (☎ 2502711; 🖥 mountmeruhotel.com), this was once the city's Novotel and the style has changed little with the change in ownership. As a result, if you've sampled the plush if uniform comforts of one of the Novotel chain you'll pretty much know what to expect from this place, though it must be said the extensive grounds are very pleasant to walk around. Rates are more reasonable than they were under the Novotel chain, too, at US$80/100 for sgl/dbl.

Finally, no review of Arusha's hotels would be complete without mention of the oldest and best of the lot, the *Arusha Hotel* (☎ 2507777; 🖥 www.arushah otel.com), discreetly hidden away in the very heart of the action by the clock tower. Opened in 1894 (though the current building dates 'only' from 1927) and recently restored, this is the swishest and plushest of them all, with wood-panelled walls and, to use that well-worn brochure phrase, a real atmosphere of yesteryear. The restaurant is, of course, fabulous, the swimming pool heated and the rooms sumptuous and kitted out with television, Internet ports and, of course, a bathroom. All this luxury doesn't come cheap, however, with rates starting at US$140/160 s/c sgl/dbl.

WHERE TO EAT AND DRINK

Arusha is a good place for foodies, with African, Oriental and Indian eating places abounding. Some also advertise Continental food, which basically means any dish that doesn't fit into one of the categories above. There are a couple of local hangouts specializing in Tanzania's hearty, cheap and simple brand of cuisine, of which *Khan's* stands out. Long a favourite with locals, it has also been winning a whole legion of foreign fans over the past decade or so and is now something of a tourist attraction, to the point where they now even sell T-shirts. A garage by day, at around 5pm Khan's transforms itself into a barbecue to serve up their take on the chicken-in-a-basket theme, namely 'chicken-on-a-bonnet'. They also do mixed grills for Ts5000, including chips, naan bread and a serve-yourself table full of salads. It's just to the north of the Central Market on Mosque Street; be careful around here after dark – take a cab. Just to the north of Khan's is *Old Rock*, a new and pleasant little place proffering cheap burgers and sandwiches, steaks (Ts4000) and its own pizza oven. It's one of those hygienic places with an open kitchen so you can see what's going on with your food – which is reassuring. They don't serve alcohol, however.

Another travellers' hangout lies to the north of the bus station. *Pizzarusha* (not to be confused with its inferior neighbour *Pizza Hut Arusha*), to the west of the Mashele Guest House, is unfortunately now suffering from a lack of custom due to the exodus of travellers from this part of town, a fate that it really doesn't deserve. Claiming to conjure up the finest pizzas in Africa, this is a tout-free haven and a great place for budget-conscious backpackers. What's more, the pizzas are indeed exceptional, really good value (starting at Ts3500) and the service excellent.

Down on Sokoine, if you thought Tanzanian fast food simply meant impala on the hoof then think again and pay a visit to *McMoody's* (closed Monday). Because while it may look like its near namesake in the West, and the menu is similar too, McMoody's is thankfully a whole lot more civilized, with basic restaurant formalities such as full table service still observed. The food's OK too and, according to one expat, their milkshakes are unrivalled throughout Arusha. On the same section of Sokoine, *Dolly's* is a curious place, ostensibly a patisserie though with a vast array of Indian dishes on offer too, all served in spotlessly clean surroundings, making this a favourite for Americans and travellers with children. Down the road opposite is the *Cinema Elite*, supplying basic staples served up by a talkative old Indian gentleman with one eye permanently on the telly. Not far away is the excellent *Swagat Restaurant*, an Indian place with some great curries that's criminally ignored by many people. Trust us, the food, particularly the tandooris, is great and the lady who runs it very helpful and friendly. There's another fantastic Indian on the north-east corner of the market, *Big Bite*, long a favourite with expats, and a fine one at the western end of Sokoine, part of the *Meru House Inn* and often recommended by those who stay there. Note, however, this last one doesn't sell alcohol.

Moving up Sokoine, the *Green Hut House of Burgers* is a bit of a misnomer, for burgers feature only twice on the menu. This is a great little place for lunchtimes, however, with cheap, simple but filling local fare the order of the day. Unfortunately, both locals and tourists have found out about this place so you may find yourself sharing a table with complete strangers. Still, it's one way to meet people.

Still further up Sokoine and entering into the tourist land surrounding the clock tower, the first place to catch the eye is *Patisserie*, possibly because of the huge overland trucks that stop outside so that their clients can use the Internet there. Food-wise it's OK but nothing worth travelling across Africa for. Just across the road the restaurant at the *Arusha Naaz* has gone upmarket (it's no longer on the pavement), opens only in the afternoon now and as a result has lost a little of its charm; nevertheless, the buffet is often scrumptious, though despite boasting an à la carte menu, we were told there wasn't one when we asked.

Moving up past the clock tower, on Boma Road by the tourist office is *Jambo's Coffee House* and *Makuti Garden*. The first is a little coffee house serving great coffee but pretty average food. The latter is more a bar/evening cocktail venue and, like so many places around here, it can be chock-a-block one night and deadly quiet the next. Opposite, the *Café Bamboo* is a busy place and in our opinion a better one than its rivals across the road. The African music and ethnic design on the walls can't quite eradicate the impression that this is actually a very English-style tearoom, but there's nothing wrong with that and the food is served in large portions and is reasonably priced.

With branches in Honduras, Java and Zanzibar, **Via Via** is a chain of 14 travellers' cafés scattered around the globe which are renowned for the good work they do in introducing travellers to the local cultures. Arusha's branch, in the grounds of the old German Boma, is no different, with dancing displays and music performances held regularly (see *Nightlife* opposite). And if you don't give a cuss about the culture there's always the food, which includes such travellers' staples as banana pancakes and tuna sandwiches. The Belgian managers are mines of information too.

To the south on Old Moshi Road there's a number of large-scale restaurants that are perfect as venues for that post-Kili celebration (or commiseration) meal with the trekkers you met on the way. These include two Chinese restaurants within a few hundred metres of each other. The first you'll come to is **Everest**, which is by far the more established, though it's **Dragon Pearl** that is currently attracting the customers. This can only be because of the service at Everest, which is occasionally a little slow, for the food in both places is authentic, served in very generous portions and first rate.

Just opened, and situated a few hundred metres to the north of Old Moshi Road on Church Road, **Pepe** describes itself as an Indian-Italian restaurant. Though you'd be forgiven for thinking that they've taken the concept of fusion cuisine a step too far, thankfully the restaurant keeps the two cuisines apart, with each having their own separate menu. What they have in common, however, are the same high standards of preparation and authenticity – and both are delicious too. Try one of the curries for Ts5000 or come along for the Sunday lunch of a roast leg of lamb (Ts10,000).

Back on the Old Moshi Road, past the Impala, **Stiggy's** advertises itself as a Pacific-Thai restaurant though everybody else knows it as the place to come for delicious steaks (Ts8800) and pizzas (the best in Arusha, according to more than one expat). This is also the meeting point of the local Hash House Harriers; ask Stiggy himself (who's easy to spot: he's the one in apron and colourful trousers) for details. He also runs a café, **Stiggbucks**, in the Shoprite complex (see p150). Back on Old Moshi Road and further down, **Masai Camp** is *the* campsite for the huge number of overland trucks that call in at Arusha. Their kitchen conjures up some pretty fair approximations of Mexican food as well as pizzas and other popular Western dishes, but for me the place itself is the main selling point, a fine open-sided wooden affair with pool tables and a well-stocked bar, all infused with a sociable, relaxed ambience.

For something out of the ordinary, a trip to **Spices and Herbs**, the blossom-laden Ethiopian restaurant in the hotel of the same name, could be in order. With vegetarian dishes ranging from Ts3500 to Ts9000 as well as meat dishes (Ts5000-13,000), this place has been garnering praise from hungry travellers for years. Try the lamb in Ethiopian butter, with onions, green peppers and oregano (Ts6500), and you'll see why.

Heading back west along Sokoine, just south along Station Road (the street running alongside the Hotel Da'Costa) is a new place, **The Lively Lady**. But while the food from their barbecue is first rate (the lemon pork fried with garlic, ginger, masala and lemon, Ts3500, is delicious), the subdued lighting, loud rock music and impressively stocked bar (the most complete in Arusha according to local barflies) suggest this should be considered primarily as a place for imbibing rather than scoffing, though the section out front is brighter and quieter.

As impressive and mouthwatering as these restaurants indubitably are, for the ultimate treat in Arusha head down to the Shoprite Complex and *Chocolate Temptation*, a bijou boutique that specializes in extracting every last milligram of pleasure from the humble cocoa bean. My advice? Come here before climbing Kili to admire the mouthwatering beauty of the confectionery on offer, then promise yourself that, should you reach the summit, you can gorge on anything in the shop, be it a 100g box of the finest Belgian chocolates (Ts6000), or an entire cake (Ts10,000-30,000).You never know, such an incentive might just be the difference between success and failure...

NIGHTLIFE

Arusha is the **nightclub** and **live music** capital of northern Tanzania, attracting rastas and ravers from far and wide. Unfortunately, as with any large city, the scene changes rapidly and what's recommended here may well be out of date by the time you arrive. For the latest on what's hot and what's not, speak to Jef or Frank at Via Via – they have their finger on the pulse.

At the moment *Le Barbie.grill*, opposite the New Mount Meru Hotel, is the favourite with locals. As with all these places, it's a restaurant selling typical Tanzanian fare (*nyama choma* etc) but has live music at weekends, sometimes with the same band playing for 12 hours non-stop (3pm-3am). Fun, local and very, very sweaty, it can be a bit intimidating if you're by yourself – this is not a place that sets out to cater for Westerners – but is friendly enough and fun if you can muster a group together. At the other end of town but on the same road, *Triple A* is the city's favourite radio station (currently broadcasting in Swahili only, though it's mooted that English-language programmes may start soon) which occasionally hosts live performances. If you're around when a gig is being held, don't miss it, for this place attracts the finest bands from all over East Africa. Also hosting live bands, though this time to a much more Western crowd, *Via Via* has a live-music evening every Thursday in addition to organizing the occasional three-day festival and rap competition. Visit them to find out what they've got lined up, or check out their 'what's on' publication, *Time Out*, for further details. Another Western place, *Masai Camp*, at the eastern end of Old Moshi Road, has a disco at weekends and is a pleasant place to visit at any time, with relaxed seating in a lovely open-sided building, a giant TV and, if one of the overland trucks are in town, maybe a live act too.

On the same road but a little nearer to the town centre, the *Colobus Club* (Ts3500) opens only at the weekends and has two rooms, one playing Western music, one African. Unfortunately, its said to be suffering somewhat thanks to the popularity of the places above. Finally, there's *Crystal* on Seth Benjamin St (Ts1500), a much more homely venue playing largely African tunes to a largely African crowd. Dead at weekends – once again due to the popularity of the above – it's the place to come on weekdays.

If all this sounds a bit too hectic, you can always opt to drink the night away in more relaxed surroundings, either in the gardens of the *Matongee Arusha Club* on Old Moshi Road, a couple of hundred metres east of the clock tower, a local restaurant/bar which is popular with well-heeled locals; or you can play **pool**, either at Via Via, Matongee or Masai Campsite, or challenge the locals to a game in the hall next to the Crystal nightclub.

There's also a **cinema** on Sokoine, the Metropole, showing films nightly at 6pm (Ts1500). It's a bit of a mess but there are two more cinemas due to open to the south-east of town on the Njiro Road. Ask around to see if they've opened yet. Via Via also plan to screen movies every Wednesday, and the Alliance Française, north of the AICC, have occasional free screenings.

WHAT TO DO

Very little is the short answer. There are a couple of museums that could conceivably be worth visiting but only if you're absolutely sure you've finished preparing for your trek, have written all your postcards, bought all your souvenirs, sent all your emails, cut all your toenails and done all your laundry. The better of the two is the **Natural History Museum** (Mon-Fri 9am-5.30pm, Sat & Sun 9.30am-5.30pm), housed in the old German fort, or Boma. For Ts2000 you have the chance to look at a few incomplete skulls of early hominids, one diorama of a neanderthal sitting in a cave and a fragment or two of a prehistoric rhinoceros skeleton, while in a separate building the history of the Boma is examined. There's also the Academy of Taxidermists round the back featuring the heads of a number of Tanzania's animal treasures, all taxidermically treated and mounted on a wall; and nearby a couple of cages occupied by rescued animals – namely a baboon, a monkey and an owl – which, given their proximity to the taxidermy room, must be wondering what the museum has in store for them. The Via Via Café, which is located in the grounds of the Boma, is committed to improving the museum, for which we offer both our best wishes and deepest sympathy.

Secondly, by the Arusha Monument there's the **Arusha Declaration Museum** (Ts2000; 9am-6pm daily), which manages the rather difficult feat of making the Natural History Museum seem fascinating. Consisting in the main of a few photos and a number of traditional tools and weapons, perhaps the most interesting part is the building itself, which is where Nyerere and chums met to hammer out the details of the Arusha Declaration (26-29 January 1967); that, and the torch which is supposed to be carried around the country every year to promote unity and patriotism among Tanzanian folk. Still, we suppose some might find this place provides a useful précis of the country's history from pre-colonial times to the death of Nyerere, and the authorities are to be commended for trying. Overall, worthy if not exactly worthwhile.

In a similar vein to the above, the **African Cultural Heritage Complex** lies to the west of town on the way to Arusha Airport. Once again, perhaps the most interesting exhibit is the actual building, the roof of which is designed to resemble the Kibo summit. The complex itself, however, is little more than a market

ARUSHA, MOSHI AND MARANGU

for woodcarvings with a couple of recreated Masai dwellings in the courtyard. While there's no denying the artistry that's gone into the sculptures, the designs themselves may be a bit too elaborate to appeal to Western tastes. Nearby, the **art centre** will perhaps be of more interest when it is finally completed; it aims to be the biggest in East Africa. However, it was unfinished when the first edition of this book went to print and, despite work continuing on it, it's still some way from completion now, so don't hold your breath.

With such a dearth of formal attractions, perhaps the most educational and entertaining thing you can do in Arusha is visit a **football game** (Ts1000); it will teach you more about Tanzanians (or at least the male half of the population) and what makes them tick than any papier maché diorama or reconstructed Masai dwelling. The next game is usually chalked up on the noticeboard outside the stadium's main entrance on Col Middleton Road. Some of the games are rather low-key but attend a big league match and you're in for a treat. If football's not your game then you can always play **pool** at Masai Camp, Via Via or Matongee, or go **swimming** in the pool at the New Mount Meru (Ts4000) or Impala (Ts5000) hotels. There's also a **sauna and steam room** on the way to Njiro, open 9am-8pm seven days a week, with a promotional price (which looks like it might be a permanent price) of Ts2500 for 25 minutes.

Organized tours and courses around Arusha

The Via Via Café organizes tours around the city and neighbouring hills. None of these sights will take your breath away, nor is that their intention: they are simply very pleasant escapes from the city – or, in the case of the Arusha churches tour, a different way of looking at it – and a refreshing way of discovering the country that exists outside the national parks. They also operate a number of courses including a Chagga cookery course, where you spend the morning shopping for ingredients at the local market and the afternoon cooking them into such dishes as *ndizi nyama* (green bananas and meat) or *wali na maharage* (rice with beans). Or you can take a trip to a batik workshop, a drum making factory (Ts4500, or Ts5000 including lessons) or even take a Swahili lesson (Ts3000).

For local tours that take you further afield, the Dutch development organization SNV, in association with the Tanzanian Tourist Board, have created **Cultural Tourism Programmes** where you can visit the rural areas of Tanzania and experience 'real' African life, with all profits going towards various development projects. These tend to be a bit more expensive, though still good value, and amongst the many tours they organize country-wide are trips to Machame to see the environmentally sound 'agroforestry' practices of the region (covering much the same ground as KPAP's 'Spend a day with a porter' tour; see pp44-5); and Marangu, where people have organized various tours around the area to a number of waterfalls, caves and farms (see p193 for details of these sights). Perhaps of more interest to the Kili trekker, on this latter trip you also visit the home and memorial of Yohana Lauwo, one of Hans Meyer's guides and a man who lived to be over 118 (see quote on p46) and you get a chance to see his log books. For more information, visit the Cultural Tourism Programme offices in the AICC building, contact them by phone or email (☎ 2507515; 🖳 www.infojep. com/culturaltours) or pick up brochures at the tourist office in Dar or Arusha.

TREKKING AGENCIES

In terms of value for money and choice, many will say that you're better off organizing your trek in Moshi than Arusha. Agencies in Arusha tend to be more expensive than those in Moshi for three reasons: firstly, some Arusha agencies are just acting as middlemen for those in Moshi and take their cut; secondly, most of the larger and more expensive companies prefer to base themselves in Arusha and enjoy the greater facilities there; and thirdly, the transport costs to Kilimanjaro are much higher than they are from Moshi: for the trip out to the Machame Gate from Arusha, for example, we were quoted a ridiculous US$160 return for a ride in a 4WD.

That said, there are plenty of good quality, reliable companies, many of them foreign-owned and many based out of town in one of the affluent suburbs. There are also many companies that are used by overseas agents to conduct their Kili climb too. So it is well worth investigating what the Arusha agents have to offer – which is exactly what we've done here.

To research this section we visited each of the agencies and asked them about their costs and what we can expect for our money. This gave us an idea of the price, of course, but little information about the quality of the service they offered. For this we looked at the comments books they kept (and if the company you are negotiating with doesn't keep such a book, be very suspicious) and, most importantly of all, asked other trekkers on Kili for their opinion of the agency they were with. In this way a fairly reliable and – we hope – accurate picture of the trekking agencies in both Arusha and Moshi emerged. We hope you find it useful, and would welcome feedback about any agency, whether listed in this book or not.

The prices quoted in the following list are per person. For details of what to look for in an agency, and what questions to ask, see p33. And one other tip: don't be afraid to tell the tour operator that you're shopping around; it's the quickest way to get them to give you a good deal.

● **African Environments** (PO Box 2125; ☎ 2548625; 🖳 www.africanenvironm ents.co.tz). Established in mid-1987, American-owned African Environments are at the very top end of the market, claiming a 98% success rate on the Lemosho Route – a route that they actually pioneered. They are also the only company to equip *all* their clients with Gamow hyperbaric bags and oxygen as safety precautions. No surprises, then, that they are widely regarded as just about the most luxurious operator on the mountain and are a favourite with many foreign film crews. That said, it's good to see that some of that money filters down to their staff, for they're also one of the best payers. In addition to Lemosho, they also run a Machame trail trek. Costs are vague depending on what sort of trek you want but are said by the company to be around US$350 per day.

● **African Walking Company** (☎ 2544461, 0748 788886; 🖳 African_walking @hotmail.com). Founded by American Jim Foster, despite the lack of a website and an obscure address this is one of the more ubiquitous companies on the mountain thanks to a reputation for reliability and an impressively high standard of treks. As such, they're a favourite with overseas trekking agencies (African Travel Resource being one). With so much custom coming from abroad, they don't really need independent trekkers – hence the lack of publicity. But if you've booked with an overseas agency, you may well end up with them; and congratulations if you do, for they're one of the best on the mountain.

● **Bobby Trekking** Goliondoi Rd (PO Box 14798; ☎ 2544118; 🖥 www.bob bytrekking.com). Not to be confused with the company below them both on the street and in this book, Bobby Trekking is a much smaller operation that has failed to grasp the fact that, if you can't compete with other operators on facilities and service, you need to compete on price. Currently they offer a five-night Machame Route for US$998 (though to be fair this drops to US$838 for two and US$800 for three people), or US$883/768/728 for 1/2/3 people for four nights on the Marangu trail.

● **Bobby Tours** Goliondoi Rd (PO Box 2169; ☎ 2503490; 🖥 www.bobby tours.com). Established way back in 1976, Bobby are a very slick and professional company with a whole fleet of 4WDs and the swishest offices on Goliondoi. One glance at their oh-so thorough website before you arrive in Arusha will give you some idea of how seriously they take their work. Weirdly, their prices at the start of 2006 were also the cheapest in either Moshi or Arusha, at US$650 for four nights on the Marangu Route, and US$800 for five nights on the Marangu or Machame routes. We can't help feeling that there must be some mistake with these prices because the park fees themselves come to more than US$500 on the Marangu Route; but we were quoted this price on more than one occasion. Got to be worth investigating.

● **Bushbuck Safaris** Moshi Rd (PO Box 1700; ☎ 2507779; 🖥 www.bushb uckltd.com). Huge operator housed in a suitably large building just north of the Impala Hotel on the Moshi Road. And as with most of the big companies around here, it rarely deals with individuals walking in off the street, though you may be able to join a group that's already climbing. Quoted prices: six days on Marangu for US$940 if trekking by yourself, down to US$790 if there's five or more of you. However, do note that *no* mountain equipment is included in that price. That's not such a problem on the Marangu Route but would be on Machame, where you have to camp. The prices there are US$1140 for one person, decreasing gradually to U$950 if there are five or more of you.

● **Crown Eagle** Joel Maeda St (PO Box 177; ☎ 0744 263085). A small outfit occupying second floor offices by the clock tower, Crown Eagle has been going for six years or so and its boss, Salehe Abdalah, has been in the business for more than 15. To judge from the comments books they keep, they seem to offer a pretty satisfactory service. Currently they charge around US$900 each for six days on the Machame Route for two people.

● **Easy Travel and Tours** Boma Road (PO Box 1912; ☎ 2507322; 🖥 www. easytravel.co.tz). In a prestigious location sandwiched between KLM and the New Safari Hotel, Easy Travel and Tours are an efficient organization, the representatives for airlines such as Air Mauritius and Air Zimbabwe, and indeed have so much going on that a tour up Kilimanjaro seems a little beneath them.

They do organize treks, of course, such as five days on Marangu (US$1200/1155/1100 each for 1/2/3 people) or six days on Machame (US$1155/ 1110/1045 each for 1/2/3 people) but one gets the feeling it's not their priority.

● **Equatorial Safaris** Room 211, second floor, Ngorongoro wing, AICC building (PO Box 2156; ☎ 2502617; 🖳 www.equatorialsafaris.com). Now in new offices in the AICC, Equatorial Safaris are unusual in a couple of ways. Firstly, because they have their own guides and don't subcontract out the work; and secondly, because they advertise complete Meru/Kili packages taking 16 days in total and using the Rongai Route – though other routes can be chosen if you prefer. We found them to be quite expensive, however, at US$924 for six nights on the Machame Route (minimum three people), rising to US$1308 if you're walking solo, and US$1372/988 each for Marangu for one/three or more people.

● **F&S Kiliwarrior** (PO Box 12339; 🖳 www.go-kili.com). Co-owned by Wilbert Mollel – the original Kiliwarrior, so-called because of his Masai heritage – this is one of the best locally owned agents in Tanzania. Even better, they began their company after seeing the poor way the porters were treated, are now regarded as one of the best when it comes to looking after their staff and are one of KPAP's partners (see pp40-1). With each trek now led either by Wilbert or one of his three brothers, the company offers trips on the Machame, Lemosho or Rongai routes and offers two levels of cost: a Platinum rate, in which almost everything – tips, drinks, laundry, meals and a private car in Arusha (though not airfares) – is included, and a better-value Gold rate which offers a similar deal to the other trekking agencies. Sample prices: 7-day Machame or 6-day Rongai US$2800 on the Gold Rate, or US$4200 for the Platinum Rate; 9 days via the Western Breach US$3300 Gold Rate, US$4800 Platinum. Incidentally, they now even have their own DVD, *Kilimanjaro – The Way It Is*.

● **Good Earth** AICC Building, Ngorongoro Wing, First floor, Suite 152 (PO Box 1115; ☎ 2508334; 🖳 www.goodearthtours.com). Established tour operator with offices in the AICC Building, and a second in Florida (see p28). Despite the overseas connections they are one of the Arusha companies that really do promote their tours around town, and you'll often see their posters on noticeboards advertising for trekkers to join their forthcoming trips. According to their website, they charge US$910 per person on the Marangu Route (7 days), US$1080 on Machame (8 days), though you may be able to get a discount if you contact their Arusha office directly. They've been recommended by more than one trekker, sponsor a primary school and have almost a 90% success rate amongst their clients for reaching the summit. Worth investigating.

● **IntoAfrica Eco-Travels Tanzania** (PO Box 12923; ☎ 2502139, 0745 880078; 🖳 www.intoafrica.co.uk). Office of the British-based company; see p25 for further details.

● **Kilimanjaro Crown Birds Tours and Safaris** India St (☎ 0748 281316; 🖳 www.kilicrown.com). Calling themselves the Kilimanjaro specialists, this is a branch office of the Moshi company; see p183 for details.

● **Kilimanjaro Guides and Porters Union** Diplomat House, Mianzini Street, off Nairobi Rd (PO Box 10699; ☎ 250 9215; 0744 544539; 🖳 www.kilima njaro-union.com). Half company, half union; see box below for details. Unusually they charge a per-day fee to climb Kili, currently US$208 per person on the Marangu Route, or US$215 per day on Machame and the other camping routes, with reductions if there are more than 5 of you.

● **Nature Discovery** (PO Box 10574; ☎ 027-254 4063; 🖳 www.naturediscov ery.com). Upmarket company in operation since 1992, offering all the routes though preferring the quieter ones. Sample prices: US$2964 for seven days on the Machame Route, including airport transfer and a night in L'Oasis Hotel in Arusha; the Marangu Route trek usually comes in at just under US$2500.

● **Roy Safaris** 44 Serengeti Rd (PO Box 50; ☎ 2507057; 🖳 www.roysaf aris.com). Roy Safaris are a strange company in that they don't make an effort to work with agents from Europe and the US, but nor, given their new home in a swish purpose-built edifice out of the town centre off the Old Moshi Road, do they seem to target those who turn up in Arusha without having booked a trek. Instead, most of their custom comes from individuals who've visited their stand at one of the travel trade fairs in Madrid, Berlin and elsewhere. And it seems to work, if their smart new offices – and with their own hotel in the process of

The Kilimanjaro Guides and Porters Union
Founded in 2003 by Joseph Nyabasi, a former porter and guide on Kilimanjaro, and Nzuamkende Mkoma, his business partner, together with the help of one of his ex-clients from Belgium, Jan CM Hoogenbosch, the stated aim of the union is simple: to improve the lot of those who make their living from the mountain, whether guides or, more particularly given the deprivations they're forced to endure, porters. A simple enough manifesto, but given that there are now some 4000 porters working on Kilimanjaro altogether, a hugely difficult task too.

Despite the name, the KGPU is a commercial business, a trekking agency like any other in Arusha and Moshi, with 15 mountain guides permanently on their books and more than 250 porters who've worked for them. The only difference here, of course, being that any profits earned are supposedly either ploughed back into the company or used to improve the working conditions of porters. That money is spent in a number of ways. Buying equipment that can then be borrowed by the porters free of charge (regardless of whether they are actually working for the union or not) is one way, as is the establishing of training camps at Machame and Arusha to teach porters English and train them in the arts of first aid and customer care – skills that will prove essential should the porters decide to continue working on the mountain as guides.

By becoming a company, of course, the KGPU needn't have to rely solely on donations from individual tourists and charities which, though generous, would never be enough to fulfill all the aims of the KGPU. And though it's only two years since its establishment, the decision to operate as a business seems to have been an astute one, with a number of foreign tour operators, among them Kumuka in the UK (see p26), using them to take their clients up Kilimanjaro. Before rushing off to book a trek with KGPU, however, it's worth noting that, currently, KPAP are hesitant about endorsing the KGPU, citing a lack of evidence that they truly are a union. As such, it may be worth checking both sides of the story and the latest developments before booking.

being built next door – are anything to go by. Unfortunately, they seem to have stopped really caring about the Kili market, for they usually subcontract the climbing to a Moshi-based operator. They charge US$1220 per person for six days on Marangu, which isn't special.

● **Safari Makers** India St (PO Box 12902; ☎ 2544446, 0744 300817; 🖥 www. safarimakers.com). Popular, efficient and reliable safari company, run jointly by a Tanzanian man and American woman, that also runs treks up Kilimanjaro on all the major routes. Six days on Machame costs US$1150 for one person, or US$1008 per person if there are two of you. For Marangu, *six* days is US$1207/1086 per person for 1/2 people respectively.

● **Shidolya** Room 218, at the end of the corridor on the second floor, Ngorongoro wing, AICC building (PO Box 1436, ☎ 2548506, 🖥 www.shi dolya-safaris.com). Shidolya are undoubtedly one of the more professional outfits, with a busy office and a slick style, including computer print-outs of the day-to-day itineraries of each trek. They are also, somewhat surprisingly, very cheap by Arusha standards, with six-day Machame treks for US$980/910/880 for 1/2/3 people, or US$900/830/780 for 1/2/3 people on Marangu – both including a free bottle of champagne at the end, which is a nice touch. They also run the Colobus Mountain Lodge in Arusha National Park (see p211) – a good base for exploring the park and climbing Meru. Definitely worth investigating.

● **Sunny Safaris** Col Middleton Rd (PO Box 7267; ☎ 2507145; 🖥 www.sunn ysafaris.com). One of the better budget companies in Arusha, recommended time and again although now slightly less popular than in previous years – possibly because their office on Col Middleton Road sees far fewer budget travellers than in years gone by when this part of town was backpacker-central. Their prices of US$1295 for the Machame Route (1 person; US$1045 per person for three people) and US$1270 for six days on the Marangu Route (US$1030 per person for three people) are fair without being fantastic.

● **Team Kilimanjaro** 1249 Kimandolu, Sekei (PO Box 12023; ☎ 0787 503 595; 🖥 www.teamkilimanjaro.com). Arusha branch of highly recommended British-based company. The location is an obscure one but if you give them a ring they'll pick you up. See p26 for details of their treks.

● **Thomson Safaris** (PO Box 6074; ☎ US toll free 800-235 0289; 🖥 www. thomsontreks.com). It's good to see such a highly regarded outfit that's been operating for more than 22 years and which is completely locally owned. Tends to concentrate on the American market, even offering airfares from the US to Arusha as part of their package. For more details of their treks, see p29.

● **Tropical Trekking** India St (PO Box 2047; ☎ 2507011; 🖥 www.tropicaltre kking.com). Branch office of Hoopoe UK and its sister Tropical Trekking; for information on the range of treks offered, see p25. If they have space, it may be possible to book a place on a trek from this office.

● **Victoria Expeditions** Meru House Inn, Sokoine Rd (PO Box 14875; ☎ 250 0444; 🖥 www.victoriatz.com) Run by a Norwegian lady and her husband, Victoria Expeditions appear to be a busy operation that's been going now for half a dozen years or so, a success that can be attributed in part to their location on the ground floor of one of the more popular and enduring budget hotels, and in part to a reliable and fairly priced service. They also have brochures with all their itineraries and tariffs listed, which is a relief for those with an aversion to haggling. Prices: Marangu route: 6 days US$1110 per person, 5 days US$980 per person; Machame route: 7 days US$1300, 6 days US$1140 per person.

GETTING AWAY

Buses

Moshi Those heading to Kili will find the **local buses** are the most convenient way to get to Moshi. They run throughout the day from the main bus station, with the last one at around 5pm (Ts1500, or Ts1000 if there are five of you in a four-seat row. This last option is the best way to get to know the locals, mainly because some of them will be sitting on your lap.)

It's not a particularly pleasant way to travel but other options are thin on the ground, with Moshi ill-served by the **shuttle bus** companies. One of the best is Riverside (☎ 2502639, 2503916; 🖳 www.riverside-shuttle.com), with its office in a chemists on Sokoine, who have just one bus per day at 2pm (Ts5000), as do Davanu (☎ 2504027; 🖳 www.davanu.com) who also set off at 2pm; their offices are in the Pallsons Hotel. Finally, though Impala (☎ 2507197; 🖳 www.impalahotel.com) *do* operate a daily bus to Moshi, this bus starts in Nairobi and they seem reluctant to allow passengers to board it in Arusha.

Nairobi Of the **bus** companies, Scandinavia, whose offices are just south of Arusha's Central Bus Station, remain the most popular. They run one bus daily to Nairobi's Central Bus Station at 3pm (Ts17,000). However, a new alternative, Easy Coach, has now started operating, with buses at 8am and 2pm, and at Ts10,000 they're quite a bit cheaper too. Furthermore, their offices are on Fire Street, south of the Arusha Hotel, which means you don't have to run the gauntlet of touts and tricksters at the bus station.

There are other companies at the bus station who also do the Nairobi run and are a little cheaper, though be warned: most travellers who ride in one of these buses later swear that they will never do so again.

The most popular **shuttle bus** company is Riverside (☎ 2502639, 2503916; 🖳 www.riverside-shuttle.com/) on Sokoine Road. They run two shuttles daily to Nairobi, at 8am (arrive 1pm) and 2pm (it's the one from Moshi, and arrives in Nairobi at 6.30pm). They charge US$20 for foreign tourists, though you are more likely to be charged the more reasonable residents' price of Ts10,000. Exactly the same times and fares are offered by Davanu (☎ 250 4027, 0744 846160; 🖳 www.davanu.com), now operating out of the ground floor of the Pallsons Hotel on Market Street. To these old stalwarts must be added a third, Impala, which also, surprise surprise, runs shuttles at 8am and 2pm for US$20 (Ts10,000 to residents); and a fourth, Bobby Shuttle (☎ 250 3490), recently set up by the Bobby Tours trekking agency (see p163). Taking their lead from the others they also have services at 8am and 2pm, charging US$20 to non-residents (though maybe in time this will drop to the more reasonable residents' rate of

Ts12,000). However, unlike the others their buses are equipped with TV and DVD players. What's more, from Nairobi they then travel to **Mombasa**. As with all shuttles, they should pick you up from your hotel, though you should press home this point when making the booking.

Dar es Salaam Scandinavia have five **buses** to Dar each morning: two at 7am (Ts17,000 and Ts24,000 – the different prices reflecting the quality of the buses), two at 8.30am (Ts17,000 and Ts24,000) and one at 11am (Ts24,000). Their previous domination of the luxury bus market is now being challenged, however, by Royal on Middleton Road, who offer just the same quality of service as Scandinavia's luxury buses (with refreshments served along the way and an on-board toilet) yet for just a little more (Ts18,000) than Scandinavia's 'economy service'. Just as importantly, Royal are reputedly just as safe as Scandinavia too. Their service is much more limited, however, with just one bus at 9am. Another old favourite is Dar Express, on the left hand side as you walk up Col Middleton road, with buses at 5.15am, 6am, 7am, 8am, 8.30am and 9.15am (Ts15,000). Other bus companies serving Dar can be found around the bus station.

Flights

See p147 for details of the airline offices in Arusha. Bear in mind that the times listed below are subject to frequent change. Remember, too, that there is a **departure tax**, namely US$8 for domestic flights, US$11 for international destinations – though these change frequently, so do check when reconfirming your flight.

Arusha effectively has two airports, with **Kilimanjaro International Airport** being less than an hour away. You may be able to find a direct flight to Dar on one of the international carriers from there, though most refuse or are simply not permitted to board passengers for this short journey. Precision Air, however, have flights from KIA to Dar twice daily, at 8.20am and 1.30pm. Air Tanzania also have twice daily flights (and three on Sunday).

From **Arusha Airport** direct flights to **Dar** are surprisingly limited, with local carriers preferring to go via **Zanzibar**. Coastal Aviation's 12.15pm flight arrives at Dar at 2.20pm (US$190), then continues onto Mafia, Kilwa and Selous. They also serve the Serengeti, Tanga and other Tanzanian destinations. Regional Air (🖳 www.regional.co.tz) also run flights to Manyara and on to the Serengeti, with another route taking in Zanzibar and Dar. Air Excel serve a number of other destinations in Tanzania, including **Dodoma** (and on to **Ruaha**) and **Manyara**.

❏ **Getting to Kilimanjaro International Airport**

Air Tanzania charge Ts5000 (free to flight passengers) for their KIA shuttle, their buses leaving from the Air Tanzania office on Boma Road two hours prior to the scheduled departure of their flights. Impala (☎ 250 7197) coincide their shuttle buses to meet KLM flights, their buses currently leaving their offices at the Impala Hotel at 5pm – thus allowing passengers who are joining the KLM flight enough time to check-in – and returning at 9pm (US$10 each way). Precision Air have also started a shuttle service to and from KIA for their flights (Ts2000). A taxi to the airport will cost at least Ts25,000, more at night. For **transport to Arusha Airport**, see p146.

Moshi

Cheaper, quieter, nearer and prettier, Moshi sits in the shadow of Kilimanjaro and, for climbing the mountain, is perhaps a superior base to neighbouring Arusha, 90km away to the west. As the unofficial capital of the Chagga world, most visitors find Moshi a little more interesting too. The missionaries who followed in the wake of Rebmann gave the Chaggas the advantage of a Western education and this, combined with the agricultural fecundity of Kilimanjaro's southern slopes, has enabled the Chaggas to become one of the wealthiest, most influential and most securely self-aware groups in the country. Moshi has reaped the benefits too, prospering to the point where it is now one of the smartest towns in Tanzania (though grim poverty is still not difficult to find, as anybody who has walked around Moshi at night, stepping over the sleeping bodies of the dispossessed lying on the pavements as they do so, can testify).

While the Chaggas are the dominant force in town, Moshi is still a cosmopolitan place, with a highly visible Indian minority; the colourful ethnic mixture is reflected in the architecture, with a huge Hindu temple abutting an equally striking mosque, and with dozens of small churches and chapels scattered in the streets thereabouts. There also seems to be more civic pride here in Moshi than in other parts of the country; check out the Kilimanjaro flower garden outside of Kibo House, for example. Indeed, the only dark cloud for tourists in Moshi is the inordinate amount of hassle they suffer from trekking agency touts, 'artists' and the like. Indeed, and it pains me to have to report this, but this kind of relentless badgering now eclipses even that of Arusha. Look beyond this, however, and you're sure to find Moshi a charming place, with enough facilities to enable you to organize a trek – and enjoy some long nights of celebration at the end.

ARRIVAL

Arriving on an Air Tanzania flight to **Kilimanjaro International Airport**, a shuttle bus should be waiting to take you to their Moshi office by the roundabout (make sure you get on the Moshi-bound shuttle, however, as they also run one from the airport to Arusha). Riverside used to meet the KLM flights but these days run this route only if there's sufficient demand. As a result, arriving on KLM you'll either have to catch a cab or take the Impala shuttle to Arusha. Precision Air also run a twice-daily shuttle service between KIA and Moshi to coincide with their flights (or rather, the flights of their partner Kenya Airways), one leaving at around 9am in the morning, the other around 7pm. Free for Precision Air/Kenya Airways passengers, it's Ts2000 otherwise. Or you'll have to pay for a cab from the airport, which can cost anywhere from US$35-50 (they'll ask for US$50, and insist it's the official rate, but if you argue and shop around you should get nearer US$35). Arrive by **bus** and you'll be dropped off at the terminal on Mawenzi Road, 200m south of the clock tower, within walking distance of most hotels.

ORIENTATION AND GETTING AROUND

According to Harry Johnston, Moshi could simply mean 'town' or 'settlement', though as with everything Johnston wrote, this could well be wrong. Indeed, Moshi also translates as 'Smoke' – a reference, perhaps, to its situation at the foot of a volcano? What is certain is that Moshi is compact, with almost everything of interest to the holidaying visitor lying on or near the main thoroughfare, **Mawenzi Road**, and its northern extension, **Kibo Road** (the two names borrowed from the peaks of Kilimanjaro). Together they run all the way from the market, down the hill at the southern end of town, to the roundabout at the northern end which for reasons beyond this author's understanding has a statue of a crocodile chasing an ostrich, a huddle of grazing giraffes and a monkey holding up a billboard; you'll have to see it for yourself to fully appreciate it. Separating Mawenzi Road from Kibo Road is a second roundabout adorned with a soft-drink sponsored digital clock tower, the centre of town. **Dalla-dallas** drive up and down the main Mawenzi and Market streets for Ts150, though it doesn't take long to walk anywhere, Moshi being compact. The one exception to this rule is the suburb of Shanty Town, north-west of the centre, home to a great Indian restaurant, a Chinese and a couple of fine hotels. A cab to Shanty Town will cost Ts2000 from the town centre.

SERVICES

Banks

The NBC bank in Moshi offers the best rates in town just as it does almost everywhere else in Tanzania, though there is a 0.5% commission charge for **travellers' cheques** at this branch. They are open from Monday to Friday between 8.30am and 3pm, and Saturday 8.30am-noon. Before calling in, check with the CRDB Bank in the nearby Kahawa House, who post their rates on a board outside their offices. **Moneychangers** such as Chase on Rindi Lane stay open later and their rates are only a little inferior to the banks, if at all; nor do they charge commission. There's an **ATM** at the Standard Chartered (Mon-Fri 8.30am-3pm, Sat 9am-noon) on Rindi Lane, another at the NBC (though this is usually very busy and far less reliable); and a third near the hotels on Mawenzi Rd.

Communications

The **post office** is by the clock tower, at the junction with Boma Road. Opening times are Mon-Fri 8am-4.30pm, Sat 9am-noon. The **Telecom office**, next to the post office (Mon-Fri 7.45am-4.30pm, Sat 9am-noon), runs an operator-assisted

❏ Moshi's area code is ☎ 027. If phoning from outside Tanzania dial ☎ +255-27.

service and also sell phonecards for the phone boxes outside. For **Internet**, there are two popular options. Easy.com are the fairest and friendliest. They charge the standard Ts1000 per hour and, gratifyingly, add five or ten minutes on top for free. They can be found in the basement of Kahawa House near the clock tower. Duma Cybercafé, near the Coffee Shop, is more convenient for those staying at the southern end of town and is also the smartest and, perhaps by a whisker, has the fastest connection. Fahari, next door, is fine and friendly. There are plenty of other places, particularly north of the clock tower on Old Moshi Road and west on Horombo Road.

Swimming pools
The YMCA charges non-residents Ts3000 for the use of their swimming pool, Key's Hotel charges US$5 and Ameg Lodge charge Ts4000, the latter also including use of their gym; in all of these places hotel guests can use the facilities for free.

Shopping

Trekking provisions Your agency should be able to supply you with any major bits of equipment – torches, sleeping bags etc – that you might have forgotten to bring with you. Other items that you may well have overlooked but will find extremely useful include: chapsticks (along with mosquito repellent and most other pharmaceutical needs), which can be bought from the Third Millennium **Pharmacy** on Mawenzi Road, between the New Kindoroko and Da'Costa hotels; and **bin liners** (or large shopping bags), useful for keeping clothing within your rucksack dry and available from the market or one of the little supermarkets mentioned below. **Maps and books** about Kili can be bought from the Old Moshi Bookshop on Rindi Lane at the junction with Kibo or the souvenir shop by Marangu Gate.

Supermarkets and other possibly useful stores Carina Supermarket, next to the Impala Shuttle office, is handy for those staying near the clock tower, while Safari, on Riadha St south of the market, has a slightly wider array of stock and is handy for those at the southern end of town. According to the expats the Shivam Centre has the best array of **DVDs and VCDs**. Phone Doctor in the bus station arcade can help you with all your **mobile phone** needs, including an unlocking service.

Souvenirs There are plenty of souvenirs to buy in Moshi, and plenty of places willing to flog them to you. Two in particular deserve special mention. **Shah Industries** is a leather-workshop-cum-aquarium housed in what used to be a flour mill. It's a strange combination but a beautiful place and a worthy one too: over a third of the workers at Shah Industries have some sort of disability. Definitely worth looking around, they lie to the south-east of town across the train tracks on the way to the Springlands Hotel. Much more central, **Tahea Kili** sits opposite the Coffee Shop and is another charitable concern, with the profits returning to local women's groups. **Our Heritage**, sharing the same building as the Coffee Shop, has a decent array of knick-knacks and does a nice line in 'I climbed Kili' T-shirts, postcards and jewellery. **Cranecraft**, in the Kilimanjaro Crane Hotel, has similar stock plus a decent selection of books about the country, its wildlife and, of course, the mountain. Better still is **Africulture**, on Old Moshi Road, with a variety of T-shirts, hats, wooden carvings etc. Worth a nose around. **Chui Traders**, near the New Castle Hotel on Mwalimu Nyerere Road, is the place to come for Maasai clothes and implements. **U's Variety** is on the main Mawenzi drag on the opposite side of the road to the New Kindoroko, and there are other souvenir places near here too. The **Coffee Shop** itself runs a profitable little trade in neatly wrapped Kilimanjaro coffee, though apparently you can get much the same sort of stuff for half the price at the supermarket.

WHERE TO STAY

The following is not an exhaustive list, but whilst there are some cheaper places at the southern end of town, many refuse to accept Westerners. Manage to persuade one to let you stay for the night and you can expect to pay around Ts1500-2000 per night, though the chances are it'll be assumed that you want bed and broad rather than bed and board. **Campsites** include the grounds of the *Green Cottage Hostels* and *Key's Hotel* (see p176), and at the *Golden Shower Restaurant* on the main road to Marangu and Dar. Expect to pay around US$3 per person at the last place, US$5 at the Key's and Green Hostels.

As for the hotels that definitely do welcome tourists, in **approximate price order** they are as follows:

Below US$20

Many of the hotels in town are related. Those who've been to the Da'Costa in Arusha, for example, and remember it as the Cinderella of the hotel scene, will find its two ugly sisters here in Moshi. Moshi's *Da'Costa* (☎ 2755159; 🖳 www. dacostahotel.com), for instance, may be slightly cheaper than its Arusha namesake at Ts4800/Ts7200 sgl/dbl for B&B, but it's nowhere near as smart and has poky rooms (though with fan and mozzy net); that said, those who've stayed here say that it's friendly and you can't argue with the price. Then there's the second sister, the *Haria Palace* (☎ 2751128, 0744-377795; 🖳 hariapalace @yahoo.com), a curious place with the reception, restaurant/bar and pool table located on the roof. Popular with locals, rates start at Ts6000 for a double with common facilities, or it's Ts12,000 for self-contained.

Another cheapie is the *Umoja Lutheran Hostel* (☎ 2750902; 🖳 ekctnd@ kilinet.co.tz), just south of the market; look for the sign 'KKKT Umoja Hostel'. There's nothing wrong with this place – it's clean, well-run and the *al-fresco* eating area is certainly pleasant – but I do find it lacks a little atmosphere and I can't help feeling that this place survives largely because of a) its church connections, and b) its endorsement by a well-known guidebook which apparently puts it first in its Moshi listing. Still, at Ts10,000/15,000 s/c sgl/dbl, or Ts6000/ 10,000 with common facilities, all with breakfast, it's certainly good value.

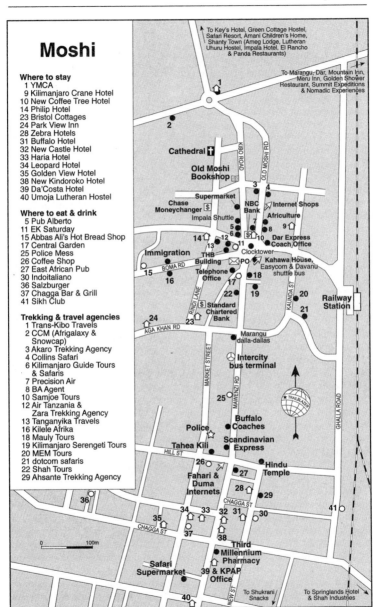

Moshi

Where to stay
1 YMCA
9 Kilimanjaro Crane Hotel
10 New Coffee Tree Hotel
14 Philip Hotel
23 Bristol Cottages
24 Park View Inn
28 Zebra Hotels
31 Buffalo Hotel
32 New Castle Hotel
33 Haria Hotel
34 Leopard Hotel
35 Golden View Hotel
38 New Kindoroko Hotel
39 Da'Costa Hotel
40 Umoja Lutheran Hostel

Where to eat & drink
5 Pub Alberto
11 EK Saturday
15 Abbas Ali's Hot Bread Shop
17 Central Garden
25 Police Mess
26 Coffee Shop
27 East African Pub
30 Indoitaliano
36 Salzburger
37 Chagga Bar & Grill
41 Sikh Club

Trekking & travel agencies
1 Trans-Kibo Travels
2 CCM (Afrigalaxy &
   Snowcap)
3 Akaro Trekking Agency
4 Collins Safari
6 Kilimanjaro Guide Tours
   & Safaris
7 Precision Air
8 BA Agent
10 Samjoe Tours
12 Air Tanzania &
   Zara Trekking Agency
13 Tanganyika Travels
16 Kilele Afrika
18 Mauly Tours
19 Kilimanjaro Serengeti Tours
20 MEM Tours
21 dotcom safaris
22 Shah Tours
29 Ahsante Trekking Agency

To Key's Hotel, Green Cottage Hostel,
Safari Resort, Amani Children's Home,
Shanty Town (Ameg Lodge, Lutheran
Uhuru Hostel, Impala Hotel, El Rancho
& Panda Restaurants)

To Marangu, Dar, Mountain Inn,
Meru Inn, Golden Shower
Restaurant, Summit Expeditions
& Nomadic Experiences

Cathedral

Old Moshi
Bookshop

KIBO ROAD

OLD MOSHI RD

Supermarket

Chase
Moneychanger

NBC
Bank

Internet Shops

Africulture

Impala Shuttle

Dar Express
Coach Office

Immigration

THB
Building

Clocktower

PO

Kahawa House,
Easycom & Davanu
shuttle bus

BOMA RD

Telephone
Office

RINDI LANE

Standard
Chartered
Bank

AGA KHAN RD

KALUNDA ST

Railway
Station

Marangu
dalla-dallas

Intercity
bus terminal

MARKET STREET

MAWENZI RD

TRAILBLAZER

Buffalo
Coaches

GHALLA ROAD

Police

Scandinavian
Express

Tahea Kili

HILL ST

Hindu
Temple

Fahari &
Duma
Internets

CHAGGA ST

Safari
Supermarket

CHAGGA ST

Third
Millennium
Pharmacy

39 & KPAP
Office

NEW ST

To Shukrani
Snacks

To Springlands Hotel
& Shah Industries

0   100m

Moving to the northern end of town, the *New Coffee Tree Hotel* (☎ 275209, 0744 485791) is a place for those for whom every *shilingi* matters. We like this place: we like the staff, we like the location right next to the clock tower and we like the restaurant on the top floor. Admittedly, the rooms are basic but they do come with sink and mozzy net and are functional, fine and fairly priced at only Ts5000 for a single with shared facilities, or Ts8000-10,000 for en-suite doubles, all including breakfast. Still further north, the *YMCA* (☎ 2751754) on the main roundabout is still open but a bit rundown now and, despite the continuing popularity of its swimming pool, feels very sleepy too. The prices (US$10/13 sgl/dbl with shared bathroom for B&B), especially when compared to those at the other end of town, are simply too high.

Though the above hotels may be the cheapest, they're certainly not the most popular places in town. For while the lion may be the king of the jungle, on Moshi's hotel scene it's the Buffalo that rules. The *Buffalo Hotel* (☎ 2750270) on New Street has clean bright rooms, all en suite and with mosquito nets, and a fairly popular bar and restaurant downstairs. It's not the cheapest in town that accepts foreigners, but it is perhaps the best value. The only drawback is that some of the female waiting staff in the restaurant can be downright surly, wearing the kind of expression that could sour buffalo's milk while it's still inside the buffalo; ask them at your peril to change TV channels while their favourite soap is on. The hotel has now installed cable TV into the en-suite rooms (Ts12,000/15,000 sgl/dbl) but there are also some fairly priced doubles with common facilities (Ts10,000), all rates including breakfast.

Another member of the Da'Costa dynasty, indeed the grandmother of the chain, is the *New Kindoroko* (☎ 2754054; 🖥 www.kindoroko.com). The restaurant is good here and gives you a rooftop view of Kibo, and there's a pool room and Internet café. Check out a number of rooms because they vary widely. Rates are around US$15 per person, which is a little pricey. Virtually next-door, the *New Castle*, is cheap and has a pool table to pacify the inmates – but other than that, we could find nothing to warrant any more space in this book than we have already given it. While we're in this quarter, on Chagga St the newest place in town is the *Golden View Hotel* (☎ 275 4877; 🖥 www.goldenhotel.4t.com), which lacks for nothing except custom. Situated in the market area, it's a smart and polished establishment where all the rooms have their own balcony, bathroom and mosquito net and rates (US$12/16 s/c sgl/dbl) include breakfast.

Much further north, on the way out of town, the *Green Cottage Hostel* (aka *Green Hostels*) on Nkomo Ave (☎ 2753198; 🖥 greenhostels2@yahoo.com) is a quiet balmy retreat hidden down a leafy cul-de-sac, perfect for those who wish to get away from it all; the three non-s/c doubles are fairly priced at US$15, or US$20 en suite, whilst the one single (not self-contained) costs US$10 and the triple is US$20. Prices include breakfast. Sadly it's feeling a little run-down now.

Heading towards Shanty Town, a couple of kilometres from the centre, the *Lutheran Uhuru Hostel* (☎ 2754084; 🖥 uhuru@elct.org) sits in fairly vast grounds. It's a quiet, relaxed place, the only activity coming from the team of gardeners and cleaners maintaining the neat-and-tidiness of it all. Rooms are very pleasant – particularly those in the new Kibo or Kilimanjaro wings – and all are self-contained; indeed, our only beef is its location, a bit too far out of town to walk and thus engendering a Ts1500 cab fare when you want to go anywhere. That and the tariff which, in our opinion, is a little high at US$35/45 s/c sgl/dbl in the Kilimanjaro and Kibo wings, though US$16/22 in the older Mawenzi wing is fair. Despite these moans, it maintains a healthy trickle of customers and if you've got your own transport – or are happy doing nothing all day except watch a battalion of gardeners watering the dirt patches – it's fine.

Finally in this group, about a kilometre further along the road from the Key's Hotel (see p176) is the *Safari Resort Hotel* (☎ 2751256; Ts10,000/15,000 s/c sgl/dbl), a charmless place that, if you were to look at the location and room facilities (TV, mozzy net, air-con), you'd think would be rather pleasant. Alas, it's completely lacking in any atmosphere and as far as we could tell the only guests were courting couples who, high on love and the giddy expectation of each other's tender caresses, come here to get away from their respective spouses.

US$20-40
The *Zebra Hotels* (☎ 2750611; ✉ zebhoteltz@yahoo.com) is a large and swish new affair. The tiger-print blankets, while not entirely appropriate for this part of the world, are just one of the features of their facility-heavy en-suite rooms; they also come with satellite TV, direct-dial telephone and room service. Tariff: US$25/30 s/c sgl/dbl; US$35 executive rooms with mini-bar and air-con.

The *Moshi Leopard Hotel* on Market Street (☎ 2750884; ✉ www.leopardhotel.com) is just a rather more upmarket version of the Buffalo, though with an excellent terrace bar – from where, peering through the branches of the nearby tree, you can see Kibo – as well as an extravagantly liveried doorman and friendlier waitresses. The rooms themselves are also that little bit better than the Buffalo's and as well as being en suite also include a fridge, TV, wardrobe, fan and balcony. The non-residents' prices are rather steep at US$35/45 s/c sgl/dbl but see if you can get the residents' rates of Ts25,000/30,000 s/c sgl/dbl, which represent pretty good value.

Moving north, the *Philip Hotel* (☎ 2754746) boasts a good location in a quiet but convenient corner of town, some pleasant staff and a smart exterior and lobby. Indeed, the only drawback is the décor, for though the rooms themselves are clean and furnished with amenities such as a TV, hot and cold shower and balcony, they are all painted, along with the rest of the hotel, in a monotonous cream paint, which gives the place the atmosphere of a Victorian asylum. It's this complete lack of any homely touches that lets it down: a few pictures on the walls, for instance, wouldn't go amiss. Rates are s/c sgl/dbl US$30/40 for non-residents, including continental breakfast. The nearby *Moshi Hotel*, by the way, is currently closed for renovations, with the new management planning to reopen as the *New Livingstone Hotel* sometime in the near future. So far the sign has gone up – and very impressive it is too – but everything else appears to have fallen into a state of disrepair, dilapidation and decay. Don't expect it to reopen anytime soon.

ARUSHA, MOSHI AND MARANGU

US$40 and above

The ***Bristol Cottages*** (☎ 2753745; ✉ briscot@kilionline.com) describe themselves as 'The country hotel in the heart of town', and though the noise from the buses revving up the hill outside rather shatters that boast, it's true that this is a little blossom-filled haven and perhaps the most convenient upper-bracket hotel in Moshi. The smart cottages, all with large TV and mozzy net, go for US$54/67.50 s/c sgl/dbl; the new wing, a little noisier due to its proximity to the road, is consequently slightly cheaper at US$40.50/54 s/c sgl/dbl. Back on Aga Khan Road, just a few metres up the hill is yet another new place – and another smart one too. The ***Park View Inn*** (☎ 2750711; ✉ www.pvim.com) is only small, with a dozen rooms or so, though the rooms themselves have the kind of smart uniformity and features – TV, telephone, air-con and bath or shower – of a large chain hotel. Thankfully, however, it has a friendly informality commensurate with its size. Rates are US$40/50 for s/c sgl/dbl.

Moving to the other side of the clock tower but staying in the same price bracket, ***Kilimanjaro Crane Hotel*** (☎ 2751114; ✉ www.kilimanjarocranehotels.com) seems to be more of a local businessman's hotel. It's a decent enough place, however, though deathly quiet at times. Singles, which have showers, TV and telephone, are US$40 each; doubles and triples have both bathtubs and showers and go for US$45/50, or it's US$50 for a double with air-con.

North again, this time on Uru Road, is the ***Key's Hotel*** (☎ 2752250/ 2751875; ✉ www.keys-hotels.com), a traditional-looking family-run hotel and the smartest address in Moshi. Oozing class, in the main building it's doubles only (US$50), all coming with TV, telephone, mini-bar, toilet and a shower with hot/cold running water; air-con is US$20 extra. There are also 15 small thatch-and-cement cottages in the grounds which are quite fun. All rates include continental breakfast.

However, for the top places in Moshi you have to go to a part of town perhaps misguidedly called Shanty Town – a smart area of jacaranda-lined boulevards that's quite unlike any other shanty town. Two of the finest, or at least priciest, hotels can be found here. The first is something of a curiosity. Maybe it's the high concrete walls surrounding the place, maybe it's the uniform white-washed, green-roofed chalets, or maybe the popular pool where everybody seems to congregate – whatever it is, there's something about the ***Ameg Lodge*** (☎ 2750175; ✉ www.ameglodge.com), off Lema Road, that's reminiscent of a 1950's British seaside holiday camp. Thankfully, the rather bland, shadeless exterior belies some rather stylish rooms, each with shower, satellite TV, fan, veranda and phone. Prices (all doubles) start at US$55, rising to US$95 for the junior suite. In addition to the pool, guests are also entitled to use the hotel gym.

Further north and on Lema Road, the ***Impala*** (☎ 2753440; ✉ impala@ kilinet.co.tz) is from the same herd as the one in Arusha, though where that one seems to be more of a business centre, this one is far more homely and all the better for it. A lovely pool and friendly staff are just two of its selling points,

---

(**Opposite**) Under the canopy of the cloud forest, Marangu Route.

along with stylish yet inviting en-suite rooms with TV and all mod-cons. In addition to the residents' rates there are also separate prices depending on whether you're a resident of East Africa or not; for those of us who aren't living in East Africa it's US$72/83 for s/c sgl/dbl B&B.

Finally, there are two places, both just a little out of town, that are owned and run by trekking agencies. Unless you have booked with one of these agencies it is highly unlikely you will stay here; if you *have* booked with these agencies, on the other hand, the chances are you will get a night or two free at the hotel before or after your trek. The first is the very comfortable ***Mountain Inn***, four kilometres from town on the way to Marangu, which is owned and run by Shah Tours (see p186 for contact details). A pool, sauna and a pretty garden are just some of the attractions here; prices start at US$35/45 for standard s/c sgl/dbl half-board, while the new deluxe rooms are US$65 dbl. The second place is the Zara-run ***Springlands Hotel*** (☎ 2753581; 🖳 www.springlands. co.tz), 2km to the south of town. Most people who stay here are happy with what they find, the pool being the main attraction, though the buffet dinners are to be recommended too. It is, however, rather isolated, and the high walls and over-zealous security really give the place a kind of them-and-us atmosphere, with the have-nots crowding to peer through the gaps in the gates to gaze upon the blessed. As it snootily calls itself a 'private residence' rather than a hotel, frequented only by those on one of Zara's tours, there are no prices available.

WHERE TO EAT AND DRINK

The most popular place in town at the moment, partly because of its location amongst the hotels near the market and partly because of its great food, is the ***Indoitaliano***. The name may conjure up all sorts of unappealing fusions – spaghetti currybonara, perhaps, or murgherita pizza – but there's no need to fear; this is really just a straightforward Indian restaurant that happens to make some delightful pizzas too (Ts3000-4000). Turn up before 8.30pm or you might find yourself queuing. A few metres east, the ***Sikh Club*** is a lovely peaceful spot overlooking a hockey pitch with great Indian food. A real secret treat!

If you're not eating at either of these then you'll probably be eating in the restaurant of your hotel, where most of the town's better food can be found. Of these, the ***New Coffee Tree Café*** on the top floor of the eponymous hotel is a light and airy place with wonderful views towards Moshi in one direction and Kili in the other – both of which you'll have plenty of time to enjoy while you wait the interminably long time for your food. When it does finally put in an appearance, it's tasty, hearty and very good value.

The ***Kindoroko*** has a restaurant with a fantastic view too, this time on its rooftop. It's also good to see a place that firmly believes that what the customer wants, the customer gets: how else can you explain the inordinately long time

ARUSHA, MOSHI AND MARANGU

(**Opposite**) **Top**: Porters strolling across the Saddle towards the Kibo summit.
Bottom: Walking through a grove of giant groundsels on the way from Barranco Huts to Lava Tower – see p246.

we had to wait for our mutton Madras, other than they were waiting for the lamb to mature first? When it did finally put in an appearance it was disappointingly unspicy, though others rave about this place so we're prepared to admit we just caught them on an off-night. There is also a restaurant at the *Buffalo*, too, though it's gone downhill recently.

If you're avoiding the hotels, the chances are you'll find yourself at the *Coffee Shop* on Hill Street instead. The travellers' number one hangout, the food

Amani Children's Home

When Hosea, aged 5, was brought to Amani he was living with his alcoholic mother, his father having died of AIDS. His friend at Amani, Andrea, 14, had been living on the streets, having fled from his abusive grandfather's house where he'd been forced to live following the death of both his parents. Then there's Oscar, aged 12, who has only just started speaking after years of begging on the streets, the only option left open to him after his grandmother refused to feed him. As for Daudi, found abandoned by the police at the central bus station, nobody knows how old he is: he's autistic, and apparently will never be able to speak.

Despite the Chaggas' reputation among Tanzanians for prosperity and power, the region is not immune from the problems afflicting the rest of the country, and that includes the malaise of street children. And while the stories of the children are unique, the general themes of neglect, poverty and desperation run like a common thread through all of them.

Whatever their reason for ending up on the streets, the gate is always open to them at the **Amani Children's Home**. Founded in 2001 by three dedicated Tanzanians, Nyaky, Godfrey and Deus, under the auspices of current director Valerie Johnson the orphanage has grown to become the largest in the region, caring for around seventy children. Most of the children are boys, though around ten of the seventy are girls. Their ages range from 4-19, though most are between 6 and 14.

They've arrived at the orphanage in a number of ways. Most have just wandered in, having been told about the place by their friends. Some have been found by social workers who are employed full time by the orphanage, or have been handed over to the orphanage by the police who have been unsure what to do with a child who has come into their custody, and has no desire to return home – or, perhaps, no home to go to. Some of these kids are orphans who've lost both their parents, in many cases to AIDS, while others have run away from home because of the physical, mental or sexual abuse they face there. Once on the streets it's a precarious existence. The boys can try to graft a living by collecting scrap metal, begging or stealing; for the girls, a life on the streets is even more dangerous, with many ending up as prostitutes.

Once in the Amani centre, they are washed, fed and, if necessary, clothed. Eventually, once their circumstances are known and their suitability for joining the orphanage has been established, they are welcomed into the orphanage and inducted into the **daily routine**. This begins with the morning clean, in which the rooms are swept and mopped by the children. After breakfast most of the kids are sent off to school or, if they have never been to school and are deemed too old to join the first grade, they are taught basic reading, writing and mathematics in the orphanage's own classroom. The afternoon is free-time, although there are duties the kids have to perform. Each must wash their own dishes and clothes, for example, as well as chop firewood, feed the orphanage's chickens or tend to the allotment. After this, for many kids the highlight of the day follows: **the afternoon football match**.

here, including salads, juices, cakes, pies and a wealth of Tanzanian coffees, is simply great, the drinks are cold and there's heaps of local information on the noticeboards and in the invaluable Moshi guidebook that they have for sale. Perhaps the best thing about this café, however, is the wonderfully tranquil little garden out back.

Back up the northern end of Mawenzi, despite an inauspicious location near the clock tower and at the junction of two main streets, *Central Garden*

Despite the security and comparative normality provided by the orphanage – at least compared to their life pre-Amani – the aim is to eventually return the children to their parents or another relative, having first checked that such a move would be appropriate. Indeed, at the orphanage they try to replicate family units, dividing the kids into *upengo* groups (*upengo* is Swahili for 'love'), with a member of staff acting as 'parent' to the group, supervising them and listening to their problems. Only one of the children has been at the orphanage since its foundation, with most staying for between 6 and 18 months.

It is both possible and worthwhile to visit the orphanage. One of the most heartwarming aspects of visiting the children is seeing how the older ones look after the newcomers and the more vulnerable. For example, Daudi, the autistic child, is looked after without complaint and treated with both kindness and respect by the other children.

The orphanage is not perfect. It was, after all, once just an average family house and as a result the rooms are cramped, with 45 boys currently sharing just ten bunk beds in one room. As such, they are sometimes forced to sleep three to a single mattress. (Having said that, the orphanage is actually due to move from its home off the Uru Road to a new building with improved facilities west of Moshi.) But that's not to deny that the orphanage is an amazing place and the dedication of the 16 staff and the expat volunteers is both a wonder to behold and the main reason Amani has been such a success. As an essentially secular organization (though many of the staff are motivated by Christian beliefs and values) the orphanage is not supported by any one church but instead relies on donations. Companies such as the British travel agents Guerba and Brighton-based search-engine marketing agency Spannerworks, the Peace House Foundation in the US, Unilever and the Montreal Canadiens hockey team's Children's Foundation have all helped to support and build upon the volunteers' hard work.

The orphanage welcomes new volunteers but needs those who have a good working knowledge of Swahili. If you don't have Swahili then you need to be willing to commit to staying for six months or more (by which time the orphanage reckons your Swahili will be of an acceptable level). But if you can't commit that kind of time, don't despair. Amani welcomes foreigners to come and look around the orphanage and spend some time with the kids. (America's Tusker Safaris and Moshi-based Tanzania Journeys are two companies who recommend their clients take time to visit.) Many tourists find that turning up to join in the afternoon football game (around 3pm daily except Wed) is a good idea, being an easy way to mix and bond with the kids without the need for a common language. To tell them you're coming, make a donation or merely to ask about their work, you can give them a call on ☎ 0744-892 456 or 0744-392 171, or email 🖳 info @amanikids.org. Or you can visit their website on 🖳 www. amanikids.org.

Trust us, if you've got a day to spare in Moshi, there's no more rewarding a way to spend it.

ARUSHA, MOSHI AND MARANGU

is actually a pleasant little spot to take the weight off your feet for a few minutes and enjoy a cold drink or snack.

The only place that can come close to the Coffee Shop when it comes to baking is **Abbas Ali's Hot Bread Shop** on Boma Road. A bit more of a local hangout (but only a bit), it's very pleasant with great fresh bread and they usually have copies of Western magazines and newspapers for sale. Also to the west of the main drag, this time on Kenyatta Street, **Salzburger** is a strange affair, a place that, to judge by the décor, is clearly in love with the Austrian city (and the birthplace of Mozart) after which it is named. The theme continues onto the small menu, with *weinerschnitzel* featuring. Despite the obscure location – it calls itself Africa's best-kept secret – it's a popular place, particularly with expats, and maybe the only place in Africa where you can dine on curry while the Von Trapp kids smile down at you from the walls.

All this Austrian-aping is fine, but for some real homegrown East African cooking there are several choices. The **Chagga Bar and Grill**, just south of the Leopard Hotel, is the place to come for authentic Chagga fare in authentic Chagga surroundings with authentic Chagga cutlery (ie: none). The menu is small but includes *mchemsho*, a kind of banana and meat stew (Ts1300 for 1/4kg of beef, for example). If you like your bananas tasteless, your atmosphere lively and your fingers dirty, this is the place for you. They also have a pool table and TV – like we said, it really is a locals' place. Another African joint, situated behind the mosque, is **Shukrani Snacks**, a Somali-run establishment that's popular and cheap. Closed in the evenings, come here at lunch to try their 'Federation' dish – a silver platter filled with samples of their greatest hits (curry, boiled bananas etc), all served with rice and yours for just Ts1000.

Moving uptown and upmarket, for a bit of a treat there are a couple of fine places in salubrious Shanty Town. The first, **El Rancho**, clearly suffers from an identity crisis, being an Indian restaurant with a Spanish name and a menu that's half-Chinese. Weirdly, it also has its own pool table, table-football pitch and even a small crazy golf course! Despite the confusion, the food can't be faulted and this is a lovely, jacaranda-shaded spot. Try the mutton kebabs (Ts3800) with vegetable rice (Ts2300). They also have an extensive alcohol selection, making this perhaps the best place for a post-trek knees-up. Finally, just south of El Rancho and also off Lema Road, **Panda Chinese** is, as you've probably already guessed from the name, a Chinese restaurant, and as you may have guessed from the Shanty Town location, a pretty smart one too. Some of their dishes, the sizzling beef in Chinese black bean sauce and pork à la Sichuan being but two, are a delight, and this is a wonderful place to sit with a jasmine tea – or something stronger – and reflect on your trek.

Nightlife

The **Police Mess** below the bus station is a bit of an eye-opener, if only because it comes as something of a surprise to find that policemen could be this much fun. The food is standard Tanzanian fare but the buzzing atmosphere is what makes it special. Its star, however, has been eclipsed somewhat with the arrival of the **East African Pub**, a real rowdy locals' hangout that lovers of English football will adore: not only do they show premiership matches live, but turn up just before kick-off on Saturday (5pm) and you can take advantage of their happy hour, when beers are buy-two-get-one-free. If you don't mind sharing the cost of a cab to Shanty Town, *El Rancho* off Lema Road is not only a fine restaurant but also has the best collection of booze in town. Out of town, the *Golden Shower* campsite on the Dar Road has a disco at weekends, though it's in a bit of an obscure location a few kilometres out of town.

Finally, for a sleazy but fun end to your time in Moshi, pay a visit to the *Pub Alberto*, Moshi's only nightclub with a couple of pool tables and a lively atmosphere – sometimes too lively, if rival street gangs are in.

TREKKING AGENCIES

Often cheaper than both Arusha and Marangu, Moshi captures the lion's share of the Kilimanjaro-trekking business, and some of the trekking companies in this town do a roaring trade. But beware: there is still a fair bit of monkey business going on here too, and you do need to be on your guard against cheetahs (!). For this reason we have compiled the following summary of some of the bigger agencies in town. Before booking with any of them, read the general advice given on pp32-6 about dealing with the trekking companies.

Please bear in mind that the following is our opinion only – an opinion that was formed by interviewing both the agencies themselves and, more importantly, their customers. By combining the information they imparted with other sources such as the Internet, the opinions of local guides and trekkers, the odd rumour and

Machame village (see p238) in the late nineteenth century. Engraving by Alexandre Le Roy from *Au Kilima-Ndjaro (Afrique Orientale)* published in 1893.

ARUSHA, MOSHI AND MARANGU

so on, we hope to have presented a fairly accurate account of the Moshi trekking scene. Remember, too, that things change very quickly in this part of the world, so some of the following will inevitably have altered by the time you reach Moshi. If you have any advice, comments, praise or criticisms about any of the following agencies, or indeed any agencies that we haven't mentioned, please write to us at the email/postal address given at the front of this book.

Agencies

● **Afrigalaxy** CCM Regional Building, Ground Floor, Taifa Road (PO Box 8340; ☎ 2750268; 🖳 www.afrigalaxytours.com). A company that does little to promote itself, probably because they get a lot of their clients from a South African agency. Nevertheless, they are worth checking out, especially as they organize cycling tours *around* Kili (US$400; see p30) as well as treks up it. Regarding the treks, they offer two types of trip, budget and luxury, with airport transfers and full-board accommodation included in the latter. Prices: five days on the Marangu Route US$740; US$880 for six days on Machame.

● **Akaro** National Social Security Fund Building, Old Moshi Road (PO Box 8578; ☎ 2752986; 🖳 www.akarotours.com). Run by the helpful and ambitious Ally with invaluable assistance from the delightful Teddy Mombury, their name is not one you hear too often but they are extremely efficient and reliable and everybody we interviewed who trekked with them seemed more than satisfied. They are also to be applauded for their refusal to use touts to drum up trade, despite an obscure location. As such, they're well worth checking out if you're in the market for a budget to mid-range trek. Costs: US$1005 Marangu for five nights; US$995 per person on the Machame trail, or US$1095 for seven days.

● **Ahsante** New Street (PO Box 855; ☎ 2753498; 🖳 www.ahsantetours.com). Though no longer the rock-bottom cheapest, Ahsante are still one of the best at the budget end of the price spectrum and have been adopted by a number of overseas travel companies as their agents on Kili, including Gap Challenge and Discover. Prices: US$1030 Machame, US$980 Marangu, both for six days, with a small reduction for groups of more than five.

● **Collins Safaris** Room 2, Aslam Garage, Old Moshi Rd (PO Box 437; ☎ 275 3070). A relatively new addition to the budget agency scene and one which, we believe, may not currently have a licence. Furthermore, they have the most persistent and annoying touts on Moshi's streets. True, their recommendations book was full of gushing praise – though the last entry was in July and it was October when we called in – and they certainly seem cheap. Their fees were US$780-850 per person for six days on the Machame Route (the higher rate applies during high season – the only company we know of to differentiate between the seasons), or US$850-950 for one person for six days on Marangu.

● **dotcom safaris** Kaunda Street (PO Box 38; ☎ 2754104, mobile 0744 317879; 🖳 www.dotcomsafaris.com). Thoroughly professional, thoroughly efficient and friendly company too, which all comes as something of a surprise given their location on dusty, unmetalled Kaunda Street. Ask for details of prices and itineraries, for example, and it's all printed out with the minimum of fuss. Much of their custom comes from outside Moshi, such as Rickshaw Travels, the local agent for Amex, who use them – and according to their recommendation books they do a good job. Do check the equipment before you set off, however: the recommendations book does occasionally mention leaky tents. Costs: US$985/915 for 1/2 people for six days on Machame, down to US$845 if there are six or more; US$800/770 for 1/2 people for five days on Marangu, down to US$725 for six or more. Competitively priced.

● **Evans** THB Bldg, 2nd Floor, Room 203 (PO Box 114; ☎ 2752612; 🖳 www. evansadventuretours.com). Evans is perhaps the least conspicuous company in Moshi, hidden away beyond the Marangu Colobus agency and not even bothering to use touts on the street to attract custom. Indeed, it took us three visits before we finally found the office open. Perhaps one reason for this unenthusiastic approach to drumming up trade is because they get most of their custom from the larger and more diligent safari operator JM Tours in Arusha, who send their climbing clients this way. Prices: US$950 if walking solo for five days on the Marangu Route, or US$820 for three people. For six days on Machame, the fee rises to US$1120 for one person, or it's US$980 if there are three of you.

● **Key's** Key's Hotel (see under hotels for contact details). Just like the hotel, a thoroughly professional, highly efficient and very satisfactory outfit with a rock-solid reputation and no pretensions towards being cheap. They boast that they pay their porters the KINAPA recommended wages too – if true, they're one of the few in Moshi who do. Prices: Marangu US$1160 for five days, or US$1270 for six days on Machame, including a couple of nights at the hotel.

● **Kilele Afrika** (PO Box 2029; ☎ 2750448, mobile 0744 679909; 🖳 www. kileleafrika.com). Due to open offices opposite the Immigration Office soon, Kilele Afrika are a relatively new company which at least talk a good talk, promising to pay their porters well and to donate part of their profits to the Amani Children's Home in Moshi. Unfortunately, we could not find anybody who'd been with them (the lack of an office was obviously hampering things, though that should have been sorted out by the time you read this). Prices: US$1235 for six days on Machame for one peron, US$1120 for three or more; Marangu US$1095 for five days for one person, US$975 for three or more. Rates include two nights accommodation. Note: this company is not licensed as yet, and though they hope to be very soon, it's advisable that you check first.

● **Kilimanjaro Crown Bird Tours & Safaris** THB Building, Room 113/114 (PO Box 9519; ☎ 2751162; 🖳 www.kilicrown.com). Another small operator but one that's been going for a few years and offers budget treks up the mountain. The prices are cheap enough at US$885 for six days on Machame and the same for the same number of days on Marangu, but their recommendations book was all a bit haphazard and some of the entries dated back almost four years, which didn't make us feel entirely comfortable with them.

● **Kilimanjaro Guide Tours & Safaris** Horombo Rd, just off the main roundabout (PO Box 210; ☎ 2750120). Sighing and rolling their eyes to the heavens when we asked them a few simple questions, this bunch were not the most

amenable of agents; their attempts to pass themselves off as a tourist information office also grated. According to trekkers who'd used them prices were too
high for the service they provided.

● **Kilimanjaro Serengeti Tours and Travel** Mawenzi Rd (PO Box 8213; ☎ 275
1287; ▣ kilimanjaroserengeti@yahoo.com). A visit to this long-standing company reminded me that, however long we stay in this country, we'll never quite
understand how it all works. First, upon our asking their prices, the young guy
whose misfortune it was to deal with me recited them with all the enthusiasm
of an automaton, as if we were the 47th people that day to enquire (which, to
judge by the slightly obscure location of their office and the fact that they were
reading the papers when we walked in, we very much doubt). Indeed, he only
became more animated when, right under the boss's nose, he told me to try
instead this new company which he appeared to be an agent for. After we told
him that we weren't interested, he then went back to try to selling me a trek with
Kilimanjaro Serengeti – who do, after all, presumably pay his wages – telling
me that the prices he quoted were negotiable and included two nights at the
Crane Hotel. To judge by the recommendations book (the last entry was about
six months ago) and the attitude of the staff, this company is going downhill,
and may soon go under, though to be fair their prices are cheap at US$715 for
one person on a four-night Marangu trek, or US$680 for three people or more;
and US$850 for five nights on Machame, or US$770 for three or more people.

● **Kindoroko** New Kindoroko Hotel (PO Box 1341; ☎ 0741 461441; ▣ www.
kindoroko.com). No-nonsense, up-front and offering a pretty good deal,
Kindoroko, like the hotel empire they seem determined to build, is gaining a
pretty good reputation and a fair bit of business. They're good value, too, at
US$835 for five days on Marangu as long as there are three or more of you, or
US$1000 for one person; or it's US$935 for six days on Machame, again with
a minimum of three people. These prices include two nights at the Kindoroko
and also any equipment. As a licenced company, these rates are competitive,
though do make sure, of course, that the savings they offer don't come directly
out of the porters' wages! Check the equipment too – the recommendations
book talks of leaky tents on occasion. Overall, however, pretty good.

● **Marangu Colobus Travels** THB Building, first floor (PO Box 8410; ☎ 275
3458, mobile 0744 588703; ▣ www.kili-colobus.com). Yet another budget
operator in the THB Building, we were greeted by the irrepressibly cheerful
Willy who seemed to pluck his trekking quotes out of the air. And to be fair, the
prices he plucked were OK – though nothing more – for a licensed company, at
US$1010 for one person on Machame, or US$940 for Marangu. Unfortunately,
I couldn't find anybody who'd actually climbed with them – so ask to see their
recommendations book before deciding anything. Happy plucking!

● **Mauly** Mawenzi Road (PO Box 1315; ☎ 2750730; ▣ www.mauly-tours.
com). Nobody can deny that Mauly are a well-run, professional agency. We did
find their prices a little – but only a little – steep for a self-professed budget outfit, but then you pay for reliability more than anything else at this end of the
market, and Mauly certainly are reliable. The thing that impressed me most

about them is their recommendation book; it's not that it was full of praise for them – indeed there were occasionally a few grumbles – but the fact that it took the form of a questionnaire that each of their trekkers had to fill in. It shows a degree of both thoroughness and confidence in the service they offer. Our only misgivings about them are that a) some readers have said that Mauly seemed surprised when they asked for a contract, as if this was both an impertinence and showed a lack of faith in them; and b) a couple of people have said that the food wasn't up to much, which is the first time we've ever heard anybody say that about their Kili trek. The wages they pay their porters are said to be poor too; ask KPAP for the latest. But these grumbles aside, this lot are fine. Costs: US$980 for six days on the Machame trail; US$850 for five days on the Marangu trail. Credit cards are accepted here for a 10% charge.

● **Moshi Expedition and Mountaineering** Kaunda Street (aka **MEM Tours and Safaris**; PO Box 146; ☎ 2754574; 🖳 www.memtours.com). Yet another very slick and professional agency that belies its location on the dusty, dishevelled Kaunda Street, MEM Tours are unusual in that they offer three standards of treks. There's Class A, which includes nights in the Impala, Protea Aishi or Salinero hotels before and after your trek and whose service on the mountain includes having one guide *per trekker*; Class B, which includes nights in the Bristol Cottages, Zebra or Mountain Park View but only one guide and assistant guide per group; and Class C, with nights at the Buffalo or Kindoroko, one guide and assistant guide per group and, perhaps most worryingly, less food on the mountain than the other classes. (When we asked for more details about this, Mohammed, the Managing Director, said classes A and B had a full English breakfast, whereas the poor class C's get only a continental breakfast.) Still, they do come recommended and a number of expats have used their services. The prices for Category B, which include, unusually, airport pick-up, are as follows: US$1140/1120 for seven days on Machame for 1/2 people; for Marangu it's US$1060/1020 for six days. Overall, an interesting and reliable company. Incidentally, they seems to be more willing than many to negotiate, and one budget trekker has written in to say that he managed to secure a trek for US$800 by paring down the number of porters, carrying his own luggage etc. Worth trying – just make sure, as always when negotiating, any saving you make on the trek hasn't come out of the porters' wages.

● **Samjoe** KNCU Building (PO Box 1467; ☎ 2751484, 0744 277825; 🖳 samjoetours@yahoo.com). Long established and still of the cheapest in town, and to be fair, though we had a problem with Samjoe once, there are plenty of trekkers who have enjoyed the experience of trekking with them. And providing you're careful in specifying exactly what you want and make sure it's written into the contract, you should have no problems. Furthermore, try to conduct your business with the founder, Betty, who seems the most competent and trustworthy. Prices are pretty reasonable at US$920 for six days on Machame. Bargain hard and you should get it cheaper – but just to reiterate: make sure everything that's specified is written in the contract.

● **Shah Tours** Mawenzi Rd (PO Box 1821; ☎ 2752370; 🖳 www.kilimanjaro-sh ah.com). Owners of the Mountain Inn, Shah are a long established and very reputable firm and Zara's nearest rivals in Moshi – so don't be put off by their rather tatty offices on Mawenzi Road. Unfortunately, just like Zara their treatment of porters has come in for much criticism of late and they really need to address this issue, particularly as they are agents for many overseas companies who would be horrified if they knew what was going on. Still, this lot are extremely reliable and their website is one of the best on the net. Costs: five days on Marangu US$935, or US$785 for three people; six days on Machame US$1160 or US$975 if there are three of you; prices include two nights at the Mountain Inn.

● **Snow Cap Mountain Climbing Camp** Rooms 404/406, Third Floor, CCM Regional Building (PO Box 8358; ☎ 2752428; 🖳 www.snowcap.co.tz). There's one reason to contact Snow Cap, and one reason only: to do the Rongai Route, which they concentrate on more than any other company and which they have done more than any other company to help popularize; indeed, they renovated the School Hut, the final hut on the Rongai ascent, and built the rather smart cottages on the Kenyan border by the start of the trek (see p276). Most of their business is actually booked in Europe (with the German agent Hauser and the French company Albert, for example), and as a consequence they expend little effort in trying to drum up trade in Moshi – hence the somewhat obscure location in the CCM building on Taifa Road. Their prices start at US$1063 per person for three people on a six-day Rongai trek, or it's US$1429 if there's just one of you. These prices include airport transfer and a night at the cottages by the Rongai Gate.

● **Summit Expeditions and Nomadic Experience** (PO Box 6491; ☎ 2753233; 🖳 www.nomadicexperience.com). Run by the irrepressible force of personality that is Simon Mtuy – an ultra-racer and the holder of the record for the fastest ascent and descent of Kili – Summit Expeditions deserve mention for the respect and kindness they show to their porters; indeed, it's usual for clients to spend a day with one of the porters at his home village before or after the trek, and the whole crew, porters included, are invited to the post-trek celebratory meal at the end. Different to other companies in Moshi, Summit Expeditions concentrate mainly on the Lemosho/Western Breach Route, for which they charge a steep US$2583, though this is for a total of 13 nights and includes a stay at Simon's cottages and farm at Mbahe village, 15 minutes west of Marangu Gate, or at Simba Farm/Poverty Gulch near the start of the Lemosho Route. Those who choose this company are often effusive in their praise, and Summit Expeditions are also partners of KPAP (see pp40-1). They're also worth contacting for details about their running and cycling holidays. Worth investigating.

● **Tanganyika Travels** Rindi Lane (PO Box 8357; ☎ 27507003; 🖳 www.tanga nyikatravels.com). Yet another bunch whose welcome made us feel that we were less a potential client than an imposition, Tanganyika, now in smart new offices opposite Chase moneychangers, rolled their eyes to the heavens when we walked in. They did warm up to the task eventually and their prices seemed reasonable too, at US$880 for six days on Machame or US$800 for five days on Marangu – which makes them worth checking for those looking for a budget deal; we just hope you catch them in a better mood.

● **Tanzania Journeys** Haria Hotel (PO Box 1724; ☎ 2750549; 🖳 www.tanza niajourneys.com). A brand new company, and one with its heart in the right place according to KPAP, Tanzania Journeys are friendly and profess an ecological and humanitarian outlook. For Kili they were charging US$1195 for one person on Machame (6 days), US$1120 for two/three people, while on Marangu it's US$1045 for five days for one person, or US$960 for two/three people; these prices, however, include return transfers to Nairobi or Kilimanjaro Airport, and two nights in the Key's Hotel.

● **Trans-Kibo Travels Limited** YMCA Building, Kilimanjaro Road (PO Box 558; ☎ 2752107; 🖳 www.transkibo.com). To be fair, Trans-Kibo Travels seemed to have pulled their proverbial socks up since the last edition, and whilst still operating out of shabby offices in the YMCA, they seem to be doing well, possibly because of patronage by Portuguese agency Rotas do Vento. Rates start at a reasonable US$913 for one person for four nights on Marangu (two climbers US$861, three or more US$802); for other routes they charge a standard US$1030 for six days, save Lemosho which ranges from a steep US$1600 for 2-3 people to a cheeky US$1840 if you're climbing solo.

● **Zara International** Rindi Lane (PO Box 1990; ☎ 2750011; 🖳 www.zaratr avel.com; if booking abroad check out 🖳 www.zara.co.tz, which will take you to EWP, the agency charged with handling their overseas bookings). They may come last in the *Yellow Pages* but in most other aspects this agency comes out

Kilimanjaro from Machame (see p238) in the late nineteenth century. Engraving by Alexandre Le Roy from *Au Kilima-Ndjaro (Afrique Orientale)* published in 1893.

ARUSHA, MOSHI AND MARANGU

either top, or very close to it. Simply put, Zara is the biggest tour leader on the mountain. A quick perusal of the recommendations from satisfied customers that have been posted on the Internet will reassure you of Zara's reliability. True, they are a little more expensive than most other companies in Moshi, but you are paying for peace of mind and quality of service. You'll also get one or two nights in their isolated Springlands Hotel thrown in.

However, there is a caveat. Despite setting up a 'porters union', there have been several complaints from trekkers about the mistreatment of porters, if not by the company themselves then by the guides they employ. So if you book with Zara, *do* keep a close eye on how the porters are treated and report any abuses to Zainab Ansell, Zara's boss, and to KPAP too. Published costs: US$1110 for six days on Machame, US$890 for five days on Marangu, including two nights B&B at Springlands. Costs *should* be reduced if you prefer to stay somewhere other than Springlands, and if you approach their offices in Moshi you may be able to bargain down the prices.

GETTING AWAY

Buses

Heading to **Arusha**, buses leave regularly throughout the day from the terminal on Mawenzi. A news report in the local press recently suggested that, while the normal fare is Ts1500, those who don't mind a little discomfort can agree to sit five to a row (normally it's four) and pay the reduced fare of Ts1000. You'd have to be desperate.

Of the **shuttles**, Impala charge a ridiculous US$10 for the two-hour journey to Arusha; the rest (Riverside, Davanu etc) charge around Ts5000.

Travellers wishing to journey to **Marangu** can catch one of the dalla-dallas (Ts800) from the adjacent terminal.

Nairobi and Mombasa **Shuttle buses** leave from their respective offices. Unfortunately, it seems to be much harder to get the residents' rates here in Moshi than it is in Arusha. Davanu (☎ 2753416) are on the ground floor of Kahawa House and are the most efficient bus office in Moshi. Their Nairobi bus leaves at 11.30am, breaking for an hour in Arusha and arriving after dark at 7pm in Nairobi (Ts15,000 residents' price, US$30 otherwise). Riverside are in Room 122 on the first floor of the THB Building (☎ 2750093); their bus to Nairobi also leaves at 11.30am, but they are slightly cheaper than Davanu at US$25 (Ts15,000 residents' rate). Impala (☎ 2751786), in the Impala Hotel and also in town next to the Pub Alberto, also operate two shuttles, at 6.30am and noon, charging US$25 to Nairobi.

Cheaper still are the big **buses**, though to Nairobi they're not recommended due to lack of comfort and the fact that they arrive at the bus terminal in Nairobi after dark – and the last place you ever want to be in this world is a Nairobi bus terminal after dark.

There is also a bus to **Mombasa**, operated by Perfect Trans, leaving at 9am daily; tickets can be bought from Hiren's Café (☎ 0748 452500), opposite Kahawa House.

Dar es Salaam There are plenty of **bus** companies plying the route to Dar. Be careful, however: as we've already stated in the Arusha chapter, this route is notorious for speeding and, as a result, horrific crashes. The cheaper companies, including both the companies attached to the Buffalo and Kindoroko hotels, are best avoided, even though they could save you Ts5000 or more. It's simply not worth it.

Scandinavian remain the one company that most locals will recommend, though at the time of writing many of their buses were being impounded due to financial problems. Currently they were still operating three buses daily at 8.15am, 10am and 12.15pm. However, only the 10.15am starts in Moshi (Ts17,000 to Dar), and thus it's the only one you can book in advance, though they will let you jump on the other two if there's room.

With the uncertainty surrounding Scandinavian you may prefer to opt for the Dar Express which, despite the rather scruffy office on the garage forecourt, actually offers a fine – and, just as importantly on this route, a safe – service (Ts15,000) with buses at 6.30am, 7.30am, 9am and 10am.

Flights

For details of flights out of Kilimanjaro International, see *Appendix B*, p305. The **Air Tanzania** office is by the clock tower on Rengua Road (☎ 2755205; Mon-Fri 8am-5pm, Sat and Sun 9am-noon). **Precision Air** are in the KNCU Building on Old Moshi Road (☎ 2753498; Mon-Fri 8.30am-4.30pm, Sat 8.30am-noon), beneath the Coffee Tree Hotel. For other airlines, call in at Emslies on Old Moshi Road, (☎ 2752701).

Getting to the airport takes about 45 minutes from Moshi. There is no public transport to Kilimanjaro International, and while you can take an Arusha-bound bus from Moshi and jump off at the junction, that still means you have to hitch down to the airport itself (it's too far to walk). Air Tanzania run shuttles daily to the airport to coincide with their flights. The shuttles leave from the Air Tanzania office by the clock tower 2hr and 10min before their flight departure times and are free to those with flight tickets, Ts5000 each way otherwise. Ask at the office the day before to check on departure times and availability. Precision Air also run a shuttle service (Ts2000), though only in the early morning (7.15am) and evening (5.40pm), so not all of their flights are covered by this service. A **taxi** should cost around US$35-50, more at night.

Marangu

According to legend, Marangu got its name when the first settlers in this part of Kilimanjaro, astonished by the lush vegetation, well-watered soils and the countless waterfalls they found here, cried out in delight 'Mora ngu! Mora ngu!' (*mora ngu* meaning 'much water'). It remains a verdant and extremely attractive place today, at least once you move away from the small huddle of shops and hustlers by the bus stop and start to climb up the hill towards Marangu Gate. The town, 14km along the Himo-Taveta highway, is extremely elongated but is in reality little more than two roads running up the mountain, with a filigree of dusty paths running off both.

ARRIVAL

Marangu is reached by a Ts800 **dalla-dalla** from Moshi, which takes about an hour. Passengers are normally dropped by the junction next to the bridge, though occasionally they will drive up the hill to drop you off on your doorstep. If not, a ride in the back of a pick-up truck up to Marangu Gate costs Ts300 (Ts500 in a shared taxi), the pick-ups leaving from the bridge when full.

SERVICES

There's a **post office** just to the east of the bridge, and a **telephone office** with some sort of broadband **Internet facility** – though at Ts2000 for 15 minutes, it's better to wait until you get back to Moshi if you can.

WHERE TO STAY

Accommodation in Marangu is fairly luxurious and survives by catering to the tour-group trade. Note that just about all of the hotels and campsites have some sort of trekking agency attached, and though they are not the cheapest, they are amongst the most reliable.

There is a **campsite** in Marangu, though this too is rather luxurious: the *Coffee Tree Campsite* (PO Box 835; ☎ 2756513; 🖳 www.alpinesafari.com), is an immaculate, manicured place to the east of main road leading up to Marangu Gate where camping alone costs US$8 per person per day, or its US$12 per person per day in one of the chalets (beds for 6 or mattresses for 16) and US$10 in the rondavel (up to four people). Tents can be hired (Ts10,000), as can stoves (Ts6000) and even a fireplace (Ts5000; firewood costs Ts1000). They now even have a sauna (US$10 for thirty minutes). Alpine Tours are based here, arranging trips to waterfalls and other beauty spots around Marangu.

A new campsite has also opened near Kilasiya Falls. Named *Gillman's Campsite* after the point where the Marangu Route reaches the crater rim, it's a very smart little place that exudes that lush, flower-filled charm that is Marangu's signature. The owner was away when we called but apparently a pitch goes for around Ts10,000 including hire of the tent (though they have only two, so you're probably better off bringing your own).

As lovely as these two places are, they pale in comparison to the grounds of the *Mountain Resort* (see p192 for contact details) where camping is also allowed. The grounds are gorgeous, the facilities spotless and huge and they charge only Ts6000, or Ts10,000 with tent hire included – plus you get to enjoy the bar/restaurant facilities of one of Marangu's most charming and luxurious hotels. Truly a lovely spot. Camping is also available at *Kibo Hotel* (see below).

Other than these, the nearest thing to budget hotel accommodation in Marangu is the **youth hostel** at Marangu Gate; usually reserved for school groups, they do *occasionally* allow trekkers to stay if it's open and there's room – though whether you'd want to sleep in the same room as a group of over-excited schoolchildren on vacation is another matter. Still, if you are desperate to stay there or you have a school group of your own, you could give KINA-PA a ring (☎ 275 6602) to see if there are places available. The cost is US$10 per person per night.

Down the hill but up the price scale, near the Coffee Tree Campsite is the friendly *Hotel Nakara* (PO Box 105; ☎ 2756571), which is clearly aiming to grab its share of the tour-group trade, though independent trekkers are welcome if there's space and rates are negotiable (rack rates US$50 per person per night for B&B, US$60 half-board, or US$70 full board).

Further down the hill and back on the main road, the *Capricorn Hotel* (PO Box 938, ☎ 2751309; ⌨ capricorn@africaonline.co.tz) is made up of a number of different buildings, some older (and therefore cheaper) than others. If you can – and don't mind spending the extra five dollars or so – try to get a room in the new wing (which opened only at the end of 2005) or, better still, the gorgeous Kisera House, up the hill behind the main reception building. More like a home than a hotel, and a particularly smart home at that, there's something decidedly colonial about the décor and furniture at Kisera House, from the plush carpets to the chandeliers and a four-poster bed that's so high it comes with its own set of steps. Then there's the splendid garden, too, a real labyrinth of flowers, birds and streams with giant Chagga storage baskets and a traditional Chagga house outside reception. Rates: B&B US$40 per person, US$45 in the new wing, or around US$50 in Kisera House.

No hotel review of Marangu would be complete without mentioning the *Kibo Hotel* (PO Box 102, ☎ 2751308; ⌨ www.kibohotel.com) which, whilst it cannot compete with most of the other hotels here in terms of luxury or comfort, cannot be beaten when it comes to character and history. A sign welcoming former US president Jimmy Carter still hangs above the door – it's a perfect symbol of the faded yet fascinating grandeur of the place, and of the time-warp it appears to be living in now. Indeed, rather comfortably, the place hadn't changed one iota since we last visited three years before. Antique German maps and other paraphernalia from the last century (and the one before that) adorn reception, while flags, T-shirts and banners from various trekking groups decorate the dining-room walls. The rooms themselves are overpriced, but it remains an absorbing place to wander around even if you don't intend staying. Prices: US$45/75 for s/c sgl/dbl half board, US$32/52 for bed and breakfast. Camping (including a hot shower) costs US$5 per person.

Further up the road, about ten minutes past the market and right by the Chagga Museum, is a new hotel that is, to be blunt, putting everything else in the village in the shade. Boasting just ten rooms – though there are plans for ten more – the *Mountain Resort* (☎ 2758950) is both luxurious and lovely, with the most sumptuous rooms in either Marangu or Moshi, each with a huge bathroom, digital TV and their own balcony. The grounds are gorgeous, the bar is beautiful and the roof terrace terrific, with views of Kili to boot. Really, we can't rave about this place enough and despite the high quality of hotels in Marangu, this place makes them all look a little tired. What's more, the rates are fair too, at US$45 B&B (US$57 full board) in a single, or US$80/104 for B&B/full board in a double. Triples are also available. A few foreign tour agencies have discovered this place but other than them there are very few people who make it here. If you have the time, energy and money, you won't be disappointed.

Finally, there are two places worth mentioning on the Himo-Taveta road: east of Marangu and just off the main road is the pleasant but slightly shabby *Babylon Lodge* (PO Box 227; ☎ 2756355; 🖳 www.babylonlodge.com), a deceptively large place with many unusually shaped rooms, some of them sunnier and cleaner than others so check a few out before checking in (US$25/40/60 s/c sgl/dbl/tpl B&B; full board US$39/68/102). Then there's the *Marangu Hotel* (☎ 2756591/4; 🖳 www.maranguhotel.com), an established favourite, standing in 12 acres of gardens (with pool) a couple of kilometres south of town on the way to Himo. The building used to be a farmhouse, built in the early 1900s. The food is great, with home-baked bread, and rates are US$50 per person per night (reduced if you join one of their Kili treks). My only gripe is with the rooms, with the hotel seemingly uncertain whether it should follow the nostalgia trail blazed by the Kibo Hotel (see p191) or try to compete with the all-mod-con luxury of the Mountain Resort. As a result the rooms lack both the charm of the former and the comfort of the latter. Still, this doesn't seem to matter too much to them for they seem to be concentrating more on organizing treks instead – something at which they excel (see below).

TREKKING AGENCIES

● **Kibo Hotel** (PO Box 102; ☎ 2751308; 🖳 www.kibohotel.com). The most interesting hotel in Marangu also organizes treks – with the shirts, banners and flags of many of those who've completed the climb with them now decorating the dining hall. Reliable and experienced, the hotel currently charges US$900 for one climber for five days on Marangu, or US$745 per person for three people or more; on Machame it's US$1225 for six days, or US$1138 per person for three people or more. Includes two nights at the hotel but not, unusually, transfer to the gate (US$30 per vehicle to Marangu, US$210 to Machame).

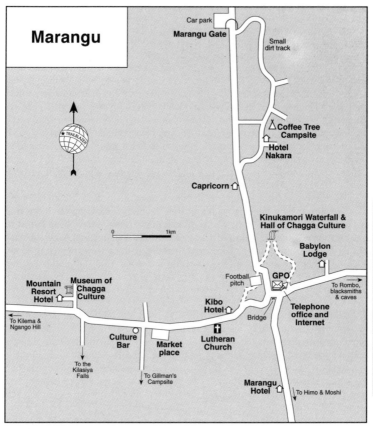

● **Marangu Hotel** (PO Box 40, Moshi; ☎ 2756594; 🖥 www.maranguhotel. com). Few companies can boast of the pedigree and experience of the Marangu Hotel, which has been sending climbers up Kilimanjaro since, wait for it, 1932! They also boast an 87% success rate among their clients for reaching the crater rim, with 70% making it to Uhuru Peak. What's more, their reputation is one of the best – superb guides who work *only* for them, and an endorsement from KPAP who reckon that this lot are amongst the best when it comes to the fair treatment of porters. Indeed, all of the porters are introduced to the clients at the beginning of the trek and at the end it's customary for them to share a celebratory meal together. They also pay extremely well! Overall, then, a highly recommended outfit. Current charges: US$895 for five days on Marangu; US$1270 for six days on Machame, with small reductions for groups.

WHAT TO DO

Always one of the prettiest villages on Kili's slopes, for some reason over the past couple of years Marangu has become the unofficial centre of Chagga culture – and it's really fascinating. You can try to find many of the attractions yourself – they're all pretty well signed – but it's much nicer and easier to hire one of the local kids who'll doubtless come up to you to offer themselves as guides (give them around Ts3000-5000 per day); they can also show you some short-cuts which will save you time. And while none of these 'Chagga' sights are going to have you rushing to the nearest phone booth in order to tell your nearest and dearest back home of the wonders you have seen, nevertheless it's good to see some sort of revival of a fascinating culture that would otherwise be confined largely to the history books. What's more, though your interest in Chagga culture may be slight, the chance to walk around one of the prettiest, homeliest parts of Tanzania should not be passed up; it's a lovely way to spend a day.

The first port of call is usually the **Kinukamori Falls** (7am-6.30pm; Ts3000), just twenty minutes' walk up from the bridge. As lovely as these are, we feel that these falls are the one sight that maybe should have been left as it was, for the addition of a **Hall of Chagga Culture** – an open-air series of statues or dioramas lining the path down to the falls, with each one depicting some aspect of Chagga culture or history – seems unnecessary and adds nothing to the beauty of the place. Indeed, with that god-awful statue of a woman about to plunge to her death that's now been installed at the top of the falls, this is one 'enhancement' that is anything but.

Still, some of the other sights are really absorbing. Falling into this category is the **Museum of Chagga Culture** (Ts2000). To reach it from the Kinukamori Falls, cross the school field, drop down to the road, turn right and continue walking for 25 minutes or so past the Kibo Hotel and the small market square (Friday is the market day here); the museum is right next to the Mountain Resort Hotel, ten minutes beyond this market square. Alternatively, you can catch a dalla-dalla (Ts100) from the main junction up to the market square. The first exhibit is a reconstruction of a thatched Chagga house complete with livestock inside. (We have been told by several people that the Chagga kept their livestock indoors not out of fear that they would be rustled by their neighbours but merely to save space.) The museum also has a display of traditional Chagga tools, farm implements, rope made from the bark of the mringaringa tree, a genealogical look at the history of the Chagga, some drums and a 'bugle' made of kudu horn. Though none of these exhibits is amazing, having them explained to you in near-faultless English by the museum's caretaker, Aloyse, really brings them to life.

Just before the museum is a turn-off to many people's favourite attraction in Marangu, the delightful **Kilasiya Falls**. These are stunning and though it costs a rather steep Ts3000 to gain entrance, you'll soon agree it's money well spent. The waterfalls are just part of the attraction, for it's the local flora that really catches the eye. Many of the plants have been labelled, and those which

Waterfall at the foot of Kilimanjaro. Engraving by Alexandre Le Roy from *Au Kilima-Ndjaro (Afrique Orientale)* published in 1893.

haven't will readily be identified by Joseph Lyimo, managing director of the falls, a relative of Aloyse and a walking encyclopaedia of all things floral. Reached via a steep muddy path, the falls are exquisite and there are even a couple of natural swimming pools in the gorge for those who fancy a cold dip. It's a great place to have lunch.

Those who've really got a taste for all things Chagga may also like to venture east along the Himo-Taveta road to the village of Mamba Kua Makunde, (about Ts300 by dalla dalla from the main junction in Marangu; look out for the Ashanti Lodge on your left as you drive along and jump out about 800m after this). Walking up the hill from the main road, you'll soon hear the sound of the **Chagga blacksmiths**, making anything from weapons to farm implements, often with little children working the bellows to keep the fires hot. It's free, though they'll sting you if you want to take a photo. Nearby, there are some underground **caves** (Ts2000) once inhabited by the Chagga. Claustrophobic, dark and difficult for anyone bigger than a smurf to negotiate, they're not the most pleasant of attractions though they are, in their own way, fascinating.

Finally, for modern-day Chagga culture look no further than the twice-weekly **markets** (Mondays and Thursdays) in the main village square by the junction, which are lively and, by the end of the day, often quite drunken too.

GETTING AWAY

Leaving Marangu, there's a bus straight from here to Dar es Salaam: every day at about 7am a Meridian bus drives through on its way from Rombo, further north. The cost is around Ts10,000, with the total travel time about six hours. The only other option is to catch a dalla-dalla to Moshi and reserve a seat there; it is in theory possible to stop a Dar-bound bus on the Moshi-Dar highway at Himo, though travellers who try this usually end up waiting for hours for one with a spare seat, and eventually most give up.

PART 6: MINIMUM IMPACT AND SAFE TREKKING

Minimum impact trekking

Manya ulanyc upangenyi cha ipfuve – 'Do not foul the cave where you have slept'
(A Chagga proverb that is said to refer to the living habits of the baboon, who do indeed 'foul their caves' until there comes a point where the stench compels them to find alternative accommodation.)

KINAPA does try to keep Kilimanjaro clean. At all huts and most campsites, every trekking group must have its rubbish weighed by the ranger and if there's any evidence that some rubbish has been dumped (ie if the rubbish carried weighs less at one campsite than it did at the previous one) then the guide could have his licence temporarily revoked and/or have to pay a heavy fine. It's a system that would appear to have many loopholes but until recently Kili *was* a very clean mountain and it also remains the only one where we've seen porters and guides voluntarily walk fifty yards from the trail to pick up a discarded water bottle or sweet wrapper. And though it can be a little frustrating to have to wait for your guide every morning while the rubbish is weighed, it's a small price to pay for a pristine peak. Unfortunately, standards appear to have slipped recently and there is now serious concern amongst trekking agents and environmentalists about the state of some of the trails. While it's easy to blame the authorities for the parlous state of Lemosho and other routes, trekkers are just as culpable. After all, much of it is our rubbish.

You can help Kilimanjaro become beautiful once more by following these simple rules that apply to almost every mountain anywhere in the world:

● **Dispose of litter properly**. In theory, all you should have to do is give your litter to your 'staff': given the stiff punishments they receive for leaving rubbish behind (see above), this should ensure all waste is taken off the mountain. Unfortunately, despite all the cleaning crews and the weighing stations at each campsite, the litter situation is getting worse. See p199 for more details. Whatever you decide to do, don't give **used batteries** to porters; keep them with you and take them back to the West where they have the facilities to dispose of them properly.

● **Don't start fires**. For some reason, many trekkers feel that lighting a fire and sitting around it in the evening is an integral part of the whole camping experience. But p109 will give you an idea of just how much damage an out-of-control fire can cause. There's absolutely no need to light a fire on Kilimanjaro: for cooking, your guides and porters should use kerosene, while for heat, put another layer of clothes on, or cuddle up to somebody who doesn't mind being cuddled up to.

● **Boil, filter or purify your drinking water**. This will help to reduce the number of non-returnable, non-reusable, non-biodegradable and very non-environmentally friendly plastic mineral water bottles that are used on Kili.

● **Use the purpose-built latrines**. True, some of them could do with emptying (especially the central toilet at the Barranco campsite, which is now so full that the pile of human waste is in danger of developing a snowy cap all of its own), but this is still better than having piles of poo behind all the bushes on the trail and toilet paper hanging from every bough. If the situation is really urgent and you cannot wait until you reach one of the purpose-built latrines along the way, deliberate before you defecate: firstly, make sure you're at least 20m away from both the path and any streams or rivers – the mountain is still the main source of water for many villages and the people who live there would prefer it if you didn't crap in their H_2O. Secondly, take a plastic spade or trowel with you so you can dig a hole to squat over, and cover this hole with plenty of earth when you've finished. And finally, dispose of your toilet paper properly, by either burning it (the preferable method) or, if this is not feasible, by putting it in the hole you've just dug and covering it with plenty of soil. One reader has written in to say that it's very difficult to burn soggy toilet paper. My editor, however, has conducted a controlled experiment and gives this advice: 'If you light the dry corner of partially wet loo paper and twist it round so the flame dries the wet bit it *does* all burn up'. Give it a go next time you need to, err, go. The reader does, in fact, go on to say that trekkers should adopt the 'pack it in – pack it out' method, ie to double-bag toilet paper (preferably in a ziplock bag) and take it out of the park; and this, to be fair, is the best way to keep Kili pristine and paper-free.

● **Leave the flora and fauna alone**. Kili is home to some beautiful flowers and fascinating wildlife, but the giant groundsels rarely thrive in the soils of Europe and the wild buffalo, though they may look docile when splashing about in the streams of Kili, have an awful temper that makes them quite unsuitable as pets. It's illegal to take the flora or fauna out of the park, so leave it all alone; that way, other trekkers can enjoy them too.

● **Stay on the main trail**. The continued use of shortcuts, particularly steep ones, erodes the slopes. This is particularly true on Kibo: having reached the summit, it's very tempting on your return to slide down on the shale like a skier and you'll see many people, especially guides, doing just that. There's no doubt that it's a fast, fun and furious way to get to the bottom, but with thousands of trekkers doing likewise every year, the slopes of Kibo are gradually being eroded as all the scree gets pushed further down the mountain. Laborious as it sounds, stick to the same snaking path that you used to ascend.

● **Wash away from streams and rivers**. You wouldn't like to bathe in somebody else's bathwater; nor, probably, would you like to cook with it, do your laundry in it, nor indeed drink it. And neither would the villagers on Kili's lower slopes, so don't pollute their water by washing your hair, body or clothes in the mountain streams, no matter how romantic an idea this sounds. If your guide is halfway decent he will bring some hot water in a bowl at the end of the day's walk for you to wash with. Dispose of it at least 20m away from any streams or rivers.

Keep Kili clean

Amidst all the hullabaloo surrounding the plight of porters, one other major concern, namely the amount of litter on Kili and the environmental degradation in general, is being largely ignored. Anybody who has climbed the mountain recently, particularly on less-popular routes such as the Lemosho trail, will have been horrified at the amount of litter lining the trail and scattered around every campsite. From the moment you set foot on the trail your eyes are assaulted by the sight of plastic bags hanging off branches, sweet wrappers and cigarette butts lying trodden in the mud and, perhaps most offensively of all, toilet paper draped across the bushes. Arrive at a campsite and used batteries lie on the ground waiting to pollute the soil, while look behind any rock and you'll find broken glass, more toilet paper, drinks cartons and plenty of orange and banana peel, which at altitude is far less biodegradable than it is at sea level.

What makes it even more depressing is that at these same campsites you'll find the official cleaning crews, usually sitting in the hut sheltering from the cold and sharing a cup of tea with the ranger, rather than carrying out the work for which they've been hired. If they're not going to clean up the camps – then who is?

As mentioned before, it is the less popular routes that seem to suffer more from the litter problem, presumably because they are less assiduously controlled and monitored, but that's not to say that the Machame and even Marangu routes – the latter often regarded as the mountain's 'show-route' and the one visiting dignitaries are usually taken on – do not from time to time suffer from the same problems.

Renata Haas from Wisconsin, a student at Colorado College, has been studying the environmental degradation Kilimanjaro has suffered due to its large and ever-increasing popularity. The amount of litter on the mountain was just one of the aspects in her study, which also looked at the condition of the campsites and their toilets and the loss of vegetation along the trail.

Some of Renata's findings are depressing but not unexpected. For instance, on one stage on the Machame trail, between Machame Huts and the Shira Caves, she found an incredible 1467 pieces of litter. On the Marangu Route, the 'dirtiest' stage was the one from Horombo to Kibo Huts, with 979 pieces of trash. When it came to campsites the picture was equally sad, with the Shira Caves recording an incredible 4850 pieces of litter. (On Marangu, the highest amount of litter was found at the Kibo Huts, where 1200 pieces of litter were counted.)

Some of her conclusions make for interesting reading too, and one in particular stands out: Renata believes that there is actually a connection between the mistreatment of porters and the amount of litter. Her reasoning is simple: if the average porter on Kilimanjaro is being paid only a small amount for his labours, the mountain for him has little intrinsic value. In other words, there is little incentive for him to tidy up his workplace. Furthermore, if you are burdening the porter with more than the regulation amount of baggage, it may actually be physically difficult for him to bend down and pick up any litter he has dropped along the way – particularly as that litter must then be carried with him all the way on the trek until the end; so the temptation to stroll on and ignore it must therefore be great. Renata's conclusion is, therefore, a simple one: improve the lot of the porters and you improve the state of the mountain.

It's a simple conclusion and one with which it's hard to argue. Hopefully, it may also help to persuade KINAPA to look at their policies aimed at cleaning up the mountain. Because one thing is for certain: their current attempts to keep the mountain litter-free, using cleaning crews and weighing stations at each campsite, are just not working.

Safe trekking

Came to cave. Men cold. Passed two corpses of young men who died of exposure, a short time ago. The vultures had pecked out their eyes, the leopards had taken a leg from each.
Peter MacQueen's diary of his expedition up Kilimanjaro, from *In Wildest Africa* (1910)

Because of the number of trekkers who scale Kilimanjaro each year, and the odd ways in which some of them choose to do so, many people are under the mistaken impression that Africa's highest mountain is also a safe mountain. Unfortunately, as any mountaineer will tell you, there's no such thing as a safe mountain, particularly one nearly 6000m tall with extremes of climate near the summit and ferociously carnivorous animals roaming the lower slopes.

Your biggest enemy on Kilimanjaro, however, is likely to be neither the weather nor the wildlife but the altitude. Unsurprisingly, KINAPA are shy about revealing how many trekkers perish on Kili each year but what is known is that, during the millennium celebrations, when the mountain was swamped by more than a thousand trekkers on New Year's Eve alone, three died and thirty-three more had to be rescued. The culprit behind at least one of the fatalities was the condition known as acute mountain sickness, or AMS.

The authorities are doing what they can to minimize the number of deaths: guides are given thorough training in what to do if one of their group is showing signs of AMS and trekkers are required to register each night upon arrival at the campsite and have to pay a US$20 'rescue fee' as part of their park fees. But you, too, can do your bit by avoiding AMS in the first place. The following few pages discuss in detail what AMS actually is, how it is caused, the symptoms and, finally, how to avoid it. Read this section carefully: it may well save your life. Following this, on p206 you'll find details of other ailments commonly suffered by trekkers on Kilimanjaro.

WHAT IS AMS?

In the last edition we stated that 'at Uhuru Peak, the summit of Kilimanjaro, the oxygen present in the atmosphere is only half that found at sea level'. We are grateful to Janet Bonnema for correcting us on this matter. As Janet explains, throughout the troposphere (ie from sea level to an altitude of approximately 10km), the air composition is in fact always the same, namely 20% oxygen and nearly 80% nitrogen. So it's not the lack of oxygen that's the problem but the lack of air pressure. As Ms Bonnema writes: 'The atmospheric pressure drops by about 1/10th for every 1000m of altitude. Thus the air pressure at the top of Kilimanjaro is approximately 40% of that found at sea level.' In other words, though each breath inhaled is 20% oxygen, just as it is at sea level, it becomes much harder to fill your lungs since the atmosphere is not pushing so much air into them. As a result, every time you breathe on Kibo you take in only about

> **If you're farting well, you're faring well — the other effects of altitude and acclimatization on the human body**
>
> In addition to AMS, there are other symptoms suffered by people at high altitude that are not in themselves usually cause for any concern. The first is the phenomenon of **periodic breathing**. What happens is that, during sleep, the breathing of a person becomes less and less deep, until it appears that he or she has stopped breathing altogether for a few seconds — to the obvious consternation of those sharing the person's tent. The person will then breathe or snore deeply a couple of times to recover, causing relief all round. Another phenomenon is that of **swollen hands and feet**, more common amongst women than men. Once again, this is no cause for concern unless the swelling is particularly severe. Another one that is far more common among women than men, is **irregular periods**. The need to **urinate** and **break wind** frequently are also typical of high altitude living and far from being something to be concerned about, are actually positive indications that your body is adapting well to the conditions. As is written on an ancient tombstone in Dorset:
>
> *Let your wind go free, where e'er you be,*
> *For holding it in, was the death of me.*

half as much air, and thus oxygen, as you would if you took the same breath in Dar es Salaam. This can, of course, be seriously detrimental to your health; oxygen is, after all, pretty essential to your physical well-being. All of your vital organs need it, as do your muscles. They receive their oxygen via red blood cells, which are loaded with oxygen by your lungs and then pumped around your body by your heart, delivering oxygen as they go.

Problems arise at altitude when that most vital of organs, the brain, isn't getting enough oxygen and malfunctions as a result; because as the body's central control room, if the brain malfunctions, so does the rest of you, often with fatal consequences.

Fortunately, your body is an adaptable piece of machinery and can adjust to the lower levels of oxygen that you breathe in at altitude. Unconsciously you will start to breathe deeper and faster, your blood will thicken as your body produces more red blood cells and your heart will beat faster. As a result, your essential organs will receive the same amount of oxygen as they always did. But your body needs time before it can effect all these changes. Though the deeper, faster breathing and heart-quickening happen almost as soon as your body realizes that there is less oxygen available, it takes a few days for the blood to thicken. And with Kilimanjaro, of course, a few days is usually all you have on the mountain, and the changes may simply not happen in time. The result is AMS.

AMS, or acute mountain sickness (also known as **altitude sickness**), is what happens when the body fails to adapt in time to the lack of air pressure at altitude. There are three levels of AMS: mild, moderate and severe. On Kilimanjaro, it's fair to say that most people will get some symptoms of the illness and will fall into the mild-to-moderate categories. Having symptoms of

MINIMUM IMPACT & SAFE TREKKING

mild AMS is not *necessarily* a sign that the sufferer should give up climbing Kili and descend immediately. Indeed, most or all of the symptoms suffered by those with **mild AMS** will disappear if the person rests and ascends no further; and assuming the recovery is complete, the assault on the summit can continue. The same goes for **moderate AMS** too, though here the poor individual and his or her symptoms should be monitored far more closely to ensure that they are not getting any worse and developing into **severe AMS**. This is a lot more serious and sufferers with severe AMS should always descend immediately, even if it means going down by torchlight in the middle of the night.

The following describes the symptoms of the various levels of AMS.

What are the symptoms?

The symptoms of **mild AMS** are not dissimilar to the symptoms of a particularly vicious hangover, namely a thumping headache, nausea and a general feeling of lousiness. An AMS headache is generally agreed to be one of the most dreadful headaches you can get, a blinding pain that thuds continuously at ever decreasing intervals; only those who have bungee-jumped from a 99ft building with a 100ft elasticated rope will know the intense, repetitive pain AMS can cause. Thankfully, the usual headache remedies should prove effective against a mild AMS headache though do be careful as they can also mask any worsening of symptoms. As with a hangover, mild AMS sufferers often have trouble sleeping and, when they do, that sleep can be light and intermittent. They can also suffer from a lack of appetite. Given the energy you've expended getting to altitude in the first place, both of these symptoms can seem surprising if you're not aware of AMS.

Moderate AMS is more serious and requires careful monitoring of the sufferer to ensure that it does not progress to severe AMS. With moderate AMS, the sufferer's nausea will lead to vomiting, the headache will not go away even after pain-relief remedies, and in addition the sufferer will appear to be permanently out of breath, even when doing nothing.

With moderate AMS, it is possible to continue to the summit, but only after a prolonged period of relaxation that will enable the sufferer to make a complete recovery. Unfortunately, treks run to tight schedules and cannot change their itineraries mid-trek. Whether you, as a victim of moderate AMS, will be given time to recover will depend largely upon how fortunate you are, and whether the onset of your illness happens to coincide with a scheduled rest day or not.

With **severe AMS**, on the other hand, there should be no debate about whether or not to continue: if anybody is showing symptoms of severe AMS it is imperative that they **descend immediately**. These symptoms include a lack of coordination and balance, a symptom known as **ataxia**. A quick and easy way to check for ataxia is to draw a 10m line in the sand and ask the person to walk along it. If they clearly struggle to complete this simple test, suspect ataxia and descend. (Note, however, that ataxia can also be caused by hypothermia or extreme fatigue. As such, ensure that the sufferer is suitably dressed in warm clothing and has eaten well before ascertaining whether or not he or she is suffering from ataxia, and deciding what to do about it). Other symptoms of severe

AMS include mental confusion, slurred or incoherent speech, and an inability to stay awake. There may also be a gurgling, liquid sound in the lungs combined with a persistent watery cough which may produce a clear liquid, a pinky phlegm or possibly even blood. There may also be a marked blueness around the face and lips, and a heartbeat that, even at rest, may be over 130 beats per minute. These are the symptoms of either HACO and HAPO, as outlined below, while the ways to treat somebody suffering from AMS are given on p205.

HACO and HAPO

Poor Mapandi, a carrier whom I had noticed shivering with fever for the last day or two, stiffened, grew cold and died beside me in the mud. **Peter MacQueen** *In Wildest Africa*

HACO (High Altitude Cerebral Oedema) is a build-up of fluid around the brain. It's as serious as it sounds. It is HACO that is causing the persistent headache, vomiting, ataxia and the lack of consciousness. If not treated, death could follow in as little as 24 hours, less if the victim continues ascending.

Just as serious, **HAPO** (High Altitude Pulmonary Oedema) is the accumulation of fluid around the lungs. It is this condition that is causing the persistent cough and pinkish phlegm. Once again, the only sensible option is to descend as fast as possible. In addition, one of the treatments outlined on p205 should also be considered.

GO *POLE POLE*[*] IF YOU DON'T WANT TO FEEL POORLY POORLY – HOW TO AVOID AMS

Haraka haraka haina baraka 'Great haste has no blessing' – a common Swahili saying.

AMS is easily avoided. The only surefire way to do so is to **take your time**. Opting to save money by climbing the mountain as quickly as possible is a false economy: the chances are you will have to turn back because of AMS and all your efforts (and money) will be wasted.

According to the Expedition Advisory Committee at the Royal Geographical Society, the recommended acclimatization period for any altitude greater than 2500m is to sleep no more than 300m higher than your previous night's camp, and to spend an extra night at every third camp. But if you were to follow this on Kilimanjaro's Marangu Route, for example, from Mandara Huts you would have to take a further *eight* nights in order to safely adjust to the Kibo Huts' altitude of 4713m – whereas most trekkers take just two days to walk between the two. The EAC realize that the short distances and high per diem cost of climbing Kilimanjaro make this lengthy itinerary impractical, so instead they recommend a pre-trek acclimatization walk on Mount Meru (see p209) or Mount Kenya (4895m to Point Lenana). This is an excellent idea if you have the time and are feeling fit; and providing you do one of these walks *immediately* before

[*] *Pole pole* is the phrase you'll probably hear more than any other on Kili. It's Swahili for 'slowly slowly' and is usually uttered by guides to dissuade their charges from ascending too fast.

MINIMUM IMPACT & SAFE TREKKING

Diamox

Acetazolamide (traded under the brand name Diamox) is the wonder drug that fights AMS, and the first treatment doctors give to somebody suffering from mountain sickness. Indeed, many trekkers use it as a prophylactic, taking it during the walk to prevent AMS.

Diamox works by acidifying the blood, which stimulates breathing, allowing a greater amount of oxygen to enter into the bloodstream. Always consult with your doctor before taking Diamox to discuss the risks and benefits. If you do take it, remember to try it out first back at home to check for allergic reaction, as Diamox is a sulfa derivative, and some people do suffer from side effects, particularly a strange tingling sensation in their hands and feet.

The disadvantage with taking it prophylactically, according to one doctor serving on the Annapurna Circuit in Nepal, is that you are using up one possible cure. That is to say, should you begin to suffer from AMS despite taking Diamox, doctors are going to have to look for another form of treatment to ensure your survival. For this reason, a number of trekkers are now buying the drug and taking it up the mountain with them, but are using it only as a last resort when symptoms are persistent. If you are unfamiliar with Diamox and uncertain about the effect it could have on you, this is perhaps the best option.

you climb Kili, these treks can be beneficial – and the views towards Kilimanjaro from Meru are delightful too (see p209 onwards for a description of this route).

But what if you don't have the time or money to do these other climbs? The answer is to plan your walk on Kilimanjaro as carefully as possible. If you have enough money for a 'rest day' or two, take them. These 'rest days' are not actually days of rest at all – on the Marangu trail, for example, guides usually lead their trekkers up from Horombo Huts to the Mawenzi Hut at 4538m before returning that same afternoon. But they do provide trekkers with the chance to experience a higher altitude before returning below 4000m again, thereby obeying the mountaineers' old maxim about the need to '**climb high, sleep low**' to avoid mountain sickness.

The route you take is also important. Some of the routes – the Machame, Lemosho and Shira trails via the Barafu Huts, for example – obey the mountaineers' maxim on the third or fourth days, when the trail climbs above 4500m before plunging down to an altitude of 3985m at Barranco Camp where you spend the night. Some of the shorter trails, however, do not: for example, it is possible for a trekker walking at an average pace on the Marangu or Rongai trails to reach the Kibo Huts in three days and attempt an assault on the summit for that third night. This sort of schedule is entirely too rapid, allowing insufficient time for trekkers to adapt to the new conditions prevalent at the higher altitude. This is why so many people fail on these trails and it is also the reason why, particularly on these shorter trails, that **it is imperative that you take a 'rest day' on the way up**, to give your body more time to acclimatize.

How you approach the walk is important too. Statistically, men are more likely to suffer from AMS than women, with young men the most vulnerable.

The reason is obvious. The competitive streak in most young men causes them to walk faster than the group; that, and the mistaken belief that greater fitness and strength (which most men, mistakenly or otherwise, believe they have) will protect them against AMS. But AMS is no respecter of fitness or health. Indeed, many experienced mountaineers believe the reverse is true: the less fit you are, the slower you will want to walk, and thus the greater chance you have of acclimatizing properly. The best advice, then, is to **go as slowly as possible**. Let your guide be the pacemaker: do not be tempted to hare off ahead of him, but stick with him. That way you can keep a sensible pace and, what's more, can ask him any questions about the mountain that occur to you along the way.

There are other things you can do that may or may not reduce the chance of getting AMS. One is to **eat well**: fatigue is said to be a major contributor to AMS, so try to keep energy levels up by eating as much as you can. Dehydration can exacerbate AMS too, so it is vital that you **drink every few minutes** when walking; for this reason, one of the new platypus-style water bags which allow you to drink hands-free without breaking stride are invaluable (see p57). **Wearing warm clothes** is very important too, allowing you to con-serve energy that would otherwise be spent on maintaining a reasonable body temperature. Although there hasn't been a serious study on this subject, many people swear that carrying your own rucksack increases your chance of suc-cumbing to AMS. Certainly, in our experience, this is true, so, finally, **hire a porter to carry your baggage** (the agencies will assume you want this anyway unless you specify otherwise).

HOW TO TREAT IT

Sat down beside P.D. in the mud. Gave him one bottle of champagne. Revived him greatly.
Peter MacQueen *In Wildest Africa* (1910)

The chances are that on your trek you will see at least one poor sod being wheeled down Kili, surrounded by porters and strapped to the strange unicycle-cum-stretcher device that KINAPA uses for evacuating the sick and suffering from the mountain. Descent is the most effective cure for AMS, but in some severe cases it is not enough. Diamox (see box opposite) is also usually given, though again, if the victim has been suffering for a while or Diamox is not avail-able, some other treatment may be used such as:

Gamow hyperbaric bag Some of the upmarket trek operators now carry a gamow bag with them. This is a man-sized plastic bag into which the victim is enclosed. The bag is then zipped up and inflated. As it is inflated, the pressure felt by the sufferer inside the bag is increased, thus mimicking the atmospheric conditions present at a lower altitude. The disadvantage with this method is that of inconvenience. The cumbersome bag has to be dragged up the mountain and, worst of all, in order to work effectively once the patient is inside, the bag must be kept at a constant pressure. This means that somebody must pump up the bag every two or three minutes. This is tricky when at least two other people are try-ing to manoeuvre the body and bag down the slopes.

Oxygen Giving the victim extra oxygen from a bottle or canister does not immediately reverse all the symptoms, though in conjunction with rapid descent it can be most effective.

OTHER POTENTIAL HEALTH PROBLEMS

Coughs and colds

These are common on Kilimanjaro. Aspirin can be taken for a cold; lozenges containing anaesthetic are useful for a sore throat, as is gargling with warm salty water. Drinking plenty helps too. A cough that produces mucus has one of a number of causes; most likely are the common cold or irritation of the bronchi by cold air which produces symptoms that are similar to flu. It could, however, point to AMS. A cough that produces thick green and yellow mucus could indicate bronchitis. If there is also chest pain (most severe when the patient breathes out), a high fever and blood-stained mucus, any of these could indicate **pneumonia**, requiring a course of antibiotics. Consult a doctor.

Exposure

Also known as hypothermia, this is caused by a combination of exhaustion, high altitude, dehydration, lack of food and not wearing enough warm clothes against the cold. Note that it does not need to be very cold for exposure to occur. Make sure everyone, particularly your porters, is properly equipped.

Symptoms of exposure include a low body temperature (below 34.5°C or 94°F), poor coordination, exhaustion and shivering. As the condition deteriorates the shivering ceases, coordination gets worse making walking difficult and the patient may start hallucinating. The pulse then slows and unconsciousness and death follow shortly. Treatment involves thoroughly warming the patient quickly. Find shelter as soon as possible. Put the patient, without their clothes, into a sleeping-bag with hot water bottles

Kilimanjaro seen from Lake Jipé
(from *The Kilima-njaro Expedition – A Record of Scientific Exploration in Eastern Equatorial Africa* HH Johnston, 1886)

(use your water bottles); someone else should take their clothes off, too, and get into the sleeping bag with the patient. There's nothing like bodily warmth to hasten recovery.

Frostbite
The severe form of frostbite that leads to the loss of fingers and toes rarely happens to trekkers on Kilimanjaro. You could, however, be affected if you get stuck or lost in particularly inclement weather. Ensure that all members of your party are properly kitted out with thick socks, boots, gloves and woolly hats.

The first stage of frostbite is known as 'frostnip'. The fingers or toes first become cold and painful, then numb and white. Heat them up on a warm part of the body (eg an armpit) until the colour comes back. In cases of severe frostbite the affected part of the body becomes frozen. Don't try to warm it up until you reach a lodge/camp. Immersion in warm water (40°C or 100°F) is the treatment. Medical help should then be sought.

Gynaecological problems
If you have had a vaginal infection in the past it would be a good idea to bring a course of treatment in case it recurs.

Haemorrhoids
If you've suffered from these in the past bring the required medication with you since haemorrhoids can flare up on a trek, particularly if you get constipated.

Snowblindness
Though the snows of Kilimanjaro are fast disappearing, you are still strongly advised to wear sunglasses when walking on the summit – particularly if you plan on spending more than just a few minutes up there – to prevent this uncomfortable, though temporary, condition. Ensure everyone in your group, including porters, has eye protection. If you lose your sunglasses a piece of cardboard with two narrow slits (just wide enough to see through) will protect your eyes. The cure for snow-blindness is to keep the eyes closed and lie down in a dark room. Eye-drops and aspirin can be helpful.

Sunburn
Protect against sunburn by wearing a hat, sunglasses and a shirt with a collar that can be turned up. At altitude you'll also need sunscreen for your face.

Care of feet, ankles and knees
A twisted ankle, swollen knee or a septic blister on your foot could ruin your trek so it's important to take care to avoid these. Choose comfortable boots with good ankle support. Don't carry too heavy a load. Wash your feet and change your socks regularly. During lunch stops take off your boots and socks and let them dry in the sun. Attend to any blister as soon as you feel it developing.

Blisters There are a number of ways to treat blisters but prevention is far better than cure. Stop immediately you feel a 'hot spot' forming and cover it with a piece of moleskin or Second Skin. One trekker suggests using the membrane inside an egg-shell as an alternative form of Second Skin. If a blister does form you can either burst it with a needle (sterilized in a flame) then apply a dressing or build a moleskin dressing around the unburst blister to protect it.

Sprains You can lessen the risk of a sprained ankle by wearing boots which offer good support. Watch where you walk, too. If you do sprain an ankle, cool it in a stream and keep it bandaged. If it's very painful you'll probably have to abandon your trek and return to your hotel. Aspirin is helpful for reducing pain and swelling.

Knee problems These are most common after long stretches of walking downhill. It's important not to take long strides as you descend; small steps will lessen the jarring on the knee. It may be helpful to wear knee supports and use walking poles for long descents, especially if you've had problems with your knees before.

MINIMUM IMPACT AND SAFE TREKKING

(**Opposite**) The famous arched fig tree on the first afternoon of the Mount Meru climb.

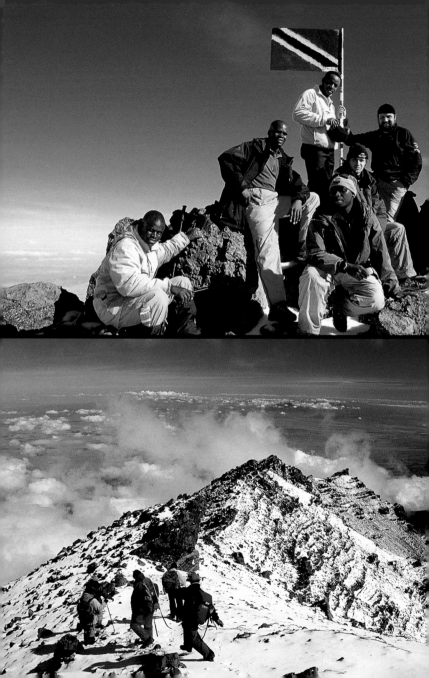

PART 7: MOUNT MERU

INTRODUCTION

Mount Meru, which overlooks Arusha from the north, is used by an increasing number of trekkers as a warm-up trek – an *hors d'oeuvre* to the main course of Kili if you like. And a perfect starter it is too: though smaller, it's also quite similar in that to reach its volcanic summit you have first to climb through a number of different vegetation zones before embarking on the final night-time march to the highest point on the crater rim and thus the summit itself. What's more, at 4562.13m, it provides the trekker with the perfect opportunity to acclimatize to Kilimanjaro's rarified atmosphere. In other words, the mountain gives one a taste of the challenges that lie ahead on Kilimanjaro, whilst also whetting the appetite for the thrills and beauty of that mountain.

However, Meru is worth doing as much for the differences as for the similarities that it shares with its neighbour. In particular, there's the greater abundance of wildlife. Lying at the heart of Arusha National Park, a reserve that's teeming with animals, it's an odd trekker who doesn't come away from the trek with his or her camera filled with pictures of buffalo, giraffe, elephant, bushbuck, dik dik, suni, colobus, blue monkey and warthog. Luckier ones may also see leopard and hyaena, while twitchers will be more than content with the number of birds on offer, from the noisy Hartlaub's turaco to the silver-cheeked hornbill and black-and-white bulbul.

If all this sounds like your idea of a perfect holiday – a safari-and-trek all rolled into one – then you're probably right, though there is one point that needs to be emphasized: do not underestimate Meru. Though it may be more than a thousand metres lower than Kili, it's still well above the altitude necessary to bring about altitude sickness and with almost everybody taking just over two days before reaching the summit, the risks are great. Indeed, though we've climbed Kilimanjaro on a number of occasions, without a shadow of a doubt our most nerve-racking ascent was on Meru. True, this had much to do with the fact that there had been heavy rain on the evening before the night-time walk to the summit, a downpour which quickly froze and caused the entire trail, from Saddle to summit, to become covered with a layer of ice. Inconvenient on the first part of that night-time walk, on the second half it became positively dangerous, causing us to scribble hurriedly a last will and testament in our notebooks. Indeed, it was only thanks to the hard work of the guides, who dug out footsteps in the ice with a piece of rock or the back of their heels – footsteps in which, taking our lead from King Wenceslas, we then trod – that we gained the

(**Opposite**) **Top**: Celebrating atop Mount Meru. **Bottom**: Making the descent from Meru, always tricky in the snow.

summit at all. And it was only by inching our way back down, bottom pressed into the ice, limbs looking for any piece of rock or other non-slippery material to put our weight upon, that we made it back down to write this guide. So though Meru may not carry the cachet, prestige or the sheer scale of Kili, it's no pushover; Meru remains an awfully big mountain, and as such it should be treated with the utmost respect.

PRACTICALITIES

The route

There is only one main route up Meru. The route begins at **Momela Gate**, around 15km from the main Ngongongare entrance gate where you pay your park fees. Having paid up and driven those 15km, past the plain known as Little Serengeti (Serengeti Ndogo) because of its similarity to Tanzania's most famous park, you arrive at Momela where you pick up your ranger and hire your porters.

The route from Momela Gate (altitude 1500m) to the summit is punctuated by two sets of accommodation huts: the first are the Miriakamba Huts (2514m), a day's walk from Momela Gate; and the second are the Saddle Huts (3570m), lying a day's walk from there. From the Saddle Huts it's a further day's walk – or rather, a night's walk – to the summit.

The cost

Trips up Meru are usually offered by the agencies in Arusha (the best place to organize such a trek) for either three or four days. Note that, unlike Kili, you don't actually need to book this trek through an agency and can do it independently; see opposite for the pros and cons of such an approach. Don't be misled, as we were, into thinking that if you book a four-day trek you are more likely to reach the summit because of the extra day's acclimatization; that extra day is actually spent on the *way down*, not up. So while we were glad to have the extra day to descend – it's a bit too much of a rush otherwise to go from the summit to Momela Gate in one day, and we were grateful to spend a second night at Miriakamba – if you're on a tight budget you'll save yourself a small fortune in park fees by taking a day less.

Regarding these park fees, they tend to be a little cheaper than the equivalent charges on Kili and are as follows:

- Park entrance fee: US$25 per day
- Rescue fee: US$20 per trip
- Hut fee: US$20 per night
- Guide/ranger fee: US$15 per day

Thus for a four-day/three night trip you're looking at a total figure of **US$240**. On top of this you'll probably need to pay the equivalent **porters/guide fees** to enable them to enter and stay in the park. Their entrance fees are charged at Ts1500 per day, while their hut fees are just Ts800. So, for example, if your agency has supplied you with a guide and three porters, the total amount you'll be paying for them will be:

- Entrance fee: Ts1500 x 4 people x 4 days = Ts24,000
- Hut fee: Ts800 x 4 people x 3 nights = Ts9600   Total: **Ts33,600**

All of these fees will be factored into the total amount the trekking agency has charged for your trek and so needn't concern you too much here. However, you may have noticed in the above that there are in fact two guides in the party: one supplied by the agency and one by the park (whom we have called a ranger to avoid confusion). The ranger/guide supplied by the park is compulsory, for it is he who carries the gun that, should any of the local fauna take an unhealthy interest in your party, could come in very handy. However, these rangers in our experience are also better guides, with better English and a greater knowledge of the park, mainly because they spend most of their time in it. Indeed, on our first day in the park we didn't even see the guide who had been supplied by the trekking agency until we got to the Miriakamba Huts at the end of the day!

Doing it independently

It is this over-supply of guides that leads several tourists to consider doing the whole thing independently without signing up to any trekking agency. True, it is tempting but there are a few things to consider first. For one thing, you will need to arrange transport to and from the park, for there is no public transport. Secondly, you'll need to bring with you all the food and supplies you need, and some form of stove in order to cook. Thirdly, all this luggage means you'll probably need to hire porters, which can be done at Momela Gate at the start of the trail, though you'll need to work out how much to pay them (the Kilimanjaro Porters Assistance Project, see pp40-1, recommends Ts8000 per day) and to organize them yourself. What's more, you will still need to take with you one of the park rangers – they're compulsory. So while the idea of doing the whole trek independently may sound attractive, you do need to have a certain amount of confidence to bring it all off, especially when it comes to organizing your porters, a job that's outside of the ranger's remit but is perhaps the most useful purpose of the trekking agency guide.

So yes, it is possible to go up Meru independently but the saving, money-wise, will be negligible. Indeed, only if you've a real aversion to agencies or really fancy the challenge should you attempt it.

Trekking with an agency

Perhaps not surprisingly, therefore, most people choose to sign up with an agency in Arusha. Rates start at around US$450-500 for four days. You may want to factor into this fee a night or two at one of the lodges near the park. This will enable you to make an early start in the morning (though treks are officially not allowed to start until 10am anyway, so as not to disrupt the animals' dawn hunt). Some of these jungle lodges are epitomes of charm. One such is *Colobus Forest Lodge* (☎ 2553632), right by the gates. Though still incomplete, the lodge has half a dozen or so lovely thatched bandas, all clean, airy and bright, while the large reception-cum-bar-cum-restaurant is a most pleasant place to sink that first beer of the day. The gardens, too, are flower-filled and attract a range of birds (as does, occasionally, the thatched roof of your banda!). Rates start at around US$25 per person.

MOUNT MERU

For rather more, ***Hatari Lodge*** (PO Box 3171, Arusha; ☎ 2553456-7; 🖳 www. hatarilodge.com) has real history and character. The lodge is named after the John Wayne film that was shot on the farm. Indeed, one of Wayne's co-stars, a German actor called Hardy Krüger, actually ended up giving up Hollywood for Arusha, and bought the farm soon after the film was completed. The Hatari Lodge lies just outside the park's northern boundary. With a small library, long bar, breakfast terrace and great views of both Kili and Meru, this is truly a luxury bush hotel. Prices are US$250 per person per night.

STAGE 1: MOMELA GATE TO MIRIAKAMBA HUTS [MAP A, p214]

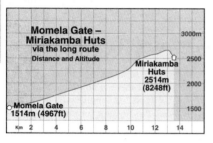

Though we stated in the introduction to this trek that there's only one path to the summit of Meru, that's not entirely true, for in fact on this first day there are two possible paths, the split between the two occurring just five minutes along the trail. Most trekkers, of course, will want to take both paths, one on the way up and the other on the way down. The question is, therefore, which path to take first?

Regarding these two trails, the first is a longer and more circuitous route that follows a 4WD dirt track as it swerves drunkenly and only very approximately along the course of the Ngare Nanyuki (the river you cross on a bridge right at the beginning of the trek) and Jekukumia rivers before turning north to cross the Crater Plain to the huts. As for the second option, this is a much more direct path and, on first sight at least, would appear to be the more tempting. It includes a crossing of the Meru Plain that's alive with Africa's tallest mammal (the giraffe) and its most bad tempered (the buffalo), and should also take in a diversion to the beautiful Tululusia waterfall that lies just off the trail.

Unless you specify otherwise the chances are your ranger/guide will take you on this shorter, steeper path; and it is indeed a wonderful walk. However, we advise you to leave this shorter path until the end and instead opt for the longer trail for your ascent. Why? Simply because, in our experience, most trekkers are too tired on the last day of their trek to attempt the longer trail on the way down, whatever their intentions when they began their trek. (Indeed, if you've only given yourselves three days to complete the trek, you probably won't have time to do the longer trail on the last day.) In other words, if you don't take the longer path now, for the ascent, the chances are you'll miss out on it it altogether. Which is a shame, as this longer trail has plenty to offer including a pretty little waterfall-cum-picnic spot and a fantastic fig tree (about which, see opposite). There's also the matter of acclimatization to consider, for taking over four hours to climb the 1000m to Miriakamba Huts is a lot more sensible than taking just two or so, as you would on the shorter trail. So don't be too eager to get amongst the animals on the plain at the foot of Meru but instead choose the longer trail for your ascent and save the shorter trail for the way down; and this is how we've described the trek below.

Though this longer trail avoids the **Meru Plain**, there's still an abundance of wildlife to be seen. In addition to the beasts of the plain that could still be espied behind the screen of acacias, within the first five minutes – no, make that three – of starting our trek we also encountered dik dik and suni standing motionless in the scrub lining the path, while a little further on a troop of baboons showed what they thought of our interrupting their elevenses by turning their backs and displaying their red-raw backsides. It's a hot and dusty start to the trek – but a distinctly memorable one. Indeed, even on this longer route we guarantee you'll see more animals within the first half-hour of your expedition than you would in a month on Kili.

The scenery changes slightly as you reach the junction with the path to the Third Campsite and the path bends right (west), with both the gradient and the size of the trees increasing. The first junipers, bearded with lichen, appear and the whole trail now takes on a lusher, greener aspect. Continuing up the hill, your guide, bored with the repetitive twists and turns of the official trail, may take you on a well-known short-cut, emerging back onto the trail just before a stream with a marshy patch of grassland to the left – often populated by bushbuck – and the Meru summit beyond. A good opportunity for a photo, methinks. A second photo opportunity occurs just a minute later with the first of several official **Kilimanjaro viewpoints**.

Regardless of whether you took photos of these places or not, one sight which we can almost guarantee will have you reaching for your Rolleiflex is the **arched fig tree**, a magnificent strangler fig (*Ficus thonningii*) which has now completely enveloped its host and arches across the track. It puts one in mind of those pictures you see of giant redwoods in California which have cars driving through them – though here it is elephants that have passed through the tunnel formed by the tree, widening the gap as they do so.

The path, now illuminated by Popcorn cassia (*Cassia didymobotrya*; incorrectly called candle bushes by many guides*)*, heads north soon after to cross an open area with a good view of the summit and possible sightings of buffaloes in the depression to the left of the trail. The northerly direction is but temporary, however, the path soon reverting south to acquaint itself with the sweetwater **Jekukumia River** (the last available water source on this climb) at the **Maio Falls**, at just over 2000m altitude a picturesque spot and a delightful place to break for lunch.

Rested and replete, you now return to the main track as it continues its weaving, wriggling way westwards up the slope. It's a pleasant stroll, the gradient seldom steep and the stands of juniper and podocarpus providing essential shade. The forest is still alive with animals, too, even though they may be more difficult to see. Your ranger/guide, however, should be able to point out the tracks of hyaena and snake, and your walk will, more than likely, be accompanied

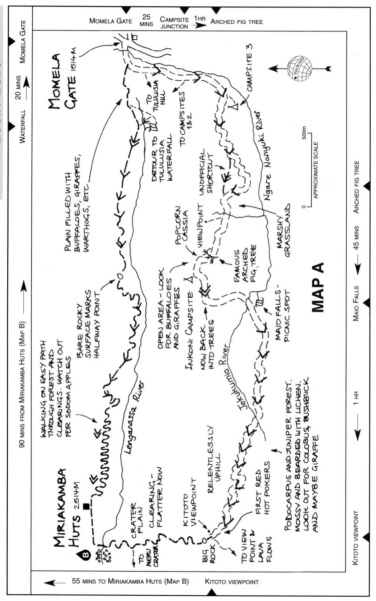

MOMELA GATE   25 MINS   CAMPSITE JUNCTION   1 HR   ARCHED FIG TREE

90 MINS FROM MIRIAKAMBA HUTS (MAP B)

MOMELA GATE 1514 M

TO TULUUSIA HILL

DETOUR TO TULUUSIA WATERFALL

CAMPSITE 3

Ngare Nanyuki River

TO CAMPSITES 1 & 2

UNOFFICIAL SHORTCUT

PLAIN FILLED WITH BUFFALOES, GIRAFFES, WARTHOGS, ETC

WALKING ON EASY PATH THROUGH FOREST AND CLEARINGS. WATCH OUT FOR SODOM APPLES

BARE ROCKY SURFACE MARKS HALFWAY POINT

POPCORN CASSIA

VIEWPOINT

MARSHY GRASSLAND

APPROXIMATE SCALE

0   500m

MAP A

OPEN AREA - LOOK FOR BUFFALOES AND GIRAFFES

INJKONI CAMPSITE

NOW BACK INTO TREES

FAMOUS ARCHED FIG TREE

MAIO FALLS - PICNIC SPOT

Lenganassa River

Jekukuma River

RELENTLESSLY UPHILL

MIRIAKAMBA HUTS 2514 M

CRATER PLAIN

TO NEW CRATER

CLEARING - FLATTER NOW

KITOTO VIEWPOINT

BIG ROCK

TO VIEW POINT & LAVA FLOWS

FIRST RED HOT POKERS

PODOCARPUS AND JUNIPER FOREST. MOSSY AND BEARDED WITH LICHEN. LOOK OUT FOR COLOBUS, BUSHBUCK AND MAYBE GIRAFFE

55 MINS TO MIRIAKAMBA HUTS (MAP B)   KITOTO VIEWPOINT

❑ For an explanation of the various symbols used on the trekking maps, please see the beginning of Part 8, p220.

by the bark of the bushbuck, the frog croak of the colobus monkey and the broken-klaxon call of Hartlaub's turaco. If you're lucky, a crash in the undergrowth or in the branches will give away the precise location of these shy creatures, or indeed of giraffe or buffalo. The scenery is just as pleasant as before lunch too, but by now tiredness and a desire for change will probably have set in, along with a wish that the track, for a few metres at least, would follow a straight line. Thankfully, about an hour after leaving the falls the first red hot pokers appear (*Kniphofia thomsonii*), a flower that heralds the imminent arrival of **Kitoto Viewpoint**, with views east-north-east over the Momela Lakes and east-south-east over the fauna-filled Ngurdoto Crater, the original centre and *raison d' être* of Arusha National Park before it merged with Meru to create the current park you find today.

From now until the end of this first stage the path feels more alpine. It's still upwards, at least until you reach a clearing with unrestricted views of the petrified lava flow that runs down from the ash cone to the plateau on which you stand – the so-called **Crater Plain**. This plain, though more than 2500m above sea level, still attracts an abundance of game including giraffe, hyaena and leopard and, to judge from the number of skulls littering the area, would also seem to be the place where old buffaloes come to die. On the northern edge of this mini plain is the dry, rocky river-bed of the seasonal **Lenganassa River**, which you follow downhill to your first night's destination. The **Miriakamba Huts** are a smart pair of accommodation huts and accompanying buildings sitting at an altitude of 2514m above sea level. The huts are divided into rooms for four people and are popular not only with tourists but also, if the amount of dung is anything to go by, with buffalo and elephant too; for this reason, we advise you to take care when nipping out to the loo at night. There are also good views across to Kilimanjaro to be had from the toilets.

STAGE 2: MIRIAKAMBA HUTS TO SADDLE HUTS   [MAP B, p217]

Everybody has their favourite section of the Meru trek and the walk from the Miriakamba Huts to the lunch stop at Mgongo Wa Tembo is ours. There's something gentle and gorgeously pastoral about the grassy slopes that put one in mind of the rolling hills of England for some reason – the exotic flora and piles of buffalo and elephant crap notwithstanding. Indeed, it's the

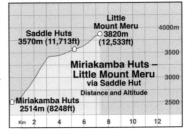

unusual flora – the *Hagenia abyssinica* with its heavy pink/brown blossom, for example, and the first senecio (*Senecio johnstonii ssp.cheranganiensis*) – and the continuing presence of the park's larger fauna that add so much to the day. Even the path is impressive, a wooden staircase leading west up the slopes of the ridge towards the Saddle. Then of course there are the views over your shoulder of Kilimanjaro glowering at its little brother, its white summit glistening in the sun. It's a great morning's walk. Nor does the interest for trekkers wane much after lunch as the path enters the alpine zone. The trees diminish in size before disappearing altogether, to be replaced by the heathers and ericas that flourish at this altitude. The only problem with the latter half of this second day is that it can become slightly monotonous after a while and impatience and ennui can set in. But don't be in too much of a hurry: from the moment you set off it's vital that you take it *pole pole* because of the altitude. This is not always easy as, unlike tomorrow when you know you're high up on a mountain, today the lush flora and burning hot sun can disguise the fact that you're more than two miles above sea level. But walk as slowly as you used to when you'd been sent to the headmaster's office.

Such a funereal speed should be adopted from the moment you set off from Miriakamba. After a few minutes traversing the ridge, the trail then heads off up the steps of the mountain's eastern flanks. The path zig-zags for much of the morning, with juniper and hagenia lining the way together with the occasional stand of *Senecio johnstonii*, whose younger plants display an impressive phallic brush growing out of their tops. Elephants can occasionally be seen along this stretch, so do make sure you stick close to the man with the gun. The path soon bends in a more northerly direction, with great views of Kili to your right framed by the local vegetation. There are some great old fallen trees here with some vivid red gladioli growing from the trunks and *Impatiens papilionacea* thriving in the shade. Following the zig-zags, **Mgongo Wa Tembo** ('Elephant's Back'; about 3200m/10,496ft) is reached, the usual lunch-stop on this second stage with views south over the **Crater Plain**.

The path continues to climb after the break, soon leaving the forest for something altogether more alpine with *Philippia excelsa* and *Erica arborea* now proliferating. If you're lucky, you may also come across chameleons that, despite being cold-blooded creatures, somehow thrive in this region. It's a bit of a relentless, monotonous trek, but it's not long before the **Saddle Huts** (3570m) are reached. The huts are very similar in style to Miriakamba, with two huts of 36 and 24 beds each, both divided into two-bunk rooms. Yet despite the altitude the huts still get the occasional visitor from Africa's animal kingdom, including elephants and buffaloes migrating to the grasslands further west. One of the huts has a fine collection of lobelias growing outside its door, but other than examining those there's little to do up here, allowing you to spend the rest of the afternoon climbing the nearby 3820m **Little Meru**, a simple 45-minute trudge that the guides will often allow you to do by yourself – remember to climb *pole pole* even though there's no one to regulate your speed! That done, you can relax and prepare yourself for the exertions of the night to come...

MAP B

GIANT BOULDERS		RHINO POINT		SADDLE HUT		MGONGO WA TEMBO		MIRIAKAMBA HUTS
2 HRS 25 MINS		1HR 10MINS	1HR 30MINS			2 HRS		

NEW STEPS THROUGHOUT THIS SECTION. PLENTY OF ZIG ZAGS TOO!

RELENTLESS SWITCHBACKS FOR LAST SECTION TO SADDLE HUTS

MGONGO WA TEMBO 3200M

LOVELY FOREST, LOOK OUT FOR HAGENIA ABYSSINICA, JUNIPER AND ELEPHANTS

FOREST NOW THINNING

GOOD STAND OF SENECIO JOHNSTONII WITH 'BRUSH' GROWING OUT OF THE TOP

MIRIAKAMBA HUTS 2514M

SADDLE HUTS 3570M

LITTLE MERU 3820M

45MINS CLIMB

TRAVERSING ROCK FACE AT HEAD OF HELICHRYSUM DEPRESSION

NOW STEEP UP ON EASIER PATH - LOOK FOR LIGHTS OF K.I. AIRPORT ACROSS CRATER

ASCENT RIDGE

STREAM

RHINO POINT 3814M

LAST HEATHERS HERE

START OF FINAL STRETCH ON CRATER RIM

GIANT BOULDERS

CAN SEE SUMMIT - AND KILI PATH FOLLOWS CRATER RIM

BIG ROCK TO SOUTH OF PATH JUST OUTER CRATER RIM

ASH CONE

LOOK FOR MOSS, LICHENS AND YELLOW EVERLASTINGS

MOUNT MERU SUMMIT 4562M

FINAL PUSH TO SUMMIT IS STEEP, SLIPPERY AND DANGEROUS

0   500m
APPROXIMATE SCALE

GIANT BOULDERS		RHINO POINT		SADDLE HUT		MGONGO WA TEMBO		MIRIAKAMBA HUTS
	1HR 30MINS		20 MINS		40 MINS		1 HR	

GIANT BOULDERS   ◄ 45MINS – 2HRS 45MINS ►   SUMMIT
(WEATHER DEPENDENT!)

MOUNT MERU

STAGE 3: SADDLE HUTS TO MERU SUMMIT   [MAP B, p217]

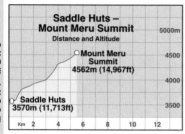

And so to the final ascent, and if the height of Meru is invaluable for acclimatizing, so this night-time march is wonderful preparation for that final push to Kili's Uhuru Peak. True, this walk is shorter and, unlike the relentless zig-zags taking you up Kibo's slopes, more varied and direct too. But the experience of waking up at some godforsaken hour to undertake a chilly high-altitude trek up a very big African volcano, before contouring around the crater rim to reach the highest point as the sun rises to the east, is useful indeed.

The stage begins with a crossing of the Saddle before bending south to the start of the climb. It's a walk that sees you leave behind the larger vegetation – the ericas and phillippias – on a winding path that eventually joins the crest of a ridge that brings you out at **Rhino Point** (3814m), the climb's first landmark. Thereafter the route bends west and, having descended to cross a rockface at the head of a lush (by the standards of this altitude) depression, then climbs to follow the lip of the Meru Crater. For the next couple of hours the path follows the course of the crater rim. Being night, of course, you'll have to wait for views of the crater itself until the morning, though beyond it you should be able to see, in the distance, the lights of various settlements as well as Kilimanjaro International Airport and the local tanzanite mine, working away through the night. Eventually, about three and a half hours after setting off, the crater rim begins to bend noticeably south. As it does, hopefully at the same time the eastern horizon will be starting to turn pink and orange with the onset of the new day, and the silhouette of Kili can clearly be discerned, with both Kibo and Mawenzi summits visible.

The summit also seems tangibly closer, too, so it's disheartening to discover that it's still a minimum of 45 minutes away. If you're hoping to capture the sight of the sun rising over Kili's shoulder you've got to time your walk quite well here. Arrive at the summit too soon and it's a chilly wait, but leave it too late and, as the last 25 minutes or so are spent clambering on the western slopes of the summit, you may miss it altogether. These timings assume, of course, that the condition of the trail and the weather situation are both amenable. If not, these last 45 minutes could, in fact, last for 2 hours and 45 minutes as your guides try to create a path in the ice using nothing but bits of rocks and the heels of their boots! It can be a little terrifying, too, with one false step sending you plummeting down the icy slopes. Take care!

At the **summit**, officially called **Socialist Peak**, there's little save a flag, a sign and a box containing a book where you can sign your name. There are also, of course, great views over Arusha to the west and Kili to the east, with

Meru's perfect ash cone below you. Photos taken and hands shaken, it's time for the descent – and isn't it wonderful to be able to walk at a speed of your choosing again! It's also interesting to see how different in daylight the path looks. Look back from Rhino Point, for example, to the climb up to the crater rim – was it really that steep? Notice, too, while renegotiating the descent from the summit, all the mini bumps and craters to the north and west of Meru which were hidden on the way up.

The descent, though wearying, shouldn't take more than a couple of hours. Those who've opted to spend four days on the mountain will take an hour or so back at the Saddle Huts, packing their bags, eating some well-earned food and maybe getting a little shut-eye, before the 100-minute return stroll down to Miriakamba, where they'll be spending the night. Those on the three-day trip will also have an hour to recover at the Saddle Huts, though for them the walk down is that much longer. If you're reading this at the Saddle Huts after your ascent to the summit, you'll probably appreciate now why we suggested taking the long route on the first stage, and saving the shorter route for now.

STAGE 4: MIRIAKAMBA HUTS TO MOMELA GATE   [MAP A, p214]

One of the advantages Meru has over Kilimanjaro is that this last stage, though short, is in no way an anti-climax, whereas the last day on Kili often feels like something to endure rather than enjoy. The descent from Miriakamba is hard on the knees, of course, but by way of compensation there's some unusual flora (check the pink impatiens growing right on the path and the hardy Sodom's apple trees, 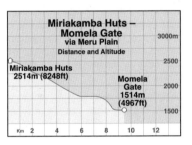 *Solanum sodomaeum*, growing by the side of it), a charming little river to cross and, of course, a crossing of the buffalo- and warthog-filled plain at the very end, with Kili as an awe-inspiring backdrop. This walk should also include (at least, it should if your guide has any concept of customer service) a brief diversion to the impressive **Tululusia Falls**, just a few minutes off the path to the south before the plain.

Even with the diversion you should find yourself back at Momela Gate less than two hours after setting off. There'll just be time to distribute tips (if you haven't already been solicited into doing so before now), collect your certificates (one for Mount Meru, possibly one for little Mount Meru too) and say your farewells to your companions and guardians of the past few days. It's been a wonderful walk, hasn't it? You've seen some beautiful birds, flowers and animals, taken in some breathtaking views and through sheer bloodymindedness climbed to the very summit of Tanzania's second highest mountain.

Now it's time for the highest...

PART 8: TRAIL GUIDE AND MAPS

Using this guide

ABOUT THE MAPS IN THIS GUIDE

Scale

Most of the **trekking maps** in this guide are drawn to the same scale, namely 19mm to 1km (1¼ inches to the mile). The exceptions are those maps depicting the routes up to the Kibo summit – ie, those maps that depict the final ascent to the top, which is usually made at night. On these maps the scale has been doubled (ie 38mm to 1km or 2½ inches to the mile) to allow for more detail to be drawn upon them.

Walking times

The times indicated on the maps should be used as an approximate guide. They refer to **walking times only**, and do not include any time for breaks and food: don't forget to add on a few minutes for breaks when estimating the total time for a particular stage. Overall you may find you need to **add between 10% and 30%** depending on your walking speed and the average lengths of the breaks you take.

Gradient arrows

You will also notice that we have drawn '**gradient arrows**' on the trekking maps in this book. The arrows point uphill: two arrows mean that the hill is

---

❏ **Altitudes**
It has long been accepted wisdom amongst many of the better trekking agencies that the official altitudes given on maps and signs are, in fact, inaccurate. Even the altitude at the summit, long accepted as 5895m, is wrong, as discussed in the box on p84 – and the summit is probably the most measured point on the whole mountain!

Although the difference between the official altitude and the actual altitude on the summit is small (2.45m), elsewhere many believe that the altitudes can be out by up to 100m. For this reason, **we have compiled our own altitudes for this book**, using the research of agencies such as Team Kilimanjaro (see p26) and our own experience to work out what we consider to be accurate, or at least *more* accurate measurements than the official ones. In most cases they differ by just 10-30 metres, though there are one or two exceptions, with Team Kilimanjaro measuring the Barafu Huts (see p248) to be at an altitude of 4681m – considerably higher than the official 4600m (which sounds like it is just an estimate anyway). The only occasion where we have used the official measurement is the summit, which we continue to refer to as being 5895m above sea level rather than the scientifically accurate one of 5892.55m, for no other reason than the former is such a universally quoted and accepted measurement.

☐ In the following descriptions, the treks have been divided into stages, with each stage roughly corresponding to a day's trekking. For this reason, throughout the text the words 'stage' and 'day' have been used interchangeably.

steep, one that the gradient is reasonably gradual. If, for example, you are walking from A (at 80m) to B (at 200m) and the trail between the two is short and steep, it would be shown thus: A– – – – >>– – – –B.

The Marangu Route

Because this trail is popularly called the 'Tourist Route' or '**Coca Cola trail**', some trekkers are misled into thinking this five- or six-day climb to the summit is simply a walk in the (national) park. But remember that a greater proportion of people fail on this route than on any other. True, this may have something to do with the fact that Marangu's reputation for being 'easy' attracts the more inexperienced, out-of-condition trekkers who don't realize that they are embarking on a **35-kilometre/22-mile uphill walk,** followed immediately by a 35-kilometre knee-jarring descent. But it shouldn't take much to realize that Marangu is not much easier than any other trail: with the Machame Route, for example, you start at 1828m and aim for the summit at 5895m. On Marangu, you start just a little higher at 1860m and have the same goal, so simple logic should tell you that it can't be that much easier.

The main reason why people say that Marangu is easier is because it is the only route where you **sleep in huts**, rather than under canvas. The accommodation in these huts should be booked in advance by your tour company, who have to pay a deposit per person per night to KINAPA in order to secure it. To cover this, the tour agencies will probably ask you to pay them some money in advance too. This deposit for the huts is refundable or can be moved to secure huts on other dates, providing you give KINAPA (and your agency) at least seven days' notice.

Unfortunately, some of the cheaper agencies prefer to trust to luck when it comes to accommodation on the Marangu Route, deciding that it is too much bother to travel all the way to Marangu Gate to pay a deposit. Instead they prefer to assume/pray that there will be room in the huts for their clients when they get there. In days gone by this resulted in some trekkers sleeping on dining tables or hall floors in situations where the huts were overbooked. More and more frequently, however, KINAPA are refusing to allow trekkers without a reservation even to start their walk if the huts are fully booked. For your own peace of mind, therefore, you should ask your agency to show you a receipt confirming that they have paid a deposit for your accommodation on the trek. Furthermore, be suspicious of any agency that doesn't ask *(Continued on p224)*

WHAT'S IT LIKE ON THE TRAIL?

Fun. It really is. Sure, the last push to the summit is hard, as some of the quotes used later in this book clearly indicate, but don't let that put you off. Kilimanjaro is a delightful mountain to climb:

But we had much to compensate us for all we had to give up. The charm of the mountain scenery, the clear, crisp atmosphere, the tonic of 'a labour we delight in' and the consciousness now and again of success achieved, all went far to make our fortnight's arduous toil a happy sequence of red-letter days. **Hans Meyer** *Across East African Glaciers*

The days are spent walking through spectacular landscapes which change every day as you pass through different vegetation zones; the pace is never exhausting, as you have to walk slowly in order to give yourself a chance to acclimatize. What's more, at the end of the day, while the guides are cooking your dinner, you are free to wander around the campsite; and, as you bump into the same people time and again over the course of the trek, a sense of community soon develops. Then as night falls, and you tuck into the huge plates of food cooked by your crew, the stars come out, stunning everyone into silence. This is the favourite time of day for most people: rested, replete with food and with a day of satisfactory walking behind and a good night's sleep ahead, it's natural to feel a sense of comfort and contentment, with the thought of wild animals possibly lying nearby serving to add a pleasing frisson of excitement.

Bed? It's too early. I feel too good. Aaah, I wonder if there'll ever be another time as good as this. **Gregory Peck**, in the film version of *The Snows of Kilimanjaro*

Of course, walking up from around 1800m to 5892.55m or thereabouts does, as you can probably imagine, take a lot of effort and the night walk to the summit is unarguably tough. But short of actually carrying you up, your crew will do everything in their power to make your entire experience as comfortable as possible. In fact, they'll spoil you: not only do they carry your bag, but at the end of the day's walk you'll turn up at camp to find your tent has already been erected, with a bowl of hot water lying nearby for you to wash away the grime of the day. A few minutes later and a large plate of popcorn and biscuits will be served with a mug of steaming hot tea or coffee.

Accommodation on the trail

I got back in time to see P.D. lying on sloping ground, slipping off the stretcher, and in great pain. Small fire had been made under the root of a great tree. Rain soon came on and wiped out the fire ... tent was not put up and we were all in great misery. Men with tent lost in the darkness. Thought if the rain stopped we could go on in the moonlight. Rain did not stop. **Peter MacQueen** *In Wildest Africa* (1910)

Unless you are on the Marangu Route, accommodation on the mountain will be in tents brought up by your porters. (Do not be tempted to sleep in any of the caves, which is against park regulations.) On the Marangu Route, camping is forbidden and instead people have to sleep in huts along the route. (You will see people camping on this route, but they are trekkers who took the Rongai Route to ascend and are now descending on Marangu.) The sleeping arrangements in these huts are usually dormitory-style, with anything from four to twenty beds per room.

Confusingly, away from the Marangu Route many of the campsites are actually called 'huts' but don't be fooled: they are called huts because of the green shacks that you'll find at these campsites which are usually inhabited by the park rangers. Trekkers used to be allowed to sleep in these huts too, but no longer. Porters and guides, however, do still sometimes sleep in them depending on the ranger's mood and the space available. The only other buildings you will possibly see along the trail are the toilets. Most are of the same design, namely a little wooden hut with a hole in the floor. Some are in better condition than others; all we will say is that some people are terrible shots, while other latrines are in desperate need of emptying before the contents become Kilimanjaro's fourth peak.

Food on the trail
Remember to tell your agency if you have any special dietary requirements – because both meat and nuts form a substantial part of the menu on Kilimanjaro.

A typical **breakfast** will involve eggs (boiled or fried), porridge, a saveloy (possibly with some tomatoes too), a piece of fruit such as a banana or orange, some bread with jam, honey or peanut butter and a mug or two of tea, hot chocolate or coffee.

Lunch is usually prepared at breakfast and carried by the trekker in his or her daypack. This packed lunch often consists of a boiled egg, some sandwiches, a banana or orange, and some tea kept warm in a flask and carried by your guide.

At the end of the day's walking, **afternoon tea** is served with biscuits, peanuts and, best of all, salted popcorn. The final and biggest meal of the day, **dinner** usually begins with soup, followed by a main course including chicken or meat, a vegetable sauce, some cabbage, and rice or pasta; if your porters have brought up some potatoes, these will usually be eaten on the first night as they are so heavy.

Drink on the trail
Porters will collect water from the rivers and streams along the trail. Some of this they will boil for you at the start of the day to carry in your water bottles. On the lower slopes you can collect water yourself from the many streams and purify it using a filter or tablets. Note, however, that as you climb ever higher the water becomes more scarce. On the Machame trail, for example, the last water point is at the Karanga Valley, the lunch-stop before Barafu; on Marangu, it's just before the Saddle. For this reason it is essential that you carry enough bottles or containers for *at least* two litres.

In camp, coffee and tea is served and maybe hot chocolate too – all usually made with powdered milk. Remember that caffeine, present in coffee and tea, is dehydrating, which can be bad for acclimatization. Caffeine is a diuretic too (ie you will want to urinate frequently – something you will already be doing a lot as you adapt to the higher conditions).

What to put in your daypack
Normally you will not see your backpack from the moment you hand it to the porter in the morning to at least lunchtime, and maybe not until the end of the day. It's therefore necessary to pack everything that you may need during the day in your daypack that you carry with you. Some suggestions, in no particular order:

- sweets
- water and water purifiers
- camera and spare film/batteries
- this book/maps
- sunhat/sunglasses and suncream
- compass
- toilet paper and trowel
- rainwear
- walking sticks and knee supports
- medical kit, including chapstick
- watch
- whistle
- lunch (supplied by your crew)

TRAIL GUIDE AND MAPS

for at least some **of your trekking fee upfront to cover these deposits**, or who agrees to accept a last-minute booking for the Marangu Route: they should have at least a day's notice in order to book the huts and pay the deposits. Of course, in most cases these agencies get away with their lackadaisical approach to hut booking simply because the huts aren't always fully booked and there are usually enough spaces for you, especially if your party is a small one of only two or three trekkers. But don't be surprised if, having booked with one of the cheaper and less reputable agencies, it transpires that there is no room for you at the huts and you get turned away at Marangu Gate. Incidentally, there are 70 spaces at Mandara Huts, 148 at Horombo – the extra beds are necessary because this hut is also used by those *descending* from Kibo – and just 58 at Kibo. If any one of those is already booked to capacity on the night you wish to stay there, you will not be allowed to start your trek and will have to change your dates.

The fact that you do sleep in huts makes little difference to what you need to pack for the trek, for sleeping bags are still required (the huts have pillows and mattresses but that's all) though you can dispense with a ground mat for this route. You may also need some small change should you give in to temptation and decide that the exorbitant price of sweets and drinks that are available at the huts is still a price worth paying. The fact that there's no tent to carry, however, means you can probably get away with just two porters per person, or fewer if you carry your own bag – something of a false economy we've found, as we believe it increases your chances of suffering from AMS. Regarding the sleeping situation, it does help if you can get to the huts early each day to grab the better beds. This doesn't mean you should deliberately hurry to the huts, which will reduce your enjoyment of the trek and increase the possibility of AMS. But do try to **start early each morning**: that way you can avoid the crowds, beat them to the better beds, and possibly improve your chances of seeing some of Kili's wildlife too.

In terms of **duration**, the Marangu Route is one of the shorter trails, taking just five days. Many people, however, opt to take an extra day to acclimatize at Horombo Huts, using that day to visit the Mawenzi Huts Campsite at 4538m. From a safety point of view this is entirely sensible and aesthetically such a plan cannot be argued with either, for the views from Mawenzi across the Saddle to Kibo truly take the breath away; assuming, that is, that you have some left to be taken away after all that climbing.

One aspect of the Marangu Route that could be seen by some as a drawback is that it is the only one where you **ascend and descend via the same path**. However, there are a couple of arguments to counter this perception: firstly, between Horombo and Kibo Huts there are two paths and it shouldn't take too much to persuade your guide to use one trail on the ascent and the other one on the way down; and secondly, we think that the walk back down the Marangu Route is one of the most pleasurable parts of the entire trek, with splendid views over the shoulder. Furthermore, it offers you the chance to greet the crowds of sweating, red-faced unfortunates heading the other way with the smug expression of one for whom physical pain is now a thing of the past, and whose immediate future is filled with warm showers and cold beers.

Trekkers' experiences
Of course, everybody's experience of climbing Kili is different. The majority of letters we receive are of the 'had the time of my life' variety, which are always lovely to receive, particularly as it's always nice to know that other people enjoy the experience as much as we do:

What a fab trip! And yes, We all made it to the top (one of us with a humungous, vice-like headache, but our good guide carried her pack on the last leg)!! And best of all, we all came back friends! Anneliese Dibetta (Canada)

A few letters also contain some useful advice:

If I can make any strong recommendations it is the truth and value of 'pole pole' ... I redefined the phrase pole pole and from the first step to the last I went with the pace I needed to do to keep my heart rate even and not get out of breath. More often than not I was way behind the group, always had one of the guides or assistant guides with me and not once did I feel pressured to go faster. It was the key to my success.
Clare Wickens (US)

I found the trail up the Western Breach to be tough but not necessarily dangerous. I think the 'toughness' came from being at the altitude we were at causing the level of exertion needed to climb and the fatigue I was experiencing from the trip so far, more than the trail itself. As I watched the porters trot by with large loads (five dozen eggs on one guy or our dining table and chairs) I realized how easy the trail really was even though at the time I was feeling taxed by it. Patti Wickham (US)

One general observation would be that although everyone said how much it was to do with altitude, I didn't realize the extent of it. I thought I'd tire easily and be breathless, but didn't understand how half the people would have headaches, and people would be running out of the dining hall to vomit. I was mentally prepared for something physically demanding, but not for feeling ill and having a headache for days on end...

As you come up to Kibo, a few people said they start to get excited and want to get it over with quickly. I'd say it's worth advising them to make sure they keep going slowly, and warn them that a lot of people suddenly feel really tired during the last 5-10 minutes of the walk. Richard Evans (UK)

One or two of them were quite encouraging too:

Two of us were not really in good enough shape to complete Kili by any route, no scrambling experience, and no strong expectation of summiting, but by taking seven days and by doing the scramble in the daylight, all made it to the summit, and back down to Mweka Gate, happy, safe and sound. John Wickham (US)

That's not to suggest, of course, that everyone has a pleasant time...

I've had a lovely few days but now I have a headache and feel like shit. Please leave me alone. Thank you. Unknown German, instructing his guide from inside his tent at Barafu Camp.

For a couple of days I thought you must have a great job: travel around the world and write about it. I now know better. I now feel sorry for you. I thought climbing Kilimanjaro was hell. I would ask for a big raise in your salary if I were you...
Mark Burgmans (Holland)

STAGE 1: MARANGU GATE TO MANDARA HUTS [MAP 1, opposite]

The woods are lovely, dark and deep, but I have promises to keep, and miles to go before I sleep. **Robert Frost** as seen on a signwriter's wall in Moshi

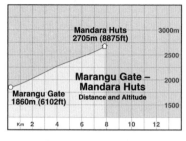

Marangu Gate –
Mandara Huts
Distance and Altitude

Mandara Huts
2705m (8875ft)

Marangu Gate
1860m (6102ft)

3000m
2500
2000
1500

Km 2   4   6   8   10   12

As the headquarters of KINAPA (Kilimanjaro National Park), you might expect Marangu Gate (altitude 1860m) to have the best facilities of all the gates, and it doesn't disappoint. Not only does the gate have the usual **registration office** but there's also a picnic area, a smart new toilet block and a **shop** that has a good collection of books and souvenirs. There's also a small booth run by the Kilimanjaro Guides Cooperative where you can **hire any equipment** you may have forgotten to bring along, from essentials such as hats and fleeces, sleeping bags and water bottles, to camping stuff that you almost certainly won't need on the trail such as stoves and so forth, which should be provided by your agency. Sample prices: ski poles US$10 per trip, sleeping bags US$20. Not cheap, as you can see.

Having gone through the laborious business of **registering** (a process that usually takes at least an hour, though it can be quicker if you manage to get here before the large tour groups arrive), you begin your trek by following the new trekkers' path which heads left off the road (which is now used solely by porters). Note the eucalyptus trees around the gate, one of the few non-native plants on the mountain; as such, the authorities are trying to slowly eradicate them from the national park. It has to be a gradual process, however: look through the trees to your right just after you start out and you'll see a big open area – the ugly result of eradicating the trees too quickly.

This first day's walk is a very pleasant one of almost 8km (5 miles), and though the route is uphill for virtually the entire time, there are enough distractions in the forest to take your mind off the exertion, from the tall and solid *Macaranga kilimandscharica* trees with their smooth grey bark by the entrance gate to troops of **blue monkeys** further along. In the early stages the path is so neat and well maintained, lined with stones and with drainage channels on either side, that it feels at first as if you are walking in the grounds of an English country house rather than on the wild slopes of Africa's highest mountain. Gradually, however, the forest closes in on all sides and the mountain's endemic flora – the vivid red *Impatiens kilimanjari* and its violet cousin *Impatiens pseudoviola* – make their first appearance by the wayside, thereby confirming that you are on Kili and not in Kent. The path soon veers towards and then follows the course of a mountain stream; sometimes through the increasingly impenetrable vegetation to your right you may be able to glimpse the occasional small **waterfall**.

After about an hour and a quarter a wooden bridge leads off the trail over this stream to the picnic tables at **Kisamboni** and a reunion with the 4WD

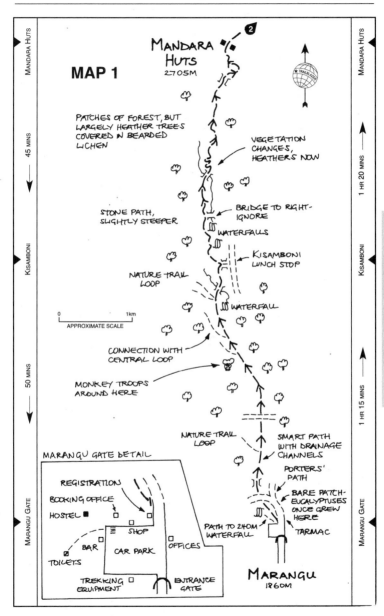

MAP 1

MANDARA HUTS 2705M

2

PATCHES OF FOREST, BUT LARGELY HEATHER TREES COVERED IN BEARDED LICHEN

VEGETATION CHANGES, HEATHERS NOW

STONE PATH, SLIGHTLY STEEPER

BRIDGE TO RIGHT-IGNORE

WATERFALLS

KISAMBONI LUNCH STOP

NATURE TRAIL LOOP

WATERFALL

0   1km
APPROXIMATE SCALE

CONNECTION WITH CENTRAL LOOP

MONKEY TROOPS AROUND HERE

NATURE TRAIL LOOP

SMART PATH WITH DRAINAGE CHANNELS

PORTERS' PATH

BARE PATCH-EUCALYPTUSES ONCE GREW HERE

MARANGU GATE DETAIL

REGISTRATION

BOOKING OFFICE

HOSTEL

SHOP

BAR

TOILETS

TREKKING EQUIPMENT

CAR PARK

OFFICES

ENTRANCE GATE

PATH TO 240M WATERFALL

TARMAC

MARANGU 1860M

MANDARA HUTS

45 MINS

KISAMBONI

50 MINS

MARANGU GATE

MANDARA HUTS

1 HR 20 MINS

KISAMBONI

1 HR 15 MINS

MARANGU GATE

TRAIL GUIDE AND MAPS

porters' trail. This is the halfway point of the first stage, and in all probability it is here that you will be served lunch.

At a height of 6,300 feet, however, all these were merged in the primaeval forest, in which old patriarchs with knotted stunted forms stood closely together, many of them worsted in the perpetual struggle with the encroachments of the parasitical growths of almost fabulous strength and size, which enfolded trunks and branches alike in their fatal embrace, crippling the giants themselves and squeezing to death the mosses, lichens, and ferns which had clothed their nakedness. Everything living seemed doomed to fall prey to them, but they in their turn bore their own heavy burden of parasites; creepers, from a yard to two yards long, hanging down in garlands and festoons, or forming one thick veil shrouding whole clumps of trees. Wherever a little space had been left amongst the many fallen and decaying trunks, the ground was covered with a luxurious vegetation, including many varieties of herbaceous plants with bright coloured flowers, orchids, and the modest violet peeping out amongst them, whilst more numerous than all were different lycopods and sword-shaped ferns.

Lieutenant Ludwig von Höhnel describing the forest of Kilimanjaro in *Discovery by Count Teleki of Lakes Rudolf and Stefanie*, 1894.

Returning to the trail and turning right, you continue climbing north for thirty minutes to another bridge, this time leading off to the right of the trail; your path, however, heads off to the left, directly away from the bridge. The trail is a little steeper now as you wind your way through the forest. It is a very pretty part of the walk, with varieties of *Impatiens* and begonias edging the path; though by now you may be feeling a little too tired to enjoy it to its fullest.

Press on, and fifteen minutes later yet another bridge appears which you *do* take. Like some sort of botanical border post, the bridge heralds the first appearance of the **giant heathers** (*Erica excelsa*) on the trail, intermingling with the camphorwood tree, with masses of **bearded lichen** liberally draped over both; and though the forest reappears intermittently up to and beyond the Maundi Crater, it's the spindly heathers and stumpy shrubs of the second vegetation zone, the alpine heath and moorland, that now dominate.

From this bridge, the first night's accommodation, the **Mandara Huts (2705m)**, lies just thirty-five minutes away. There are some smaller private rooms here, though most trekkers sleep in the large dormitory in the roof above the dining hall. If you have the energy, a quick fifteen-minute saunter to the parasitic cone known as the **Maundi Crater** (see Map 2, p231) is worthwhile both for its views east over Taveta and north-west to Mawenzi and for the wild flowers and grasses growing on its slopes. On the way to the crater, look in the trees for the bands of semi-tame blue monkeys that live here and are particularly active at dusk, as well as their more bashful and beautiful cousins, the colobus monkeys.

Incidentally, the Mandara Huts are the only huts on the mountain to be named after a person rather than a place. Mandara was the fearsome chief of Moshi, a warrior whose skill on the battlefield was matched only by his stunning greed and cupidity off it. Mandara once boasted that he had met every white man to visit Kilimanjaro, from Johannes Rebmann to Hans Meyer, and it's a fair bet that all of them would have been required to present the chief with a huge array of presents brought from their own country. Failure to do so was not an option, for those who, in Mandara's eye (he had only one, having lost the other in battle), were insufficiently generous in their gift-giving, put their lives in peril. The attack that led to the death of Charles New (see p98), for example, was said to have been orchestrated by Mandara after the latter had 'insulted' him by refusing to give the chief the watch from his waistcoat. Read any of the nineteenth-century accounts of Kilimanjaro and you'll usually find plenty of pages devoted to this fascinating character – with few casting him in a favourable light.

STAGE 2: MANDARA HUTS TO HOROMBO HUTS
[MAP 2 p231; MAP 3, p232]

On this 11km-plus stage, in which you gain almost a kilometre in altitude, you say a final goodbye to the forest and spend the greater part of the day walking through the bleaker landscape of Kilimanjaro's moorland. If the weather's clear you will get your first really good look at the twin peaks of Kili, namely spiky Mawenzi and snow-capped Kibo; they will continue to loom large, and will doubtless appear in just about every photo you take,

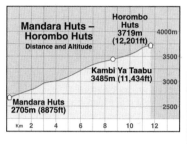

from now to the summit. The giant groundsels (*Senecio kilimanjari*) and phallic lobelias (*Lobelia deckenii*) also make their first appearance in this stage, with the former growing in some abundance towards the latter part of the walk.

The whole landscape as far as the eye could reach was a medley of dull grey lava slabs, dotted with the red-leafed protea shrub (Protea Kilimandscharica) and stunted heaths, which became smaller and smaller as we rose higher. Not a sound disturbed the silence of this uninhabited mountain mystery; not a sign of life broke the stillness save a little ashy-brown bird that hopped about the boulders, flipping its tail up and down. And to add to the impression created by the eerie scene, huge senecios lifted to a height of 20ft their black stems and greyish-yellow crowns and stood spreading out their arms in the deep moist gullies, like ghostly sentinels of the untrodden wilds.

Eva Stuart Watt *Africa's Dome of Mystery* (1930)

The day begins with a stroll through the monkey forest towards the Maundi Crater. After fifteen minutes you cross the small bridge and, leaving the last significant expanse of forest behind, enter a land of tall grasses and giant heathers. **Wild flowers** rarely seen elsewhere in the park, such as the pinkish *Dierama cupiflorum*, abound in this bumpy little corner of the mountain. Crossing bridges over (often dry) water courses, you eventually come to gently undulating fields. Passing through these, the path continues north-west through slopes of heather directly towards Kibo, with Mawenzi peering over the horizon to your right and **Kifunika Hill** – the main water source for many of the villages on the southern slopes – on your left.

The vegetation here has clearly suffered from the fires of the past few years, the new growth of green heathers emerging between the blackened sticks of

TRAIL GUIDE AND MAPS

burnt bushes. If it's a clear day you may be able to make out, atop one of the many undulations, a small green hut; this will be your lunch stop, reached after a fairly trying thirty-minute climb from the sloping bridge. The guides typically call this the halfway point in the day but they're being unnecessarily pessimistic: the Horombo Huts lie just 90 minutes away, the path tracing a generally westward course across a number of (dry) stream beds including the head of the Whona River which runs through a valley known as **Kambi Ya Taabu**, which translates, rather melodramatically, as the 'Camp of Trouble'!

The **Horombo Huts** (3719m) are generally regarded as the most pleasant of those on the route: small A-frame shelters partitioned down the middle, with each side holding beds for four people. They cater for a transient population of almost 150 trekkers plus porters and guides, as well as a more permanent population of four-striped grass mice whose numbers are now almost at plague proportions; indeed, some of them have now forsaken their grassy homeland to scavenge in the main dining hall. The huts are also the busiest on the mountain, catering not just for those ascending the mountain, but those coming back down from Kibo too, as well as those who spend the day here acclimatizing. As such the whole place tends to get rather busy, which can be a problem when it comes to feeding-time, there being only one dining hut at Horombo and a rather offi-

Mawenzi

Though less than 6km of nothingness (namely the Saddle) separates the foot of one from the foot of the other, the twin peaks of Kibo and Mawenzi could not be more different. Where Kibo is all gentle slopes and a perfectly circular crater, Mawenzi is spiky, steep, and rises to a series of peaks like the back of a stegosaurus; where the former is at least partially covered in glaciers, the latter stands naked, or at least wears no permanent raiment of ice, its sides too steep to allow the glaciers a secure enough footing; and while Kibo is easily accessible to walkers, any assault on Mawenzi involves some serious preparation, specialist equipment and no small amount of technical skill.

Indeed, the only similarity between the two peaks is their enormity: Mawenzi's **Hans Meyer Peak**, at 5149m, is the third highest in Africa (after Kibo and Mount Kenya, 50m taller). Its smaller size when compared to Kibo can be ascribed to the fact that the Mawenzi volcano died out first, while the forces that formed Kibo continued to rage for a few thousand years after Mawenzi had become extinct, pushing Kibo above the height of its older brother. Erosion then caused the collapse of Mawenzi's entire north-east wall, releasing the waters of a lake that had formed in its crater down into the valley below.

The jagged appearance of its summit is due to the formation of **dykes**. This is where lava, pushed into gaps in the crater rim, solidified over time and, being harder than the original rock, remained while the softer rock eroded. Today, this hardened lava is also rather shattered, which, combined with its steep gradients, makes Mawenzi extremely dangerous to climb. John Reader tells of two Austrian climbers who perished on their descent from the summit of Mawenzi, with the body of one of them found dangling by a rope snagged to the rocks. Such is the difficulty associated with any climb of Mawenzi that, rather than risk climbing up the peak to recover the corpse, the park authorities decided instead to hire a marksman to shoot at the rope with a rifle.

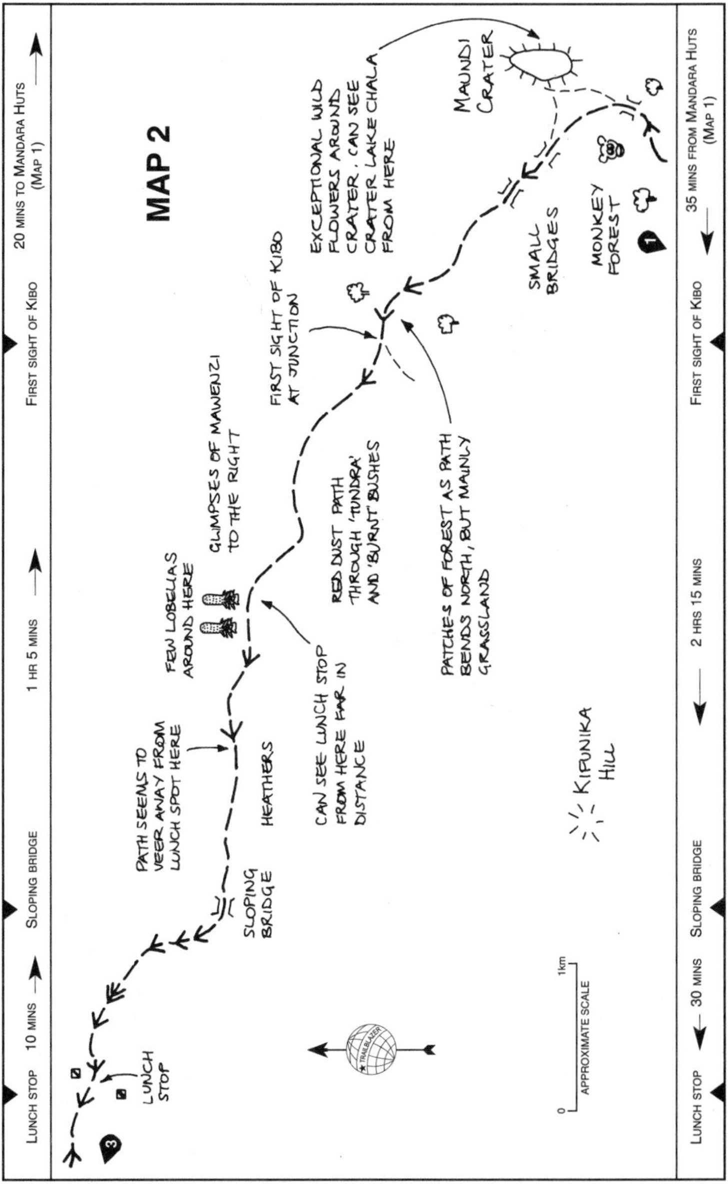

MAP 2

FIRST SIGHT OF KIBO

FIRST SIGHT OF KIBO

1 HR 5 MINS

2 HRS 15 MINS

SLOPING BRIDGE

SLOPING BRIDGE

10 MINS

30 MINS

LUNCH STOP

LUNCH STOP

MAUNDI CRATER

EXCEPTIONAL WILD FLOWERS AROUND CRATER. CAN SEE CRATER LAKE CHALA FROM HERE

FIRST SIGHT OF KIBO AT JUNCTION

SMALL BRIDGES

MONKEY FOREST

GLIMPSES OF MAWENZI TO THE RIGHT

RED DUST PATH THROUGH 'TUNDRA' AND 'BURNT BUSHES'

PATCHES OF FOREST AS PATH BENDS NORTH, BUT MAINLY GRASSLAND

FEW LOBELIAS AROUND HERE

PATH SEEMS TO VEER AWAY FROM LUNCH SPOT HERE

HEATHERS

SLOPING BRIDGE

CAN SEE LUNCH STOP FROM HERE FAR IN DISTANCE

KIPUNIKA HILL

LUNCH STOP

APPROXIMATE SCALE

0   1km

TRAILBLAZER

TRAIL GUIDE AND MAPS

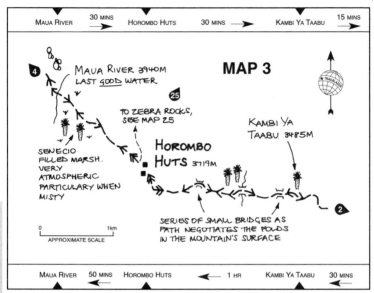

MAUA RIVER —30 MINS→ HOROMBO HUTS —30 MINS→ KAMBI YA TAABU —15 MINS→

MAP 3

MAUA RIVER 3940M
LAST GOOD WATER

TO ZEBRA ROCKS,
SEE MAP 25

HOROMBO
HUTS 3719M

KAMBI YA
TAABU 3485M

SENECIO
FILLED MARSH.
VERY
ATMOSPHERIC
PARTICULARY WHEN
MISTY

0   1km
APPROXIMATE SCALE

SERIES OF SMALL BRIDGES AS
PATH NEGOTIATES THE FOLDS
IN THE MOUNTAIN'S SURFACE

MAUA RIVER ←50 MINS HOROMBO HUTS ←1 HR KAMBI YA TAABU ←30 MINS

cious caretaker who refuses to allow eating in the dorms. Try to arrange with your guide to have dinner slightly earlier than normal to avoid the main dinner-time rush, or you could be waiting for hours.

If you have opted for the **acclimatization day**, the chances are you'll be led by your guide on the northern route (aka Mawenzi Route, see p292) past the **Zebra Rocks** and up to the **Mawenzi Huts** at 4538m (see Map 25, p293). Not only will this exercise allow you to cope with the thin air of Kibo later on but it also affords magnificent views of your ultimate destination across the Saddle, yet is near enough to allow you to return to Horombo for a late lunch.

STAGE 3: HOROMBO HUTS TO KIBO HUTS
[MAP 3 above; MAP 4, opposite; MAP 5, p236]

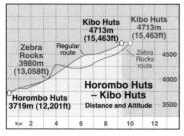

Kibo Huts 4713m (15,463ft)

Zebra Rocks 3980m (13,058ft)

Regular route

Kibo Huts 4713m (15,463ft)

Zebra Rocks route 4500

4000

Horombo Huts – Kibo Huts
Distance and Altitude 3500

Horombo Huts 3719m (12,201ft)

Km 2   4   6   8   10 12

The path to Kibo from the Horombo Huts now divides into two; almost invariably you will be led along the southern (left-hand) route, which we describe now. If your guide is amenable, however, you may like to ask him on the return from Kibo to use the more northerly route, particularly if you did not take a day to acclimatize at Horombo (those who did will be familiar with much of this northerly path, which we have called the Mawenzi Route and describe, in reverse, on p292).

The 9.2km **southern path** seems rather steep at first as it bends left (northwest) and up through the thinning vegetation of the moorland. Looping north, just under an hour after leaving Horombo you come to the tiny mountain stream known as the **Maua River** (3940m/12,923ft). You should fill up your water bottles here, for the water from this point on is rather brackish. The terrain gradually levels out after Maua, passing the junction with the **Southern Circuit** as it does so, and some of Kili's many parasitic cones move into view for the first time. Still bending north, the path leaves the scant vegetation behind for even more barren terrain. The **Last Water Point**, well signposted and rather incongruously furnished with picnic tables, marks the beginning of the uphill approach

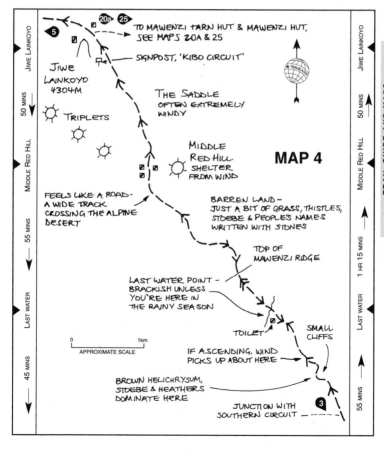

to the **Saddle**, the dry, barren terrain separating Kilimanjaro's two major peaks which lies on the other side of **Middle Red Hill**, the small parasitic cone you see ahead of you to the right of the path. You are now in a rather flat, extremely windswept and dramatic landscape, the only decoration provided by a few tufts of grass, some hardier floral species such as the aptly named everlastings, and a number of boulders and smaller stones, some of which have been arranged into messages by previous trekkers. The path begins to loop north between the Kibo summit on your left and the Middle Red on your right, whose western slopes shelter trekkers from the often howling wind and usually provide the venue for **lunch**.

Your path for the afternoon continues northwards across the Saddle; it's a bit of a weary trudge on a steadily inclining path to **Jiwe Lainkoyo**, a former campsite with some toilet huts and a huge boulder. (Jiwe means 'Rock' in Swahili.) It is also the meeting point between the two main paths from Horombo. Thereafter the path turns sharply westwards towards the **Kibo Huts**, which nestle snugly at the foot of the summit after which they were named. Though the huts look close, you still have more than an hour of walking from Jiwe Lainkoyo, and it's a tough walk too, a gradual but relentless uphill slog to round off what has already been a fairly wearying day. The huts themselves are basic, built of stone and rather chilly. A sign on the door of the main hut tells you that you are now at 4750m (though we think it's a fair bit lower than this at 4713m); a second sign warns you that Gillman's Point is still five hours away...

STAGE 4: KIBO HUTS TO GILLMAN'S POINT AND UHURU PEAK
[MAP 5, p236, MAP 28, p301]

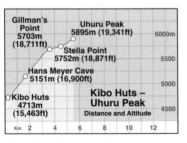

And so you come to the testing part of the walk. No matter how tough you have found the trekking so far, it has been but a leisurely stroll compared to what lies ahead of you tonight. The path to Gillman's Point on the crater rim has been in your sights since the previous afternoon when you crossed the Saddle and saw it rearing up at an angle of 16° (John Reader's estimate) on your left behind the Kibo Huts. By common consent, it is the easiest of the three leading up to the crater rim. But don't be fooled by this, for it is still an extremely demanding hike: the chances of failure are high – and those of making it, but throwing up or passing out along the way, are even higher. Just remember the golden rule: when it comes to climbing Kibo, there is no such thing as too slow.

I find a rhythm and try to lose my thoughts to it but feel the first pain of a stomach cramp and then another, and I feel the nausea starting and the headache that I recognise all too well ... The pain is sharp in my head and my cramping is still with me; if I feel this way how is Danny doing with no sleep and nothing in his stomach from the vomiting after dinner?
Rick Ridgeway, *The Shadow of Kilimanjaro – On Foot Across East Africa*

What you can't see from Kibo Huts, and yet what is rather good about this path, is that there are a number of landmarks on the way – the main ones being William's Point at 5000m (16,400ft) and Hans Meyer Cave at 5151m (16,900ft) – that act as milestones, helping both to break up the journey and to provide you with some measure of your progress. **William's Point** – or rather, the large east-facing rock immediately beneath it – lies 1hr 45min from Kibo Huts and is usually the first major resting point. Reach here and you can take some pride from the fact that you have already passed the highest altitude achieved by Jon Amos in 1998. Mind you, Mr Amos did have something of a disadvantage when he made his attempt: he was in a wheelchair raising money for the British Wheelchair Sports Foundation. Though he failed to go any further, he still set a new world record for the highest altitude – 4812m (15,788ft) – reached by somebody in a wheelchair. **Hans Meyer Cave**, a small and undistinguished hollow adorned with a plaque commemorating the Hungarian hunter, count and *bon viveur* Samuel Teleki who rested here in 1887, is another 30min further on from William's Point.

From Hans Meyer Cave, it's a case of following the scree **switchbacks**; if you've mastered the art of walking in a zombie-like trance, now is the time to put that particular technique into action. This part, as you pinball back and forth on a stretch of fine scree bounded by two boulder-strewn slopes, is extremely exposed, and if there's any wind about, you will almost certainly feel it here. If you bought one in Moshi, now is the time to put on your balaclava: your friends will be too concerned with their own situation to laugh at you now anyway.

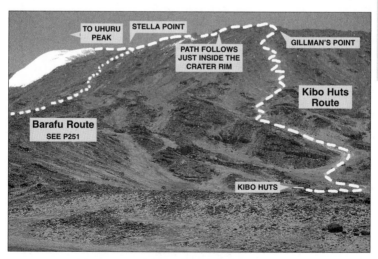

Kibo Huts Route

TRAIL GUIDE AND MAPS

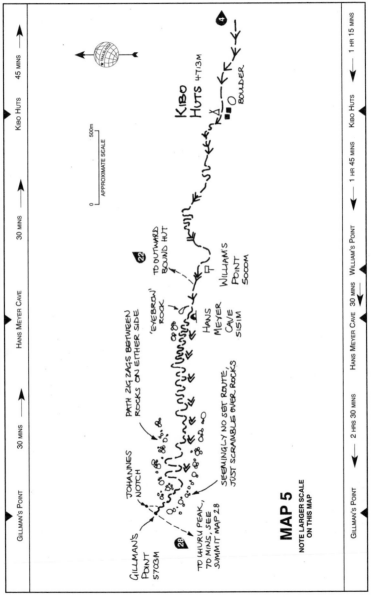

GILLMAN'S POINT →30 MINS→ HANS MEYER CAVE →30 MINS→ KIBO HUTS →45 MINS→

APPROXIMATE SCALE
0 _____ 500m

JOHANNES NOTCH

PATH ZIG ZAGS BETWEEN ROCKS ON EITHER SIDE

'EYEBROW' ROCK

TO OUTWARD BOUND HUT

HANS MEYER CAVE 5151M

SEEMINGLY NO SET ROUTE, JUST SCRAMBLE OVER ROCKS

GILLMAN'S POINT 5703M

TO UHURU PEAK, 70 MINS, SEE SUMMIT MAP 28

WILLIAM'S POINT 5000M

KIBO HUTS 4-7.3M

BOULDER

MAP 5
NOTE LARGER SCALE ON THIS MAP

GILLMAN'S POINT ←2 HRS 30 MINS← HANS MEYER CAVE ←30 MINS← WILLIAM'S POINT ←1 HR 45 MINS← KIBO HUTS ←1 HR 15 MINS←

Gradually the switchbacks begin to reduce in size like the audiograph of an echo, and 1hr 30min after leaving Hans Meyer Cave you begin to clamber between and then over rocks. This is the final phase of the climb to Gillman's, though it takes an hour to complete and you'll probably be breathless the whole way. There doesn't seem to be a set course to take through these rocks, so don't be too surprised if you see other trekkers to the left and right of you on a different path. If your guide is at least halfway competent, however, you should find yourself at the crater's edge at **Gillman's Point**. (If, upon arrival at the crater rim, you find no signpost welcoming you to Gillman's, then the chances are the guide has got his bearings slightly wrong and has led you to the slightly lower point of **Johannes Notch**. No matter: Gillman's is just a three-minute scramble up to your left.)

Gillman's Point is 960m above Kibo Hut, that is almost the equivalent of three Empire State Buildings standing one on top of another. The horizontal distance between Kibo Hut and Gillman's Point is roughly 3000 metres, so the gradient averages about 1:3.3 and the distance covered on the way up is about 3300m – the equivalent of nine Empire State Buildings laid end to end up the incline. **John Reader** *Kilimanjaro*

If the wind is not too high, Gillman's is a good spot to sit for a few minutes, get your head together, contemplate the star-spangled night with the silhouette of Mawenzi to the east, and congratulate yourself on having completed the hardest part of the trek. At least, it's the hardest part physically; the hardest part from a psychological point of view now awaits you, as you try to muster up the energy and enthusiasm to tackle the walk to **Uhuru**. Though the time varies throughout the year, as a rough guide you need to be at Gillman's at around 4.30am, in order to have a chance of seeing the sunrise at Uhuru at 5.30-6am. If you've no chance of making it by then, consider seeing the sunrise from somewhere along the way: from Stella Point, for example, or overlooking the Rebmann Glacier, or from one of the lesser peaks before Uhuru.

See Map 28 on p301 for details of the summit. The first part of this walk to Uhuru is easy enough, being either flat or, in some places, even slightly downhill. You will, however, need your head torch, because you will be walking in the moon-shadow of the crater rim for at least the first few minutes. The difficult part starts after **Stella Point**, twenty-five minutes to the south-west of Gillman's, when the path begins to climb steadily again. Though nothing like as steep as that which has gone before, at this stage any incline is a major challenge. Don't be too disheartened by the many false summits you will encounter along the last part; instead, distract your mind from the pain you are feeling by looking at the huge and beautiful icefields to your left. A golden dawn at the summit, and a golden certificate back at Marangu Gate, are the prizes that await...

For details of what you can actually see at the summit, turn to p300, while for a description of the designated descent route, turn to the **Marangu Route descent** on p292.

TRAIL GUIDE AND MAPS

The Machame Route

Then they began to climb and they were going to the East it seemed, and then it darkened and they were in a storm, the rain so thick it seemed like flying through a waterfall, and they were out and Compie turned his head and·grinned and pointed and there, ahead, all he could see, as wide as all the world, great, high, and unbelievably white in the sun, was the top of Kilimanjaro. And then he knew that there was where he was going.
Ernest Hemingway, *The Snows of Kilimanjaro*

Ask any guide or tour agent which is the best walk to do on Kilimanjaro and more often than not they will choose this, the Machame-Mweka Route (usually just shortened to the Machame Route, a convention we have adopted here). Though some of them doubtless say this because it's easier to organize – requiring no hut-booking or long-haul driving – it is not difficult to see why the route is so popular with everyone: beginning on the south-western side of the mountain, the trail passes through some of the mountain's finest features, including the **cloud forest** of Kili's southern slopes, the dry and dusty **Shira Plateau** and the delightful senecio-clad **Barranco Campsite**. Furthermore, you have a choice of ascent routes to the summit, with the courageous opting for the daunting **Western Breach Route** to the summit, while the majority head for the lengthy, long-winded climb up the **Barafu trail**, with the Rebmann Glacier edging into your field of vision on your left as dawn breaks behind Mawenzi on your right; unlike the Marangu Route, on the Machame Route you don't use the same path to descend as you took to climb up the mountain, but instead you come down via the Mweka Route, a steep but very pretty descent encompassing inhospitably dry mountain desert and lush lowland forest in a matter of a few hours.

Curiously, though the Machame Route is widely reckoned to be that much harder than the Marangu Route (and is thus nicknamed the Whiskey Route, in opposition to Marangu's softer soubriquet of the 'Coca Cola trail'), the proportion of trekkers who reach the top using this route is marginally but significantly higher. Whether this is evidence that the Machame Route allows people to acclimatize better because it's longer, particularly if you opt to take the Barafu Route to the summit, or whether this higher success rate is merely an indication that more experienced, hardened trekkers – ie the very people who are most likely to reach the summit – are more inclined to choose this route, is anyone's guess.

The following description assumes that you will be taking the Barafu Route to the summit. The entire walk up and down via Barafu traditionally lasts for six days and five nights, though it is becoming more common for trekkers to opt for an extra night during the ascent, usually in the Karanga Valley. Not only does the extra day aid acclimatization, but this also reduces from almost six to three the number of hours walked on the day that precedes the exhausting midnight ascent to the summit, thereby allowing trekkers more time to recover their faculties, relax and prepare themselves for the final push to the top.

For those daredevils wishing to try their hand at Kibo's most challenging path, the Arrow Glacier/Western Breach Route, they will leave the regular Machame Route on the third day; the text on p246 and the map on p245 will indicate where. They can then find a description of their path to the summit on p267.

STAGE 1: MACHAME GATE TO MACHAME HUTS
[MAP 6, p240; MAP 7, p241]

Coming from Moshi, the drive to the Machame Gate, at an altitude of 1828m, takes just under an hour; the tarmac doesn't last that long, petering out after about 40 minutes. On the way to the gate ask the driver to point out the house of the local chief, a simple yet large bungalow on the left-hand side of the road. Passing through Machame village you'll soon arrive at the gate itself, a small collection of

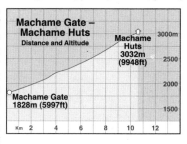

buildings huddled around a 4WD car park. Register in the office and make sure you use the toilet facilities on site – you may not think much of them now but, believe me, compared to some of the latrines on the trail these are heavenly.

Back at the car park, porters are busy haggling over who is going to take what, water-sellers and walking-pole vendors are accosting new arrivals, while the trekkers themselves are packing away their Chrisburger lunchboxes and quietly steeling themselves for the rigours ahead. To one side of this chaos is the beginning of the trail...

The **10.5km** (7 mile) first-day starts with a three-kilometre amble up a 4WD track, a wide snaking trail that cuts through the kind of deep dark enchanted forest that Hansel and Gretel would be familiar with. Green moss hangs thickly from the branches that creak and groan in the wind. It's a magical start to a wonderful adventure. After 45 minutes, the track arrives at a sign advising hikers that Machame is for those ascending the mountain only. The sign also marks the end of the 4WD road, the gentle curves and steady incline giving way to a narrower, steeper but now beautifully renovated pedestrians-only path. Looking up from the path you'll notice that the vegetation is already changing as you progress deeper into the **cloud forest**. The scarlet and yellow *Impatiens kilimanjari* and the violet *Viola eminii* and *Impatiens pseudoviola* now flourish between the roots of the huge 30-metre tall trees; tree ferns also proliferate here.

Ninety-five minutes or so from the end of the 4WD track, the path widens momentarily to form two small **clearings** (the first with en-suite toilet facilities) that make for popular lunch stops. Those who've already drunk their water bottles dry can replenish their supplies from the stream down in the valley to the west. Listen out for the primate-like call of the black (actually dark green) and red turaco which nests around here, and watch your lunch too: it's not uncommon for the forest rodents to sneak into lunchboxes and drag off a samosa or two.

TRAIL GUIDE AND MAPS

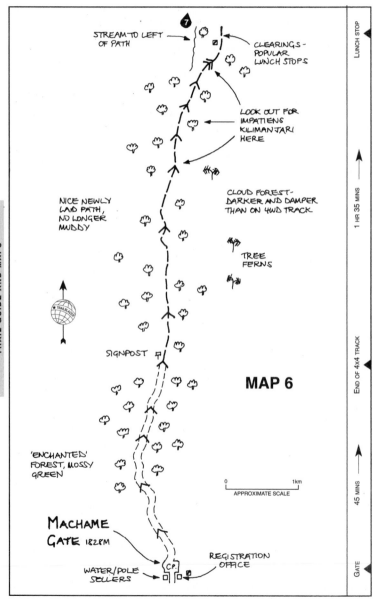

STREAM TO LEFT OF PATH

CLEARINGS - POPULAR LUNCH STOPS

LOOK OUT FOR IMPATIENS KILIMANJARI HERE

CLOUD FOREST - DARKER AND DAMPER THAN ON 4WD TRACK

NICE NEWLY LAID PATH, NO LONGER MUDDY

TREE FERNS

TRAILBLAZER

SIGNPOST

MAP 6

'ENCHANTED' FOREST, MOSSY GREEN

0   1km
APPROXIMATE SCALE

MACHAME GATE 1828M

REGISTRATION OFFICE

WATER/POLE SELLERS

C.P.

LUNCH STOP

1 HR 35 MINS

END OF 4X4 TRACK

45 MINS

GATE

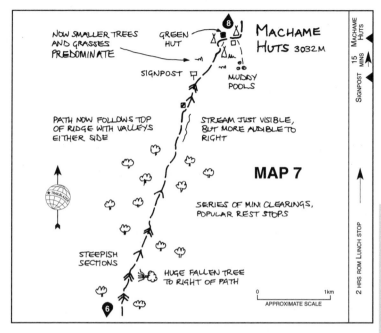

NOW SMALLER TREES AND GRASSES PREDOMINATE

GREEN HUT

MACHAME HUTS 3032M

MACHAME HUTS

15 MINS

SIGNPOST

SIGNPOST

MUDDY POOLS

PATH NOW FOLLOWS TOP OF RIDGE WITH VALLEYS EITHER SIDE

STREAM JUST VISIBLE, BUT MORE AUDIBLE TO RIGHT

TRAIL BLAZER

MAP 7

SERIES OF MINI CLEARINGS, POPULAR REST STOPS

2 HRS ROM LUNCH STOP

STEEPISH SECTIONS

HUGE FALLEN TREE TO RIGHT OF PATH

0   1km
APPROXIMATE SCALE

6

TRAIL GUIDE AND MAPS

The post-prandial path varies little from that which has gone before, though the gradient increases slightly the higher you climb. As the forest gradually begins to thin out you'll notice that you are actually walking on a narrow forested spine between two shallow valleys. A stream – more audible than visible – runs briefly to the right of the trail.

Around two hours after lunch a second signpost of the day appears, this time warning against the careless discarding of cigarette butts; as well as dispensing some sound advice, this signpost also marks the border between the cloud forest and the heath, where the long grasses dominate and the robust trees of the forest give way to the spindly, tree-like giant heathers. *Kniphofia thomsonii* (known to you and me as red hot pokers) make their first appearance at this altitude, as do several other wild flowers and shrubs such as the bushy *Phillippia excelsa*. With the forest thinning, the **Kibo peak** hoves into view for the first time to the east.

It is only fifteen minutes from the signpost to **Machame Huts** (3032m), a series of level pitches cut into the grass, each with its own toilet. Make sure you sign your name in the **registration book** and aim to pitch your tent as high as possible for the best views: by the green hut is a good spot, affording views to the east up to Kibo and south-west towards Mount Meru.

STAGE 2: MACHAME HUTS TO NEW SHIRA CAMP[MAP 8, opposite]

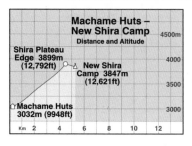

This leg of the trek is short but a little strenuous as you ascend from 3032m up to the Shira Plateau, finally coming to a halt at the New Shira Camp at just over 3847m. Parts of this walk are a bit steep and the skinny, naked giant heathers at this altitude provide little shade from the heat; what's more, the path is extremely dusty, at least after lunch, so if you have gaiters you'll probably be thankful of the protection they provide (and remember to keep your camera bag tightly closed too). In spite of all this, by taking it slowly, resting frequently and enjoying the en-route views that encompass Kibo, Meru and all points in between, this day needn't be too taxing – indeed, it's probably the easiest day of the whole ascent.

The walk starts as it goes on for much of the day, with a steepish climb north up through forests of stunted, twisted heather bushes that are still recovering from the fire a few years ago; ahead of you in the distance is the lip of the **Shira Plateau**. The path winds its way up to the top of a ridge formed by a petrified lava flow, occasionally allowing trekkers some splendid views over last night's campsite, Machame village and the flat Tanzanian plains beyond. Giant groundsels (*Senecio kilimanjari*), the squat, dry-looking trees with the green-leaf crown, begin to dot the path and Kilimanjaro's dessicated **helichrysums**, ubiquitous above 3000m, appear here for the first time too, like living pot pourri. Note, too, how most of the vegetation not only diminishes in size as you climb higher but the taller plants seem to bend as one towards the plateau, as if pointing the way. After passing a number of viewpoints and clambering from one side of the ridge to the other, the gradient of the trail increases exponentially towards the **lunch stop**, hidden from view behind a rocky outcrop. The effort expended in reaching there is worth it, for while munching your sandwiches you can savour yet more views of Kibo as well as all points south. Note, however, that the renovated path ends here.

Observing the line of porters and trekkers on the path ahead, you can also pick out the afternoon's trail, which initially continues north and up, before bending fairly sharply to the north-west, cutting a near horizontal line beneath the rim of the plateau. But though the worst of the day's climbing is now behind you, don't be fooled into thinking this is an easy section, for the path on this north-westerly trail undulates considerably as it climbs over rocks and boulders, and it can be fairly tiring in the searing afternoon heat. As a distraction, the first of Kilimanjaro's celebrated **lobelias** (*Lobelia deckenii*), both phallic and cabbage-shaped and growing to a height of two metres or more, appear by the trail.

Just under an hour after lunch the plateau is gained and the path continues northwards. Note how much more barren the landscape is up here, with trees

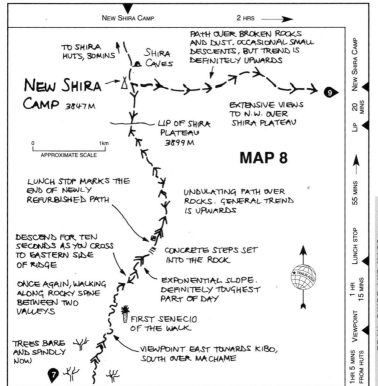

now all but extinct and only the dry white helichrysums and yellow everlastings thriving. Look out, too, for the Shira Plateau's distinctive, shiny black **obsidian** rock. Your camp for the night, which we have called the **New Shira Camp** to distinguish it from other sites around here, lies just 20 minutes into the plateau. On most maps this relatively new, sprawling campsite is not marked, leading many trekkers to think mistakenly that they are actually camping at Shira Huts. In fact, this New Shira Campsite lies just a few minutes' walk to the south of the **Shira Caves** – which *are* marked on most maps – which in turn are located a good 30 minutes to the south of the Shira Huts. Looking west from the New Shira Camp, ask your guide to point out the **Shira Cathedral** and the **East Shira Hill** which line the southern boundary of the Shira Plateau, and, behind them to the far west, **Johnsell Point** and **Klute Peak**, the highest points of the Shira Ridge, the western rim of the oldest of Kili's three craters. Mount Meru, too, is still visible to the west on the horizon.

STAGE 3: NEW SHIRA CAMP TO BARRANCO HUTS
[MAP 8, p243; MAP 9, below; MAP 10, opposite]

Camp-life on Kilimanjaro is a capital school for the practice of self-denial.

Hans Meyer *Across East African Glaciers*

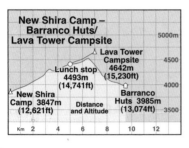

New Shira Camp –
Barranco Huts/
Lava Tower Campsite

5000m

Lava Tower
Campsite
4642m
(15,230ft)

4500

Lunch stop
4493m
(14,741ft)

4000

New Shira
Camp 3847m
(12,621ft)

Distance
and Altitude

Barranco
Huts 3985m
(13,074ft)

3500

Km   2   4   6   8   10   12

During this section of the trek you cover a total of almost **10km** as you move from the western to the southern slopes of Kilimanjaro; by the end of it you may feel slightly disappointed to learn that, for all your efforts, you will have gained just 138m in height, from the New Shira Camp at 3847m to Barranco, situated at an altitude of 3985m. Nevertheless, this leg of the trek is vital for acclimatization purposes, for during the day you will climb to a respectable **4530m (14,858ft)**. Don't be surprised, therefore, if by the end of it you have a crashing headache: this is normal and is only cause for concern if it is accompanied by other symptoms of mountain sickness or if the pain hasn't disappeared by the morning.

The day begins with a steady, gentle ascent towards the western slopes of Kibo through the dry, boulder-strewn terrain of the Shira Plateau. At first the path meanders somewhat and rises and falls regularly as it negotiates the gentle folds of the plateau, before finally settling on a roughly easterly direction, with a steady, shallow incline, for most of the next 6km. Notice how the vegetation has deteriorated to such an extent that only a few everlastings and lichen successfully cling to life up here. Soon after the **junction with the Lemosho Route** the path loops to the south-east before dividing into two.

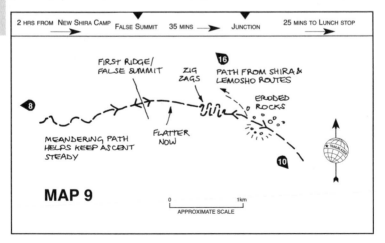

2 HRS FROM NEW SHIRA CAMP FALSE SUMMIT 35 MINS JUNCTION 25 MINS TO LUNCH STOP

FIRST RIDGE/
FALSE SUMMIT

ZIG
ZAGS

16
PATH FROM SHIRA &
LEMOSHO ROUTES

ERODED
ROCKS

8

MEANDERING PATH
HELPS KEEP ASCENT
STEADY

FLATTER
NOW

10

MAP 9

0   1km
APPROXIMATE SCALE

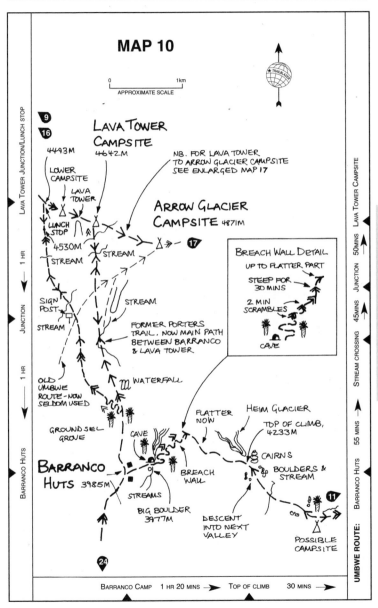

MAP 10

0   1km
APPROXIMATE SCALE

9
16

4493M

LOWER CAMPSITE

LAVA TOWER

LAVA TOWER CAMPSITE 4642M

NB. FOR LAVA TOWER TO ARROW GLACIER CAMPSITE SEE ENLARGED MAP 17

ARROW GLACIER CAMPSITE 4871M

LUNCH STOP

4530M

STREAM

STREAM

17

SIGN POST

STREAM

STREAM

FORMER PORTERS TRAIL. NOW MAIN PATH BETWEEN BARRANCO & LAVA TOWER

BREACH WALL DETAIL

UP TO FLATTER PART

STEEP FOR 30 MINS

2 MIN SCRAMBLES

CAVE

OLD UMBWE ROUTE - NOW SELDOM USED

WATERFALL

GROUNDSEL GROVE

CAVE

FLATTER NOW

HEIM GLACIER

TOP OF CLIMB, 4233M

CAIRNS

BARRANCO HUTS 3985M

BREACH WALL

BOULDERS & STREAM

STREAMS

BIG BOULDER 3977M

DESCENT INTO NEXT VALLEY

11

POSSIBLE CAMPSITE

24

BARRANCO CAMP   1 HR 20 MINS ➤   TOP OF CLIMB   30 MINS ➤

Side bar (top to bottom):

LAVA TOWER JUNCTION/LUNCH STOP

1 HR

JUNCTION

1 HR

BARRANCO HUTS

TRAIL GUIDE AND MAPS

LAVA TOWER CAMPSITE   50MINS   JUNCTION   45MINS   STREAM CROSSING   55 MINS   BARRANCO HUTS

UMBWE ROUTE:

❑ **Ascent of Kibo via the Western Breach/Arrow Glacier Route**
The Western Breach Route is a harder, shorter, more dangerous and less popular alternative trail than the standard route via Barafu Huts. But it's also a great walk that allows you to explore Kibo's crater floor and all its features – the Furtwangler Glacier, Reusch Crater and Ash Pit, to name but three – and allows supreme views of the Shira Plateau, Barranco Valley and the summit of Mount Meru. You can find a full description of the Arrow Glacier/Western Breach Route starting on p267.

It is here that those people who have opted to tackle the summit on the more difficult Western Breach Route branch off and head east towards the **Lava Tower**, while the rest (the majority) follow the more southerly, gentler trail as it bends round to the right. Just one minute after the fork the latter route comes upon a large flat, rocky surface – the **lunch stop** on this third leg.

The highest point of the day's walk, 4530m, lies just 15 minutes further on. At the top, by walking just off the path to the left, you can enjoy unrivalled views of the strange and isolated Lava Tower, with Lava Tower Camp sitting in its shadow to the east, and the path to the Arrow Glacier Campsite leading off behind it. (For details of this ascent, see p267.)

'...an extraordinary arborescent plant, since named *Senecio Johnstonii*... Its trunk was so superficially rooted and so rotten that, in spite of its height and girth, I could pull it down with one hand.
(from *The Kilima-njaro Expedition*, HH Johnston, 1886)

The Lava Tower continues to loom to your left for the next ten minutes as you descend quickly via a series of zigzags into the gully separating you from Kibo's southern slopes. Crossing the tiny stream at the bottom, the path bends south-east once more, following the contours of Kibo's lower reaches as it crosses two more streams. Less than an hour later the trail meets with the old **Umbwe Route**, a junction that is marked by a proliferation of signposts. From here it's downhill all the way as the route descends once more, this time into the delightful **Barranco Valley**, rich in senecio and lobelia. A huge gouge in the southern face of Kibo to the south-west of Uhuru Peak, the valley is in places 300m deep and was formed when a huge landslide swept southwards down from the summit about 100,000 years ago.

From the **Barranco campsite** (3985m) and its environs you'll have spectacular views of Kibo's southern face, the Western Breach and the mighty Heim Glacier, with glacial moraine tumbling southwards towards the camp. Few are the trekkers who do not rank this campsite as their favourite on this trail – we just hope the toilets have been cleaned up before you arrive.

STAGE 4: BARRANCO HUTS TO BARAFU HUTS
[MAP 10, p245; MAP 11, p248]

This is a long stage, so long that many trekkers now prefer to tackle it over two separate days, camping for the night in the Karanga Valley. Make sure you fill your containers in this valley as this is the last place to get water on the Machame Route and, if the cold wind's rushing through, it's possibly the last place you'd want to be stopping at too, though its beauty cannot be denied. As you walk along the path today the great

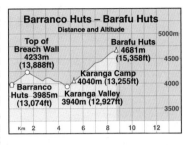

glaciers of Kili's **Southern Icefields** – the Heim, Kersten and Decken glaciers – will appear on your left one after the other. Curiously, although this stage sets you up nicely for the final push to the summit, by the end of the day you will actually be further away from Uhuru Peak (as the mountain buzzard flies) than you were at the start of the day at Barranco.

The hardest part of the day occurs right at the beginning, with a near-vertical scramble up the **Great Barranco Wall** (or **Breach Wall**) to the east of the campsite. You'll have to stash your walking poles away for this first section, because at times you'll need to use both hands to haul yourself up the senecio-dressed slopes. False summits along the way further sap the strength and spirit, but after about an hour and twenty minutes you'll reach the true summit of the wall; here you can sit on the bare rock and enjoy the views south and east, with the great **Heim Glacier** over your shoulder to the north, and relish the prospect of the relatively gentle descent into the next gully below.

At the bottom of this pretty little gully, and having crossed the small stream that flows through it, you come to a **flat gravel area**, a possible camping spot and, by the amount of loo roll hanging from the bushes, a popular pit stop too. To the north-east a path snakes towards a high pass, but this is a dangerous route that even porters blanch at the prospect of joining. In all probability your guide will lead you away from this short-cut to Barafu, and bring you instead along an easier trail cutting south-east into a series of mini-valleys. Climbing out of these valleys, the path then cuts across a barren, desert slope where the silence and stillness are positively deafening, before finally descending down the western, lusher slopes of the **Karanga Valley**. Ferns, heather and other greenery reappear for a while as you descend along the rock-and-mud path, a path that you share in places with a mountain stream. The Karanga Valley is, in the words of John Reader, 'narrow, steep and exquisite'. It is also your last place to collect water before the summit, so it is vital you fill all your water bottles here. Try to collect your water from as high a point in the stream as possible and purify it: giardia could be present. The valley itself is like a small oasis of green, albeit a cold and windswept one; the beautiful shimmering green **malachite sunbirds** nest around here; you may spot them feeding on the lobelias.

TRAIL GUIDE AND MAPS

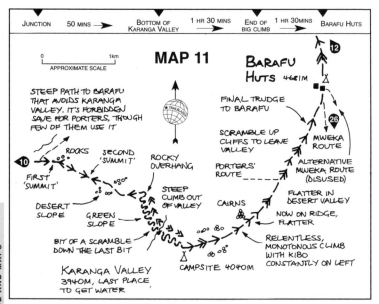

JUNCTION 50 MINS → BOTTOM OF KARANGA VALLEY 1 HR 30 MINS → END OF BIG CLIMB 1 HR 30MINS → BARAFU HUTS

MAP 11

BARAFU HUTS 4681M

0 ——— 1km
APPROXIMATE SCALE

STEEP PATH TO BARAFU THAT AVOIDS KARANGA VALLEY. IT'S FORBIDDEN SAVE FOR PORTERS, THOUGH FEW OF THEM USE IT

FINAL TRUDGE TO BARAFU

SCRAMBLE UP CLIFFS TO LEAVE VALLEY

ROCKS SECOND 'SUMMIT' ROCKY OVERHANG PORTERS' ROUTE

MWEKA ROUTE

ALTERNATIVE MWEKA ROUTE (DISUSED)

FIRST 'SUMMIT'

DESERT SLOPE GREEN SLOPE

STEEP CLIMB OUT OF VALLEY

CAIRNS

FLATTER IN DESERT VALLEY

NOW ON RIDGE, FLATTER

BIT OF A SCRAMBLE DOWN THE LAST BIT

RELENTLESS, MONOTONOUS CLIMB WITH KIBO CONSTANTLY ON LEFT

KARANGA VALLEY 3940M, LAST PLACE TO GET WATER

CAMPSITE 4040M

Those who plan to split this leg into two days will camp at the top of the next climb, a very steep twenty-minute ascent on a switchback path. This is the somewhat misnamed **Karanga Valley Campsite** (I say misnamed because, of course, it's above the valley and not in it). At the camp the trail takes a leftward turn, heading in an easterly or north-easterly direction on a relatively gentle incline, with the Decken Glacier a permanent presence to your left. The scenery now becomes even more barren as you make your way between the boulders and over the shattered rocks and stones of this misty mountain slope. Even the trail is faint. Only the occasional cairn marking out the way gives an indication that man has passed this way before (unless, of course, some bastard has dropped some litter). If George Lucas is looking for somewhere wild, inhospitable and unearthly as a location for his next Star Wars instalment, he could do a lot worse...

At the top the path bends more to the right (east) and descends into a shallow valley that, if anything, is even drier and more blighted than the previous section. Once again, the Southern Icefields loom ominously to your left, with the **Rebmann Glacier** appearing for the first time.

Barafu Huts (4681m), your destination for this leg, lies at the end of this valley, reached after a short scramble up the cliff-face and a 25-minute walk almost due north. Barafu means 'Ice' in Swahili and the camp is probably called this because of its proximity to the Rebmann Glacier, away to the north-west. Try to get some food and rest as soon as possible and sort out your equipment for the next stage before it gets dark: you've got a long night ahead.

STAGE 5: BARAFU HUTS TO STELLA POINT AND UHURU PEAK
[MAP 12, p250, MAP 28, p301]

But now, apparently, the mountain was inhabited by fiery beings who baffled man's adventurous foot: the mountain receded as the traveller advanced, the summit rose as he ascended; blood burst from the nostrils, fingers bent backwards... even the most adventurous were forced back. **Richard Burton** in *Progress of Expedition to East Africa*, reporting the rumours he had heard about Kilimanjaro while residing in Tanga (circa 1857).

And so you come to the final ascent, a rigorous, vigorous push to Stella Point and the crater rim, followed by a 45-minute trudge up to Uhuru Peak, the highest point in Africa. It's tough, no doubt about it, but if you manage to avoid sickness or injury there's no reason why you, too, shouldn't be clutching a golden certificate come tomorrow evening. This final stage usually begins at around midnight; this not

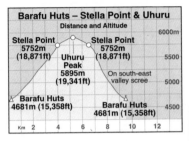

only allows trekkers the chance to see sunrise from the summit but also leaves enough daylight to allow for the long descent to the next night's campsite, with an hour's recuperation back at Barafu on the way. As such, you can leave most of your **luggage** at Barafu while you tackle the ascent, though you should take any valuables with you (there have been a few robberies from tents left unguarded), as well as your **camera**, spare film and batteries and all your **water** (which should be kept in **insulated bottles** or it'll freeze up and be useless on the ascent). Cameras, particularly digitals and feature-heavy SLRs, have been known to freeze in these conditions as well so keep them insulated. Wear all your **clothes** too – you can always take a layer or two off in the unlikely situation that you find yourself getting too hot – and have your **head-torch** readily to hand when you wake up so you don't have to spend time and energy looking around for it before you go.

  Good luck!

At 4am by the light of a hurricane lamp, and wrapped in everything that could give warmth, I started with Mawala, the headman, and Jonathan, our guide, on the long uphill pull of 4000ft over loose scree and fissured rocks. The cold was intense, and Mawala got two of his toes frost-bitten ... our breathing had become so difficult that we could barely drag ourselves along and had to sit down every few yards to recover breath, now and again sucking icicles and nibbling Cadbury's Milk Chocolate. Yet the steep ascent was mostly over projecting ridges of lava slabs and presented no real obstacle beyond the extreme altitude. Here and there, however, we struck a bed of loose shingle, which mockingly carried us backwards at every footstep almost the whole distance of our tread.
Eva Stuart Watt climbing Kili in *Africa's Dome of Mystery* (1930)

The way to the summit starts, as you've probably already observed from Barafu, by scrambling over the **small cliffs** at the northern end of camp; after fifteen minutes or so the path flattens a little as you walk in the moon-shadow of a second set of cliffs rising up to your left. Twenty-five minutes on from there the path descends minimally; we mention this not because the descent is in any way remarkable or extensive – it lasts for maybe ten seconds in total – but merely because it is the only descent we can recall for the whole of the next six hours.

Immediately after this the path takes a fairly sharpish turn to the left (north-west). You are now heading directly for the summit and Stella Point, a direction

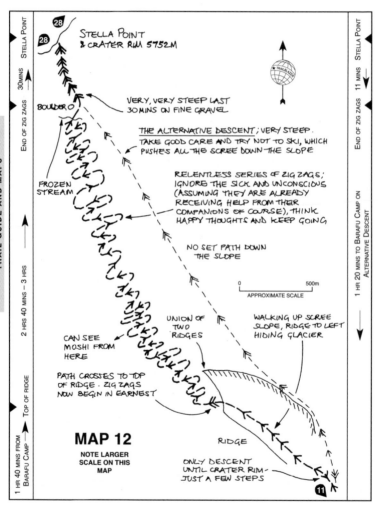

TRAIL GUIDE AND MAPS

MAP 12

NOTE LARGER SCALE ON THIS MAP

you will maintain for nearly the entire night. After another fifteen minutes or so you begin to walk on the distinctive **shale and gravel slopes** of Kibo, which if they're not frozen may cause you to slip back with every step. Everybody has their own way of tackling this, with some trekkers stabbing their poles hard into the ground to aid their balance, while others walk with a Chaplinesque gait, their feet splayed outwards to stem the slide back. Whatever way you choose, you'll find it hard work.

The situation was appalling, there was a grandeur and a magnificence about the surroundings which were almost too much for me; instead of exhilarating, they were oppressive.
Charles New *Life, Wanderings, and Labours in Eastern Africa* (1873)

An hour or so after turning north-west you take another left turn and cross to the top of the ridge that has been a constant companion on your left-hand side for the past hour or so. The **switchback path** begins in earnest now and continues for most of the next three hours. It is pointless describing the scenery on this section, for the chances are you won't be able to see much beyond the radius of your torch-beam, and won't be keen on surveying the landscape now anyway. If it's a clear night, however, you may be able to see the **Rebmann Glacier** ahead of you to your left, with the snow-less Stella Point a little to your right in the distance. Picking your way through the trail of knackered trekkers and exhausted assistant guides, ignore the sound of people retching and sobbing and remember to keep your pace constant and very slow, even if you feel fine: you've come this far, and now is not a good time to get altitude sickness.

Barafu Route

Though you probably won't notice it, the path actually drifts slightly to the north over these three hours, before crossing a frozen stream and passing a **large boulder** which marks the end of the zigzags. You are now just thirty minutes from Stella Point (5752m), a painful, tear-inducing half-hour on sheer scree. The gradient up to now has been steep, but this last scree slope takes the biscuit; in fact, it takes the entire tin.

Lift one foot and then the other, just enough to place it higher; don't use any more energy than you need to and breathe deeply between each move. Rhythm is everything, rhythm and pacing, and when you are in it your thoughts go and it is dreamlike, but you are still here in the moment, the cone beam of light coming from your forehead tying you through the blackness to the lava slope of this mountain that in your mind you see rising to a rare glacial height above the acacia-studded plain of Africa.
     Rick Ridgeway *The Shadow of Kilimanjaro – on Foot across East Africa (1999)*

Make it to the top and you can afford to relax a little. If you really, absolutely, positively, definitely can't do anymore, take comfort from the fact that you have already matched the feat of respected climber HW Tilman, for whom Stella Point was the highest point reached on his first attempt on the summit; and you can always use his excuse – that he thought that this *was* the highest point – too. (Mind you, as if to prove that it was ignorance and not a lack of fortitude that prevented him from reaching Uhuru, he then went on to conquer the much harder Mawenzi Peak a few days later). Take comfort, too, from the fact that you have also earned yourself an impressive green certificate. Those who want an even more impressive gold one, however, must push on for another 45 minutes around the crater rim, turning left (south) and then bending right (west), passing minor pinnacles such as **Hans Meyer** and **Elveda** points before finally arriving, just as Hans Meyer himself did over a century ago, at Uhuru Peak: the true summit of the mountain and the highest point in the whole continent (see Map 28, p301). You are now enjoying an unrivalled view of Africa – nobody on this great, dark continent is currently gazing down from as lofty a vantage-point as you.

From the summit, it's usual for trekkers who took the Machame Route up to take the **Mweka Route** back down; and this you'll find described on p294.

The Shira Plateau and Lemosho routes

Without doubt Kibo is most imposing as seen from the west. Here it rises in solemn majesty, and the eye is not distracted by the sister peak of Mawenzi, of which nothing is to be seen but a single jutting pinnacle. The effect is enhanced by the magnificent flowing sweep of the outline, the dazzling extent of the ice-cap, the vast stretch of the forest, the massive breadth of the base, and the jagged crest of the Shira spur as it branches away towards the west.

Hans Meyer *Across East African Glaciers* (1891)

These two treks have been put together simply because they have a lot of features in common, the main one being that both involve a crossing of the expansive Shira Plateau which stretches out for around 13km to the west of Kibo. This plateau is actually a **caldera**, a collapsed volcanic crater: when you are walking on the plateau, you are walking on the remains of the first of Kilimanjaro's three volcanoes to expire, around 500,000 years ago; it was then filled by the lava and debris from the later Kibo eruption.

The plateau also has a reputation for its **fauna**, largely thanks to its proximity to Amboseli National Park in Kenya from where herds of elephant, eland, buffalo, and big cats such as the lion have been known to wander. Indeed, not so many years ago (and occasionally still today) trekkers on these routes had to be accompanied by an armed ranger (for which they had to pay) to protect them against encounters with predators. That said, the rule is seldom enforced these days and, to be honest, you will be very, *very* lucky to see any evidence of wildlife existing on the plateau, save for the odd hoofprint or two and the occasional sun-dried lumps of scat and spoor. So while the proximity of Africa's finest wild beasts adds a certain frisson of excitement to the walk, don't choose either of these trails purely on the strength of their reputation for spotting game: it's an awful long way to come just to see some dessicated elephant shit.

The first thing to know about these two routes is that **it is common for the relatively new Lemosho Route to be referred to as the Shira Plateau Route**, particularly by foreign agencies keen to promote the fact that you'll be walking across the Shira Plateau. This, of course, is confusing so you should ask your agency to indicate *exactly* which of the two routes you will be taking. Another way to check is to see where your first night's accommodation will be; if it's the Big Tree Campsite – or Mti Mkubwa in the local language – where you'll be staying, then it's actually the Lemosho Route that you'll be following, regardless of what your trekking agency calls it.

Furthermore, there are **many paths** on the plateau and a number of possible campsites too, and each year the guides alter slightly the routes taken by their trekkers. For these reasons, the following descriptions of the Lemosho and Shira Plateau trails may not tally exactly with your own experience on the plateau, though the difference should be negligible.

The journey to Londorossi

The starting point for both of these trails is the **Londorossi Gate**, reachable via a long drive from Moshi or Arusha. As a result of the extra effort and petrol required to get here, these two trails often cost a little more than the more popular, and nearer, Marangu, Umbwe and Machame trails.

Thus, for much of the first day you won't be walking anywhere but will be strapped into the back of a jeep as it glides along the Arusha–Moshi highway, before turning off at **Bomaya Ya Ng'ombe** ('Cattle Corral'; 26km/16 miles from Moshi). From there it bounces along for another hour past **Sanya Juu** (22km/13 miles from the turn-off and virtually the last place to get supplies), **Ngarenairobi** and **Simba Farm** (a huge estate to the left of the road) before finally pulling up at the village and gate of Londorossi. It's a weird place, a Spaghetti Western outpost stuck in the middle of Africa, made entirely of wood, divided up and shut off from the outside world by high wooden fences designed to keep the local fauna at bay. At Londorossi you can register, pick up a **permit** (the only other place outside of Marangu and Machame gates where this is possible) and check out the troop of colobus monkeys in the trees near the park rangers' accommodation. If your company hasn't already collected all your fees from you and is expecting you to pay at the gate, do try to bring the correct amount of cash/travellers' cheques with you; if the office here doesn't have the correct change, it's highly unlikely anybody else in Londorossi will have.

From here, the two trails divide, and are described separately below.

The Lemosho Route

The Lemosho Route is a relatively new variation on the traditional Shira Plateau Route, (described on p272), which is seldom used nowadays. Indeed, though many people book what they think is a trek on the Shira Route – as that is what the trekking agencies often call it – almost invariably it is the Lemosho Route on which they will actually be walking.

This new route across the Shira Plateau has quickly gained in popularity, to a point where it is now the third most popular route on the mountain – and it is not difficult to see why: a six- or seven-day yomp (though some companies take as many as ten) through the remote and pristine forest of west Kilimanjaro and across the Shira Plateau precedes an assault on the summit via either the tricky **Western Breach Route** (see p267) or via Barranco, Karanga Valley and Barafu to Stella Point on the **Barafu Route**, (a description of which begins on p246). Either way, the usual **descent route is the Mweka trail**.

It is the first day or so, when you are walking through the forests on Kilimanjaro's western slopes, that is the main reason why this trail has overtaken the old Shira Plateau Route as the main path attacking Kilimanjaro from the west. With the latter you usually take a car all the way up to the plateau, thereby missing out not only on some fine forest, which you experience only through a car window, but also on some useful acclimatization. And although the walk up to the plateau on the Lemosho Route is an exhausting one, the benefits of trekking rather than driving up will manifest themselves later on as you saunter up Kibo with scarcely a headache, while littering the trail around you are the weeping, retching bodies of the AMS-sufferers who took the car up to the Shira Plateau.

What's more, because Lemosho is a more southerly route, so it allows side trips to the minor peaks of Kilimanjaro's third summit, the Shira Ridge. In particular, the **Shira Cathedral**, on the southern side of the plateau, has become a very popular excursion on the third day of the trek. Again, such a side trip is useful for acclimatization purposes and no extra days need to be taken to do this either. Other side trips that *do* require an extra day include a trek to the Moir Huts, on the north-western side of the mountain; and, if taking the Western Breach Route to the summit, a diversion to see the Reusch Crater and Ash Pit. Indeed, one of the joys of the Lemosho Route is the variety of different trails one can take and itineraries one can build – there is no one standard 'Lemosho Route'.

Though it's a great route, Lemosho is not without its drawbacks. For one thing, we reckon it to be the wettest route; though meteorology doesn't back us up, it always seems to rain on this side of the mountain more than anywhere else. Unfortunately, the rise in Lemosho's popularity has also led to problems. For one thing, the amount of **rubbish** on the trail and especially at the campsites is little short of distressing. How anybody could be stupid enough to drop sweet wrappers in somewhere as lovely as the western forest is beyond me, while those who leave used batteries lying on the ground at campsites deserve shooting. There are cleaning crews employed to clear up the litter but either they're not doing their job properly or the job is too big for them. The problem needs to be addressed, and addressed soon. Hopefully, by the time you read this, KINAPA will have pulled their proverbial finger out and all will be lovely once more. If not, don't hesitate to leave messages in the suggestion boxes at the campsites along the way or write to KINAPA to express your views. I, too, would welcome your reports on the latest situation – for better or worse; send us an email to the address at the front of the book or contact us via the website.

STAGE 1: LONDOROSSI GATE TO MTI MKUBWA/BIG TREE CAMP
[MAP 13, p257]

Getting to the start of the Lemosho Route is a bit of a bind. Your first port of call is Londorossi. Park fees paid and luggage weighed, you must then return through wheat fields and cypress forests ten minutes' back south to **Simba**, curiously also occasionally called **Lemosho Glades** and, indeed, Londorossi too. Whatever it's called, you have to pay Ts15,000 here (Ts3000 for residents) to the Forest

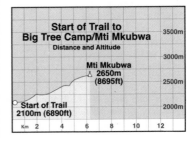

Start of Trail to
Big Tree Camp/Mti Mkubwa
Distance and Altitude

Mti Mkubwa
△ 2650m
(8695ft)

Start of Trail
2100m (6890ft)

3500m
3000m
2500m
2000m

Km 2   4   6   8   10   12

TRAIL GUIDE AND MAPS

Authority who maintain the road up to the trek's start. From here the road you take winds up the slopes past largely denuded hills and little wooden shacks incongruously furnished with satellite dishes. (As these dishes indicate, the inhabitants aren't particularly poor even though the conditions of their houses would indicate otherwise; in fact, the reason why they live in crudely erected wooden shacks is because they aren't actually allowed to build any permanent construction this high up on Kili.) Some of these settlements have even been dignified with names, including **Gezaulale** and the last 'village' before the forest, **Chaulale**. Considering the cold climate, it won't surprise you to learn that as well as the tree plantations that abound, potatoes and carrots are the main crops in these parts.

Eventually, twenty minutes after Simba and having entered into the forest, your vehicle will give up trying to negotiate the muddy path and it will be time to alight, grab your rucksack and make your own way up the slopes. At the end of the road there are a couple of toilets here but little else to delay you. It will already be late in the day by the time you start walking, although the first night's camp lies just two hours from the end of the road. There are enough steep gradients in these two hours to check all your equipment is comfortable and your limbs are in full working order. The conditions are often misty and quite cool on this first stage through the forest: ideal weather for walking, if not for taking photos.

As you can tell from the map opposite, landmarks in the forest are few; nevertheless, it's still a splendid start to your trek. After all, you're sharing the forest with colobus and blue monkeys and the rarely encountered buffalo, elephant, lion, leopard and porcupine. Indeed, though rarely seen now as the trail has grown in popularity, it wasn't uncommon a few years back for trekkers to be accompanied by armed rangers to ward off buffalo attacks. In addition to the fauna, you'll be sharing the path itself with many of the celebrities of Kilimanjaro's floral kingdom, including the two most prominent *Impatiens* species, *kilimanjaro* and *pseudoviola*, as well as millions of soldier ants; while watching over the whole shebang are those giants without which there would be no forest, in particular the camphor, podocarpus and hagenia trees. Look out, too, for the *Senecio johnstonii sp. cheranganiensis* with its phallic brush rising from it, more common on Meru and virtually non-existent on Kilimanjaro, except in this western forest and one place on the Umbwe Route. Ask your guide, too, to point out the *Dracaena afromontana*, locally known as the yucca plant, which though seemingly unimpressive is held in high esteem by the Chagga (see box p258).

Colobus monkey
(from *The Kilima-njaro Expedition*, HH Johnston, 1886)

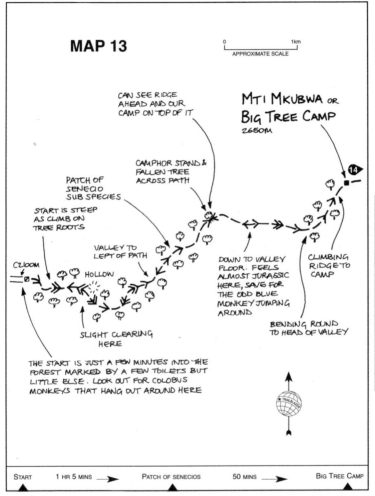

MAP 13

0 _____ 1km
APPROXIMATE SCALE

CAN SEE RIDGE
AHEAD AND OUR
CAMP ON TOP OF IT

MTI MKUBWA OR
BIG TREE CAMP
2650M

CAMPHOR STAND &
FALLEN TREE
ACROSS PATH

PATCH OF
SENECIO
SUB SPECIES

START IS STEEP
AS CLIMB ON
TREE ROOTS

VALLEY TO
LEFT OF PATH

C2100M

HOLLOW

DOWN TO VALLEY
FLOOR. FEELS
ALMOST JURASSIC
HERE, SAVE FOR
THE ODD BLUE
MONKEY JUMPING
AROUND

CLIMBING
RIDGE TO
CAMP

BENDING ROUND
TO HEAD OF VALLEY

SLIGHT CLEARING
HERE

THE START IS JUST A FEW MINUTES INTO THE
FOREST MARKED BY A FEW TOILETS BUT
LITTLE ELSE. LOOK OUT FOR COLOBUS
MONKEYS THAT HANG OUT AROUND HERE

TRAILBLAZER

| START | 1 HR 5 MINS ➞ | PATCH OF SENECIOS | 50 MINS ➞ | BIG TREE CAMP |

TRAIL GUIDE AND MAPS

Your destination for this first stage is the campsite known officially (ie by nobody) as the **Forest Camp**, and unofficially (ie by everybody) as Mti Mkubwa, or the **Big Tree Camp** (2650m), for obvious reasons. Lying at the top of a ridge in the shade of a wonderful spreading podocarpus, as with all the campsites on Kili there's little to it other than a piece of flat ground, a couple of

Dracaena afromontana* – the Chagga's constant companion
Known as *masale* by the locals, the inedible and – at least compared to some of the beautiful plants on Kilimanjaro – rather unedifying *Dracaena afromontana* has nevertheless been cultivated and used by the Chagga since time immemorial, to the extent where it's now almost their tribal emblem. Nobody knows why this should be but it's clear that where the outside world sees an unspectacular green plant of little practical use, the Chagga see a shrub whose spiritual qualities and symbolism are far more important than the practical and nutritional value inherent in other plants.

You'll probably first come across the *dracaena* in one of the mountainside villages where it's still commonly used as a boundary marker, with a row of them planted to form a fence to demarcate the extent of a person's property. According to some Chagga guides, this is because the *dracaena* is able to ward off evil spirits, which are unable to pass through a line of them. The plant is also traditionally a symbol of contrition and an appeal for clemency. If you are in dispute with a neighbour, for example, or have somehow wronged somebody, the best way to ask for forgiveness is to give them a *dracaena* plant. Do so, and they'd have to have a very strong reason for not forgiving you.

Indeed, in some Chagga villages it is said that the *dracaena* is a Chagga's constant companion, accompanying a person throughout their life from their first breath to their last. There's some truth to this, too, because in some Chagga villages it was customary to give the sap of the plant to newborns before they took their mother's milk for the first time; while when it came to burying a village chief, the corpse would traditionally have been wrapped in dracaena leaves before being interred.

long-drop toilets and a ranger's hut. But it's still many people's favourite stopping point on the trail, with the noise of the turaco and colobus in the trees at both dusk and dawn making for a quintessential African night.

STAGE 2: MTI MKUBWA/BIG TREE CAMP TO SHIRA 1
[MAP 14, opposite]

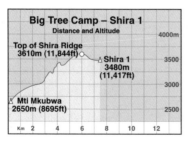

Big Tree Camp – Shira 1
Distance and Altitude
Top of Shira Ridge 3610m (11,844ft)
Shira 1 3480m (11,417ft)
Mti Mkubwa 2650m (8695ft)

You've spent a whole day travelling, registering and walking, and you are still some way short of the plateau, which you will finally reach towards the end of this second stage, leaving the forest for the moorland as you do so. Many trekkers' favourite stage on the trail, this four hour-plus walk (though with all the breaks you'll need it will take a full day) is something of a red-letter day too. For not only do you forsake forest for moorland and get your first proper views of the Shira Plateau and its accompanying ridge and peaks, but it is on this stage that, finally and famously, you get your first views of Kibo.

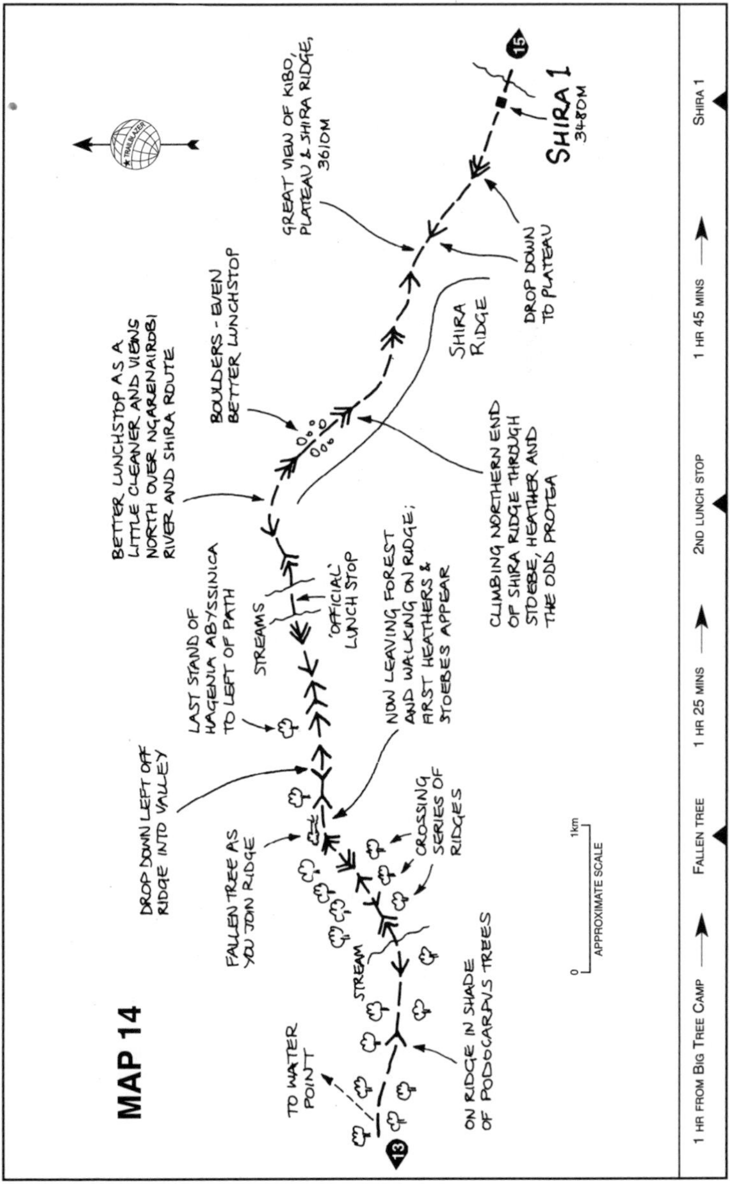
MAP 14
TRAILBLAZER
13
TO WATER POINT
ON RIDGE IN SHADE OF PODOCARPUS TREES
STREAM
FALLEN TREE AS YOU JOIN RIDGE
CROSSING SERIES OF RIDGES
DROP DOWN LEFT OFF RIDGE INTO VALLEY
NOW LEAVING FOREST AND WALKING ON RIDGE; FIRST HEATHERS & STOEBES APPEAR
LAST STAND OF HAGENIA ABYSSINICA TO LEFT OF PATH
STREAMS
'OFFICIAL' LUNCH STOP
BETTER LUNCHSTOP AS A LITTLE CLEANER AND VIEWS NORTH OVER NGARENAIROBI RIVER AND SHIRA ROUTE
BOULDERS - EVEN BETTER LUNCHSTOP
CLIMBING NORTHERN END OF SHIRA RIDGE THROUGH STOEBE, HEATHER AND THE ODD PROTEA
SHIRA RIDGE
GREAT VIEW OF KIBO, PLATEAU & SHIRA RIDGE, 3610M
DROP DOWN TO PLATEAU
SHIRA 1
3480M
15
0
1km
APPROXIMATE SCALE
1 HR FROM BIG TREE CAMP
FALLEN TREE
1 HR 25 MINS
2ND LUNCH STOP
1 HR 45 MINS
SHIRA 1

These rewards are not gained without effort, however, and during today you'll be climbing almost 1000m, taking you above 3000m and into the realm of dastardly HACO and its evil twin, HAPO (see p203). So do make sure you go *pole pole* if you don't want to feel poorly poorly.

Today begins just as the last one left off, as you head in a general easterly direction and generally upwards too, though with plenty of minor variations as you negotiate the folds and creases of Kili's forested slopes. Eventually you find yourself heading north-east to climb to the top of a ridge, the point where you actually gain the top being marked by a large fallen tree. As with many of the larger trees in this neck of the woods, this giant shows signs of having been scorched around the trunk – the unmistakable signs of honey-seekers who burn the hollow inside of the tree in order to smoke out the bees, making it easier to gain access to their produce. Climb a little further and you'll also find an artificial, man-made 'hive' – just a hollowed out piece of wood – lodged in a tree. As all forms of honey collection are now banned within the boundaries of the national park, one can assume only that these date back to pre-KINAPA times...

Heading east and up along the ridge, it's not long before the trees start to diminish in size and number, to be replaced by their hardier cousins of the heather and stoebe family. These soon begin to crowd you in on both sides but not enough to obscure your view north over the valley. It's a valley you eventually join, too, as you continue your eastward and upward progress, briefly contouring the ridge's slopes as you drop gently to the valley floor to reacquaint yourselves with the decorative *Hagenia abyssinica*, here making one last stand.

The relentless uphill is finally interrupted by a short descent to what was once a popular **lunch stop** – popular, that is, until the litter left by these lunching parties drove guides and their trekkers to find another dining-room to frequent and, no doubt, despoil too. That alternative lunchspot lies at the top of the next ridge and while there's no water up here (whereas there is in the older picnic site down below), the views are better, particularly to the north over the Ngarenairobi River and the 4x4 road of the Shira Plateau Route beyond. From this new lunchspot the path once again turns east before bending south, following the ridge, before heading east once more to contour around the slope of what is – though you may not realize it just yet – the northern extremity of the **Shira Ridge**.

The path's gradient, steep since lunch, flattens out as you contour along this northern slope and drops at the first sight of the Shira Plateau. This is the moment you've been waiting for all day: standing at 3610m above sea level, the Shira Ridge to your right and snow-capped Kibo straight ahead, with the plateau unfurled at your feet and your next two day's trekking mapped out for you upon its face. More immediately, beneath you lies a green uniport, marking the site of the **Shira 1 Campsite** (3480m), a spot that's popular with four-striped grass mice, streaky seed-eaters and white-necked ravens as well as the usual foreign itinerants in lurid Gore-tex.

STAGE 3: SHIRA 1 TO SHIRA HUTS/FISCHER CAMP
[MAP 15, p262]

As mentioned in the introduction, one of the advantages of the Lemosho Route is the number of different variations one can take upon it. And this third stage is perhaps the one with the greatest number of options, for not only are there a number of different destinations, there are a number of different ways of reaching them too. In order to introduce some sort of clarity, we've chosen as our destination for

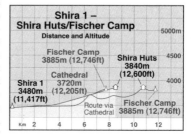

this third stage two possibilities, Shira Huts and Fischer Camp, that lie just twenty minutes apart and are by far and away the most popular destinations. But it is not unheard of for some companies, such as Tusker Safaris, to use Fischer merely as a place for lunch before moving on to Moir Huts, on the north-western side of Kibo. The gain in altitude of doing this is great but then your company will have built in acclimatization days after this to compensate.

There are two main ways of getting to Shira Huts/Fischer from Shira 1: the regular direct trail slicing west-east across the plateau, or the new and increasingly popular alternative detour via the Shira Cathedral on the plateau's southern rim. This latter route was devised by African Environments and though it's not strenuous, it does provide some useful acclimatization as you climb to 3720m before dropping again. Furthermore, as if the lack of a blinding AMS headache later on wasn't reward enough, there are also the views from the top of the Cathedral across the plateau and towards Kibo; and as it takes only a day, and thus no more time than the regular route, we recommend that you select this option if given the choice. However, as it is the alternative route to the main trail, we have described it second (beginning on p263) after the regular, traditional trail which we look at now.

Shira 1 to Shira Huts/Fischer Camp: the regular route

This 'traditional' trail may lack the pazzazz of the younger alternative but that's not to dismiss it altogether. After all, no stroll across the Shira Plateau could ever be described as dull! There are two main destinations to this walk. The first, Shira Huts, is, as with all such places, equipped with a green uniport, toilets and a particularly prominent suggestions box, as if it's inviting criticism; and given the filthy state of the campsite, it's probably going to get it too. The ranger here also oversees the campsite at Shira Caves on the Machame Route and Fischer Camp, the other 'usual' destination on this trail. Quieter and slightly cleaner, Fischer is frequented only by the more expensive trekking agencies (African Environments, Tusker Safaris etc), mainly because they are the only

TRAIL GUIDE AND MAPS

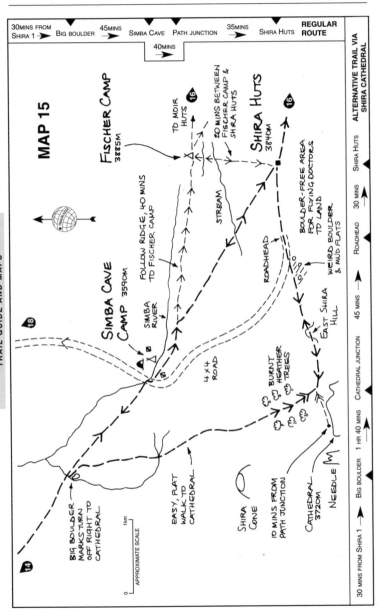

MAP 15

REGULAR ROUTE

30MINS FROM SHIRA 1 → BIG BOULDER → 45MINS → SIMBA CAVE → PATH JUNCTION → 35MINS → SHIRA HUTS

40MINS →

ALTERNATIVE TRAIL VIA SHIRA CATHEDRAL

30 MINS FROM SHIRA 1 → BIG BOULDER → 1 HR 40 MINS → CATHEDRAL JUNCTION → 45 MINS → ROADHEAD → 30 MINS → SHIRA HUTS

FISCHER CAMP 3885M

TO MOIR HUTS

20 MINS BETWEEN FISCHER CAMP & SHIRA HUTS

SHIRA HUTS 3840M

FOLLOW RIDGE, 40 MINS TO FISCHER CAMP

SIMBA CAVE CAMP 3590M

SIMBA RIVER

STREAM

BOULDER-FREE AREA FOR FLYING DOCTORS TO LAND

ROADHEAD

WEIRD BOULDER & MUD FLATS

4x4 ROAD

EAST SHIRA HILL

EASY, FLAT WALK TO CATHEDRAL

BURNT HEATHER TREES

SHIRA CONE

10 MINS FROM PATH JUNCTION

CATHEDRAL 3720M

NEEDLE

BIG BOULDER MARKS TURN OFF RIGHT TO CATHEDRAL

1km

APPROXIMATE SCALE

0

ones with mobile toilets to compensate for the complete lack of facilities on site. Named after the famous Seattle mountaineer Scott Fischer (1955-96), founder of climbing outfit Mountain Madness (see p29) and one of the victims of the vicious storm on Everest that killed eight climbers in one day, the campsite has one slight advantage over Shira Huts in that it is located on the way to Moir Huts, two-and-a-half hours away, and is thus used as a stopping point by those agencies who have Moir on their itineraries.

To get to either Shira Huts or Fischer Camp involves at least two hours and thirty minutes of steady uphill walking. From Shira 1 you head south-east through the heath and moorland of the plateau, still bearing the charred remains of heather trees immolated in a fire in 2002. Watch out for buffalo tracks and other animals that cross the plateau in search of salt and fresh grazing. Come to think of it, watch out for the buffaloes themselves – encountering one can ruin your holiday. Crossing the unimpressive trickle of the waterway that will, further down the slopes, become the torrent of the Ngarenairobi, after about 75 minutes you reach the plateau's major junction. It is here that the Lemosho Route meets the 4x4 track of the Shira Route; here too that you meet the deepish creek of the Simba River. Shame, then, that such an important landmark should be marked only by a couple of toilets belonging to the **Simba Cave Campsite** (3590m), the cave itself a rather forlorn effort lying north-east of the junction.

From here it's another 40 minutes or so up to the top of a ridge and another path junction, with the trail to **Fischer Campsite** (3885m) heading off left. A further forty minutes will bring you to this campsite on top of the ridge, a climb that's mainly conducted over rocks with giant heathers and horsetail grass lining the path and the Simba Valley a constant companion on your left. Those staying at **Shira Huts** (3840m), however, the green roof of which is visible from the junction, should continue straight ahead on the main trail. It's a fairly direct 35-minute path that takes you there, crossing a couple of shallow ridges and a stream along the way.

Shira 1 to Shira Huts/Fischer Camp via the Shira Cathedral

This route begins by following the regular trail as it heads south-east across the southern reaches of the plateau, turning off south by a big and distinctive boulder just after crossing the Ngarenairobi. It's a long trek across to the foot of the Cathedral, with the **Shira Cone** (aka Cone Place) the only major landmark nearby, but it's not a trek that's lacking in interest. In all probability you should see the first lobelias of your trek, standing sentinel-straight as they peer above the grass to check on your progress. You may also see many animal tracks on the trail, including klipspringer, eland and dik dik, hoofprints that betray this path's origins as a trail used by animals in search of salt and fresh grazing. Crossing many (probably dry) stream-beds, all feeding into the Ngarenairobi, you start to climb through burnt heather trees – the legacy of another fire, though thankfully new heather bushes are flourishing amongst the roots of the blackened remains – to the foot of the rounded hump known as the **Cathedral** (c3720m). The summit is gained soon after, the whole expedition from Shira 1 taking two hours and ten minutes or so. Panorama-wise, not only are there the delights of the plateau ahead and Kibo to your right but behind and to the east of the Cathedral your guide should be able to point out the faint traces of the Machame Route etched into the slopes. As a further reward, this is also said to be the first place on the Lemosho trail with mobile phone reception.

From the summit a stretch of ridge walking follows as you make your way north-east across the **East Shira Hill** and the other undulations of the crater rim. Eventually you come to a strange muddy area sprinkled with boulders, the lack of vegetation being due to poor drainage, according to one guide. The eastern end of this area has been converted into a **helipad** for the local flying doctors. This was also the spot used by IMAX to reprovision during the 40 days they spent on the mountain to film their *Kilimanjaro: To the Roof of Africa* documentary. Just a couple of minutes later you come to the **roadhead** – it's amazing to think that some trekkers on the Shira Route don't actually start walking until this point, though really the road should be used only by rescue vehicles beyond the Morum Barrier (see p272). It may be the end of the road for some, but you still have a further 30 minutes up to the **Shira Huts** (see p263 for description) and the day's end; and, if you're going to **Fischer Camp** (3885m), it's another twenty to thirty minutes further on from there.

STAGE 4: FISCHER/SHIRA HUTS TO LAVA TOWER
[MAP 16, opposite, MAP 10, p245]

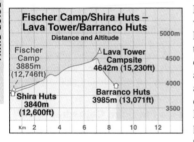

Fischer Camp/Shira Huts –
Lava Tower/Barranco Huts
Distance and Altitude

Fischer Camp 3885m (12,746ft)

Shira Huts 3840m (12,600ft)

Lava Tower Campsite 4642m (15,230ft)

Barranco Huts 3985m (13,071ft)

If you've spent the last three days marvelling at the silence and solitude of the Lemosho Route and wondering what all those newspaper articles about overcrowding on Kilimanjaro are talking about, today should provide you with an answer. For it is on this stage that the quiet but increasingly popular Lemosho Route (where, if you're lucky, it is still possible to feel like you're the only one on the mountain) merges with the already popular Machame Route. As a consequence, you won't be alone on the mountain anymore. Nor is it just solitude that you'll be bidding farewell to on this stage. The Shira Plateau takes a final bow, and as a result you'll be leaving the World of Heather for the Land of Lichen. True, those opting for the trek round the southern side of Kilimanjaro and the Barafu Route will reacquaint themselves with heathers, stoebes, lobelias and senecios at the magical Barranco Valley. But from now until the summit, the Barranco and other valleys excepted, it is the alpine desert that prevails.

What's more, as we are joining the Machame Route so there are two alternative routes to the summit – and it's on this stage that the two paths diverge. You can read about both of them on p246 onwards (regular route via Barranco Valley and the Barafu Route) and p267 onwards (Western Breach Route).

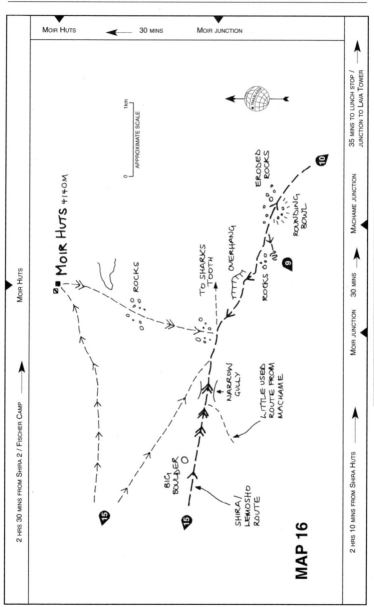

MOIR HUTS ← 30 MINS MOIR JUNCTION

1km

0

APPROXIMATE SCALE

MOIR HUTS 4140M

ROCKS

TO SHARKS TOOTH

OVERHANG

ERODED ROCKS

ROUNDING BOWL

ROCKS

10

9

NARROW GULLY

LITTLE USED ROUTE FROM MACHAME

BIG BOULDER

SHIRA/LEMOSHO ROUTE

15

15

MAP 16

2 HRS 30 MINS FROM SHIRA 2 / FISCHER CAMP →

MOIR HUTS

← MOIR HUTS

MOIR JUNCTION ↑

30 MINS ↑

MACHAME JUNCTION ↑

35 MINS TO LUNCH STOP / JUNCTION TO LAVA TOWER ↑

2 HRS 10 MINS FROM SHIRA HUTS ↑

TRAIL GUIDE AND MAPS

THE PATH TO THE MOIR HUTS

From the junction a thirty-minute path picks its way between boulders and around or over petrified lava flows before descending steeply down to the **Moir Huts** (4140m/13,579ft). Used mainly by those taking a 'rest' day to acclimatize – or by those few doing a complete circuit of Kibo – this campsite is set in a lovely sheer-sided valley. The valley sees few visitors and, as a result, the campsite is cleaner, tidier and certainly more peaceful than almost any other on the mountain. Indeed, even the white-necked ravens don't bother scavenging around here, the pickings presumably being too slim, and the silence as a result can be positively deafening. Apart from the three toilets, the only other building is a ruined pyramid-shaped hut, built as a sleeping shelter but now sadly vandalized. There are also some old elephant bones that somebody has carefully placed on one of the boulders, presumably to replace the buffalo bones that were once here but have now disappeared we know not where.

But you have to get to the Machame Route first, and that involves about 2 hours 40 minutes of uphill walking. As you probably expect, it's an easterly climb up the fairly gentle slope of the Shira Plateau, gradually forsaking the heather and moorland for something altogether more barren, where lichen-covered boulders predominate. Look out for the shiny black obsidian rock on the trail, not forgetting to look up occasionally to see Meru in the distance over your right shoulder. There are few steep passages to this stage, save for a brief clamber up a narrow gully on the route from Shira Huts, soon after which the trail from Fischer Camp merges with it. Ten minutes more of clambering on a fairly steep gradient and suddenly you find the path flattening out, just before the junction with the path to Moir Huts, which lie about 30 minutes away (see above). This junction is a popular place to rest and, if the mist that swirls around Kibo is in a particularly benign mood, a great place for photos too. There's also a 25-minute path from here to the foot of **Shark's Tooth**, the pointy little peak sitting to Kibo's north-west. The regular trail, however, bends right (south) to chop through a gully, from where it bends again to follow, approximately, a line of overhanging rocks. Bending south again, you now climb up to the top of the neighbouring ridge... and there, marked by some weird mushroom-rock formations, you meet the main Machame Route that has been contouring that ridge from the New Shira Camp.

Soon after, the path loops to the south-east and divides into two. It is here that those people who have opted to tackle the summit on the more difficult Western Breach Route branch off and head east towards the **Lava Tower**, a long and fairly steep uphill trek to this charmless campsite; while the rest (the majority) follow the more southerly, gentler trail as it bends round to the right. Just one minute after the fork the latter route comes upon a large flat, rocky surface – the **lunch stop** on this third leg. If you are taking the longer, easier route via Barafu, turn to p246 for a description of your trek; while if you're continuing on the Western Breach Route, read on.

STAGE 5: LAVA TOWER TO ARROW GLACIER CAMPSITE
[MAP 17, p269]

By our reckoning this particular leg, even taken *pole pole*, lasts little longer than an hour, yet it's not unusual for trekking agencies to set aside an entire day for it. In one respect this seems a little over-cautious and does lead to a situation where, that hour aside, you'll be spending the rest of your day freezing your butt off inside your tent. On the other hand, it's a good idea to take your time at this altitude. After all, save

Lava Tower – Arrow Glacier – Crater Rim – Uhuru Peak

Uhuru Peak 5895m (19,341ft)	6000m
Crater rim 5725m (18,783ft)	
Crater Campsite 5729m (18,796ft)	5500
Arrow Glacier Huts 4871m (15,981ft)	5000
Lava Tower Campsite 4642m (15,230ft)	Distance and Altitude 4500
Km 2 4 6 8 10 12	

for the crater camp this is the highest place where you can pitch your tent on the mountain at 4871m (15,981ft); and that kind of altitude should always be taken seriously.

Furthermore, the walk, though only sixty minutes or so in duration, is still quite exhausting, it being uphill just about all the way. You begin by crossing a stream or two (the same one, Bastions Stream, that runs below Lava Tower) before climbing steeply in a south-easterly direction to the top of a ridge. Near the top of the climb you pass an old trail running directly from Lava Tower to the Western Breach Route that bypasses the Arrow Glacier Campsite altogether; it's a path that's seldom used these days and unless your guide points it out to you, it's easily missed. Descending for a few seconds to a stream and then climbing to a second ridge, by following the direction of that ridge eastwards you soon come to the **Arrow Glacier Campsite** (4871m/15,981ft). Engulfed by avalanches and often subject to the vagaries of the extreme conditions up here, this place has always been a bit of a mess and little has changed. Whilst the rubbish is depressing, it's the toilets that are the most revolting spectacle, with the ones that haven't been destroyed now home to an entirely new geological form: neither stalactite nor stalagmite, but stalagshite. Console yourself with the thought that, if you're not spending a night on the summit, you won't be spending a full night here but should be away by 2am. Happy Camping!

STAGE 6: THE WESTERN BREACH ROUTE: ARROW GLACIER CAMPSITE TO UHURU PEAK   [MAP 17, p269, MAP 28, p301]

Over the years the Western Breach Route has acquired a certain aura and a reputation as the hardest of the summit routes. Nor is this reputation entirely undeserved. Though it's the shortest route, time-wise, it's also the steepest (with the mean gradient of the route said to be 26 degrees) and there's a bit of non-technical and very basic scrambling involved. What's more, and most worryingly, this trail is subject to frequent rockfalls and there are a couple of places where your guide will stop and listen out for any heading in your direction. At the very start of 2006 three American climbers perished due to a rockslide near Arrow Glacier

TRAIL GUIDE AND MAPS

Camp, with a fourth member of their team and four porters all very badly injured (about which, see the box on p270). That said, to hear some people talk about the Western Breach you'd think that you'd have to have the climbing capabilities of your average bluebottle in order to make it to the top. Suffice to say you don't. Yes, this route is a little trickier in parts. And yes, after snowfall the route up can be icy and an ice axe may be required in really extreme conditions, though it is only in extreme conditions. But as with all the trails in this book no technical climbing know-how is necessary – just the ability to haul yourself up by your hands on occasion when required.

So what are the benefits of doing this route? Well, firstly, the Western Breach is the only one that enters directly into the crater as opposed to the top of the rim that rises above it. As such, this is the route to take if you want to explore the Ash Pit, Reusch Crater, Furtwangler Glacier and other features of the summit. (Though it's possible to visit these features even if you climbed to the summit on other routes, we've yet to meet anyone who's actually done so; whatever their intentions before they reach the top of Kibo, by the time trekkers get there via Gillman's or Stella Point they're usually too knackered or in too much pain to spend the two hours-plus necessary to explore the crater.)

Another advantage of the Western Breach Route is that it is the one trail to the summit that's often tackled during the day rather than at night, traditionally by those intending to camp on the summit. (That said, the general consensus amongst Kili connoisseurs is that it's much easier to tackle this route at night,

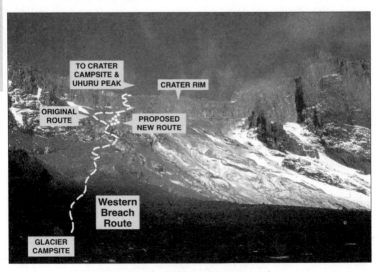

Western Breach Route

TRAIL GUIDE AND MAPS

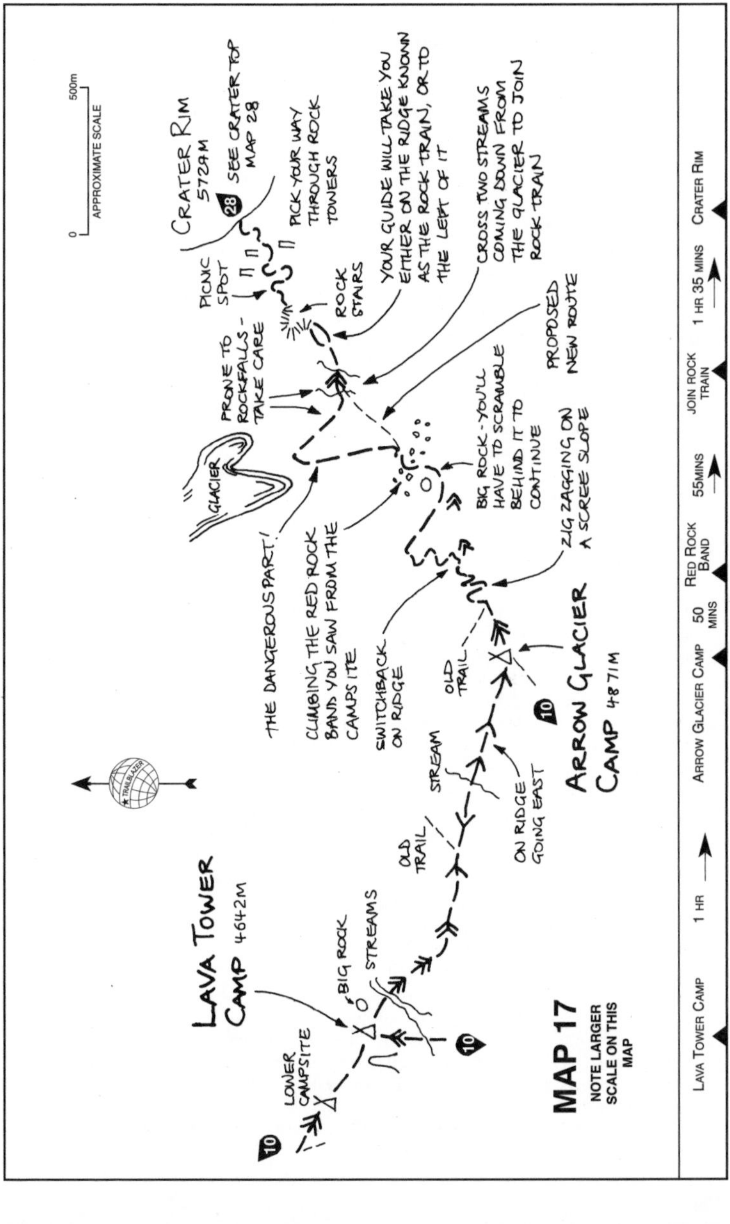

APPROXIMATE SCALE

0 ____ 500m

CRATER RIM
5729M

28 SEE CRATER TOP
MAP 28

PICK YOUR WAY
THROUGH ROCK
TOWERS

PICNIC SPOT

YOUR GUIDE WILL TAKE YOU
EITHER ON THE RIDGE KNOWN
AS THE ROCK TRAIN, OR TO
THE LEFT OF IT

ROCK STAIRS

PRONE TO
ROCKFALLS -
TAKE CARE

CROSS TWO STREAMS
COMING DOWN FROM
THE GLACIER TO JOIN
ROCK-TRAIN

GLACIER

PROPOSED
NEW ROUTE

THE DANGEROUS PART!

CLIMBING THE RED ROCK
BAND YOU SAW FROM THE
CAMPSITE

BIG ROCK - YOU'LL
HAVE TO SCRAMBLE
BEHIND IT TO
CONTINUE

SWITCHBACK
ON RIDGE

ZIG ZAGGING ON
A SCREE SLOPE

OLD
TRAIL

STREAM

ARROW GLACIER
CAMP 4871M

10

ON RIDGE
GOING EAST

LAVA TOWER
CAMP 4642M

OLD TRAIL

BIG ROCK

STREAMS

LOWER CAMPSITE

10

10

MAP 17
NOTE LARGER
SCALE ON THIS
MAP

TRAIL·CO

TRAIL GUIDE AND MAPS

| LAVA TOWER CAMP | 1 HR | ARROW GLACIER CAMP | 50 MINS | RED ROCK BAND | 55MINS | JOIN ROCK TRAIN | 1 HR 35 MINS | CRATER RIM |

The Western Breach Tragedy 2006

On 4 January 2006, three members from an American group were killed in a rockslide on Kibo. In addition, a fourth member was very badly injured, along with several porters. The accident happened near Arrow Glacier when a glacial deposit, estimated to weigh some 39 tonnes, collapsed and tumbled down the slope. According to early studies, the rocks tumbled some 150m and were falling at a speed of around 39m per second when they collided with the climbers. With an estimated wind speed of 177km/h that day – which may have been one of the reasons why the rocks fell in the first place – the climbers would have been unable to hear the rocks coming until just before they were struck, giving them no opportunity to take evasive action.

Once the dust had settled on the tragedy, the focus turned to what had actually happened and how to prevent it from happening again. To this end KINAPA, in conjunction with John Rees-Evans of Team Kilimanjaro, the trekking company that organizes the speed records on the mountain (see p26) and who regularly use the Western Breach Route, organized a reconnaissance party to explore the western side of Kibo.

Their conclusions seemed to back up John's initial theory that the tragedy was linked to the disappearance of Kilimanjaro's snowy summit. As the ice and glaciers melt, so the rocks and stones that have previously been bound to the mountain within the ice are released. In particular, John pointed to what he dramatically (but not inaccurately) termed a 'death zone' a hazardous stretch of the trail between about 5220m and 5310m (17,120-17,417ft) on the Western Breach Route. Though it takes less than an hour to cross, this zone is particularly vulnerable to rockfalls and is the riskiest part of this stage.

Having ascertained the causes, the next step was to find a solution. An initial proposal to dynamite the ice and outcrops to release the stones was eventually dismissed in favour of a route change to divert walkers away from the dangerous section. By opting for this new route, drawn on the map on p269, the estimated time that it would take trekkers to cross areas that were vulnerable to rockfalls (ie the 'death zone') would be dramatically reduced from just less than an hour to around five minutes.

Furthermore, they also recommended erecting a sign at Arrow Glacier to highlights the risks associated with this route and the dangers of climbing during the day (when the sun is high up in the sky, the ice melts and, as a result, rockfalls are more likely). Regular inspections of the trail and the surrounding rocks were also proposed, as well as consultations with geologists, seismologists and meteorologists to assess the chances of further rockfalls – both in the near future and the long term – due to the rapidly changing climatic situation on Kilimanjaro. It was also suggested that trekkers should be surveyed to see if they want the Western Breach Route to close altogether, even if the proposed new 'safer' route was opened.

At the present time the route remains closed while these recommendations are considered. But there is one point that is worth making here. Though you may believe rockfalls to be a hazard peculiar to the Western Breach Route and a concern only to the small number of trekkers who climb that trail each year, nothing could be further from the truth. The area between Hans Meyer Cave and Gillman's Point on the Kibo Huts Route (see p235), used by those on the Marangu and Rongai trails, and a couple of areas on the Barafu Route, used by those on the Lemosho/Shira, Machame and Umbwe paths, have also been subjected to rockfalls in the past and could do so again. And in these days of climate change and the melting of glaciers and snowcaps worldwide, the situation is likely only to get worse. Indeed, and though we shudder to think of such a possibility, is it possible that could we be seeing the beginning of the end of climbing on Kilimanjaro altogether?

when the scree, shale and rocks are frozen and thus less likely to move when you step on them; and that, furthermore, after dark the occasionally vertiginous drops are invisible, which makes climbing for vertigo sufferers much easier.)

And the third benefit of climbing via the Western Breach is, of course, the kudos that comes with having conquered the hardest non-technical route Kilimanjaro has to offer.

Do note, finally, that this route, though the shortest way to the top, is often the most expensive if you intend to camp at the summit because it is usual for porters to ask for a premium (US$50 per porter is the usual quote) to climb up there. This is understandable; on all other routes they don't go above 5000m (ie the altitude of the last campsite/huts), whereas here they have to go to the crater (above 5700m), and carry all their load up the trickiest route too.

Though we've talked as if there is one set path from the campsite to the crater rim, this isn't actually the case. With the land around this part of the mountain constantly shifting and the freezing conditions causing snow and ice to build up where once there was a trail, so the path changes as snow and rock-falls dictate. Every guide, too, has his own way of tackling the ascent, with only certain features common to each. As such, the map on p269 and the description that follows may differ from the exact route you end up taking. But whatever route you take, rest assured it will be steep, and it will be exhausting.

Having said that each path up the Western Breach is unique, your guide will doubtless aim for the rocky ridge that you can see from the Arrow Glacier Campsite which runs from the rock towers near the crater down towards the camp (often called the 'stone train'). It will take around an hour and three quarters before you properly join this ridge (soon after crossing a second stream), a walk that includes the most dangerous part of the ascent, where rockfalls are frequent. Furthermore, this area is often also covered in snow and many a guide has lost the path here. Successfully gain the ridge and about 15 minutes later you'll find yourself at the foot of the so-called **Rock Stairs** – natural steps that, after the shifting scree and rocks of the previous hour and three quarters, come as something of a relief. These stairs are also viewed as a 'Point of No Return' by the porters who, once they see that you've reached here, consider that there's no turning back and thus break camp and march off to Mweka (unless you're planning to sleep on the summit, of course, in which case they'll be right behind you).

The stairs take about 40 minutes to tackle altogether, at the end of which you find yourself on a small, flat space that's often used as a **picnic spot** by those tackling the Western Breach during the day. Dirty and chilly, a more inhospitable picnic spot it would be hard to find, though you do get great views down to the Barranco Campsite. Beyond the picnic site the stairs are replaced by a path that's just as steep, though you have to tackle this section without the benefit of any stairs. The trail picks its way between the rocky towers guarding the crater; but persevere for another 40 minutes and you'll find yourself finally gaining the crater rim, with the **Furtwangler Glacier** on your left the first of many spectacular sights up here. Walking on level ground for a change, it takes around ten minutes to reach the **Crater Campsite**, set amongst boulders at the foot of the climb up to Uhuru. The path up to the Reusch Crater and **Ash Pit Viewpoint**, 40 minutes away, bends north round and behind the Furtwangler Glacier. For more details on what's up here, see p300.

The stiff switchback climb up to Uhuru, 50 minutes away, lies to the south of the campsite, clearly etched into the crater wall. It's a hard climb and you'll be cursing every zigzag and switchback on the way. But keep going: the sense of achievement at the top is beyond compare. And it's a feeling that will stay with you all the way down, and all the way back to your home country. Because if you get to the summit, you'll believe you can do anything.

Oh, to be able to bottle that feeling...

The Shira Plateau Route

[MAP 18, opposite; MAP 15, p262; MAP 16, p265; , MAP 10, p245]
This is the older of the two trails and definitely inferior. The main problem is that for much of the first part you'll be walking on a 4WD road. Of course you could opt to drive to the end of the road, or at least the Morum Barrier which is as far as non-emergency vehicles can drive; but then you'll be missing out on the entire forest zone and, more importantly, some precious acclimatization, for you'll be starting your trek at around 3500m (11,480ft). Still, if this route does have one thing in its favour it is that, apart from the odd rescue car zooming past, you'll be just about certain to have the first part of the walk all to yourself.

Assuming you choose to start your walk in the forest, the first day is about six hours long (depending on where, exactly, the car drops you). During those six hours you'll leave the forest – which is, to be fair, gorgeous around here – for the heather and moorland zone, with the Ngarenairobi River an almost permanent presence to your right. The **first campsite** on the trail is sandwiched between the road and the river. Away to the south the northern slopes of the Shira Ridge loom up, while to your east lies the Morum Hill. But that's for tomorrow...

For the first couple of hours of the **second stage** the path winds mercilessly up the slope towards, and then to the south of, **Morum Hill**. At the foot of the hill is the **Morum Barrier**, where many Shira trekkers are dropped off – only emergency vehicles are allowed beyond here. If you *have* alighted here, depending on what time of day it is you can either walk for a couple of hours to one of the campsites on the plateau, or set up tent by the barrier and begin walking tomorrow.

This barrier marks the start of the Shira Plateau, where you'll be spending the next couple of days. The road continues south-south-east from the barrier, from where it's about another two hours to the junction with the Lemosho route and the **Simba Cave Campsite**. For details of the trail from here, please see p263.

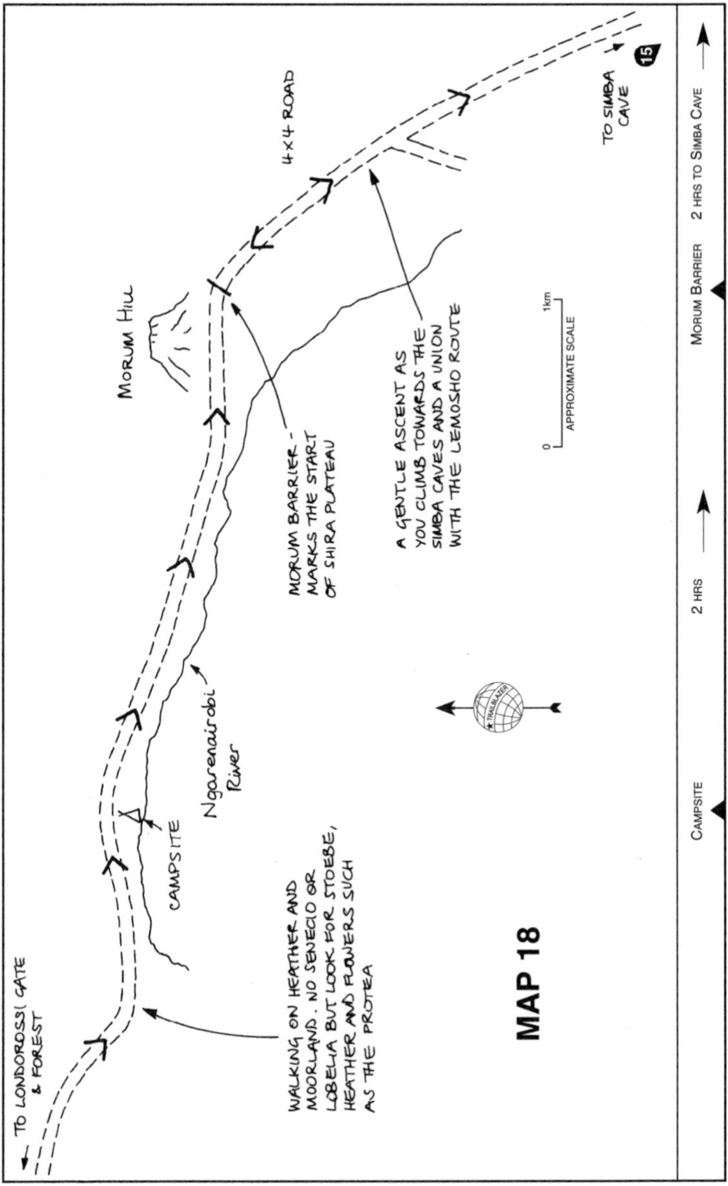
TO LONDOROSSI GATE & FOREST
WALKING ON HEATHER AND MOORLAND. NO SENECIO OR LOBELIA BUT LOOK FOR STOEBE, HEATHER AND FLOWERS SUCH AS THE PROTEA
MAP 18
CAMPSITE
Ngarenairobi River
MORUM HILL
MORUM BARRIER MARKS THE START OF SHIRA PLATEAU
A GENTLE ASCENT AS YOU CLIMB TOWARDS THE SIMBA CAVES AND A UNION WITH THE LEMOSHO ROUTE
0
1km
APPROXIMATE SCALE
4x4 ROAD
TO SIMBA CAVE
15
TRAILBLAZER
CAMPSITE
2 HRS
MORUM BARRIER
2 HRS TO SIMBA CAVE

The Rongai Route

Please convey to the seven blind climbers who reached the summit of Kilimanjaro my warm congratulations on their splendid achievement. **Queen Elizabeth II** in a telegram to Geoffrey Salisbury who, with his team of young, blind African trekkers, used the Rongai Route for their attempt on the mountain.

The name **Rongai Route** is actually something of a misnomer. Sure, it's the name that everybody uses but, strictly speaking, it's not the correct one. The real, original Rongai Route used to start at the border village of the same name but was closed several years ago by the authorities who decided that two trails on a side of the mountain that few trekkers visit was unnecessary. You will still see this route marked on many maps, but today all trekkers who wish to climb Kili from the north now follow a different trail, also known as the **Loitokitok Route** after the village that lies near the start. (Just to confuse the issue still further, this isn't officially the correct name either, for along the trail you'll see various signs calling this trail the **Nalemuru Route** – or, occasionally, Nalemoru – though this name is rarely used by anybody.)

At first glance, this trail seems decidedly unattractive. The lower slopes at the very start of the trail have been denuded by farmers and present a bleak landscape, while the forest that follows is little more than a narrow band of woodland which soon gives way to some rather hot and shadeless heathland. Indeed, the parched character of Kili's northern slopes often means trekking parties have to carry water along the way (often all the way from the Third Cave Campsite to the Outward Bound Hut); your agency should have supplied you with enough porters for this. Furthermore, because of its proximity to Kenya this route is also prone to the occasional foray by opportunist bandits from the Kenyan side who indulge in a little light larceny, before escaping Tanzanian jurisdiction by hot-footing it back to their homeland again. For this reason, groups trekking on the Rongai Route are accompanied by an armed guard (though to be honest, we didn't realize our party had one until he appeared out of the heather on the second day to bid his farewells). And then there's the expense: if you are booking your trek in Moshi, Arusha or Marangu, the cost of transporting you to the start of the trail can be quite exorbitant, pushing the price up above most other trails.

So why, if this route is more expensive, dangerous and barren than all the others, should anybody do it at all? Well for one thing, there's the **wildlife**. Because this side of the mountain sees fewer tourists, and because animals tend to gather where humans don't, your chances of seeing the local wildlife here are greater than on any other route bar, perhaps, those starting in the far west on the Shira Plateau. During the research for the first edition of this book we encountered a troop of colobus monkeys, while later that same day we came across an elephant skull, with elephant droppings and footprints nearby; and at night our little party was kept awake by something snuffling around the tents (a civet cat, according to our guide, though presumably one wearing heavy hobnail boots to judge by the amount of noise it was making). Buffaloes also frequent the few mountain streams on these northern slopes (though, as previously mentioned, these streams, never very deep, are almost always dry except in the rainy season, and consequently the buffaloes choose to bathe elsewhere for most of the year). The **flora** is different here too, with its juniper and olive trees. And if at the end of the ascent you do feel you've somehow missed out on some of the classic features of Kili – lobelias, for example, or the giant groundsels, which don't appear regularly on the northern side – then fear not, as both can be found in abundance on the Marangu Route, **the designated descent** for those coming from Rongai. Furthermore, opt for the extra day (see pp280-1) – which we strongly advise, for reasons not only of acclimatization – and you will spend that extra night at the **Mawenzi Tarn Hut**, which not only allows you to savour some gobsmacking views across to Kibo, as well as a grove of splendid senecios on this northern side, but also gives you the chance the following day to walk across the Saddle, many people's favourite part of the mountain. And finally, when it comes to the ascent, we found the walk from the Outward Bound Huts to Gillman's Point to be *marginally* easier than that from Kibo Huts, (though admittedly the two do share, for the last three or four hours to the summit, the same path).

Other advantages include the drive to the start: if you're coming from Kenya you'll drive through a landscape populated by giraffes and zebra, while from Moshi the road passes through a rural Chagga heartland, so giving you the chance to see village life Chagga-style (see p118), which we heartily recommend. Furthermore, if you manage to find other trekkers to join you and split the cost, the transport should not be too expensive.

But perhaps the best thing about the Rongai Route is the fact that it is **so unpopular**. Choose to undertake this route and you'll often be the only party on the whole of this side of the mountain. According to the only statistics available, 130 people climbed it in 2000. That's 130 out of more than 20,000 who climbed the mountain that year. When compared with the human jungle on Kili's southern side, the sense of isolation one feels when walking the Rongai Route is simply wonderful – and that is reason enough to recommend this trail.

PREPARATION

When booking your trek, it is important to get details right: are you staying at the cottages by Rongai Gate for the first night (in which case you won't need to pay any park or camping fees to the authorities for that first day, though you will have to pay something to Snow Cap – see p186 – for using their campsite)? Check too that lunch on the first day is included, for this is usually taken at a café in Tarakea. Finally, permits have to be collected at Marangu Gate; make sure your guide has that permit before embarking on the long drive to the gate.

The journey to Loitokitok

From Marangu Gate, the car returns down the hill to the bus station before continuing round the dry, eastern side of the mountain, through the villages of Mwika and Mrere, host to a big market on Saturday, in the heart of the **Rombo District**. After them, in order, the villages of Shauritanga (site of a horrific tragedy in June 1994, when 42 schoolgirls were burnt to death in a dormitory fire started by a candle), Olele, Usseru, Mashima and Kibaoni emerge through the dust before, finally, around an hour and a quarter from the Marangu junction, you arrive at Tarakea, the largest settlement in the district and the usual venue for lunch. Don't let your guide drink too much here – we've heard some horror stories about this.

There is also a border post with Kenya in Tarakea; presumably your guide will know *not* to take the road leading to it but instead to keep on hugging the main track which now heads north-west. The road continues to deteriorate until it is little more than pure sand and dust; keep your windows wound up.

Forty-five minutes after leaving Tarakea, you reach the wooden settlement of Loitokitok, where a track on the left branches up to the park gate, situated at around 2000m. From the gate you can see the smart **Snow Cap Cottages**, which resemble Swiss-style chalets... though only a bit. Still, it's a pleasant spot, with an open fire, TV room and a well-stocked bar that charges US$25 per night. Book through Snow Cap in Moshi (see p186 for contact details).

STAGE 1: LOITOKITOK TO FIRST CAVE CAMP [MAP 19, opposite]

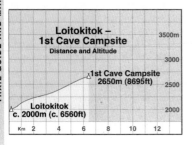

Loitokitok –
1st Cave Campsite
Distance and Altitude

1st Cave Campsite
2650m (8695ft)

Loitokitok
c. 2000m (c. 6560ft)

It is an inauspicious start to the trek. Having registered with the park official in his little wooden booth, your guide will then take you up the slopes through what, for many trekkers, is the ugliest part of Kilimanjaro, a hot and dusty blemish of corn and **cypress plantations** pockmarked here and there with the wooden shacks of those who eke out a living from the soil.

It is almost an hour before you escape this desolate scene for the lush green haven of the forest. When you do so, you'll be disappointed to find just how quickly the tall trees of the montane forest give way to the smaller, less robust varieties. The forest does make a second, equally brief appearance later on in the day fifteen minutes after the first one, but even then the **heathland** is quick to assert itself and thereafter remains the dominant landscape for the rest of the day.

It's tempting to blame the untrammelled agriculture for the paltry amount of decent rainforest here. No doubt the farmers have played their part, but the truth of the matter is that this side of Kili has never had much in the way of rainforest – simply because it never gets much in the way of rain. Besides, this narrow band of forest is still teeming with wildlife, in particular **colobus monkeys**, with a troop often grazing in the first tree by the entrance to the forest.

Leaving the forest on a trail that slowly steepens, half an hour afterwards you cross a stream and a few minutes later reach the first campsite on this route, known as the **First Cave Campsite** (though there are no significant

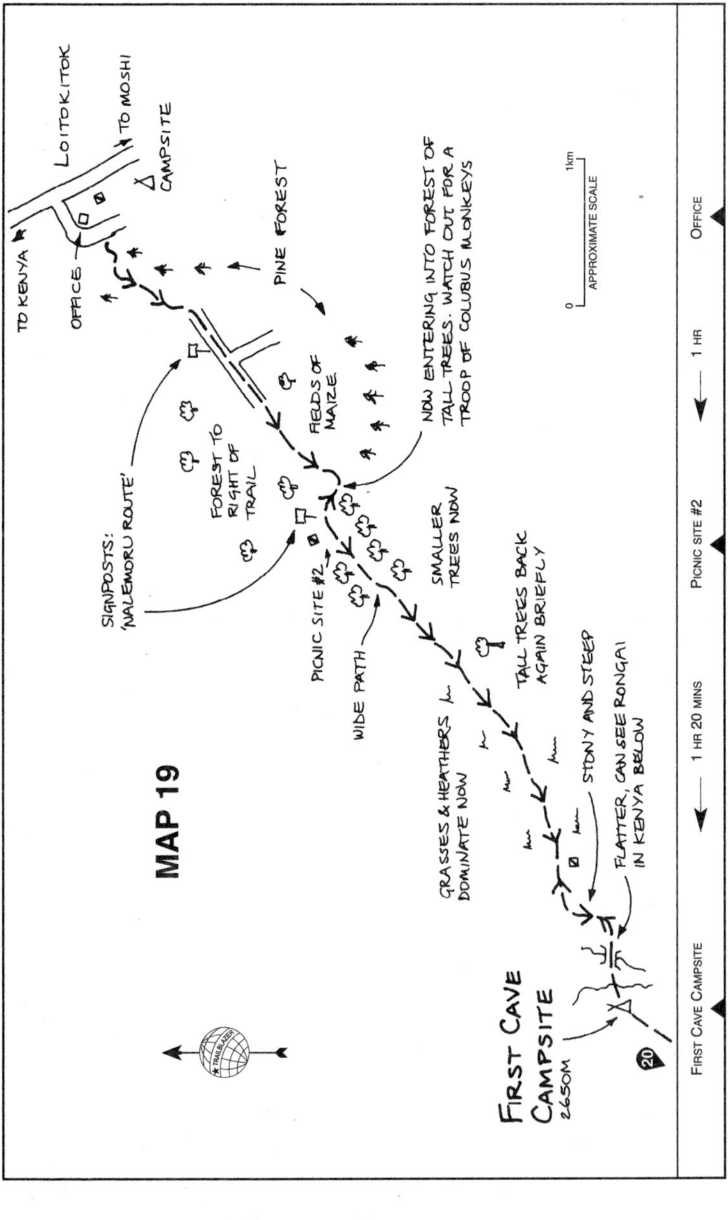

MAP 19

TO KENYA

LOITOKITOK

TO MOSHI

OFFICE

OFFICE

△ CAMPSITE

PINE FOREST

SIGNPOSTS:
'NALEMORU ROUTE'

FOREST TO
RIGHT OF TRAIL

FIELDS OF MAIZE

NOW ENTERING INTO FOREST OF
TALL TREES. WATCH OUT FOR A
TROOP OF COLOBUS MONKEYS

PICNIC SITE #2

SMALLER TREES NOW

WIDE PATH

TALL TREES BACK
AGAIN BRIEFLY

GRASSES & HEATHERS NOW
DOMINATE NOW

STONY AND STEEP

FLATTER, CAN SEE RONGAI
IN KENYA BELOW

FIRST CAVE CAMPSITE
2650M

20

0   1km
APPROXIMATE SCALE

| FIRST CAVE CAMPSITE | 1 HR 20 MINS | PICNIC SITE #2 | 1 HR | OFFICE |

TRAIL GUIDE AND MAPS

caves nearby), at an altitude of 2650m. You have already gained 650m in altitude in the 6km or so since you started walking. It's always good to get to a campsite, and this one in particular is pleasant: with creatures snuffling about the tent at night and birdsong from the Hunter's cisticolas in the morning, this spot has a pleasingly wild, isolated ambience.

STAGE 2: FIRST CAVE TO THIRD CAVE CAMP   [MAP 20, opposite]

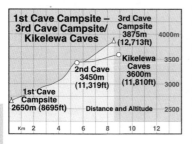

This stage perhaps lacks the variety of other stages. For most of the day you will be walking up slopes flanked with heather and erica, with the twin peaks of Kilimanjaro keeping a watchful eye as you progress. If you're on a five-day trek, during this stage you will bid farewell to those lucky trekkers who opted to take the extra day and visit the Mawenzi Tarn Hut; they will go their own way after lunch. (That route is described on p280.) For the 'five-dayers', by the end of today you will have ascended more than 1100m, from 2650m at the First Cave Campsite to 3875m at the campsite at the end of this stage, the Third Cave. But there's no gain without pain, and today is long, involving almost four and a half hours of steady walking on a steep, dusty path. Take comfort from the fact that tomorrow is much easier, and that you have already ascended more than 1775m from the gate, and are now well over halfway to the summit.

The path at the start of this 8.5km stage is, perhaps surprisingly, a westward one, its goal seeming to be the northern slopes of Kibo rather than the eastern slopes that you will eventually climb. The heathers are gradually shrinking in size now too, and while there are still some trees clinging on at this altitude, they are few in number and scattered. For these reasons, the first part of this stage is rather shadeless and very hot. After 45 minutes a **river bed** (dry for the best part of the year) joins you from the left and the path follows its course for most of the next hour. Look back occasionally and, weather permitting, you should be able to see a number of villages on the Kenyan side of the border, the sunlight glinting off the metal roofs. Continuing upwards, the path steepens slightly and begins to turn more to the south, passing the **junction** with the old Rongai Route, where an armed guard you never knew you had may suddenly appear and bid you farewell. It's just as well you don't have to pay for him. Most strange.

The terrain up here is rather rocky and bumpy. The path continues south-south-west, rounding a few minor cliffs and hills and crossing a number of false summits, before eventually flattening out and arriving at a small, waterless cave. As inviting as the cave and the shade it offers now appear, this is not your lunch stop, known as the **Second Cave** (3450m), which lies twenty minutes further on through lizard country of bare rocks and long grasses.

(Continued on p282)

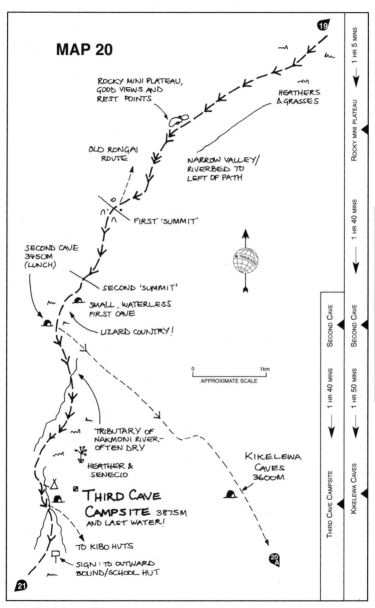

MAP 20

ROCKY MINI PLATEAU, GOOD VIEWS AND REST POINTS

HEATHERS & GRASSES

OLD RONGAI ROUTE

NARROW VALLEY/ RIVERBED TO LEFT OF PATH

FIRST 'SUMMIT'

SECOND CAVE 3450M (LUNCH)

SECOND 'SUMMIT'

SMALL, WATERLESS FIRST CAVE

LIZARD COUNTRY!

TRAIL GUIDE

0   1km
APPROXIMATE SCALE

TRIBUTARY OF NAKMONI RIVER— OFTEN DRY

HEATHER & SENECIO

THIRD CAVE CAMPSITE 3875M AND LAST WATER!

KIKELEWA CAVES 3600M

TO KIBO HUTS

SIGN : TO OUTWARD BOUND/SCHOOL HUT

1 HR 5 MINS → ROCKY MINI PLATEAU

1 HR 40 MINS → SECOND CAVE

SECOND CAVE

1 HR 50 MINS → KIKELEWA CAVES

1 HR 40 MINS → THIRD CAVE CAMPSITE

TRAIL GUIDE AND MAPS

❏ THE MAWENZI TARN HUT ROUTE [MAP 20, p279, p20A, opposite]

As alternative paths go, this is wonderful. Great views, great scenery and a useful way to acclimatize, if you can afford the extra day on the mountain, don't hesitate. From the Second Cave, the usual lunch stop on the second day, the path takes an abrupt south-easterly turn directly towards the jagged peak of Mawenzi. Traversing open moorland, the path is straightforward if occasionally a little indistinct through lack of use. Your camp on this second day is near a small set of grottoes known as **Kikelewa Caves**. These lie just below the Saddle, set in a valley of the same name that is rich in senecios. The caves lie at an altitude of around 3600m; since the Second Cave you have walked about 3.5km, but have gained just 150m in altitude. It's an easy, gentle walk. The campsite lies on the heathland and is surrounded by heathers and stoebes.

Kikelewa Caves to Mawenzi Tarn Hut

Though the next two days are short, this second day is also steep. Initially, the path continues its idle south-east-erly course, before rising on an expo-nential gradient to your destination, shedding the moorland vegetation as it does so, though a wealth of senecios line the path. The **Mawenzi Tarn Hut** (4330m) is situated in one of the most spectacular settings of any camp, in a cirque right beneath the jagged teeth of Mawenzi. There is a small wooden

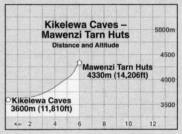

Kikelewa Caves –
Mawenzi Tarn Huts
Distance and Altitude

Mawenzi Tarn Huts
4330m (14,206ft)

Kikelewa Caves
3600m (11,810ft)

5000m
4500
4000
3500

Km 2   4   6   8   10   12

hut here and a dining hall too, though most companies these days prefer their clients to camp. You are now at an altitude of 4330m and assuming the walk here was trou-ble-free you should have most of the afternoon to explore the barrancos and towers of this secondary peak. Make the most of it: few people get here, and there's plenty to see and discover, including, of course, the tarn itself – though really it's little more than a puddle. Nevertheless, a few brave (ie 'foolish') souls insist on taking a dip. Wherever you go, take a guide.

Mawenzi Tarn Hut to Kibo Huts or School Huts

On the third day you strike a direct westerly course, tiptoeing along the northern edge of the beautifully barren Saddle. Having rounded the northern slopes of Mawenzi, the path descends gently on its western slopes before hitting the Saddle itself, with wonderful views north, south, east and west. The vegeta-tion is sparse but do look out for eland, which are said to occasionally stroll up here. You have two destinations at the end of this third day: the School Huts (the more usual destination on this route) or the Kibo Huts. Both lie on the lower

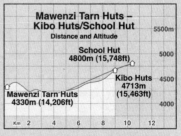

Mawenzi Tarn Huts –
Kibo Huts/School Hut
Distance and Altitude

School Hut
4800m (15,748ft)

Kibo Huts
4713m
(15,463ft)

Mawenzi Tarn Huts
4330m (14,206ft)

5500m
5000
4500
4000

Km 2   4   6   8   10   12

slopes of Kibo and both are just a few hours' walk away along the largely flat Saddle.

Depending on which hut you end up at, please see either p234 or p283 for the con-tinuation of your walk up to Gillman's and Uhuru.

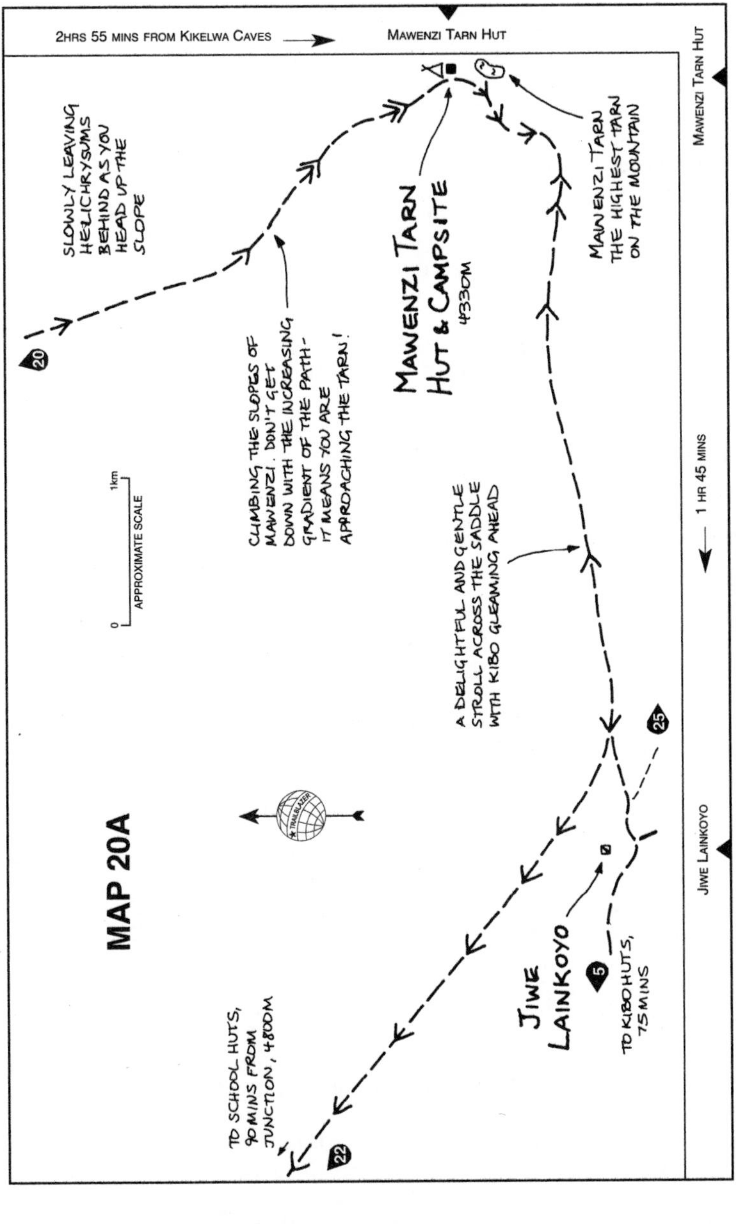

MAP 20A

2HRS 55 MINS FROM KIKELWA CAVES →

MAWENZI TARN HUT

SLOWLY LEAVING HELICHRYSUMS BEHIND AS YOU HEAD UP THE SLOPE

20

0 1km
APPROXIMATE SCALE

CLIMBING THE SLOPES OF MAWENZI. DON'T GET DOWN WITH THE INCREASING GRADIENT OF THE PATH— IT MEANS YOU ARE APPROACHING THE TARN!

MAWENZI TARN HUT & CAMPSITE 4330M

MAWENZI TARN THE HIGHEST TARN ON THE MOUNTAIN

A DELIGHTFUL AND GENTLE STROLL ACROSS THE SADDLE WITH KIBO GLEAMING AHEAD

25

JIWE LAINKOYO

5

TO KIBO HUTS, 75 MINS

22

TO SCHOOL HUTS, 90 MINS FROM JUNCTION, 4800M

MAWENZI TARN HUT

1 HR 45 MINS

JIWE LAINKOYO

TRAIL GUIDE AND MAPS

Before setting off in the afternoon, make sure you are on the right trail, for the path to the Mawenzi Tarn Hut branches off at this point (see p280), so if your destination is the Third Cave Campsite but you find yourself heading south-east, reconsider. The path to the Third Cave begins behind and above the caves, from where it now bears off in a more southerly direction than heretofore. Crossing a wide and usually dry riverbed, which in the rainy season is a popular playground for buffaloes, the path continues drifting southwards across increasingly arid terrain, the 'dry flower' helichrysum now interspersed amongst the heathers. As huge rocks begin to appear to left and right, temporarily obscuring Mawenzi and Kibo, the unmistakable outline of toilet huts appear ahead on the trail, a sure sign that the campsite is nearing, this time to your left across another broad riverbed. This is the Third Cave Campsite and the **last water point** before the summit.

STAGE 3: THIRD CAVE CAMPSITE TO SCHOOL HUT
[MAP 20, p279, MAP 21, opposite, MAP 22, p284]

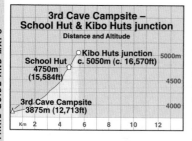

**3rd Cave Campsite –
School Hut & Kibo Huts junction**
Distance and Altitude

Kibo Huts junction
c. 5050m (c. 16,570ft)   5000m
School Hut
4750m
(15,584ft)   4500

3rd Cave Campsite
3875m (12,713ft)   4000

Km   2   4   6   8   10   12

This stage is little more than an *hors d'oeuvre* for the main course, which will be served at around midnight tonight. Yet it may surprise you to find out that over the course of this stage you climb 875m – just 300m less than the previous stage, even though today's walk takes less than half the time. By the end of it you'll be on the eastern slopes of Kibo, with splendid views across the Saddle to Mawenzi just a few minutes' walk away.

If you haven't already been doing so, this is also the time to take things deliberately *pole pole* ('slowly slowly' in Swahili) – you're reaching some serious altitudes now, and mountain sickness stalks the unwary. Looking south-west from the Third Cave Campsite, you should be able to see today's path snaking over the undulations of Kibo. The path begins by retracing the last few steps of yesterday back to the river bed, which forks just a few minutes after the campsite into two distinct tributaries. The path, too, divides at this junction and is signposted, with your trail heading off to the right, crossing the western tributary and continuing on towards the foot of Kibo. It's a slow slog southwards up the hill. Even the heathers struggle to survive up here, disappearing for the last time less than an hour outside camp; only the *helichrysum*, including the occasional yellow everlasting, continue to thrive, providing a welcome relief from the relentless greys and browns of the rocky soil.

After about 75 minutes a summit of sorts is reached, whereafter the path now heads more to the west, directly towards Kibo. The Northern Circuit bisects our trail around here, though this path is so seldom used that the junction is easily missed. No matter, for your path is clear as it bends more to the south, traversing Kibo's eastern slopes with the western face of Mawenzi now in full view to your

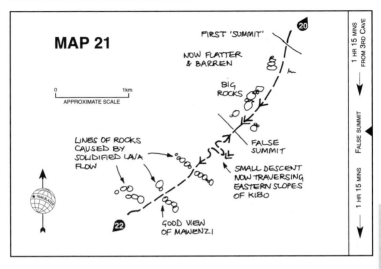

MAP 21

FIRST 'SUMMIT'

NOW FLATTER
& BARREN

BIG
ROCKS

0   1km
APPROXIMATE SCALE

LINES OF ROCKS
CAUSED BY
SOLIDIFIED LAVA
FLOW

FALSE
SUMMIT

SMALL DESCENT
NOW TRAVERSING
EASTERN SLOPES
OF KIBO

★ TRAILBLAZER

GOOD VIEW
OF MAWENZI

20

1 HR 15 MINS FROM 3RD CAVE

FALSE SUMMIT

1 HR 15 MINS

22

TRAIL GUIDE AND MAPS

left. This last bit of the walk is steep, and with the drop in oxygen at this altitude, quite exhausting. But after little more than an hour from the western bend in the path, you finally reach the **School Hut** (marked as the Outward Bound Huts on some maps, though this is its former name and one that KINAPA would prefer you didn't use), sitting in the shadow of some rather daunting cliffs. The huts sit at an altitude of about 4750m. If there are no tour groups that day, the chances are you'll have the place to yourself, save perhaps for an impressive mountain buzzard that likes to scavenge here from time to time when the place is deserted. Officially you should still use your tent rather than the hut to sleep in; for a small consideration, however, (namely a beer or two) the caretaker might consider letting you use the hut if that is what you prefer. Incidentally, if you need to fetch help for any reason, the Kibo Huts, larger and permanently manned by park staff, lie just 25 minutes to the south, the path beginning by the southernmost toilet hut.

STAGE 4: SCHOOL HUT TO THE KIBO HUTS ROUTE AND GILLMAN'S POINT   [MAP 22, p284]

The higher we climbed the rarer grew the atmosphere and the more brilliant the light of the stars. Never in my life have I seen anything to equal the steady lustre of this tropical starlight. The planets seemed to grow with a still splendour which was more than earthly, ... Assuredly, the nights of lower earth know nothing of this silver radiance.
Hans Meyer *Across East African Glaciers* (1891)

There is no direct trekking route from the School Hut to the crater rim. Instead, the path heads south from the huts to join up with the 'Tourist trail' running from Kibo Huts towards Gillman's Point – the trail that we have dubbed the Kibo Huts Route. Your trail joins it between William's Point (about 5000m) and

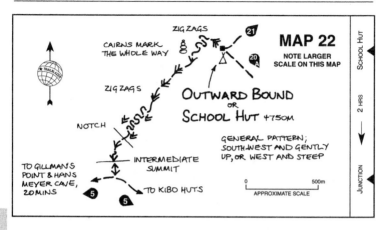

Hans Meyer Cave (5151m). In our experience, it takes slightly – though only slightly – less time from the School Hut to this junction than it does from Kibo Huts, so you may wish to start this stage a little later than you would if walking from Kibo Huts – say at 12.15-12.30am rather than midnight.

Finding the start of the path from the School Hut can be a little tricky in the dark, so we recommend that you or your guide conduct a little reconnaissance while it's still light to ensure you knows where you're supposed to go. Once you're on the path, which starts with a scramble up the rocks behind the School Hut, the trail becomes fairly clear, being marked with cairns the whole way. A repetitive pattern emerges during the walk: generally you are walking in a south-westerly direction over scree, but every so often the path turns more westerly and climbs more steeply over solid rock – these being petrified lava flows. At the end, a short descent brings you into the Kibo Huts 'valley' and a union with the path up to Gillman's. After the isolation of the last three days, the number of trekkers on this path comes as something of a shock. Hans Meyer Cave lies just twenty minutes above you along a series of switchbacks. For details of the path up to Gillman's Point from Hans Meyer Cave, turn to p235. For the descent you'll be using the Marangu Route, details of which can be found on p292.

The Umbwe Route

If Marangu is the 'Coca Cola Route' and Machame has the nickname 'The Whiskey Route', then what does that make Umbwe, (in)famous as the hardest of the trails on Kili. Sure, Machame is *fairly* steep here and there. But on Umbwe, the gradient is such that in a couple of places on the first day you can stand upright on the trail and kiss it *at the same time*. What's more, since the Machame path has been renovated, it's now only on the Umbwe trail that you'll be trekking on tree roots for much of the first day. So while Machame is still popularly called 'The Whiskey Route', since its recent renovation that whiskey has been rather watered down; and when compared to the unadulterated Umbwe Route, Machame starts to seem like pretty small beer.

That said, the Umbwe Route is still **a non-technical climb**. Taxing, but not technical. All you need are an iron will and calves of steel; this is truly a trek to test your mettle. The difficulty is that it's so damn relentlessly uphill. Indeed, looking back on the first couple of days we can think of very few places where you actually descend, the longest being the five minutes or so at the end of the second stage when you walk down to the Barranco Campsite.

As far as rewards go, while your calves and thighs will curse the day God paired them with somebody who would want to undertake such a climb, your heart and lungs will be thankful for the workout. Your eyes, too, will be grateful you chose Umbwe as they feast upon the scenery, particularly on the second morning as you leave the forest and find yourself walking on a narrow ridge between spindly heathers. The gobsmacking views on either side of the trail here are amongst the most dramatic the mountain has to offer, save for those on the summit itself. Your ears, too, will be glad that they're stuck to the side of your head rather than anyone else's for they'll enjoy the break, this being the quietest trail of them all – at least until the second day when you find yourself joining the hordes at Barranco Camp, the busiest on the mountain. Once at Barranco, you can either follow the majority round to Barafu and access the summit via Stella Point; or, if you hanker after the quieter, more dramatic option once again, you can join the path up to Lava Tower and continue to the summit via the Western Breach (see p267). This latter option is the connossieur's choice, no doubt, though be warned that it's an extremely risky strategy unless you take at least one – and preferably two – acclimatization days en route to the Arrow Glacier Hut. Otherwise, the trip from Moshi up to Arrow Glacier Hut, an increase in altitude of almost 4000m, will have taken you just three days which is far too rapid. Do this and you can kiss your golden certificate – and possibly a lot more – goodbye.

So that's Umbwe: dramatic views, blessed solitude and some terrific, invigorating walking – and all without the clutter and chatter of other trekkers. Those who know the mountain consider it Kili's best-kept secret. And it's hard to argue with that.

STAGE 1: UMBWE GATE TO UMBWE CAVE CAMPSITE
[MAP 23, opposite]

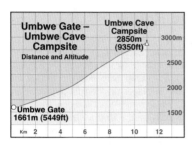

The first stage of this route transforms itself from a tiring tramp on a 4WD trail to a terrific trek on tree roots. It's normal to start this stage fairly late in the day, for permits for this route are issued not at Umbwe Gate but at Marangu, and they have to be fetched before you can begin. If you specifically want to start early it might be worth asking your agency if they can fetch the permit the day before. (This may be not be such a bad idea, for our guide on this trail told us of one occasion when, due to torrential rain that washed away the road leading to Umbwe, the group he was leading didn't actually arrive at Umbwe Campsite until 10pm!)

As the closest gate to Moshi, getting to the start of the trail should be uncomplicated. Turning off the Moshi-Arusha road just ten minutes after leaving the former, you bid farewell to the joys of tarmac by heading north on a mud track to Umbwe. Incidentally, if you want to get any last minute supplies for the trail, you're best off doing so in Moshi or Arusha; from Moshi the last reliable place is the Highway Supermarket and those other, smaller stalls near the Karanga River. There are some others on the Umbwe Road but both the stock and opening times of these establishments are unreliable.

Passing banana plantations (with much of the produce in this region going to make banana wine, bottled in Arusha) you soon reach the gate itself, where there's little save for some toilets and a couple of friendly and under-worked rangers. This is also the place where you should pay your forest fee – the only route other than Lemosho where you must fork out for the forest before you can begin (your trekking agency should have already sorted this out).

After the usual pfaffing around at the gate, you eventually begin your walk by setting off on a 4WD road. With monkeys (blue and colobus) crashing in the trees, turacos gliding above them, chameleons stalking amongst the shrubbery and some of Kilimanjaro's more celebrated flora putting in an appearance, including a profusion of *Impatiens pseudoviola* and, further on, its more glamorous, beautiful, and rarer cousin, *Impatiens kilimanjari*, it's a fine start. Look out, too, for *Senecio Johnstonii sp. cheranganiensis*, with their strange phallic brush growing out of the top of the plant. This route is one of the few places where you can find them on the mountain (the Lemosho Route is another), though they appear in greater abundance on Mount Meru. If it's the weekend, you'll also be sharing the path with dozens of kids collecting fodder, probably illegally, from the forest.

No matter how interesting this initial walk is, after almost two hours it comes as something of a relief when the road finally ends and the Umbwe trail 'proper' begins. It's a path that continues the north/north-north-east trend of the

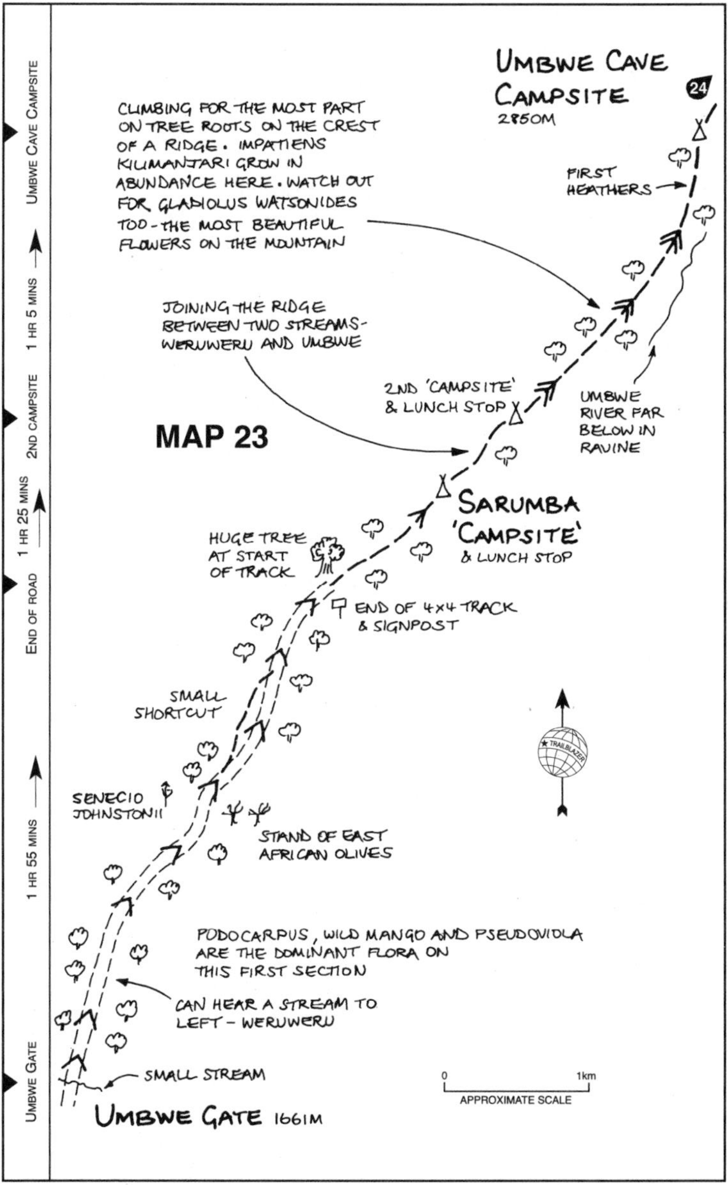

UMBWE CAVE CAMPSITE

1 HR 5 MINS →

2ND CAMPSITE

1 HR 25 MINS →

END OF ROAD

1 HR 55 MINS →

UMBWE GATE

UMBWE CAVE CAMPSITE 2850M

24

FIRST HEATHERS →

CLIMBING FOR THE MOST PART ON TREE ROOTS ON THE CREST OF A RIDGE. IMPATIENS KILIMANJARI GROW IN ABUNDANCE HERE. WATCH OUT FOR GLADIOLUS WATSONIDES TOO - THE MOST BEAUTIFUL FLOWERS ON THE MOUNTAIN

JOINING THE RIDGE BETWEEN TWO STREAMS - WERUWERU AND UMBWE

2ND 'CAMPSITE' & LUNCH STOP

UMBWE RIVER FAR BELOW IN RAVINE

MAP 23

SARUMBA 'CAMPSITE' & LUNCH STOP

HUGE TREE AT START OF TRACK

END OF 4×4 TRACK & SIGNPOST

SMALL SHORTCUT

SENECIO JOHNSTONII

STAND OF EAST AFRICAN OLIVES

PODOCARPUS, WILD MANGO AND PSEUDOVIOLA ARE THE DOMINANT FLORA ON THIS FIRST SECTION

CAN HEAR A STREAM TO LEFT - WERUWERU

SMALL STREAM

UMBWE GATE 1661M

0   1km
APPROXIMATE SCALE

TRAIL GUIDE AND MAPS

road, though in our opinion it's considerably more charming. For much of it you'll be walking not on the soil but actually on tree roots. These can be your best friend, providing steps up a trail which would otherwise be too steep; or, if it's been raining, they can be your worst enemy, causing you to slip and swear.

Almost an hour after leaving the road you reach the first of two lunch-stops, this one known amongst guides and porters as **Sarumba** after the guide who frequently used it as a campsite for the first night. Halfway between here and a second possible campsite/lunch stop you realize that you've actually joined a ridge – and a spectacular one at that, with the great forested ravine of the Umbwe River on one side and the more modest dip of the Lonzo Stream on the other. No doubt you've also noticed that the trail is getting increasingly steeper. Indeed, this ridge is one of the steepest parts of the entire trek, and in places you'll be using the tree roots to haul yourself up with your hands. Luckily, there are plenty of tree roots around. The forest around here is rich and dark, the forest canopy minimizing the amount of light that filters through to the path. Distract yourself from the muffled screaming coming from your calf muscles by admiring the beauty of the forest here, the trees all knobbled, gnarled and heavy with moss. In between breaths, check out the beautiful red *Impatiens kilimanjari*, too, growing between those same tree roots that are helping you progress along the path.

An hour after joining the ridge you reach the first heathers on the trail. As those who've trekked on other routes will know, this change from forest to heathland often heralds the end of the first day and so it is here, with the end of the first stage, Umbwe Cave Campsite, lying just ten minutes away. More a glorified overhang than a proper cave, the adjacent campsite dribbles up the ridge and is a charming spot, a quiet place hidden in the upper reaches of the forest with *Impatiens kilimanjari* dotted here and there amongst the tents.

Let's just hope you started your trek in time to reach it.

STAGE 2: UMBWE CAVE TO BARRANCO HUTS [MAP 24, opposite]

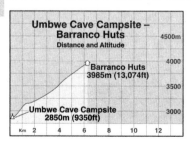

Umbwe Cave Campsite – Barranco Huts
Distance and Altitude

4500m

4000

Barranco Huts
3985m (13,074ft)

3500

Umbwe Cave Campsite
2850m (9350ft)

3000

Km 2   4   6   8   10   12

This second stage of the Umbwe Route is a showcase for the weird and wonderful. It's the stage where you move from the forest, past a magical stretch of giant heathers and on to the moorland zone where giant groundsels – surely the strangest plants on Kilimanjaro – grow in abundance. The walking, as with yesterday's stage, is pretty much uphill all the way, though again is tiring rather than technical and thus nothing to fear. By the end you will have reached Barranco Campsite, a wonderful spot at the junction of a number of routes and on the border of the alpine

(**Opposite**) The beautiful scenery and strange flora of the Barranco Huts make this the most popular campsite on the mountain.

desert. Note that Machame Route trekkers will have taken three days to get to this camp, and those on the Lemosho Route four. It gives you some idea of just how steep the Umbwe Route is; it should also remind you, if you didn't know before, of the importance of building in rest days and of taking it *pole pole* from now on.

The stage starts with a tramp through one of the prettiest sections – no make that *the* prettiest section – of heathland on the entire mountain, the sunlight penetrating through the giant heathers to dapple the carpet of soft mossy grass. We've never seen heather forest so thick, so uniform, so laden with bearded lichen nor so gorgeous. Though normally lumped together with the moorland

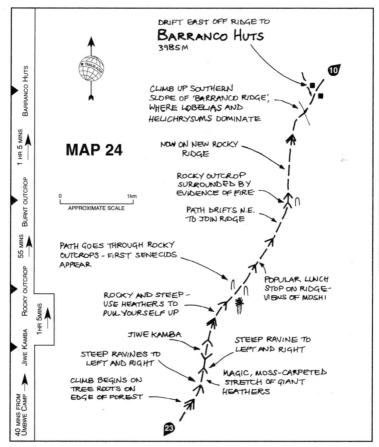

MAP 24

DRIFT EAST OFF RIDGE TO
BARRANCO HUTS
3985M

CLIMB UP SOUTHERN SLOPE OF 'BARRANCO RIDGE', WHERE LOBELIAS AND HELICHRYSUMS DOMINATE

NOW ON NEW ROCKY RIDGE

ROCKY OUTCROP SURROUNDED BY EVIDENCE OF FIRE

PATH DRIFTS N.E. TO JOIN RIDGE

PATH GOES THROUGH ROCKY OUTCROPS - FIRST SENECIOS APPEAR

POPULAR LUNCH STOP ON RIDGE - VIEWS OF MOSHI

ROCKY AND STEEP - USE HEATHERS TO PULL YOURSELF UP

JIWE KAMBA

STEEP RAVINE TO LEFT AND RIGHT

STEEP RAVINES TO LEFT AND RIGHT

MAGIC, MOSS-CARPETED STRETCH OF GIANT HEATHERS

CLIMB BEGINS ON TREE ROOTS ON EDGE OF FOREST

0   1km
APPROXIMATE SCALE

Barranco Huts — 1 HR 5 MINS — Burnt outcrop — 55 MINS — Rocky outcrop — 1HR 5MINS — Jiwe Kamba — 40 MINS FROM UMBWE CAMP

TRAIL GUIDE AND MAPS

(Opposite) Top: Smiling (or grimacing) at the summit (see p300).
Bottom: The Ash Pit sits at the heart of the Reusch Crater (see p302); few people get here.

above it, here, as with the Mweka Route that you'll be tackling on the way down, the heather zone is so very distinct from it. As the path veers to the left you realize you're overlooking the vertiginous valley of the Lonzo Stream, (a tributary of the Weru Weru) while veer right and you find yourself staring down the giddying ravine of the Umbwe – and you suddenly realize you're balanced on a knife-edge ridge. Vertigo sufferers should perhaps concentrate instead on Kibo which, if the weather's on your side, glistens magnificently ahead.

Around 40 minutes after breaking camp you reach **Jiwe Kamba**, or 'Rope Rock', the name providing a clue as to how trekkers used to tackle this section. The rope's gone now and though the larger groups still bring their own, it's no problem if you didn't – it's just a few careful steps to the top, rope or no rope. The going is a little rockier from now on and you'll soon find yourself using the vegetation flanking the path to haul yourself up on occasion. As you progress further north the first helichrysums appear, their paper texture and white colour contrasting with the scarlet *Gladiolus watsonides* which survives in both the forest and heathland zones and is surely the most beautiful flower on the mountain. Continue still further and amongst the tussock grass and rocky outcrops the first senecios also put in an appearance.

The ridge which you've been following eventually merges with a new one which you also climb and then follow, still heading north and with Mount Meru now a spectator in the distance. Climbing to yet another rocky ridge, this one with clear signs of having suffered fire damage, you continue your progress north towards what we will call Barranco Ridge, which you start to climb before turning off right and down to the Barranco Huts themselves. For a description, please turn to p246.

It is at Barranco that you have a choice to make: left, north-west and up for the Lava Tower Campsite, Arrow Glacier Campsite and the path via the Western Breach to the summit. Or right, east and up to Karanga, Barafu and the path up to the summit via Stella Point. Presumably you will have already decided one way or the other. If you've opted for the more popular route via the Barafu Campsite, turn to p247 for the continuation of this trail. Whereas if you're gunning for the Western Breach, read on...

STAGE 3: BARRANCO HUTS TO LAVA TOWER CAMPSITE
[MAP 10, p245]

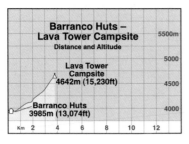

It is the nature of the trails on Kili that many started as porters' routes. That is to say that the porters originally established them before the guides and their clients also adopted them and, eventually, the authorities too. Furthermore, it is of course the nature of porters to find the quickest route from A to B, with little thought given as to whether it's a pretty or attractive route.

And so it is with today's trail from Barranco up to Lava Tower, the start of the climb up to the Western Breach. It's a short-cut that was established by porters hurrying down from Arrow Glacier or Lava Tower round to the Mweka Route, in order to meet their clients arriving down from the summit. This trail has become so established as to render the previous route just about obsolete. (That previous route, by the way, continued along the crest of the ridge to the west of the Barranco Campsite to the signposted junction at the head of the Barranco Valley and is still marked on most maps, though it's a rare guide who'll follow it these days.)

The only problem with this new route is that, as previously mentioned, it *is* a short-cut, and one moreover used by porters to *descend* from the mountain. As such, as an ascent route many people find it entirely too short and will have succumbed to the pain of altitude sickness by the stage's end. We therefore recommend you take this into consideration and maybe factor two nights at Barranco into your itinerary, with the rest day spent sauntering up to the head of the valley to help you get used to the rarified atmosphere.

The stage begins with a walk up the Barranco Valley. Come here later in the day and you'll find yourself hiking against a tide of trekkers on the Machame, Lemosho and Shira trails all coming the other way down the same path. But assuming that you've started walking in the morning it will probably be just you and your crew, allowing you to enjoy views of Kibo through the stands of senecios. About 25 minutes after setting off you leave the main path – or rather, it leaves you – by a waterfall as you continue north, eventually crossing the stream you've been following since the day's beginning (and, indeed, as it eventually turns into the Umbwe River, since the start of the whole trek). Recrossing it further upstream, two paths present themselves, the first a one-hour short-cut to Arrow Glacier Campsite – to be taken only if thoroughly acclimatized – or a slightly gentler trail heading north up to a crossroads. Your path is the latter, which continues straight ahead over two streams and on, steeply, up to Lava Tower. The entire walking, without breaks, would have taken you just two-and-a-half hours and you'll probably be at Lava Tower by lunch, allowing you plenty of time to savour this grim campsite's uniquely chilly, god-forsaken 'charm'.

For details of the rest of the walk from Lava Tower to the summit, please turn to p267.

TRAIL GUIDE AND MAPS

The descent routes

MARANGU ROUTE

Stage 1: Gillman's Point to the Horombo Huts
[Map 5, p236; Map 4, p233; Map 3, p232]

Few people remain at the summit for long: weariness, the risk of hypothermia and the thought of a steaming mug of Milo at the Kibo Huts are enough to send most people scurrying back down. There are two main ways of doing this: the first is to follow exactly the course you took getting up here, carefully retracing every zig and zag like somebody who has dropped a contact lens on the way up but can't quite remember when or where. Curiously, it is precisely those people who are in greatest need of getting down fast who are the ones who usually use this slower method to descend.

The second way is to cut straight through the switchbacks and simply head vertically downwards in a sort of ski-style, using the now defrosted scree to act as a brake on your momentum. After the tedium of the previous night's heel-to-toe exercise, the sheer abandon of this method and the rapid progress made – it takes just over 60min to travel from Gillman's to the huts this way – comes as something of a relief. Take care, however: far more people are injured going

Returning via the Mawenzi Route　　　　[Map 25, opposite]
This is the more interesting path between Kibo and Horombo, encompassing not only entire groves of giant groundsels (*Senecio kilimanjari*) and the Zebra Rocks, but also the best panorama of them all on Kilimanjaro. It is, however, one that is seldom used, mainly because the majority of trekkers will already have done a lot of it during their acclimatization day up to Mawenzi Hut.

From Kibo Huts the path descends once more to **Jiwe Lainkoyo**. Though there appears to be but one path from Jiwe, there is in fact another, much fainter path heading almost due east across the Saddle towards Mawenzi. If you cannot make it out at first don't worry, just aim for Mawenzi and you will soon notice a faint but distinct path etched into the earth bisecting the Saddle. Ten minutes after Jiwe a junction with the even fainter **Northern Kibo Circuit** is reached (a signpost is the only evidence that there is a junction here at all), and twenty-five minutes after that the path begins to rise and fall as it follows the contours of Mawenzi's lower reaches. After another twenty-five minutes of following this undulating terrain you come to a summit of sorts, from where you can rest and gaze back over the finest **panorama** this mountain has to offer: the alpine desert of the Saddle, with a string of parasitic cones leading from the foreground to the foot of Kibo and with Mawenzi just over your shoulder. Spectacular.

From here, the path runs due south through heather, past the path leading to Mawenzi Hut, to the **Zebra Rocks** (a collection of rockfaces that resemble the flanks of a zebra), then down between the groundsel gullies until, 70 minutes from the unforgettable panorama and 2 hours 10 minutes since leaving Jiwe Lainkoyo, the roofs of the **Horombo Huts** appear beneath you once more.

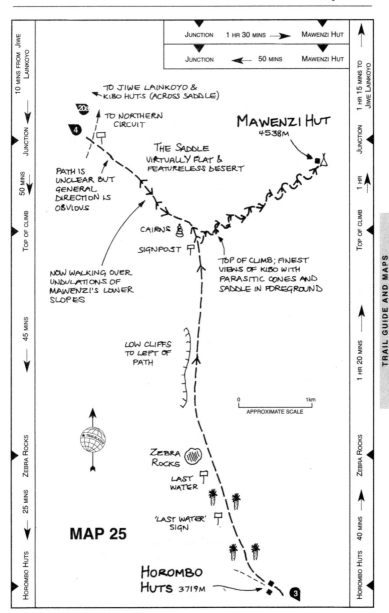

| Junction | 1 HR 30 MINS → | Mawenzi Hut |
| Junction | ← 50 MINS | Mawenzi Hut |

10 MINS FROM JIWE LAINKOYO

TO JIWE LAINKOYO & ← KIBO HUTS (ACROSS SADDLE)

← TO NORTHERN CIRCUIT

20s

4

MAWENZI HUT 4538M

THE SADDLE VIRTUALLY FLAT & FEATURELESS DESERT

PATH IS UNCLEAR BUT GENERAL DIRECTION IS OBVIOUS

CAIRNS

SIGNPOST

NOW WALKING OVER UNDULATIONS OF MAWENZI'S LOWER SLOPES

TOP OF CLIMB; FINEST VIEWS OF KIBO WITH PARASITIC CONES AND SADDLE IN FOREGROUND

LOW CLIFFS TO LEFT OF PATH

TRAILBLAZER

0   1km
APPROXIMATE SCALE

ZEBRA ROCKS

LAST WATER

'LAST WATER' SIGN

MAP 25

HOROMBO HUTS 3719M

3

1 HR 15 MINS TO JIWE LAINKOYO

JUNCTION

1 HR

TOP OF CLIMB

1 HR 20 MINS

ZEBRA ROCKS

40 MINS

HOROMBO HUTS

10 MINS FROM JIWE LAINKOYO

JUNCTION

50 MINS

TOP OF CLIMB

45 MINS

25 MINS

ZEBRA ROCKS

HOROMBO HUTS

TRAIL GUIDE AND MAPS

down than going up. Furthermore, do remember that every year at least ten thousand other pairs of feet tread on this part of the mountain and, at the risk of sounding like a killjoy, pushing down all that scree cannot be doing the mountain any good. Indeed, may we politely request that you use this faster method only if you need to descend rapidly? Otherwise, stick to the switchbacks which will be far less damaging to the mountain – and safer too!

Upon returning to camp, your guide should allow you to rest for an hour before moving on again to the **Horombo Huts**. If you ascended on the Marangu Route, heed the advice given at the beginning of Stage 3 (see p232) and ask your guide to take you back via a different route to the one on which you ascended. This usually means returning via the Saddle on the Mawenzi Route, a route we have described in the box on p292. If you return via the southerly route, expect it to take four hours. If you took the Marangu Route up the mountain, you'll be sleeping in the huts again; while those who took a different route up (eg the Rongai Route which also uses this path to descend) will be camping outside them.

Stage 2: Horombo Huts to Marangu Gate
[Map 3, p232; Map 2, p231; Map 1, p227]

Don't be in too much of a hurry to finish your trekking, for today holds lots of treats for those who take the time to enjoy them. If you have come from the Rongai Route this is the first time you will have seen forest so thick and vast on Kilimanjaro, and it's worth taking the time to appreciate the different flora on this side of the mountain. But even if you ascended by the Marangu Route, it still warrants a second look on the way down. Much of the scenery may be old hat to you by now but remember that you've still paid US$60 in park fees alone for the privilege of walking in the forest today, so you may as well make the most of it. And just as Lee Marvin in *Paint Your Wagon* sang that he'd never seen a town 'that didn't look better looking back', so most people will agree that the forest seems so much more welcoming when you're walking *downhill* through it; and the views of Kibo are that much more appealing from over the shoulder, knowing that you'll never have to climb it again.

It takes about 2 hours 20 minutes to return from Horombo to the **Mandara Huts** which are, typically, the final lunch-stop of the trail. This is also your last chance to buy beer while it's still cheaper than water. From there, it's back into the forest and down to the **gate**, a journey of some 95 minutes. Name registered, tips dispersed and with certificate clutched close to your bosom, it's time to return to the land of hot showers and flush toilets. Your adventure is at an end; civilization will rarely have felt so good.

THE MWEKA ROUTE

Stage 1: Uhuru Peak to Barafu and Mweka Huts
[Map 12, p250; Map 26, p296]

What goes up must come down, and that includes you. The path back to Barafu is little more than a retracing of your steps of the previous night (assuming you climbed this way and not the Western Breach Route), though there is a slightly quicker, if more hair-raising approach: descending from Stella Point, after ten minutes or so you reach a boulder which earlier that morning you would have walked around: it's the same boulder that marks the very steep last thirty minutes or so to the crater rim. This boulder also marks the start of a straight ski-run down through the gravel that bypasses the zigzags of the regular route. Some people prefer to make

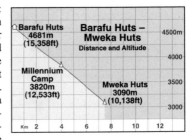

it down as quickly as possible and so choose this trail; others find it too taxing on both nerves and knees, and opt for the gentler descent. Before deciding which is for you, read the advice about erosion on p198 and if possible take the gentler descent. Either way, the two paths reunite back near the foot of the cliffs above Barafu. The entire descent takes about an hour and thirty minutes (plus breaks) from Stella Point.

You probably feel, on returning to camp, that you have earned the luxury of a brief rest at Barafu, and indeed you have. But make sure it *is* brief, for you still have another two hours and twenty minutes of knee-knackering downhill before you reach Mweka Huts, your probable home for the night. A pretty monotonous two hours and twenty minutes it is, too, as you head off due south and down for the entire 7.5km. In its defence, the descent is both large (dropping from 4681m to 3090m) and fairly gradual, which can only be good news for AMS sufferers. There is also some interest to be had in seeing how the vegetation changes along the way: at first, only the incredibly hardy yellow everlastings are able to survive at the high altitude, but they are soon joined by their dry-looking cousins in the *helichrysum* family, and soon after that the first heathers appear, to be joined a little later by the proteas.

After forty minutes or so you come to a huddle of **signposts** warning you about the danger of starting fires around here; the signs also mark the junction with the little used Southern Circuit: to your left on the slopes you can see paths from the Horombo Huts on the Marangu Route, while to your right are those coming from the Karanga Valley. Another path, an emergency trail from Karanga Campsite for those suffering from altitude, joins the Mweka trail just above the green-roofed rescue hut. This hut was originally established to help out the suffering during the millennium, when the mountain was swamped by thousands hoping to see the new era in from the summit. It's remained ever since and, now called the **Millennium Huts**, is a campsite for those who prefer something a little quieter than the Mweka Huts. It also has a water source nearby – another advantage over the Mweka Huts and one of the reasons, perhaps, why more and more groups are choosing to stay here. Coke and beer are available here too.

Immediately to the south, giant heathers grow for the first time by the dusty path and, further down, the vanilla-coloured **protea** makes its first appearance, and thereafter dominates the pathside vegetation. The proteas' presence in these

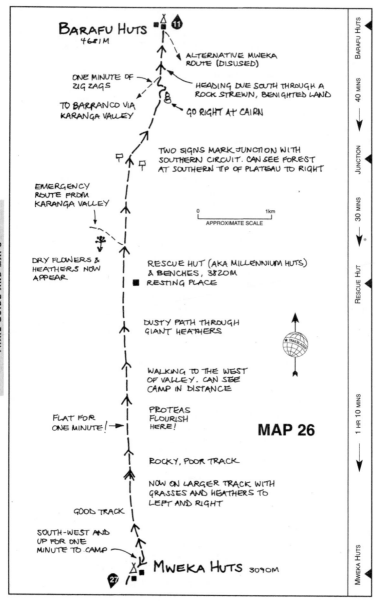

BARAFU HUTS
4681M

ALTERNATIVE MWEKA ROUTE (DISUSED)

ONE MINUTE OF ZIG ZAGS

HEADING DUE SOUTH THROUGH A ROCK STREWN, BENIGHTED LAND

TO BARRANCO VIA KARANGA VALLEY

GO RIGHT AT CAIRN

TWO SIGNS MARK JUNCTION WITH SOUTHERN CIRCUIT. CAN SEE FOREST AT SOUTHERN TIP OF PLATEAU TO RIGHT

EMERGENCY ROUTE FROM KARANGA VALLEY

0   1km
APPROXIMATE SCALE

DRY FLOWERS & HEATHERS NOW APPEAR

RESCUE HUT (AKA MILLENNIUM HUTS) & BENCHES, 3820M
RESTING PLACE

DUSTY PATH THROUGH GIANT HEATHERS

WALKING TO THE WEST OF VALLEY. CAN SEE CAMP IN DISTANCE

FLAT FOR ONE MINUTE!

PROTEAS FLOURISH HERE!

MAP 26

ROCKY, POOR TRACK

NOW ON LARGER TRACK WITH GRASSES AND HEATHERS TO LEFT AND RIGHT

GOOD TRACK

SOUTH-WEST AND UP FOR ONE MINUTE TO CAMP

MWEKA HUTS 3090M

TRAIL GUIDE AND MAPS

BARAFU HUTS
40 MINS
JUNCTION
30 MINS
RESCUE HUT
1 HR 10 MINS
MWEKA HUTS

parts has ensured a healthy population of **malachite sunbirds** live around here too, as well as the little green **white-eyes** – so-called because of the distinctive white ring around their eyes. **Chameleons**, surprisingly, also make the heather their home.

You first glimpse **Mweka Huts** (3090m) about 40 minutes before you actually get there as you descend on a ridge between two valleys towards a small heather-clad hill. Rounding this, the path widens and flattens before turning south-west and climbing for one minute to the camp – the only ascent of the entire walk from Barafu. By the way, you may wish to share out your tips at Mweka Huts before you depart on this last leg: as porters all walk at different speeds, this may be the last time the whole group is together.

Stage 2: Mweka Huts to Mweka Gate [Map 27, p298]

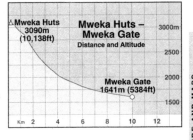

Mweka Huts – Mweka Gate
Distance and Altitude

By now you'll probably just want to get off the mountain as quickly as possible – which would actually be rather a shame, for this last section follows a very pretty forest trail alive with birdsong and flowers. Indeed, the variety, quantity and sheer beauty of the flora is incredible. This path has now thankfully been fully restored following years of over-use. Towards the end of 2001 it was so eroded that in parts trekkers found themselves walking in a two-foot deep trench. The worst bits of that path have now been abandoned altogether (in one place a bridge has been built to convey the new path across the old), and the new trail is in much better shape. The only complaint we have is that the authorities have decided to build steps on the steep parts, which we are sure is good for combatting erosion – but after five days or so of climbing, your knees will be screaming for mercy by the end. It's a lovely section of forest, but whether your mind can concentrate on anything other than the pain in your joints is another matter.

This 10km (6 mile) stage begins in similar fashion to much of the previous one, by heading south and down. Less than five minutes after you start walking, you find yourself in cloud forest, the border between this and the giant heather forest so definite and distinct that you could almost draw a line in the ground between the two. Once again walking on a narrow ridge between two valleys, look around and notice how the trees now grow in height and girth, how the moss that grows upon them is thick, green and hearty where before it was stringy and limp, and how flowers such as the *Impatiens kilimanjari* once again make an appearance on the trail, and in abundance too. Its cousin *Impatiens pseudoviola* also lines the path, while the occasional beautiful vivid red *Gladiolus wastonides* flourishes here and there, the delicate white flowers of the wild blackberry grow in clusters and the lily-white petals of the *Begonia meyeri johannis* litter the trail towards the end.

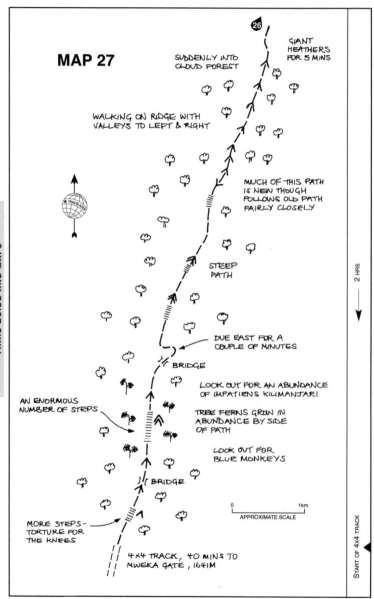

MAP 27

26

GIANT HEATHERS FOR 5 MINS

SUDDENLY INTO CLOUD FOREST

WALKING ON RIDGE WITH VALLEYS TO LEFT & RIGHT

MUCH OF THIS PATH IS NEW THOUGH FOLLOWS OLD PATH FAIRLY CLOSELY

STEEP PATH

DUE EAST FOR A COUPLE OF MINUTES

BRIDGE

LOOK OUT FOR AN ABUNDANCE OF IMPATIENS KILIMANJARI

AN ENORMOUS NUMBER OF STEPS

TREE FERNS GROW IN ABUNDANCE BY SIDE OF PATH

LOOK OUT FOR BLUE MONKEYS

BRIDGE

MORE STEPS - TORTURE FOR THE KNEES

0   1km
APPROXIMATE SCALE

4X4 TRACK, 40 MINS TO MWEKA GATE, 1641M

2 HRS

START OF 4X4 TRACK

TRAIL GUIDE AND MAPS

Almost two hours after breaking camp, you'll find yourself walking on the start of the 4WD track down to **Mweka Gate** (1641m), a further 40 minutes away. At the gate you can buy a souvenir T-shirt to advertise the fact you reached the summit (curiously, there are no suitable T-shirts for those that did not). You must also sign the last **registration book** at the nearby park office, from where those who were successful can collect the appropriate certificate. If you're with a company that has four-wheel drive vehicles you might be met at the gate; the rest have to walk ten minutes further down the hill to the lower station, where there are a couple of shops and a bar, the *Tobit Kilimanjaro View Centre*. Those who succeeded in reaching Uhuru Peak can usually be seen standing around, their golden certificates dangling casually yet deliberately from their hands so that they catch and glint in the sun, in much the same way that Ferrari owners are wont to display their car keys. Your mountain odyssey is almost at an end: from here, it's a 30-minute drive back to the land of power showers, flush toilets and cold, cold beer. You've earned it – though if you do plan to celebrate in Moshi, please take more care than Meyer did upon his return to town:

In the evening, to show there was no ill-feeling, I treated the natives to a display of fireworks, in the course of which a spark from a rocket set fire to one of the men's huts.

TRAIL GUIDE AND MAPS

PART 9: THE SUMMIT

What's at the top?

The crater of Kilimanjaro is a primeval place and decidedly uncomfortable, yet I was drawn to it. The idea of spending some days and nights awoke a compelling mixture of reverential fear and wonder; similar, I suspect, to the compulsion which draws some people unquestioningly to church. And like churches, the crater also invites contemplation of the eternal mysteries. **John Reader** *Kilimanjaro* (1982)

It's only when you reach the top of Kibo that you realize that the mountain really is a volcano, and all you have done is climb to the crater rim.

The rim itself is largely featureless, though as the highest point on the mountain it has assumed a pre-eminent role and is the focus of all trekkers. The few bumps and tumescences on it have been dignified with the word 'Spitze' or 'Point' as if they were major summits in their own right. Heading clockwise around the rim from **Gillman's** (named after the first man to reach the crater rim after the mountain had come under British protection), these bumps in order are: **Stella** (the aim of those climbing from Barafu), **Elveda**, **Hans Meyer**, **Uhuru** and **Furtwangler** (named after the man who first used skis to descend); while just to the north of Gillman's is **Leopard Point**. The distance between Gillman's to Uhuru is about 1.5km, with the crater rim rising 189.55-192m (depending on which estimate of the summit's altitude you're using) between the two. The floor of the crater, covered in brown shale and rocks and boulders of all shapes and sizes, lies between 25m (at Gillman's) and 200m (at Uhuru Peak) beneath this rim.

Trudging around the rim to Uhuru is achievement enough. There are, however, plenty of other diversions to keep you on the summit for longer ...

WALKING ON THE SUMMIT [Map 28, opposite]

For most people the conquest of Uhuru Peak, and a shiny gold certificate that says as much, is reason enough to climb Kilimanjaro. Some trekkers, however, always want to do just that little bit more, and if you still have some energy to burn once you've reached the summit you may care to take a quick tour around the crater itself. **Warn your guide in advance** of your intentions – preferably before you've even started your trek – for some react badly to the idea of spending any longer on the summit than is absolutely necessary; a little gentle cajoling along with a few hints about the size of the tip that awaits them at the end of the trip should do the trick. Make sure, too, that your guide knows his way around up there: you'll probably be a little short of humour as well as breath on the crater rim and following an ignorant guide while he tries in vain to locate the correct path to the Reusch Crater will do little to lighten your mood.

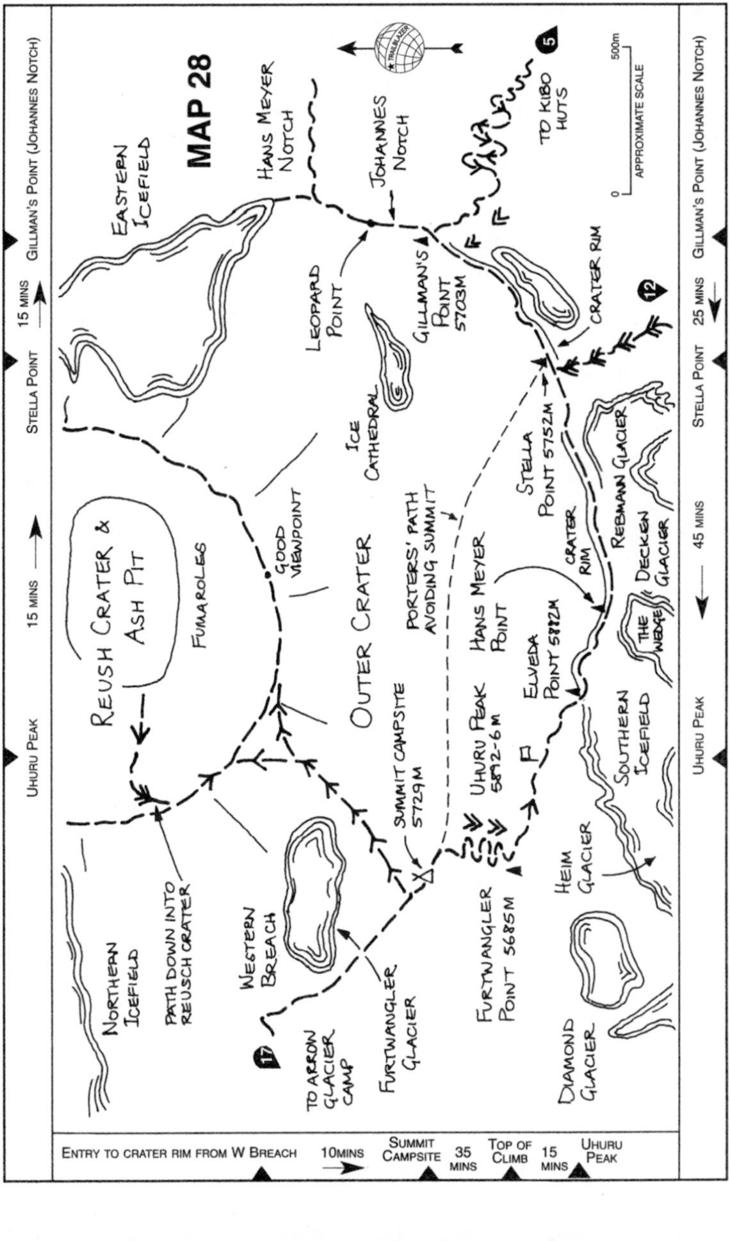
MAP 28
Gillman's Point (Johannes Notch)
15 mins
Stella Point
15 mins
Uhuru Peak
Gillman's Point (Johannes Notch)
25 mins
Stella Point
45 mins
Uhuru Peak
Eastern Icefield
Hans Meyer Notch
Johannes Notch
Leopard Point
Gillman's Point 5703M
Ice Cathedral
Crater Rim
To Kibo Huts
5
12
17
0
500m
Approximate scale
Reusch Crater & Ash Pit
Fumaroles
Good Viewpoint
Outer Crater
Porters' path avoiding summit
Stella Point 5752M
Crater Rim
Rebmann Glacier
Decken Glacier
The Wedge
Hans Meyer Point
Elveda Point 5882M
Uhuru Peak 5892-6 M
Summit Campsite 5729M
Southern Icefield
Northern Icefield
Path down into Reusch Crater
Western Breach
Furtwangler Glacier
To Arrow Glacier Camp
Furtwangler Point 5685M
Heim Glacier
Diamond Glacier
Entry to crater rim from W Breach
10mins
Summit Campsite
35 mins
Top of Climb
15 mins
Uhuru Peak

THE SUMMIT

The standard way to reach the **Reusch Crater**, the Kibo summit's very own parasitic cone, is to ascend via the Western Breach, where a trail of sorts heads off to the north round the Furtwangler Glacier away from Uhuru Peak. For this reason, it is far more common for those who have climbed via the difficult Arrow Glacier/Western Breach Route to visit Reusch than those who ascended by one of the other paths. But those who arrived at the crater rim at either Gillman's or Stella Point needn't despair, for there is also a porters' trail from near Stella Point that crosses the crater floor to join up with the path to Reusch. The actual climb up to the rim of the Reusch Crater is relatively short but surprisingly tiring; if you didn't know you were at altitude before, you will do now! This walk can take as little as thirty minutes from the campsite, though that's assuming that you are in fairly good shape; and on the summit this is a very big assumption. Having reached Reusch, check out the bright yellow sulphurous deposits, largely on its western side, and the fumaroles that occasionally puff smoke – proof not only that Kili is a volcano, but that it is also an active one. The smell of sulphur is all-pervasive in this crater, and the earth is hot to touch.

Within the Reusch Crater is the 120m/394ft-deep **Ash Pit** which, though it does not conspicuously contain ash, is said to be one of the most perfect examples of this sort of formation in the world. At 360m (1181ft) across, it's also one of the largest. If you reach the Ash Pit, you can truly say that you have conquered this mountain.

APPENDIX A: SWAHILI

Of the two main languages you will encounter, Swahili, the national tongue, is undoubtedly the more useful and the one you will see written on signs and notices. There are plenty of Swahili dictionaries around; street vendors sell little green Swahili dictionaries in Arusha for about Ts3000, or you can pick one up in souvenir stores for about a sixth of that. The other language, Chagga (along with all of its various dialects), is more common around Kili but it is unlikely you will hear it outside the region. You will, however, curry favour with porters and guides on Kilimanjaro by learning a few words; see the box on p117 for a brief introduction to the language. Chagga dictionaries are rare, though you'll find one mentioned in *Appendix E*.

Basics

Yes	Ndiyo
No	Hapana
Good Morning	Jambo
My name is...	Jina langu ni...
How are you?	Habari gani?
Please...	Tafadhali...
Thanks (very much)	Ahsante (sana)
Do you speak English?	Unasema Kiingereza
Help!	Saidia!
How much is it?	Kiasi gani?
Slowly, slower	Pole, pole-pole
Let's go!	Twendai!

Numbers

1	moja
2	mbili
3	tatu
4	nne
5	tano
6	sita
7	saba
8	nane
9	tisa
10	kumi
11	kumi na moja
12	kumi na mbili
20	ishirini
21	ishirini na moja
30	thelathini
40	arobaini
50	hamsini
60	sitini
70	sabini
80	themanini
90	tisini
100	mia
200	mia mbili
1000	elfu
2000	elfu mbili

Places

Bank	Banki
Laundry	Kufulia
Post office	Posta

Days of the week

Monday	Jumatatu
Tuesday	Jumanne
Wednesday	Jumatano
Thursday	Alhamisi
Friday	Ijumaa
Saturday	Jumamosi
Sunday	Jumapili

Travel

Bus station	kituo cha mabasi
Airport	kiwanja cha ndege
Port	bandari
Train station	stesheni
Ticket office	wanapouza tikiti
When will we arrive at...?	tutafika...jini?
Is this the direct way to...?	hii ni njia fupi kwenda...?

Food and drink

Beans	Maharagwe
Bread	Mkate
Chicken	Kuku
Coffee	Kahawa
Cold	Baridi
Eggs	Mayai
Fish	Samaki
Meat	Nyama
Orange	Chungwa
Pork	Nyama ya nguruwe
Vegetables	Mboga
Venison	Nyama ya porini
Water	Maji

APPENDIX B: FLIGHTS TO KILIMANJARO

FLIGHTS TO KILIMANJARO INTERNATIONAL AIRPORT

Currently there are four main **international carriers** flying into Kilimanjaro: Air Kenya, Air Ethiopia, Air Tanzania and the Dutch airline KLM.

Ethiopian Airways (⌨ www.flyethiopian.com) operate a pretty comprehensive pan-African network and are renowned for being cheap, and one of the most reliable of African airlines. From London they have flights to Addis Ababa thrice weekly, usually leaving at night and arriving around 8.30am. At Addis Ababa you'll have to wait for a few hours before catching the 12.15pm flight to Kilimanjaro, a journey of 2hr 15min. This latter flight operates six times a week, though all but one fly via Nairobi first.

KLM (⌨ www.klm.com) fly everyday in the high season to Dar, touching down first in Kilimanjaro. The flight currently leaves Schipol (Amsterdam) at 10.35am, arriving the same day at Kili at 8.50pm (total travel time 8hr 15min). This is certainly the most convenient way to get to Kili from Europe, particularly if you're coming from the UK and can get an early morning connecting flight to Amsterdam (there is a flight from London to Amsterdam at 6am, for example, making this the best connection from the UK).

Kenya Airways (⌨ www.kenya-airways.com) have flights from Nairobi to Kili three times a day at 8am, 10am and 6pm. They also operate thrice-weekly flights from London to Nairobi, though currently only the Friday one, which leaves in the evening at 7pm and arrives at Nairobi at 6.30am, has a reasonable connection with their Kili flights.

Air Tanzania (⌨ www.airtanzania.com) operate a complicated schedule. Flights to Kilimanjaro depart from the following:
- **Entebbe** Twice a week (Tues, Sat) via Dar, and direct on Sun
- **Mwanza** Daily
- **Dar es Salaam** Twice a day except only one on Mon
- **Johannesburg** Daily via Dar and possibly Zanzibar
- **Zanzibar** Daily, with Mon and Thurs flights via Dar

Precision Air (⌨ www.precisionairtz.com) also have flights to Kilimanjaro from various places in East Africa, including:
- **Mombasa** Tues & Fri 12.50pm, Thurs & Fri 10.35am & 12pm, Mon, Wed & Sun 10.05am
- **Nairobi** Twice daily at 9.50am & 6pm
- **Shinyanga** Twice weekly on Mon & Fri
- **Dar es Salaam** Twice daily direct at 8.20am and 1.30pm
- **Zanzibar** Twice daily via Dar at 12.30pm

APPENDIX C: TANZANIAN & KENYAN EMBASSIES

TANZANIAN EMBASSIES ABROAD

Belgium 363 Avenue Louise, 1050 Brussels; ☎ (32-2) 640-6500; 💻 tanzania@skynet.be

Canada 50 Range Road, Ottawa, Ontario KIN 8J4; ☎ (613) 234702; 💻 tzottawa@synapse.net

China 53 Dong Liu Jie, Beijing; ☎ (86-1) 532-1491, 532-1719; 💻 tzbejing@info.iuol.cn.net

Congo (DRC) 142 Boulevard 30 Jin BP 1612, Kinshasa; ☎ (0982) 34364

Egypt 9 Abdel Hamid Loutfy, Street, Dokki-Cairo; ☎ 20-2 3374286; 💻 tanrepcairo@infinity.com.eg

Ethiopia P.O. Box 1053, Addis Ababa; ☎ 251-1 634353; 💻 tz@telecom.net.et

France 13 ave Raymond, Pointcare, 75116 Paris; ☎ 00331 4755 0546; 💻 tanzanie@infonie.fr

Germany Eschenalle 11, 14050 Berlin; ☎ 49- 30 30308000; 💻 tzberlin.haban@gonx.de

India 10/1 Sarv Priya Vihar, New Delhi 110016; ☎ 6853046/7; 💻 tanzrep@del2.vsnl.net.in

Italy 9 Via Giambattista Vico, 00196, Rome; ☎ 06 3610901; 💻 tanzarep@pcg.it

Japan 21-9, Kamiyoga 4, Chome Setagaya-Ku, Tokyo 158; ☎ (03) 425 4531/3; 💻 tzrepjp@japan.co.jp

Kenya Continental House, Harambee Ave/Uhuru Highway, PO Box 47790, Nairobi; ☎ (254) 331 056/7; 💻 tanzania@users.africaonline.co.ke

Mozambique Ujamaa House, PO Box 4515, Maputo; ☎ (263-4) 721870; 💻 safina@zebra.uem.mz

Nigeria 15 Yedseram Street, Maintama, PMB 5125, Wuse, Abuja; ☎ 234 9 413 2313; 💻 tanabuja@lytos.com

Russia Pyatnitskaya, Ulitsa 33, Moscow; ☎ 231 8126; 💻 tanmos@wm.west-call.com

Rwanda 15 avenue Paul VI, BP 3973, Kigali; 💻 tanzarep@rwandatell.rwandal.com

Saudi Arabia PO Box 94320, Riyadh 11693; ☎ 4542839, 4542833 💻 tanzania@mail.gcc.com.bh

South Africa PO Box 56572, Arcadia, 0007, Pretoria; ☎ 3424371/93; 💻 tanzania@cis.co.za

Sweden Oxtorgsgatan 2-4, Box 7255, 103-89, Stockholm; ☎ 08 244870; 💻 mailbox@tanemb.se

Switzerland 47 Avenue Blanc, CH 1201 Geneva; ☎ (004122) 731 8920; 💻 mission.tanzania @itu.ch

UAE 56 Al-Nasser Street, Khalidiya, PO Box 43714, Abu Dhabi; ☎ 971 2 66626; 💻 tanrep@ emirates.net.ae

Uganda 6 Kagera Road, PO Box 5750, Kampala; ☎ (41) 257357; 💻 tzrepkla@imul.com

UK 3 Stratford Place, London W1C 1AS; ☎ 44 020-7569 1470; 💻 www.tanzania-online.gov.uk

USA 2139 R Street, Washington DC 20008; ☎ (202) 9939 6129; 201 East 42nd St, Suite 1700, New York, NY 10017; ☎ (212) 972 9160; 💻 tzrepny@aol.com

Zambia Ujamaa House, No 5200, United Nations Ave, PO Box 31219, 10101 Lusaka; ☎ 227698/227702; 💻 tzreplsk@zamnet.zm

Zimbabwe Ujamaa House, 23 Baines Ave, Harare; ☎ (263-4) 721870, 722627; 💻 tanrep@icon. co.zw

KENYAN EMBASSIES ABROAD

Australia 6th Floor, O.B.E. Building, Ainslie Ave 33-35, PO Box 1990, Canberra, ACT 2601; ☎ 062-2474788; 🖳 kenrep@austarmetro.com

Austria Neulinggasse 29/8 1030 Vienna; ☎ 7123919; 🖳 kenyarep-vienna@aon.at

Botswana 5373 President's Drive, Private Bag Bo 297, Gaborone; ☎ 267-351408/430; 🖳 kenya@info.bw

Canada 415 Laurier Avenue East, Ottawa, Ontario K1N 6R4; ☎ 1-5631773/4/6; 🖳 www.kenyahighcommission.ca

China 4 Xi Liu Jie, San Li Tun, Beijing, 100600; ☎ 65323381; 🖳 koenyla@iuol.cn

Congo (DRC) 4002 Ave De Louganda, Zone Degombe, PO Box 9667, Kinshasa; ☎ 1-212-372 3641

Egypt 7 El Mohandesseen, Giza, Cairo PO Box 362 Dokki; ☎ 2-3453628/3453907; 🖳 embaci@hotmail.com

Ethiopia Fikre Mariam Road, Hiher 16 Kebelle 01, PO Box 3301, Addis Ababa; ☎ 1-610033; 🖳 kenya.embassy@telecom.net.et

France 3 Rue Freycinet, 75116 Paris; ☎ 45533500; 🖳 kenparis@wanadoo.fr

Germany Markgrafenstrasse, 63 10969, Berlin; ☎ 259266-0; 🖳 embassy-kenya.bn@wwmail.de

India 66 Vasant Marg, Vasant Vihar, New Delhi, 10057; ☎ 11-6146537, 26146538, 6146540; 🖳 www.kenyamission-delhi.com

Israel 15 Rehov Abba Hillel Silver, 3rd Floor, Ramat Gan 52522, PO Box 52136, Tel Aviv; ☎ 3-5754633; 🖳 kenya04@ibm.net

Italy Via Archimede 16400197, Roma; ☎ 6-8082717/18; 🖳 www.embassyofkenya.it

Japan No 24-3 Yakumo, 3-Chome, Meguro-Ku, Tokyo 152; ☎ 37234006/7; 🖳 kenrepj@ma.kcom.ne.jp

Namibia 134 Luetwein Street, PO Box 2889, Windhoek; ☎ 61-225900; 🖳 kenya-net@iwwn.com.na

Netherlands Nieuwe Parklaan 21 2597 La, The Hague; ☎ (70) 3504215; 🖳 kenre@dataweb.nl

Nigeria 52 Oyinkan Abayomi Drive, PO Box 6464, Ikoyi, Lagos; ☎1-2670221; 🖳 kenya@alpha.linkserve.com

Pakistan Islamabad House No 10, Street No 9, Sector F-7/3, PO Box 2097, Islamabad; ☎ 51-279540, 279542; 🖳 kenreppk@apollo.net.pk

Russia Bolshaya Ordinka, Dom 70, Moscow; ☎ 095-2374702

Rwanda Prima 2000, Apartment 202 BP 6159, Kigali; ☎ 583173

Saudi Arabia Riyadh 11693, PO Box 94358; ☎ 1-4881238; 🖳 kenya@shaheer.net.sa

South Africa 302 Brooks Street, Menlo Park, 0081; ☎ 12-3622249; 🖳 kenp@pta.lia.net

Sudan Street 3, Amarat, PO Box 8242, Khartoum; ☎ 11-460386

Sweden Birger Jarlsgatan 37, 2nd Floor, PO Box 7694 103 95, Stockholm; ☎ 8✍ 218300; 🖳 kenya.touristoffice@swipnet.se

Switzerland Bleicherweg 30 8002 Zürich; ☎ 2022244

Tanzania 14th Floor, NIC Investment House, Samora Avenue, PO Box 5231, Dar-Es-Salaam; ☎ 51-112955-7; 🖳 khc@raha.com

UAE PO Box 3854, Abu Dhabi; ☎ 2-6666300; 🖳 kenyarep@emirates.net.ae

Uganda Plot No 41, Nakasero Road, PO Box 5220, Kampala; ☎ 41-258235/6

UK 45 Portland Place, London, WIN 4AS; ☎ 020-76362371/5; 🖳 kcomm45@aol.com

USA 2249, R Street NW Washington DC 20008; ☎ 3876101; 🖳 klqy53a@prodigy.com

Zambia 5207 United Nations Avenue, PO Box 50298, Lusaka; ☎ 1-250722; 🖳 kenhigh@zamnet.zm

Zimbabwe 95 Park Lane, PO Box 4069, Harare; ☎ 4-704820; 🖳 kenhicom@africaon line.co.zw

APPENDIX D: USEFUL WEBSITES

You could easily spend a happy decade or two simply by typing the word Kilimanjaro into your search engine and sifting through the results. In fact, a quick check just now with the search engine Google found 3,060,000 relevant sites; you can add a few hundred thousand more by typing in Marangu or Machame.

Most of these sites fall into two categories, being either websites promoting trekking companies or personal accounts of people's experiences on Kilimanjaro. Some of the former are rather good and packed full of useful info; these sites have not been listed below, though details of the best of them can be found in the sections on trekking agencies on p22-32, p161, p182 and p192. As for the personal accounts, these tend to be short on practical information and long on both pretty pictures and phrases such as 'spiritual awakening', 'inner drive' and other guff, though you should find some goodies if you look hard enough.

We hope that by the time you read this the website to accompany this book, namely 🖳 www.climbmountkilimanjaro.com will be up and running; a website that, we hope, will have all the latest news and reviews on Kili, have comments and reactions from our readers, and provide links to other relevant sites – as well as a whole load of other stuff. Details of this site can be found on p16. Other useful sites include:

● **http://kili50.blogspot.com/** Humorous and well-written blog by an Englishman as he approaches both his fiftieth birthday and a climb up Kilimanjaro to celebrate it.

● **http://news.nationalgeographic.com/news/2003/09/0923_030923_kilimanjaroglaciers. html** Spectacular, if rather worrying, photos by Dr Vincent Keipper of a section of Kili's Furtwangler Glacier collapsing.

● **http://whc.unesco.org/pg.cfm?cid=31&id_site=403** Webpage of the Kilimanjaro entry on the list of UNESCO world heritage sites.

● **www-bprc.mps.ohio-state.edu/Icecore/TimesArticle.html** Useful, sober overview of the controversy surrounding the disappearance of Kilimanjaro's glaciers.

● **www.expedia.co.uk/daily/resources/currency/** One of the few currency converters to feature the Tanzanian shilling in its list.

● **www.geo.umass.edu/climate/kibo.html** University of Massachusetts' geoscience website covering their study of the climate on Kibo and the rate of disappearance of the glaciers, using a weather station they have installed on the summit.

● **www.high-altitude-medicine.com/** Website covering everything you need to know about altitude sickness.

● **www.kilimanjarotrust.org** Website of the Kilimanjaro Environmental Conservation Management Trust Fund, an African body working towards the preservation of Kilimanjaro's natural resources and the prevention of degradation of the mountain through man's activities such as fires, forestry and farming.

● **www.mos.org/kili/index.html** Site of the Museum of Science in Boston which includes a trailer for their IMAX film *Kilimanjaro – to the Roof of Africa*.

● **www.ntz.info/** Unusual personal scrapbook of northern Tanzania, recommended partly because of the author's obvious passion/obsession for the place, and partly because of the interesting collection of news clippings/quotes/song lyrics and indeed anything else he or she can find about Kili. A bit haphazard but well worth a browse.

● **www.summitpost.org** Website dedicated to all things mountainous worldwide. Very comprehensive, up-to-date and impressive. Check it out.

● **www.tanzaniawebsiteaddresses.com** List of Tanzanian firms' web addresses.

● **www.tanzania.go.tz/** Official website of the government of Tanzania.

● **www.teamkilimanjaro.com** Website of UK trekking agency that arranges record attempts on Kili.

APPENDIX E: RECOMMENDED READING, LISTENING AND WATCHING

MAPS

Maps of Kilimanjaro are available in Arusha, Moshi and your own country, though we've yet to find one that is entirely satisfactory. The most common map is the cartoonish *New Map of the Kilimanjaro National Park*, published by the safari-cum-trekking agency Hoopoe Adventure & Tropical Trekking (see p25 and p166). It's not a bad map – bright and colourful, and drawn in 1998, which makes it one of the newest – though in all honesty it's very inaccurate. Its cartoon-style means it's of little practical use, too, though it's packed full of information and the flora guide on the reverse is useful. The scale, by the way, is about 1.1cm to 1km (or 1:90,909), with a close-up of the summit on the reverse drawn at a scale of 5.4cm to 1km (about 1:18,518.5). They also publish a similar-style map to Meru.

The *Tourist Map of Kilimanjaro* (1:100,000) by the Ordnance Survey is the biggest and most beautiful, though once again of little practical use: the routes themselves have been drawn, seemingly without thought of precision, over the top of what looks an accurate topographical map. Well over a decade old, it's a little out of date too.

A third map, *Kilimanjaro* (1:50,000), by Mark Savage, is harder to track down – though the shop at Marangu Gate stocks some. The descriptions of the trails are not brilliant and the map itself is a little ugly, though it is more up to date than the above and the black-and-white drawings of wild flowers are good – though would be far more useful in colour.

Finally, the Canada-based ITM (International Travel Maps) series has recently produced *Kilimanjaro*, a colourful 1:62,500 map of the mountain, as well as a separate 1:6,250,000 road map of the area.

RECOMMENDED READING

Please note that many of the following books are rare and a number are extremely difficult to find except at the British Library or a similar institution. Among those that are readily available are Hemingway's *The Snows of Kilimanjaro* (and the recently published *Under Kilimanjaro*, the rather long-winded novel-cum-memoir-cum-tribute to Africa that recounts Papa Hemingway's time in Kenya); the comprehensive and wonderful book-of-the-IMAX-film *Kilimanjaro, Mountain at the Crossroads*, by Audrey Salkeld – possibly the most beautiful and absorbing souvenir of your climb that money can buy; and John Reader's excellent (though rather bulky) *Kilimanjaro*, which you may have more luck tracking down in Tanzania than in your home country. If you're visiting Zanzibar after Kilimanjaro, you may want to wait and buy your reading material for the mountain there: some of the bookshops in Stonetown have fine selections.

Biographies and personal accounts

Many of the following books, particularly those written during the great days of exploration in the 1800s, are now out of print and, short of a miraculous find in a secondhand bookstore, the only place you're going to find them is at the British Library in London or a similar institution abroad. The Internet is, of course, another place. For example, I've successfully tracked down online the English translation of Hans Meyer's account of his conquest of Kili (see first entry below); now all I've got to do is find the £5750 that the dealers are asking for it. The online auction house eBay is a good place to begin your search, with companies such as Bibliografi, who trade through eBay, frequently offering some rare tomes. The Canadian-based Voyager Press also have some good stuff on Kili, particularly old reports from the Royal Geographic Society.

For those books that *are* still in print, your best bet is in Tanzania itself, either in the small souvenir shop by Marangu Gate or, somewhat surprisingly, in the large bookshops in

Stonetown, Zanzibar. Failing that, you could always try the Internet (Amazon etc) which will usually be able to track a copy down for you.

The explorers...

Across East African Glaciers – An Account of the First Ascent of Kilimanjaro Dr Hans Meyer, translated from the German by EHS Calder (George Philip and Son, 1891). Perhaps the most fascinating book ever written about the mountain, Meyer's beautiful work describes his unprecedented ascent of Kilimanjaro, all illustrated with some lovely sketches by ET Compton. Splendid stuff.

An Essay on the Sources of the Nile in the Mountains of the Moon Charles T Beke (Neill and Company, 1848). This short work is of interest not only because it was published at the same time as Rebmann's groundbreaking visit of Kilimanjaro but also, though written around 160 years ago, the author still takes as his starting point the work of Ptolemy written 1800 years before, thus giving an indication of just how little was known about Africa at that time.

Discovery by Count Teleki of Lakes Rudolf and Stefanie Lieutenant Ludwig von Höhnel, translated by Nancy Bell (Longmans, Green and Co, 1894). Lengthy, two-volume account of the Hungarian count as he shoots and slaughters his way through East Africa's fauna, written by his companion von Höhnel. Only about a sixth of the book deals specifically with Kili, though that sixth is interesting both for the account of their attempt to climb Kili, and in their dealing with Chagga chiefs Mandara (whom they try to avoid) and Mareale.

Life, Wanderings, and Labours in Eastern Africa Charles New (Cass Library of African Studies, 1971, originally 1873). Charles New set off in 1871 to spread the gospel to Africa's heathen population but it was as an explorer that he is remembered, becoming the first white man to cross the African snow-line during a visit to the Chagga region. This book was written in the months spent in England between his first and second trips, on the latter of which he fell ill and died. Once again, though the account of his time on the slopes of Kili occupies only about a third of the book, it is for the most part fascinating, as much for his description of Mandara and the Chaggas as it is for his climb up the mountain.

The Church Missionary Intelligencer (Seeleys, 1850). Definitely one you'll have to look for in the British Library, this august organ was the first to publish Rebmann's accounts of his three trips to Kilimanjaro, as well as Krapf's subsequent visit to the Usambara region. Volume 1, May 1849, contains most of the relevant texts.

The Kilima-njaro Expedition – A Record of Scientific Exploration in Eastern Equatorial Africa HH Johnston (Kegan Paul, Trench and Co, 1886; republished by Gregg International Publishers Ltd, 1968). Widely dismissed as exaggeration going on fabrication, this is nevertheless a very entertaining read thanks to Johnston's sense of humour and the scrapes he gets into. Just about possible to pick up secondhand.

Tracts Relating to Missions (Printed by A Lankester, 1878) Yet another work whose habitat is restricted almost entirely to the British Library these days, this collection of missionary accounts includes one by the Rev A Downes Shaw entitled *To Chagga and Back – An Account of a Journey to Moshi, the Capital of Chagga, Eastern Equatorial Africa*.

...and those who followed in their wake

Africa's Dome of Mystery Eva Stuart Watt FRGS (Marshall, Morgan and Scott Ltd, 1930). Brought up in East Africa, Ms Stuart-Watt describes her life among the Chagga people, including an account of her climb to Kibo's crater rim. Interesting, if only for the fact that there are few accounts of Kibo from this period under British rule.

Bicycles up Kilimanjaro Richard and Nicholas Crane (Oxford Illustrated Press 1985). These two cycled up Kili with Mars Bars taped to their handlebars to finance the construction of windmills for pumping water in East Africa. The only other person I met who had read this book said he enjoyed it, but I didn't.

Duel for Kilimanjaro Leonard Mosley (Weidenfeld and Nicolson, 1963). Account of the East African campaign during World War I.

Snow on the Equator HW Tilman (Bell and Son Books, 1937, republished as part of ***The Eight Sailing/Mountain Exploration Books*** by Baton Wicks, 1989). Inaccurate account (Kilimanjaro is not an extinct volcano, for example, but a dormant one) by coffee planter, explorer, mountaineer and all-round show-off Harold William Tilman. Nevertheless a very entertaining read and, for all his bluster, Tilman comes across as an entirely likeable fellow.
The Road to Kilimanjaro Geoffrey Salisbury (Minerva Press, 1997). Though mainly autobiographical, recounting Salisbury's busy life, this book includes a heart-warming, humbling account of an expedition in 1969 by the author to the summit of Kilimanjaro on the Loitokitok (Rongai) Route with a group of eight totally blind African youths, all but one of whom made it to the top.
The Shadow of Kilimanjaro – On Foot Across East Africa Rick Ridgeway (Bloomsbury 1999). Well-written account of a walk that begins on the summit of Kilimanjaro and ends at Malindi on the Kenyan coast. Though Kili is dealt with in a matter of pages at the front of the book, the narrative style is absorbing and this book is well worth reading.
On Top of Africa – the Climbing of Kilimanjaro and Mount Kenya Neville Shulman (Element Books, 1995). Tale of the conquering of these two African giants by the author, along with the help of Zen philosophies and his own personal *shin* spirit.
In Wildest Africa Peter MacQueen, FRGS (George Bell and Sons, 1910). Account of one of the first tourists to visit Kilimanjaro, coming here during the German occupation. Includes a description of their ascent up Kili, during which some of their porters died, more were frightened by snow and fled (taking the food with them) and MacQueen himself only managed to find his way down by following the trail of porters' corpses left behind from an expedition five months previously. MacQueen went on to reach a highly credible 19,200 feet, the highest, at that time, by an English speaker.

Fiction
Home on Kilimanjaro Margaret Chrislock Gilseth (Askeladd Press, 1998). Novel written by a lady who spent four years teaching in Marangu for the Lutheran Church, written largely from the point of view of her 11-year-old son.
The Snows of Kilimanjaro Ernest Hemingway (Heinemann, 1941; Arrow Books, 1994). Short story about a writer plagued by both a gangrenous leg and a rich wife, written by an honorary game warden based in Loitokitok. Was always regarded as his most autobiographical work until the publication of...
Under Kilimanjaro Ernest Hemingway (Kent State University Press, 2005). Hemingway called it fiction but with himself and his wife as the lead characters and the events that are described presumably pretty close to the truth, this book could just as easily have been pigeonholed in the *Biography* category above. Long and funereally paced, it has its moments but is probably for fans and aficionados only.

Chagga language, history and lifestyle
Chagga – A Course in the Vunjo Dialect of the Kichagga Language of Kilimanjaro, Tanzania Bernard Leeman and Trilas Lauwo (published in Europe by Languages Information Centre). The best Chagga language book we could find, this tome, written by an Australian who worked as a teacher in the region, deals with the basic structure and grammar and is an ideal introduction to the tongue.
History of the Chagga People of Kilimanjaro Kathleen M Stahl (Mouton & Co, 1964). Highly detailed account of the Chaggas, probably more for those with an academic interest in the subject.
Hunger and Shame – Child Malnutrition and Poverty on Mount Kilimanjaro Mary Howard and Ann Millard (Routledge). Comparatively rich by African standards it may be but, as this book proves, Kilimanjaro still suffers from more than its fair share of grinding poverty. With views from family members, health workers and government officials, this book discusses the moral and practical dilemmas of malnourishment.

Kilimanjaro and its People The Honourable Charles Dundas OBE (H, F and G Witherby, 1924; reprinted by Frank Cass & Co, 1968). Probably still the most authoritative account of the Chagga people, this tome is a little dry in places (particularly the rather involved history section), and outdated too (very few of the more extreme Chagga practices, described on p116 of this book, are still conducted today); nevertheless the sections on religion, witchcraft and ritual ceremonies are completely fascinating and offer the most comprehensive insight into how the Chaggas *used to be*, at least, if not how they are today.

Fauna and flora
Birds of Kenya and Northern Tanzania Popular guide by Dale A Zimmerman.
Field Guide to the Birds of East Africa Guide in the Poyser series.
Kilimanjaro – Animals in a Landscape Jonathan Kingdon (BBC Publications 1983). Born in Tanganyika, Kingdon is an artist specializing in the flora and fauna of his homeland. This book, based on a BBC series, contains examples of his work as well as an extended commentary on the creatures that live on the mountain.

Coffee table books
Kilimanjaro John Reader (Elm Tree Books, 1982). Excellent, beautifully written coffee-table book with detailed accounts both of the history and geology of Kili, and the author's own experience of photographing it.
Kilimanjaro: The Great White Mountain David Pluth (Camerapix, 2001). Another tome that will have your coffee-table groaning.
Kilimanjaro: To the Roof of Africa Audrey Salkeld, (National Geographic Books). The best-looking book on Kilimanjaro, this mighty coffee-table tome includes detailed sections on history and geology, as well as some excellent photographs of the mountain. If you only buy one book on the mountain – other than the one you're holding now, of course! – make it this one.

FOR YOUR LISTENING PLEASURE

The following is some appropriate music to take up the mountain with you; appropriate, but not necessarily any good. And we have to wonder: have any of the following artists actually been anywhere near the mountain?
Babyshambles *Kilamangiro* Celebrity junkie and Kate Moss's on-off boyfriend is also, apparently, a rock star. This 2005 offering was Pete Doherty's first single with new band Babyshambles following his acrimonious departure from The Libertines. Not bad but the question remains: will we know who he is come the next edition of this book?
Miles Davis *Filles de Kilimanjaro* Before he went all funky and weird on us with his *Bitches Brew* album – great album cover, unlistenable tunes – Miles Davis recorded this album in 1968 with his 'second great quintet', featuring Wayne Shorter on trumpet and keyboard god Herbie Hancock.
Medwyn Goodall *Snows of Kilimanjaro* 'As uplifting as catching the first sight of the mountain rising up out of the African plains – as inspirational as gazing down from the summit – *Snows of Kilimanjaro* is a perfect musical tribute to the inner strength of those who rise above adversity.' At least, that's what the blurb says; and as it was made in support of a charity climb, I'm not going to disagree. Whatever I may really think.
Iration Steppas Meet Dennis Rootical *Kilimanjaro* A 1995 ten-inch single from British dubmasters. Rare; check out the Summit Mix on side two.
Lange presents Firewall *Kilimanjaro* Trance-dance CD from 2004, including 8-minute long original mix, 9-minute 23 seconds Lange remix and 7 minute 51 second 'B-side', *Touched*. Not special.

Letta Mbulu *Kilimanjaro* Soulful disco with Afrobeats. Quite groovy but difficult to find unless on compilation.

The Rippingtons *Kilimanjaro* Guitarist Russ Freeman's instrumental follow-up to *Moonlighting*, their successful debut. Jazzy, smoothish and with world-music influences.

Teardrop Explodes *Kilimanjaro* One of Britain's loveable oddballs, Julian Cope – last seen in public travelling around Britain to write about stone circles – first came to public attention with the release of this 1980 debut album. Includes their greatest hit, 'Reward', which is bound to stir up memories amongst those who grew up in the eighties. Like me. Described as post-punk by aficionados – shorthand for passionate, angry yet melodious.

Toto *Africa* Bearded eighties crooners worldwide smash includes the line 'Sure as Kilimanjaro rises like Olympus above the Serengeti'. Which, of course, it doesn't.

The Twinkle Brothers *Kilimanjaro* A 2000 Roots-reggae release. I must confess, I've never actually heard it but I like the look of the cover.

...AND FIVE FILMS WITH KILIMANJARO IN THE TITLE

Kilimanjaro – to the Roof of Africa The film of the book – or was it the book of the film? Whatever, this IMAX film recounting the experiences of a group of trekkers on the mountain is beautifully shot by film-maker David Breashears. It's the best documentary if you want to know what it's like to climb the mountain, as well as a gorgeous and evocative souvenir for those who have already done so.

Killers of Kilimanjaro With scarcely a swash left unbuckled, this tale follows the adventures of trouble-shooter Robert Adamson (Robert Taylor) who, arriving in deepest Africa with Jane Carlton (played by the luscious Anne Aubrey) to oversee the completion of a cross-continental railroad, finds he has all manner of continental clichés to contend with, from slave traders (ruthless) to tribes (savage) and, of course, the local fauna (Grrrr!). Will he make it out alive? And complete the railroad too? And get together with Jane? Probably, yes. It's not great but I quite enjoyed it, and it has a certain charm. Usually available on eBay, if you're interested.

The Mines of Kilimanjaro Italian offering from 1986 that's been dubbed into English. Tobias Hoesl stars as Dr Ed Barkely who travels to East Africa in search of his professor's killers. But as Robert Taylor (see *Killers of Kilimanjaro*, above) could have told him, this part of the world is chock-a-block with danger, from savage tribes (in this case, the Gundors), Chinese gangsters (?) and even Nazis (???). And after that, things get *really* weird! But as Robert Taylor could also have told him, there are compensations in the form of some lovely scenery and equally comely female company, with Elena Pompei as Eva Kilbrook. All in all, an appalling film but unfortunately not bad enough to be funny – making it possibly the worst couple of hours of cinematic 'entertainment' you will ever experience.

In the Shadow of Kilimanjaro It's 1500 men versus 90,000 flesh-eating baboons that have been driven mad by a drought. The odds look bad but if anybody can find a way out of this dilemma, John Rhys Davis and Timothy Bottoms can.... Grab a beer and some chocolate, settle into your favourite armchair, disengage your brain and enjoy this truly rubbish but succulent slice of eighties' ham and corn. Said to be hard to track down – but not on eBay it isn't.

Snows of Kilimanjaro Henry King's 1952 film version of Hemingway's semi-autobiographical work, with Gregory Peck in the leading role, Susan Hayward as his devoted belle and Ava Gardner as the lost love he pines for – and when you see Ava in this film, you can't blame him. Of course it's the most highbrow film of the ones listed here and I should like it – but, personally speaking, give me killer baboons anyday.

WE GIVE YOU THE LION'S SHARE OF AFRICA

Try as you might, unless you've seen Africa, you can't begin
to imagine the depth of its beauty. Ethiopian has the pleasure
of flying to more African countries than any other airline.
Our growing international network provides a growing
number of people with the opportunity to travel all the way
there and back with one airline.
Ethiopian... there's no better way to see Africa.

Ethiopian
የኢትዮጵያ

AFRICA'S WORLD CLASS AIRLINE

INDEX

Abbreviation for Mount Meru : MM

TRAILBLAZER'S BRITISH WALKING GUIDE SERIES

We've applied to destinations which are closer to home Trailblazer's proven formula for publishing definitive route guides for adventurous travellers. Britain's network of long-distance trails enables the walker to explore some of the finest landscapes in the country's best walking areas and they are an obvious starting point for this series. These are guides that are user-friendly, practical, informative and environmentally sensitive.

● **Unique mapping features** .In many walking guidebooks the reader has to read a route description then try to relate it to the map. Our guides are much easier to use because walking directions, tricky junctions, places to stay and eat, points of interest and walking times are all written onto the maps themselves in the places to which they apply. With their uncluttered clarity, these are not general-purpose maps but fully-edited maps **drawn by walkers for walkers**.

● **Largest-scale walking maps** At a scale of just under 1:20,000 (8cm or 3¹/₈ inches to one mile) the maps in these guides are bigger than even the most detailed British walking maps currently available in the shops.

● **Not just a trail guide – includes where to stay, where to eat and public transport** Our guidebooks are a complete guide, not just a trail guide. They include: what to see, where to stay, where to eat: pubs, hotels, B&B, camping, bunkhouses, hostels. There is detailed public transport information for all access points to each trail so there are itineraries for all walkers, both for hiking the route in its entirety and for day walks.

West Highland Way *Charlie Loram*   2nd edn out now
ISBN 1 873756 90 9, 192pp, 53 maps, 16pp colour, £9.99, $17.95

Hadrian's Wall Path *Henry Stedman*   1st edn out now
ISBN 1 873756 85 2, 192pp, 60 maps, 16pp colour, £9.99, $17.95

Pennine Way *Ed de la Billière & Keith Carter*   1st edn out now
ISBN 1 873756 57 7, 256pp, 140 maps, 16pp colour, £9.99, $16.95

Coast to Coast *Henry Stedman*   2nd edn out now
ISBN 1 873756 92 5, 224pp, 110 maps, 16pp colour, £9.99, $17.95

Pembrokeshire Coast Path *Jim Manthorpe*   1st edn out now
ISBN 1 873756 56 9, 208pp, 96 maps, 16pp colour, £9.99, $16.95

Offa's Dyke Path *Keith Carter*   1st edn out now
ISBN 1 873756 59 3, 208pp, 53 maps, 16pp colour, £9.99, $16.95

Cornwall Coast Path *Edith Schofield*   2nd edn out now
ISBN 1 873756 93 3, 224pp, 100 maps, 16pp colour, £9.99, $17.95

The Ridgeway *Nick Hill*   1st edn Nov 2006
ISBN 1 873756 88 7, 176pp, 60 maps, 16pp colour, £9.99, $17.95

North Downs Way *John Curtin*   1st edn Oct 2006
ISBN 1 873756 96 8, 208pp, 53 maps, 16pp colour, £9.99, $17.95

South Downs Way *Jim Manthorpe*   2nd edn Jan 2007
ISBN 1 873756 95 X, 192pp, 60 maps, 16pp colour, £9.99, $17.95

*'The same attention to detail that distinguishes its other guides has been brought to bear here'. **The Sunday Times***

OTHER TRAILBLAZER TITLES – SEE OVERLEAF FOR FULL LIST

Dolomites Trekking Alta Via 1 & Alta Via 2 *Henry Stedman*,
192pp 52 trail maps, 7 town plans, 38 colour photos
ISBN 1 873756 83 6, £11.99, US$22.95 *2nd edition*
AV1 (9-13 days) & AV2 (10-16 days) are the most popular long-distance hikes in the Dolomites. Numerous shorter walks also included. Places to stay, walking times and points of interest, plus detailed guides to Cortina and six other towns.

Trekking in Ladakh *Charlie Loram*
288pp, 75 maps, 24 colour photos
ISBN 1 873756 75 5, £12.99, US$18.95, *3rd edition*
Fully revised and extended 3rd edition of Charlie Loram's practical guide. Includes 75 detailed walking maps, guides to Leh, Manali and Delhi plus information on getting to Ladakh.
'Extensive...and well researched'. **Climber Magazine**
'Were it not for this book we might still be blundering about...'
The Independent on Sunday

The Inca Trail, Cusco & Machu Picchu *Richard Danbury*
320pp, 65 maps, 35 colour photos
ISBN 1 873756 86 0, £11.99, US$19.95, *3rd edition*
The **Inca Trail** from Cusco to Machu Picchu is South America's most popular trek. Practical guide including detailed trail maps, plans of Inca sites, plus guides to Cusco and Machu Picchu. This expanded third edition includes new guides to the **Santa Teresa Trek** and the **Choquequirao Trek** as well as the **Vilcabamba Trail**.   *'Danbury's research is thorough... you need this one'.* **The Sunday Times**

Trekking in the Annapurna Region *Bryn Thomas*
288pp, 55 maps, 28 colour photos
ISBN 1 873756 68 2, £11.99, US$19.95, *4th edition*
Fully revised guide to the most popular walking region in the Himalaya. Includes route guides, Kathmandu and Pokhara city guides and getting to Nepal. *Good guides read like a novel and have you packing in no time. Two from Trailblazer Publications which fall into this category are* 'Trekking in the Annapurna Region' *and* 'Silk Route by Rail'. **Today**

New Zealand – The Great Walks *Alexander Stewart*
272pp, 60 maps, 40 colour photos
ISBN 1 873756 78 X, £11.99, US$19.95, *1st edition*
New Zealand is a wilderness paradise of incredibly beautiful landscapes. There is no better way to experience it than on one of the nine designated Great Walks, the country's premier walking tracks. Also includes detailed guides to Auckland, Wellington and six other access towns.

Scottish Highlands – The Hillwalking Guide *Jim Manthorpe*
312pp, 86 maps 40 colour photos
ISBN 1 873756 84 4   £11.99, US$19.95
Covers 60 day-hikes in the following areas: ● Loch Lomond, the Trossachs and Southern Highlands ● Glen Coe and Ben Nevis
● Central Highlands ● Cairngorms and Eastern Highlands
● Western Highlands ● North-West Highlands
● The Far North ● The Islands
● Plus: 3- to 4-day hikes linking some regions

TRAILBLAZER GUIDES – TITLE LIST

Adventure Cycle-Touring Handbook	1st edn out now
Adventure Motorcycling Handbook	5th edn out now
Australia by Rail	5th edn out now
Azerbaijan	3rd edn out now
The Blues Highway – New Orleans to Chicago	2nd edn out now
Coast to Coast (British Walking Guide)	2nd edn out now
Cornwall Coast Path (British Walking Guide)	2nd edn out now
Corsica Trekking – GR20	1st edn Feb 2007
Dolomites Trekking – AV1 & AV2	2nd edn out now
Good Honeymoon Guide	2nd edn out now
Himalaya by Bicycle – a route and planning guide	1st edn mid 2007
Inca Trail, Cusco & Machu Picchu	3rd edn out now
Indian Rail Handbook	1st edn mid 2007
Japan by Rail	1st edn out now
Kilimanjaro – the trekking guide (with Mt Meru)	2nd edn out now
Mediterranean Handbook	1st edn out now
Nepal Mountaineering Guide	1st edn May 2007
New Zealand – The Great Walks	1st edn out now
North Downs Way (British Walking Guide)	1st edn Oct 2006
Norway's Arctic Highway	1st edn out now
Offa's Dyke Path (British Walking Guide)	1st edn out now
Pembrokeshire Coast Path (British Walking Guide)	1st edn out now
Pennine Way (British Walking Guide)	1st edn out now
The Ridgeway (British Walking Guide)	1st edn Nov 2006
Siberian BAM Guide – rail, rivers & road	2nd edn out now
The Silk Roads – a route and planning guide	1st end out now
Sahara Overland – a route and planning guide	2nd edn out now
Sahara Abenteuerhandbuch (German edition)	1st edn out now
Scottish Highlands – The Hillwalking Guide	1st edn out now
South Downs Way (British Walking Guide)	1st edn out now
South-East Asia – The Graphic Guide	1st edn out now
Tibet Overland – mountain biking & jeep touring	1st edn out now
Trans-Canada Rail Guide	4th edn Mar 2007
Trans-Siberian Handbook	7th edn Dec 2006
Trekking in the Annapurna Region	4th edn out now
Trekking in the Everest Region	4th edn out now
Trekking in Corsica	1st edn out now
Trekking in Ladakh	3rd edn out now
Trekking in the Moroccan Atlas	2nd edn Jan 2007
Trekking in the Pyrenees	3rd edn out now
West Highland Way (British Walking Guide)	2nd edn out now

For more information about Trailblazer, for where to find your nearest
stockist, for guidebook updates or for credit card mail order sales visit:

www.trailblazer-guides.com